TAKING SPORT SERIOUSLY

Social Issues in Canadian Sport

Second Edition

*Sport as a popular art form is not just
self-expression, but is deeply and necessarily a
means of interplay within an entire culture.
Rocket Richard, the Canadian hockey player,
used to comment on the poor acoustics in some
arenas. He felt that the puck off his stick rode
on the roar of the crowd.*

—Marshall McLuhan

Cinq à zéro by Normand Hudon. Mix media, dated 1987, size 18 X 24 inches.
Reproduced by permission of Multi Art Ltée, Saint Lambert, Quebec.

TAKING SPORT SERIOUSLY

Social Issues in Canadian Sport

Second Edition

Edited by

Peter Donnelly
University of Toronto

Thompson Educational Publishing, Inc.
Toronto

Information on how to obtain copies of this book may be obtained from:
 Web site: www.thompsonbooks.com
 E-mail: publisher@thompsonbooks.com
 Telephone: (416) 766-2763
 Fax: (416) 766-0398

Canadian Cataloguing in Publication Data

Main entry under title:

Taking Sport Seriously : social issues in Canadian sport

2nd ed.
Includes bibliographical references.
ISBN 1-55077-116-7

1. Sports—Social aspects—Canada. I. Donnelly, Peter.
GV585.T34 2000   306.4'83'0971   C00-930847-4

Copy Editing: Elizabeth Phinney
Cover Design: Elan Designs
Cover image: Cinq à zéro by Normand Hudon. Mix media, dated 1987, size 18 X 24 inches. Reproduced by permission of Multi Art Ltée, Saint Lambert, Quebec.

Photos: p.11, the news media, courtesy of Canadian Sport Images, photo by F. Scott Grant; p.39, the 1996 Atlanta Olympics, courtesy of Laura Robinson; p.69, rugby match, courtesy of Ontario Secondary School Sports Association; p.77, women's volleyball competition, courtesy of Ontario Volleyball Association; p.112, indigenous games, courtesy of Laura Robinson.

Every reasonable effort has been made to acquire permission for copyright materials used in this book and to acknowledge such permissions accurately. Any errors or omissions called to the publisher's attention will be corrected in future printings.

We acknowledge the support of the Government of Canada through the Book Publishing Industry Development Program for our publishing activities.

Printed in Canada.
1 2 3 4 5   06 05 04 03 02 01 00

Table of Contents

Introduction

Peter Donnelly

The sociology of sport is concerned with the relationship between sport and other social institutions (the family, education, politics, and the economy), the social organization, social relations and group behaviour associated with different types of sport (e.g., elite or mass, amateur and professional, the class, gender or race relations that sport involves), and the social processes (such as ideological incorporation) that occur in conjunction with sport (Jary and Jary, 1995, p.638).

One of the great advantages of teaching the sociology of sport (whether we call it "Sport and Social Issues," "Sport in Canadian Society," or whatever) is the continuing possibility of using current events as source material. It seems that there is always something of social interest happening in sport, and such current events are usually of interest to both students and teachers. One of the great disadvantages of teaching the sociology of sport in Canada used to be the lack of Canadian textbooks. This was resolved to a great extent in the 1990s with the publication of Jill LeClair's (1992) *Winners and Losers: Sport and Physical Activity in the 90s* (Toronto: Thompson Educational Publishing) and Hall, Slack, Smith and Whitson's (1991) *Sport in Canadian Society* (Toronto: McClelland & Stewart).

But, even with the availability of textbooks, both students and teachers are exposed to a second great Canadian disadvantage—American media dominance. We are likely to hear more, and know more, about the Final Four than the Vanier Cup, to obtain our information about sports events from American media sources, and to have our "branch plant" status reinforced by the major American professional sports—two NBA teams; two Major League baseball teams; two less Canadian NHL teams; and in football, the continuing attempt to acquire an NFL franchise for Canada while we observe both the decline and Americanization of the CFL.

The first edition of this collection, published in 1997, represented one small skirmish in the fight against American media domination. More importantly, it represented an attempt to provide a current collection of (primarily) Canadian readings for students and teachers of sport in Canadian society at the high school, community college, and university levels. The collection was intended to supplement the sport textbooks being used in Canada by providing current readings from various relatively popular sources on issues of relevance to sport in Canadian society. I found many of these readings to be of use in my own teaching. They combined readability and concern over current issues with a significant awareness of, and sensitivity to, the relationships between sport and the larger society.

The success of that experiment, that intervention to provide current Canadian materials for sport and society courses in this country, is evident from the fact that this is the *second* edition. A number of those who used the first edition have told me how useful it was in generating student discussion about issues relevant to Canadians.

But current materials fade quite quickly; news becomes "old news;" and new events come along to remind us of older issues, or sometimes there are even new issues. Therefore, out of the 59 articles in this new edition, 41 are published here for the first time. I have saved some of the "oldies but goodies," but the vast majority of the selections are new. Again, there is no particular sequence to the topics in the collection—they represent a variety of current issues in Canadian sport, and the sections may be read in any order, although I have reorganized them more thematically.

The themes are those commonly taught in sociology of sport and sport management courses. The second edition of this book begins with a section on

The Significance of Sport, followed by three sections on major issues which have become even more significant since the first edition: **Drugs**, the **Olympics**, and **Health, Fitness and Injury**. The section on **Violence and Masculinity** is a natural segue from the previous section, and begins a group of five sections dealing with issues in the various demographic categories of sport participants: **Women**; the **Sexual Orientation of Athletes**; **Youth**; and **Heritage**. The next two sections are concerned with two major institutions that dominate our view of sport: the **Economics of Sport**; and **Sport and the Media**. And, to conclude, there is a new section on the **Crisis in Hockey**. Some articles are relevant to more than one section and where appropriate I have noted the overlap.

The absence of a section on the environment in this edition is obviously not because the environment is no longer an issue in sport—far from it. Concerns range from the environmental impact of golf and ski resort development to the environmental consequences of hosting major sport events or participating in extreme sports. The average golf course requires 3,000 cubic metres of water per day—a quantity that could meet the total daily water needs of 14,000 people; 2.7 tons of chemicals are used on the average golf course in a year; and only 8 percent of Canadian golf courses participate in the Audubon Society environmental plan to encourage golf courses to double as wildlife sanctuaries (Brunt, 2000). I hope that the environment will continue to be a topic for discussion in "sport and society'" and "sport management" courses, but I have not discovered any new and accessible articles on the issue—although Chernushenko's (1994) book represents an important Canadian and international source on the topic.

The new section on the **Crisis in Hockey** introduces a new line of discussion for those who wish to take sport seriously—and, as Canada's premier winter sport, hockey needs to be taken seriously. Among other things, there is justifiable concern about the globalization of hockey, inadequacies in player development programs, and violence and injury. For these reasons, in this edition I have included an entire section on the crisis in Canadian hockey.

As you will see, many of the articles are critical and raise controversial issues that are useful for discussion and debate. Students often think that the criticism evident in the sociology of sport is a sign that those teaching the courses and writing the articles hate sport. The opposite is the case. The criticisms are almost always made by teachers and professors who have a passionate interest in improving the current sport system and in making participation in sport accessible to as many people as possible. I have substituted "sport system" for "country" in the following quote from the American senator, John Fulbright:

> To criticize one's sport system is to do it a service and pay it a compliment. It is a service because it may spur the sport system to do better than it is doing, it is a compliment because it evidences a belief that a sport system can do better than it is doing (cited by Sage, 1990, p.11).

Of course, to "do better" does not necessarily mean winning more medals and championships, and setting more records. Most sport "criticism" looks to ways in which more people might experience the benefits of participating in sport and fewer people might be damaged by such participation.

Most of the topics discussed here deal with ongoing issues in Canadian sport, and the last few years have produced a number of interesting topics. The Olympic crisis broke at the beginning of 1999, with revelations about corruption in the awarding of the 2002 Winter Olympics to Salt Lake City. Although such corruption was not news to those who have been concerned about the Olympics for some time, U.S. government investigations and worldwide media coverage of the scandals are producing a period of major reform in the Olympic movement.

Likewise, the drug crisis seems to have deepened in sport, with continuing revelations about Chinese athletes, growing information (and criminal trials) about the East German doping program during the 1970s, widespread use of suspect nutrition supplements, widespread reported use of supposedly undetectable substances such as EPO and HGH, and a major drug crisis during the Tour de France bicycle race in 1998. And, in Canada, a crisis in hockey became a national concern after the poor performance of the men's team at the Nagano Olympics and a number of instances of violence and injury. A major federal report on sport (Mills, 1998) was also published, and the Liberal government appointed a new Minister of State for Sport (Denis Coderre) who has made it his mission to support Canada's national team athletes.

The growing significance of social issues concerning sport is evident in the number of "special issues" of magazines that have been devoted to the topic in the last few years. For example, in Canada, *Canadian Issues/Themes Canadiens* (Autumn 1999); in North America, the *Nation* (10/17 August 1998) and *UTNE Reader* (February 2000); and internationally, *Peace Review* (December 1999) and the *UNESCO Courier* (April 1999). These are all signs of the growing significance of sport studies, and sport sociologists are well represented in all these magazines.

Four limitations of the previous edition are still evident, though to a lesser extent, in this second edition. First, my own location in Toronto has resulted in the readings still being somewhat Toronto/Ontario-centric, although I have tried, wherever possible, to include materials representing sport in other parts of Canada. Second, the collection overemphasizes corporate-professional sport rather than the sports we are actually involved in. This is a consequence of the nature of the sources used—newspapers and magazines are frequently involved in a symbiotic relationship with corporate interests and the ownership of professional sport teams. The section on the **Economics of Sport** has been cut down substantially from the previous edition, but it is still a major section; and the new section on hockey also overemphasizes the professional elements of the game. Third, and related to the second limitation, the majority of the articles are about men's sport. This, too, is less an indication of the amount of sport actually being played by men and women respectively than it is an indication of whose sport the media attends to (see the section on **Sport and the Media**). Fourth, and finally, a great deal of insightful writing on sport in Canada is published in French, and translation is unfortunately beyond the means of this collection.

Despite these limitations, I was able to collect many more interesting articles than it was possible to include in this collection (and I have included references to these wherever possible), but I am also well aware that there are numerous useful and interesting articles from all over Canada in sources that I have not been able to track down. Thus, for future issues, I would again like to recruit the help of those who find this collection useful. If you come across articles (or papers, radio or television scripts, speeches, etc.) that you as teachers have found useful for your own students, or that you as students think would be of interest to other students, please send a copy (or reference) to me at the address listed below. All topics on, or of interest to, Canadian sport, physical activity, and society are acceptable. I would be particularly grateful to receive any insightful articles that deal with levels of sport other than the corporate-professional level and those that represent all of the regions of Canada.

I hope that the collection will continue to prove useful and I look forward to hearing your suggestions for sources and topics for future collections. I would like to thank Keith Thompson of Thompson Educational Publishing for his continuing faith in this project.

PETER DONNELLY

Director, Centre for Sport Policy Studies
Faculty of Physical Education and Health
University of Toronto
55 Harbord Street
Toronto, ON   M5S 2W6
Phone: 416 946 5071 / Fax: 416 978 4384
E-mail: peter.donnelly@utoronto.ca

References

- Brunt, S. (2000). Golf: The stupidest game in the world. *The Globe and Mail,* 6 May, R1, R18.

- Chernushenko, David. (1994). *Greening Our Games: Running Sports Events and Facilities That Won't Cost the Earth.* Ottawa: Centurion.

- Jary, D. & Jary, J. (1995). *Collins Dictionary of Sociology* (2nd ed.). Glasgow: HarperCollins.

- Mills, Dennis (M.P.; Chair). 1998. *Sport in Canada : Everybody's Business (Leadership, Partnership and Accountability).* Standing Committee on Canadian Heritage, Sub-Committee on the Study of Sport in Canada. December.

- Sage, G. (1990). *Power and Ideology in American Sport: A Critical Perspective.* Champaign, IL: Human Kinetics.

Part 1
The Significance of Sport

Sport is about play, games, fun. It is not supposed to be serious; it is "the toy department of life." Look at the status of sport, physical education or kinesiology in your own institution. Ask any physical education or kinesiology student about the taunts they have to suffer ("What are you going to be when you grow up—a phys-ed teacher?"; "Do you spend all of your time in the gym?"). In the teachers' room hierarchy at any high school, the physical education teacher ranks below the shop teacher. And the "dumb jock" image is pervasive in educational institutions.

Yet, despite this image problem, sport commands attention in developed societies today:

... sports cannot be ignored because they are such a pervasive part of life in contemporary society. It does not take a sociologist to call our attention to the fact that during the twentieth century the popularity and visibility of sports have grown dramatically in many countries around the world, especially those in which industrialization has occurred. A survey of the mass media shows that newspapers in most cities devote entire sections of their daily editions to the coverage of sport. This is especially true in North America, where space given to sports coverage frequently surpasses the space given to the economy, politics, or any other single topic of interest. Radio and television stations bring numerous hours of live and taped sporting events to people all around the world. Sport personalities are objects of attention—as heroes and antiheroes. Young people in many countries are apt to be more familiar with the names of top-level athletes than with the names of their national religious, economic, and political leaders. For a large segment of people of all ages in industrialized countries, sport is likely to be included in their every-day lives through their involvement as participants or spectators, through their reading, or through their conversation with friends and acquaintances (Coakley, 1994, p.5).

It is quite evident, then, that although sport is pleasurable and entertaining, and many people feel uncomfortable with the idea of "taking sport seriously," it is a pervasive and significant part of our lives and is worthy of our serious academic attention. The three articles in this first section raise different issues about the significance of sport.

The millennium witnessed a great many articles about the greatest sporting feats and celebrated athletes of the past, but few are as insightful as Stephen Brunt's piece on the history of sport and its significance in the modern world. He concludes that sport is one of the few experiences that brings people together and creates a sense of community.

Elliott Gorn and Michael Oriard lend the title to this collection in one of the few American articles. Much of the best current research in the sociology of sport may be classified under the general heading of "cultural studies." And, although Gorn and Oriard may underestimate the amount of influential work that has been done, they certainly provide a strong argument for the use of a cultural studies approach to researching and understanding sport. Finally, Jean Harvey, in an article that was adapted as an introduction to a special issue of the *UNESCO Courier* devoted entirely to sport, looks at the complexity as well as the significance of sport in the modern world. As Harvey notes, "in some case sport serves the establishment; in others it can be a seedbed for social activism."

These three articles go a long way towards making the case that sport is both significant and worthy of serious attention in Canada today.

Reference
- Coakley, J. (1994). *Sport in Society: Issues and Controversies* (5th ed.). St. Louis: Mosby.

Additional Sources
Videos:
- *Ultimate Athlete: Pushing the Limit.* Discovery Channel.
- *Home Game*, the hockey classic, is available through CBC in Canada.

Print Resources:
- Smith, G. (1996). The roar of the greasepaint, the smell of the crowd? *Queen's Quarterly*, 103(3), Fall, pp.503-519. [Asks a number of key questions about Canadian sport.]
- Boniface, P. (1998). Soccer and geopolitics. *Queens Quarterly*, 105(3), Fall, pp.345-49. [Looks at the global significance of soccer after the 1998 World Cup.]
- Also, the introductory chapters of most sociology of sport textbooks provide support for the significance of sport.

1.

How Sport Became a Religion

Stephen Brunt

A sense of community in a world where other communal institutions have broken down

Astylus could run like the wind. He was the fastest man in the world, so fast than in successive Olympic Games he won the two glamorous sprints. They loved him in Croton, the city of his birth, the city he represented and made famous. A statue was erected in his honour.

By then, the ancient Olympics had outgrown their relatively pure and amateur origins, tainted by the commercial and the political. The champions were regarded as greater heroes than ever, as embodiments of the limits of human potential, as nearly divine—statues of some dead athletes were even believed to have curative powers.

They had also become disconnected from the real world, from real jobs and real lives, training full time, richly rewarded, super men among men. And so, before the next Games, when Astylus received a better offer from the tyrant ruler of Syracuse, his choice was simple and obvious. For the Olympics of 480 BC, he wore the Syracusan colours, and again ran to glory. In Croton, they destroyed the statue and turned what had been his house into a prison.

That story should seem oh so familiar now, be it Alexei, once of Ottawa, or Shawn, once of Toronto, or Wayne, once of Edmonton, where they graciously left his statue alone, or Lennox, once of Kitchener, now of London. Not since ancient Greece, two millennia ago, has sport held such a central, dominant position in the culture as it does, now, in the waning moments of this 1,000 years.

Spectator sport now is not just a pastime, not just a diversion, but something approaching a belief system—a belief system with a hollow core, where "winning" has replaced the religious goal of redemption, where the players are not only made wealthy, but are also assumed to possess qualities of character based solely on how they perform in the arena, or the stadium, or in front of the interviewer's microphone.

"Although there are myriad evils throughout Greece, there is nothing worse than the race of athletes," the poet Euripides wrote. "...Yes, and I blame the Greek custom of assembling to watch these men and of honouring useless pleasures for the sake of a feast....We ought then to crown with garlands the wise and the good, and whatever temperate and upright man best leads the state, and whoever by his counsels rids it of evil deeds."

We ought to, but we don't, because, as the multimillion-dollar salaries paid to professional athletes attest, we desperately need something that the sports spectacle provides—a sense of community, a sense of shared purpose in a world where other communal institutions have broken down.

Change came then. Greek sport collapsed, as the glorious society which it reflected eventually collapsed. And where are we now?

There has always been play—animals do it as well as human beings. There have nearly always been some kind of contests pitting man against man (or, more rarely, woman against woman). There were games of combat—wrestling and boxing. There were ball games, played by the aboriginal peoples of North and South America, including the Inuit, played by Maoris and by Europeans. There were equestrian sports, chariot races and horseback riding. For the ruling classes in the Middle Ages, there were war games, in the form of elaborate tournaments featuring jousting and swordplay. For the underclasses, diversion came more often in the form of mass games of a primitive form of football, pitting village against village, with matches lasting all day, and each side featuring hundreds of players.

Still, those are only in the most distant sense the antecedents of the games we know now. The roots of modern sport—and the modern attitude toward sport—don't appear until the 17th and 18th centuries. The philosopher John Locke was one of the first to suggest that exercise was a necessary component of developing the whole man. Jean-Jacques Rousseau wrote that, "The body must be vigorous in order to obey the soul."

That notion was taken to heart in Germany, where physical education was considered of paramount importance, and in England, where sport as we now understand it, began. It did not develop in isolation, but as has been the case with every aspect of its continuing evolution, in tandem with technological and social changes. Something as simple as the invention of the stopwatch in the 18th century would completely change the perception of athletic achievement. Until then, there may have been conventional wisdom regarding the fastest people or the fastest horses, but there was no sure means of recording times for covering a specific distance.

Now, there was a standardized means of measurement, and the whole idea of "record setting" became almost a mania. The first "miracle horse," Flying Childers, was said to have reached the speed of a mile a minute in 1721. The first timed foot races took place (originally they had been contests among the footmen whose job it was to run alongside the coaches of the aristocracy). Wagering became widely popular, both in the form of the first pari-mutuel betting on horse races, and in betting on various extraordinary physical feats, as far-fetched as the possibility of an 18-month-old walking the length of The Mall in London in less than 30 minutes (she did it in 23).

The first sports celebrities since the days of Ancient Greece were Robert Barclay Allardice (1779-1854), known as Captain Barclay, the great pedestrian who won renown for his feats of distance walking—in 1809 he walked one mile in each of 10,000 successive hours—and the heavyweight boxing champion James Figg. The fights had been made more civilized and socially acceptable, with gloves and rounds and rules, and Figg, beaten just once in more than 300 bouts, would become the first in a long line of larger-than-life champions extending in an unbroken line to the present day.

The rise of spectator sport coincided with the age of industrialization, for reasons that are obvious, and less so. The factory worker had both defined hours on the job (unlike a farmer), and defined hours of leisure, which would eventually creep beyond the Christian Sabbath, into Saturdays. (It's because of the five-day work week that soccer matches traditionally begin at 3 o'clock on Saturday afternoon.)

Sports that were increasingly directed toward efficiency, rationalization, standardization, calculation, measurement and following rules mirrored the qualities required of the new industrial work force. Workers were being subtly indoctrinated by the very games that allowed them to forget their toil for a few hours.

The first written rules for soccer appeared in 1842—though "football" in one form or another had been played for hundreds of years. Twenty years later, the split between that sport, and the sport as played at the Rugby School became permanent—mirroring a class split between the two games.

"Modern football can only be played, theatrically presented and joyously observed in societies that have been at least partially deracinated, partly tamed, and partly regularized for modern, industrial market production," writes the social historian Richard Mandell. "For modern life demands a rigid sectioning and observance of time, treasures and rewards verifiable accomplishment, and demands the sublimation of aggression."

With that, and with the codification of baseball in the United States at about the same time, the stage was set for the sports explosion of the early 20th century. Once again, social and technological factors also came into play. The growth of the railroads made it simpler for teams and their fans to travel from place to place to compete. Increased leisure time—and increased disposable income—fuelled the sports economy. And the birth of mass communications allowed for the instant transmission of the details from far-away contests. When the heavyweight boxing champion John L. Sullivan—the first sports superstar of North American origin—fought Jake Kilrain in New Orleans in 1889, Western Union paid 50 operators to transmit 208,000 words describing the fight over the telegraph wires.

The business of sport follows two parallel lines through this century, converging near the end. The first is that of the modern Olympic Games, modelled on those of Ancient Greece, and steeped in the 19th-century ideals of the whole man (and less explicitly, preparing those whole men to go out and fight European wars). While its beginnings, in 1896, were rooted in the notion of gentlemanly amateurism, the modern Olympics would never have survived without its commercial and propaganda potential.

The Games as we now understand them were shaped over a four-year period during the 1930s. First the Americans had their crack in 1932 in Los Angeles, where they made the pageant their own, with massed flags, marching bands, the release of pigeons, and with the invention of the Olympic flame. In 1936, it was the turn of Nazi Germany to do the Americans one better. Initially, the National Socialists had rejected sport (other than that required to build physical fitness), and of course rejected any mixing of the races in competition. But the Nazis would come to understand the propaganda value of athletic success, and especially of the Olympic spectacle. They added the Olympic torch relay, elaborate medal ceremonies, and of course Leni Riefenstahl, whose six-hour film *Olympia* would fully reveal the Games' image-making potential.

The Olympics offered a potent mix—nationalist passion, the veneer of amateurism, the possibility of political statement, the notion of "pure" competition in an ever more mercenary sporting world. As a propaganda vehicle, the protest of 1968, the boycotts of 1976, 1980, 1984 and 1988, and the massacre of Israeli athletes in 1972, were a natural, if horrific extension on what had taken place in 1936. As a commercial vehicle, none of that would set the Olympics back, nor would the shift from faux amateurism to overt professionalism, nor, apparently, would the myriad scandals of the International Olympic Committee. This was a sporting event with a belief system built in (the amorphous creed known as "Olympism"), a sponsor-friendly vehicle that could still pretend to be above mere monetary concerns. At century's end, the Olympics' power in the public imagination and the marketplace showed no signs of abating.

The parallel line through the 20th century, especially in North America, is that of professional sport, both team and individual, and the elevation of athletes to iconic figures. Unlike the Olympics, it came without ideological trappings,

and was purely and unapologetically commercial. In North America, that current is most easily traced to the 1920s, the first golden era of sport, when the combination of the development of mass communications—especially radio—with the savvy marketing of sports heroes who were, or who would be made to seem, larger than the games in which they competed. Babe Ruth in baseball. Red Grange in U.S. football. Bill Tilden in tennis. Bobby Jones in golf. First and foremost Jack Dempsey, in boxing, a onetime hobo turned hero through the promotional genius of Tex Rickard, the spiritual father not just of Don King, but of Nike's Phil Knight and all other sports hucksters of every stripe. With Dempsey, who fought only occasionally during his championship reign, Rickard proved that it was possible to sell the athlete away from the arena, the stadium, the playing field.

There would be no setbacks, no pauses. Sport would only grow, speeding past a series of landmark events: the first television experiments in the 1930s, the beginning of a medium that would be from his infancy linked with sport; the Joe Louis-Max Schmeling fight in 1938, the first time a black athlete was hailed as hero by white America, paving the way for Jackie Robinson, for Muhammad Ali, and for the first race-neutral sports hero, Michael Jordan; the National Football League's landmark television deal in 1960, and the implementation of a revenue-sharing scheme that allowed it to leap past baseball as the continent's dominant sport; Ali's victory over Sonny Liston in 1964, the coming-out party for the first sports hero to cross every line, black-white, First World/Third World, Christian/Muslim, and become the most famous man in the world; the Curt Flood case, and the rise of the Major League Baseball Player's Association, the first hint that athletes would be free to claim their share of the pie; Billie Jean King's victory over Bobby Riggs, a circus, but a circus without which it would have been hard to imagine an event such as last year's women's soccer World Cup.

All of that mattered, but none of it would have mattered had the need not been there, had there not existed a void that only sport could fill. In the closing moments of the millennium, sports delivers more than entertainment. It offers the possibility of a communal experience, of coming together with other people (either live or through television—or the Internet) at the same time to care passionately about the same thing, of self-affirmation—an experience difficult to come by anywhere else. The spectacle may be empty, but the power of the spectacle is enormous in a world where there is no common faith, where political ideologies have been devalued, where cynicism reigns. The sports fans can suspend disbelief, can temporarily forget about salaries and labour disputes and drug use and scandal, can embrace mercenary athletes as super men and super women and role models because of what the games deliver. Thus the television ratings, thus the salaries and franchise values, thus the sense that sport has never before been this important—at least it hasn't for the last 2,500 years.

We know what happened then.

Source: Stephen Brunt is a sports writer with *The Globe and Mail*. This article was originally published in *The Globe and Mail*, Saturday, January 1, 2000. Reproduced by permission of *The Globe and Mail*.

2.
Taking Sports Seriously

Elliott J. Gorn and Michael Oriard

Studying sport as a part of cultural studies

The West Indian scholar C.L.R. James's 1963 work, *Beyond a Boundary*, is a remarkable book of history and memory. It is about the game of cricket. More, it is about the West Indies, poverty, being black, and colonialism. Cricket is James's microscope, and through it he magnifies whole areas of life and thought. He presents cricket as both sport and metaphor, the property of colonizers and colonized, in which struggles over culture, power, hegemony, and resistance are played out. Many scholars consider *Beyond a Boundary* to be the most profound and moving book ever written about sports.

So we were greatly interested when we received a brochure for a conference at New York University last month entitled "Beyond the Boundary." The conference was held in conjunction with the Whitney Museum of American Art, whose show "Black Male: Representations of Masculinity in Contemporary American Art" had included some images of blacks engaged in sports. A conference on black masculinity, borrowing its title from James's book, looked promising for scholars in American studies who, like us, have tried to take the study of athletics seriously. Yet as well looked at the program more closely, we found that it did not include a single session or paper concerning sports.

Of course, scholars can choose to discuss whatever they want to. But how is it possible to understand American culture, particularly African-American culture, and ignore the role played by sports?

We see all around us team logos, images of athletes, and expensive clothing endorsed by famous athletes. Michael Jordan's is perhaps the most recognized face in the world, just as Muhammad Ali's was a generation ago. Nor is there a lack of experts who might participate in scholarly discussions of sports. Harry Edwards, a professor of sociology at Berkeley, opened up the academic study of blacks in sports 25 years ago. His chief concern was the exploitation of black athletes by the sports establishment. He has been succeeded by other distinguished writers–including Gerald Early, a literary scholar at Washington University, and Jeffrey Sammons, a historian at New York University–who have broadened the inquiry into many other aspects of the relationship between race and sports.

Despite the obvious importance of sports in American life, only a small number of American academics have made a specialty of analyzing the relationship between athletics and culture, and their work remains ghettoized. Historians, sociologists, psychologists, anthropologists, and even philosophers and literary scholars have established subspecialties on sports, but their work hovers at the margins of their disciplines.

Moreover, the booming field of cultural studies seems oblivious to the work done on athletics. This is ironic, because cultural studies–the interdisciplinary analysis of history, cultural expression, and power–is exactly where the study of sports is most needed. Where is there a cultural activity more freighted with constructions of masculinity than football, more deeply inscribed with race than boxing, more tied in the public mind to the hopes and hopelessness of inner-city youths than basketball? Gender, race, and power are central theoretical and methodological concerns of cultural studies.

Despite the continuing discussion in American studies of "the body" (of how human beings conceive of themselves physically), athletes' bodies remain curiously off-limits. Yet power and eroticism meet most conspicuously in the athletic body –Florence Griffith-Joyner's, Greg Louganis's, or Michael Jordan's.

Is "the body" as conceived in cultural studies a rhetorical construction, while the bodies of athletes are too palpably real? Are we, as intellectuals, just uncomfortable with physicality, because our own bailiwick is the life of the mind? Could it be that professors are creatures of words while the language of athletics is fundamentally non-verbal? Or are we simply playing out the

long-standing faculty antagonism to the distorted priorities of universities with multimillion-dollar athletics programs?

Furthermore, although critical scholarship about television's place in American life is an important part of cultural studies, amazingly little of that scholarship is concerned with televised sports. Yet the mass media have always depended on athletics to reach large audiences, from the invention of the sports pages in the first large-circulation metropolitan newspapers in the 1880s and 1890s, to the first World Series radio broadcasts in the early 1920s, to the baseball and football games and boxing matches telecast at the beginning of the television age. Today, international broadcasts via satellite, cable superstations, and pay-per-view television all thrive on sporting events. Sports have been the cash cow of the increasingly pervasive (some would say invasive) entertainment media.

In an age that (properly) embraces multiculturalism, athletics represent both our diversity and our common culture. It is almost a cliché to mention that sports are the *lingua franca* of men talking across divisions of class and race. Sports also reveal just how interdependent particular subcultures and the larger consumer culture can be. Think, for example, of the symbiotic ties between inner-city playground basketball and the National Basketball Association championships.

Sports keep bringing us back to the ever-shifting relationship between commercialized mass culture (the Olympics come immediately to mind) and subcultures of difference (the Gay Games, for example).

Sports also are clearly about gender, although, until recently, this often has been overlooked. Certainly athletics have shaped American masculinity. One hundred years ago, in an essay called "The American Boy," Theodore Roosevelt exhorted young men to follow the same principles in life as in football: "Hit the line hard; don't foul and don't shirk, but hit the line hard."

For women, organized sports became available as feminism grew and they gained access to higher education and other areas from which they had previously been excluded. Even as Roosevelt wrote his essay, women at Vassar, Smith, Mount

Holyoke, and Wellesley Colleges were playing baseball—not softball; baseball. By the turn of the century, a particularly aggressive form of basketball had become a source of pride and passion at women's colleges and on countless playgrounds. We are just beginning to ask what such facts say about definitions of feminism and femininity.

The general banishment of sports from cultural studies is not merely an omission of an important expressive form; leaving out sports distorts our view of culture. Sports present unique challenges to theories about cultural power and personal freedom, which cultural-studies scholars discuss using such categories as "representation," "commodification," "hegemony, " and "subversion." One of the challenges is that sports differ from movies, novels, music, and television shows, all of which scholars view as wholly "constructed." Sports, however, are essentially "unscripted." They are real contests, in which many people have participated, at least at an amateur level.

This makes sports different from the other forms of entertainment, which are packaged by their creators. Knowledgeable fans can understand the games on their own terms and ignore the silly prattle of the "colour" commentators. Baseball officials cannot script a "Cinderella season" on demand. What sports "means" to their vast audiences cannot be ordained by either owners or media pundits.

The great virtue of cultural studies has been to take seriously the idea of "otherness," a concept that, in part, relates to how a group defines itself by the images that it creates of outsiders. But otherness is a slippery term. To many scholars—whose values are cosmopolitan, whose politics are progressive, and whose incomes are upper middle class—the "other" is not necessarily the same as for most Americans. Young, verbally dexterous, and entrepreneurial rappers—modern-day rebels against a narrow-minded and prissy culture—may be far less alien to hip young intellectuals than the gifted and disciplined athlete. "Otherness," for scholars, may reside even more in the polyester-clad fan who drinks with his buddies and roots for the home team, or in the middle-aged woman out bowling in her weekly league game. What, in the eyes of many in the academy, could be more

unhip, uncool, "other" than American working-class pleasures?

Some scholars have suggested that, after Martin Luther King, Jr., Jackie Robinson may well have been the most influential black American of the past 50 years. Not everyone would agree with this proposition, but it is plausible, and it speaks volumes about American culture that the artistry, grace, fierce will, and embattled restraint of a baseball player could become a symbol of courage and strength to so many people. There is no getting around it: For African Americans, sports have been a fount of creativity, of art, of genius. Sports have also been a source of respect for black Americans among people of all races. Any list of the most culturally influential African Americans of the 20th century would have to include Robinson, as well as Jesse Owens, Joe Louis, Jack Johnson, Wilma Rudolph, and Muhammad Ali.

C.L.R. James was so convinced of the importance of sports that he declared cricket and soccer to be "the greatest cultural influences in 19th-century Britain." Although a bit hyperbolic, James's point is well taken. That athletics have remained so far beyond the boundary of most intellectual discourse is beyond belief. As James so brilliantly demonstrated, the study of sport can take us to the very heart of critical issues in the study of culture and society.

Source: Elliot J. Gorn is a professor of History and American Studies at Miami University, Ohio. Michael Oriard is Professor of English at Oregon State University. This article was originally published in *The Chronicle of Higher Education*, March 24, 1995, A32. Reproduced by permission.

3.

What's in a Game?

Jean Harvey

Does sport create harmony or foment division? Or both at once?

Basketballer Michael Jordan's announcement on January 13, 1999, that he was retiring made headlines all around the world. He was up there with Pelé, they said. The American superstar's skill dazzled everyone who had watched him dashing around a basketball court; as he leaped to dunk the ball in the net he seemed to be momentarily suspended in the air. They call him "Air Jordan."

But Jordan, the Chicago Bulls star whose income during his last season as a player was estimated at $30 million, is also at the head of a business empire. His impact on the U.S. economy is reckoned by *Fortune* magazine at $10 billion. His link with the sporting goods firm Nike is believed to have generated about $5.2 billion in sales of shoes and clothing.

Idol of the world's youth he may be, but people argue about the role in society that he has—or hasn't—played. The basketball shoes carrying his name have been stitched by child workers in sweatshops, say U.S. trade unions. He has never spoken up for Black causes, say leaders of the Black American community. Has he not set up thousands of young people for a big fall because he is such a symbol of social advancement and success? Try as they might to emulate him, their chances of succeeding are close to nil.

In fact, has he not been a huge publicity machine which has strengthened social inequalities in the U. S. and other countries and helped big transnational companies to conquer a world market?

In August 1998, 40 Iranian women footballers [soccer players] were given permission to train in a stadium in Teheran for the first time in 20 years. In a sense, they are the heirs of the pioneers, led by Frenchwoman Alice Millat, who founded the International Women's Sports Federation and then, in 1922, launched the first women's

Olympic games. Women athletes are still in a minority in the Olympics, after making their debut in tennis and golf. Only a little more than a third of the competitors at the last summer Olympics were women. Even today women are still battling for complete equality and fair treatment in sport.

People with physical disabilities have removed one barrier that discriminated against them in sport. More and more disabled athletes, using special facilities, are today playing the same sports as the non-disabled. They have their own sports meetings, and since 1960 they have had their own Olympic games. However, the presence of the disabled in mainstream clubs is still rare.

So is sport an instrument manipulated by the powerful? Or is it a lifeline for those who are marginalized and excluded by society? Can it be an outlet for social discontent? The examples cited above provide no straightforward answer to these questions. In some cases sport serves the establishment; in others it can be a seedbed for social activism. At one and the same time it plays a host of contradictory social roles at local, national and international levels.

Sport does not speak with a single voice. It is not monolithic. It holds different meanings for different social groups, partly depending on what they want to get out of it. For the well-heeled,

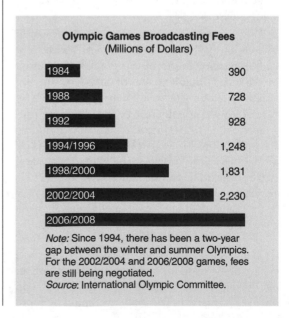

Olympic Games Broadcasting Fees
(Millions of Dollars)

1984	390
1988	728
1992	928
1994/1996	1,248
1998/2000	1,831
2002/2004	2,230
2006/2008	

Note: Since 1994, there has been a two-year gap between the winter and summer Olympics. For the 2002/2004 and 2006/2008 games, fees are still being negotiated.
Source: International Olympic Committee.

sport can be a way of advertising their social status. Playing at exclusive golf, tennis or cricket clubs can be an opportunity to display membership of a privileged group. Amateur sport was controlled for a long time by such people.

At the other end of the spectrum, sport practiced with the most rudimentary facilities can be a great form of self-expression for disadvantaged young people the world over, and may—in exceptional cases—offer them a way out of poverty and deprivation. Here the myth of sport as a ticket to upward mobility can be seen in its quintessential form.

The kaleidoscope of sport also includes the big-time spectacular events which have become first and foremost a commodity whose economic importance and presence in the media are growing nonstop. And finally there's sport, as it is enjoyed by so many people around the world—a pastime that helps to keep them fit and brings them together in a convivial setting. But here too the competition can be intense, and the atmosphere may turn sour. It's among amateur sportsmen and sportswomen that drug abuse is rife and where on-the-field clashes can be the most violent.

Sport is something more than a mirror of the societies in which it is played. It is not a carbon copy of their inequalities and problems. It is a world in its own right, with its own life and its own contradictions. Through the medium of sport, countless volunteers, for example, organize activities and events that make a positive contribution to their communities. Through sport, a strong feeling of comradeship develops among athletes at all levels. In short, major social issues influence sport, just as sport can play a big part in them.

Globalization of sport is a good illustration of the sport paradox. Be it virtual or a reality, globalization has an impact on society and sport. The acceleration of communications and rapid movement of capital leave the impression that the planet is getting smaller, that local frontiers are more and more porous, although contradictory tendencies can also be witnessed. As a vector of cultural homogenization, globalization is also a factor in the resurgence of all forms of local nationalism.

Globalization of sport, and through sport, occurs through separate, albeit interconnected, processes. Michael Jordan's example touched on some aspects of economic globalization. Sporting goods, manufactured multinationally, penetrate what is now known as the world market through the production of products that are marketed globally. Economic globalization is also a vector

---

The Economics of Sport (estimates)

- Overall annual turnover: *over $400 billion**
- U.S. annual turnover: *nearly $200 billion**
- Soccer annual turnover: *over $200 billion**
- Annual growth: *between 6% and 10%*
- Share of GDP in rich countries: *between 1% and 1.5%*
- Share of world trade: *2.5%*
- Sponsorship worldwide: *nearly $7 billion*
- Stock exchange value of the English football club Manchester United: *more than $1 billion*
- Ferrari's annual budget: *nearly $150 million*
- Michael Jordan's earnings in 1997: *nearly $80 million*

*These totals include equipment, construction of facilities, broadcasting fees, sponsorship and players' and competitors' earnings. *Source: L'Économie du sport,* by Jean-François Bourg, to be published in the *Encyclopedia Universalis.*

of cultural globalization trends. Gigantic entertainment conglomerates are now developing the structure and the contents of global mass culture. For example, multinational firms like News Corp and Disney make large investments in professional sport franchises, broadcasting world class sporting events, such as the Olympic games, while also investing in the cable industry, specialty channels, pay TV, cinemas and theme parks.

But is not globalization also a vector of social change? The women's movement, pressing national as well as international sport authorities for more equity in sport, is but one example. Networks of women's groups are forming, helped in part by the increasing speed of communications offered by the Internet, which thus creates virtual global communities closely knitted together and therefore more effective in their action. Another example is linked to the protection of the environment. The Global anti-Golf Movement is a network of organizations fighting against the homogenization of green space generated by the world expansion of golf, and against the massive use of chemicals and scarce water resources by golf clubs, which diminish the access to green land for local people. Finally, a third example is the Gay Games, a world event where gays and lesbians freely celebrate their identities through sport.

No doubt the power of sport is in its ambivalence, in the diversity of experiences it may provide; for better or worse.

Source: Jean Harvey is a professor in the School of Human Kinetics, University of Ottawa, Ontario. A slightly different version of this paper first appeared in *The UNESCO Courier*, April 1999. Reproduced by permission of the author.

Part 2
Drugs and Sport

Canadian sport still lives under the shadow of Ben Johnson (whose 100m. gold medal and world record at the 1988 Seoul Olympics were withdrawn after he tested positive for Stanozolol, a banned steroid) and the 1989 Commission of Inquiry into the Use of Drugs and Banned Practices Intended to Increase Athletic Performance (known as the Dubin Inquiry). The shadow was still evident in the reaction of the world press in 1995 to Donovan Bailey and Bruny Surin taking the gold and silver medals respectively at the Track and Field World Championships. Bailey was tested for drugs 20 times that year and many more in 1996. It was almost possible to feel Canada holding its collective breath while we waited for Donovan Bailey's test results following his world-record, gold medal run in the 100m. at the Atlanta Olympics, and the celebrations did not fully begin until the negative result was announced.

But the spectre of drugs is now even more widespread in sport, with numerous reports of the use of erythropoietin (EPO) and human growth hormone (HGH)—neither of which is evident in dope testing at the time of writing—as well as "designer" steroids. The numerous positive tests for nandrolone in the last two years and the widespread use of "andro" in the U.S. (not illegal in baseball) has now begun to cast light on the dietary supplements industry.

This section begins with a re-visit to Dubin and Johnson. Varda Burstyn places the use of performance-enhancing drugs firmly in the context of modern values. Although in the final analysis it is the athlete who must ingest the drug, she or he does not make that decision in a moral, social, or cultural vacuum. Burstyn, in a critique of the Commission, notes that they were not taking into account the role of government policy and funding, the role of commercial and media interests, or the larger issues of drug use in elite and professional sport. (Burstyn's article also relates to the sections on the **Olympics**, **Violence and Masculinity**, and the **Economics of Sport**.)

John Hoberman's article (which also relates to the section on the **Olympics**) examines why anti-doping policies have failed at the Olympics and recommends ways in which international sport might make a serious anti-doping effort. The World Anti-Doping Agency (WADA), recently established by the IOC in light of critiques such as Hoberman's, only goes a little way towards resolving the problem. Gillmor's controversial article on women's bodybuilding reminds us that the vast majority of steroid use is not for performance enhancement, but for body enhancement (see also Article No. 19, and the sections on gender). And, finally, journalist Laura Robinson situates drug use firmly in a wider range of biotechnologies in order to warn us of the dangers of narcissism.

Reference

- Dubin, C. (1990). *Commission of Inquiry into the Use of Drugs and Banned Practices Intended to Increase Athletic Performance.* Ottawa: Ministry of Supply and Services.

Additional Sources

Videos:

- *Steroids: Crossing the Line*, available from Films for the Humanities & Sciences (Princeton, NJ), is an account of David Jenkins, former British Olympic medalist turned steroid smuggler/dealer in the U.S.; good information on the complexities of steroid use.
- *Dying to Win* is a recent (2000) CBC documentary giving up-to-date information on the drug issue.

Print Resources:

- Leonard, J. (1996). The last race. *Inside Sport*, May, pp. 50-57. [The Executive Director of the American Swimming Coaches Association challenges the IOC and major Olympic sponsors such as Coca Cola to take a stand against drug use in his sport.]
- Bamberger, M., & D. Yaeger (1997). *Sports Illustrated Special Report on Drug Use in Sport*, 14 April, pp.60-85. [Two articles: the first examines the widespread use of drugs in modern day high-performance sport; the second considers whether Michele Smith, the Irish swimmer, used performance-enhancing drugs.]
- Hoberman, J., & C. Yessalis (1995). The history of synthetic testosterone. *Scientific American*, February, pp.76-81. [Looks at the increasing medical use of steroids, particularly to combat the "male menopause."]

4.

The Sporting Life

Varda Burstyn

Ben Johnson seemed almost superhuman

Flying down the straightaway in a breathtaking lead that left Carl Lewis sucking air, Ben Johnson seemed almost superhuman at the Seoul Olympics. When he crossed the finish line metres ahead of the field, the stadium rose in a roaring ovation, while in Canada millions cheered and yelled in front of their television sets. We worshipped Ben Johnson, and what he represented: living proof that hard work could make a poor boy from Jamaica a demigod. His career was a matter of national pride. When he fell from grace, we lamented him as we would a dishonoured hero: with vicious attacks, with breast-beating, and with a national commission of inquiry.

At first the Commission of Inquiry into the Use of Drugs and Banned Practices Intended to Increase Athletic Performance (known as the Dubin inquiry after Mr. Justice Charles Dubin who presided over it) held out a lot of promise. When the hearings convened in January, 1989, Dubin declared in his opening remarks that drugs were "the single greatest threat to the integrity of sport" and that "cheating is the antithesis of sports competition." The implication was that his investigations would be pursued with rigour and determination and, further, that the inquiry would move from description to analysis, addressing the context that had produced the steroids phenomenon. The impression was strengthened only seven weeks later when Charlie Francis, former Sport Canada darling and Ben Johnson's coach, named names and described the institutionalization of steroids in Olympic athletics. Certainly, context was what was needed. As David Steen, the Olympic bronze medal decathlete who partly redeemed Canada's tarnished image at Seoul, observes, "Many people say that it's Ben's fault, or the fault of the people immediately around him. But if they look a little deeper, they'll see that it's society and its values that are also at fault. We've lost the original ethics and

morals of sport, and that's the context for the individual acts of athletes."

Meeting alternately in Toronto and Montreal, and broadcast live on TSN to thousands of addicted daytime viewers, the inquiry was the closest thing to a show trial Canadians had seen in a long time. The parade of witnesses included hulking weightlifters (Jacques Demers and David Bolduc), fleet track stars (Angella Taylor Issajenko and Desai Williams), and suited sports-medicine experts (Norman Gledhill, Andrew Pipe, Robert Kerr) as well as defiant or shamed coaches and Olympic and government officials. In all, the commission interrogated 122 people and produced 15,000 pages of evidence. It was an extraordinary pageant of irony, tragedy, and farce.

But as the months passed the investigation seemed to veer away from examining the factors underlying the revelations it chronicled so unflinchingly. To understand the real causes of the Ben Johnson scandal it was not nearly enough to solicit detailed accounts of who prescribed what for whom, when, and in what sequence. Though the final report may yet surprise us, the hearings themselves failed on three crucial counts. They minimized the importance of governmental policy and funding in promoting performance-enhancing drugs. They ignored the role of commercial and media interests in the evolution of an athletic drug culture. They avoided examining the larger issues of drug use in elite and professional sport. Thus the central issue was never addressed: that today, Olympic athletes–like professional athletes–are no more than paid gladiators whose sacrifices our sporting rituals celebrate and we willingly support.

If it is the postwar proliferation of drugs in Olympic sport that needs explaining, an excellent place to start looking for the explanation is in Berlin in 1936. The Olympic stadium is monumental, built to symbolize Aryan supremacy. The games themselves are an orchestrated showpiece for fascism, and Hitler presides over them like an emperor, reviewing the spectacle from his dais in the stands. Eight rows behind him, taking it all in, sits a young John Diefenbaker. "Diefenbaker told me that he was in Europe to attend the unveiling of the Vimy memorial," says Bruce Kidd, a sport historian and former Commonwealth champion who has written extensively about the period. "And because he had always wanted to see the Olympics, he went on to Berlin. Throughout the entire track-and-field competition, he said, he watched the athletes with one eye and Hitler with the other. When the Korean runner Son Ki-Chong won the marathon, which the Germans had been favoured to win, Diefenbaker said Hitler stormed out of the stadium."

Son Ki-Chong and Jesse Owens, the black American athlete who won four gold track-and-field medals and who emerged as the real *Übermensch* of the games, foiled the Nazis' plan. "But Diefenbaker told me that it was a powerful eye-opener to the tremendous mobilizing power of sport," Kidd recalls. "When in 1961 he announced a sport policy that seriously committed government to Olympic sport, he talked about it as crucial in the struggle, as he put it, 'for the hearts and minds of men.'" Diefenbaker declared to the House of Commons that "in the field of sports today, there are tremendous dividends in national pride from some degree of success in athletics. The uncommitted countries of the world are now using these athletic contests as measurements of evidence of the strength and power of the nations participating." Thus the 1961 Fitness and Amateur Sport Act—the foundation for Canadian Olympic policy—was marked from the outset by a political agenda.

Certainly, by the early sixties, the Cold War in sport was hot. The Soviets, eschewing their tradition of separate Olympics throughout central and eastern Europe, had been accepted into the International Olympic Committee (IOC) fold in 1952. Though the IOC was fiercely anti-Communist by political instinct and tradition, when the Soviets applied, the spirit of postwar reconstruction and the IOC's intense commitment to the "internationalism" of the games won out. The Soviets' debut at Helsinki far surpassed Western expectations and appalled the U.S., by now the standard-bearer for capitalism. The Soviets followed this performance with another dazzling one in Melbourne in 1956.

It became increasingly apparent that the Soviets had developed intensive methods of training and physical conditioning in a system of sport schools and sports medicine that made Western athletics appear dilettante by comparison. Especially amazing was Soviet prowess in events involving strength. John Ziegler, a physician to American strength athletes in many of the major international competitions during the fifties, marvelled. In Vienna in 1954, he had occasion to spend an evening with his Soviet counterpart and for the first time to learn something about the Soviets' training methods. They included the use of the hormone testosterone which had dramatically boosted the performances of a number of Soviet and Eastern-bloc athletes. But even at that early date it was clear that testosterone also had disastrous consequences: androgynization of users, followed by liver and heart damage.

Ziegler wanted something for his athletes too—but he wanted something better. In the late 1950s, working with Ciba Pharmaceuticals, he helped to develop the first anabolic steroids for use in sport. These synthetic derivatives of testosterone were designed to deliver most of testosterone's benefits with fewer of its drawbacks. Under Ziegler's influence, a small elite group of American weightlifters began to use steroids. Steroids got results. More effectively than any other drugs developed to date, steroids open a breach in the body's natural limitations. They are thought to stimulate the development of bone, muscle, and skin. But many experts believe their real secret lies in the extra kick they give to the nervous system. Steroids help athletes override the alarm signals of fatigue, emotional exhaustion, and pain. By the late sixties, Ziegler has since written, he was appalled by the monster he had unleashed. Strength athletes were taking huge doses of the anabolic steroid Dianabol—not the small dosages he had recommended—and seriously jeopardizing their health.

The use of steroids spread rapidly from strength to other sports, and penetrated commercial team sports (especially football). Steroids have since turned up in the urine of, among other athletes, Tour de France cyclists, male and female short- and middle-distance runners, swimmers of both sexes, hockey and baseball players, boxers, and gymnasts. Throughout the 1970s, steroids and other drugs became increasingly normal to the athletic scene, part of a more general intensification of sport training, which gave birth to a new and distinct subbranch of both the medical profession and the drug industry: sports medicine.

During the same period, under the leadership of Pierre Elliott Trudeau, who believed that "sport is important for the way Canadians see themselves," the federal government was increasing its financial support of high-performance sport as a means of shoring up federalism (primarily in opposition to Quebec separatism). "By the early 1970s, Canada had recognized the importance of paying athletes," says Janet Borowy, a sport researcher and former national team field-hockey player. "So they established the carding system, by which athletes were paid a monthly stipend. The system was patterned on that of West Germany, which in turn copied a number of East German features. But with direct government funding came incredible pressure to perform. Those were the years that Rob Beamish [Queen's University sport sociologist] and I have called 'the hothouse period.' The carding system institutionalized funding for elite athletes, but did it on the basis of an international ranking system that set up impossible performance standards."

The basic structure of the 1970s carding system remains in place today even though it's based on a faulty assumption, namely, that athletes, being amateurs, have a job and simply work at sport in their spare time. "A" cards are awarded to athletes with records equal to those of the top eight in the world. For this extraordinary achievement, they receive $7,800 per year, an income well below the poverty line. "B"-card athletes, who must rank on a par with the top nine to sixteen worldwide, get $6,600 per year, and "C" cards go to athletes who show good international potential (they are worth $5,400 per year). There are fewer than 1,000 carded athletes in Canada; last year, 66 percent of them relied on their subsidies as their sole source of income. (According to Beamish and Borowy only one in a hundred elite athletes in Canada ever gets a major corporate sponsorship or an endorsement.) Though Sport Canada's budget grew from $8.9 million in 1972 to $58.5 million in 1988, athletes as a group have not been getting rich.

"When Canadian athletes are ranked not against other Canadians but against international competitors, then there are a number of negative consequences," says Bruce Kidd. "Most athletes are living hand-to-mouth. When their livelihood is so totally dependent upon athletic performance, there is an enormous temptation to use any means

necessary to get ahead. To demand that athletes rank among the top eight in the world to qualify for an 'A' card, as Sport Canada now does, puts an enormous premium on performance enhancement. How many Canadians are in the top eight in the world in any field? Imagine making the salaries of Canadian lawyers or judges dependent on that criterion. But that's what we do to our athletes. We tell them, unless you win, you don't eat."

The concentration on Olympic sport during the 1970s also bled money from community fitness and recreational sport. In 1972 Sport Canada designated $6.8 million for elite athletics and $2.1 million for community sport. By 1979 the budget for elite athletics was $21.6 million, for community sport, $3.9 million. But the growth of a bureaucratic sport superstructure and the increasingly specialized nature of athletic training seemed to outdistance even these larger budget allocations. Feeling the strain of the long international recession of the 1970s, the federal government entered the 1980s burdened with the task of maintaining the sport sector with fewer resources. This set the stage for the development that has been the hallmark of this decade, the corporate transformation of Olympic sport.

In the 1950s and 1960s, the official Olympic code of pecuniary disinterest, the philosophic cornerstone of the amateur-sport system, prevailed, at least in the West. It is true that, for its own members, the IOC had always been a passport to high living, financial gain, and international power broking. And it is true that the de facto professionalism of many Eastern-bloc countries, and the commercialization of team sports in Europe and North America, already presented an "industrial" model of sport in which athletes worked full time ("professionally") for the state or a corporate boss. But most of the athletes whose performances made up the meaningful core of the Olympics, and the sports associations whose labour sustained the games, were volunteer and part time. They engaged in amateur sport because it gave them pleasure and fulfilled important aspirations to fitness and fraternity.

When athletic associations did look for patronage they sought out businesses that would donate funds and services with few strings attached. In return, the companies could expect to benefit from the same kind of goodwill they earned when they gave to the opera or ballet. The relationship of the private sector to Olympic sport was still at arm's length. "A qualitative change began to take place in corporate expectations of sport in the early 1970s," says sport sociologist Richard Gruneau, a former high-performance athlete, now a communications professor at Simon Fraser University. "Corporations began to want to see measurable returns for their funds. They started to see themselves as investors, not patrons, and they began to shape sport more directly to their own purposes. They wanted value as well as prestige for their money."

The International Olympic Committee's burgeoning commercial links with major corporations coincided with the "hothouse" period in Canadian Olympic sport. As those relationships evolved, corporations began to discover—just as the state had—that they too could harness the symbolic energy of a particular sport to their marketing purposes. Especially through television. First televised live and internationally in 1956, the Olympic games have since been used to organize ever larger audiences for paying sponsors—in 1984 and 1988, close to a billion viewers. Despite a prediction by *Sports Illustrated* in 1986 that television would begin to lose interest in covering the Olympics, NBC bid $300 million for Seoul and $401 million for the 1992 Barcelona games, up about $175 million from ABC's then-extravagant $225 million coverage of the 1984 Los Angeles games. If Toronto wins its Olympic bid for 1996, it is expecting $750 million—maybe even $1 billion—for world TV rights; the U.S. share alone would be between $500 and $600 million. For television, sport is the goose that lays golden eggs. The IOC is equally enthralled with television. One widely told story illustrates the point. When the IOC confronted the U.S. delegation with the news that a prominent American athlete had apparently tested positive for steroids at Seoul, the Americans are said to have threatened to kill U.S. media coverage of Barcelona, and the $401 million payment that goes with it, if the information were made public. The information remained secret. Even if the story is apocryphal, the scenario is believable.

The 1984 Los Angeles games are considered by many to have been the watershed in the commercialization of the Olympics. "A lot of people called

them the McLympics," Richard Gruneau remembers with some amusement, "because of the blatant role of corporate financing and advertising." By 1988 in both Calgary and Seoul, the corporate transformation was almost complete. And it had a profound effect on the way high-performance sport was presented. "Watching the games on television, I realized you often couldn't tell the difference between the real Olympics and the advertising content," Gruneau says. "The athletes, the camera sequences, the music in the ads merged right into the athletic events and the media commentary. They were one seamless fabric. The athletics and the marketing had fused."

Gruneau is one of a number of people in Canadian sport and sport studies who are highly critical of the values promoted by the media's presentation of sport. Andy Higgins, University of Toronto's head track coach, president of the Canadian Association of National Coaches, and a long-time opponent of drugs in sport, has little that's complimentary to say on the subject: "As I told the reporters who descended on me in Seoul after Johnson tested positive, we don't have a drug problem, we have a values problem, and you guys are a big part of it. Watch any television broadcast, pick up any newspaper, listen to any radio, and the only thing of consequence is winning. Winners are heroes, even when their choices and their lives are, shall we say, very far from exemplary."

Many opponents of drugs in sport concur with Higgins's view that the obsession with winning is damaging. "I was at the Saddledome in Calgary the night that Brian Orser and Brian Boitano competed for the men's figure-skating medal," Bruce Kidd remembers. "Orser skated stunningly, but Boitano got the gold. On the way out, I listened to what people were saying. 'Too bad Orser didn't come first, but my God, what an incredible athlete,' and 'He's given us four glorious years,' that kind of thing. What did the papers have to say the next morning? They called him a loser. They devalued his magnificent athleticism and artistry. They only cared about the medal."

The focus on winning has saturated Olympic sport, and it affects every coach, athlete, and athletic association. "Without thinking, perhaps, Sport Canada has bought in to the commercial enterprise values promulgated by the media," says Andy

Higgins. "Winning is important and we don't care if you do it like Pete Rose or Ben Johnson or whoever, just go on out and bring us a medal. But I certainly found it objectionable that Charlie Francis was held up by Sport Canada and the Canadian Track and Field Association as an example of the kind of coaching we should be doing to get winners, when the rumours about steroid use had abounded for years."

Sport can be the vehicle for many different kinds of experience. It can model and deliver physical well-being, sharing, and sociability. Or it can highlight authoritarian, materialistic, and sacrificial values. The sport forms and values that work best for the corporate sector are the ones that encourage the audience to consume. "The media favour a star-studded, highly visible, personality-driven form of sport," says Richard Gruneau, "because they believe this is the most effective way to organize and exploit their markets. And since the late seventies, the corporations have given Olympic sport a very clear message: you tell us how your sport will get us a larger market share, and then we'll talk. That's the climate in which sport associations, faced in many cases with trebling costs in the eighties, have had to seek their financing."

Commercialization has been the byword of the eighties, and in Canada, since their election in 1984, the Conservatives have aggressively pursued it. Not satisfied with the pace of corporate involvement in Olympic sport during the first half of the decade, in 1986 Otto Jelinek, then minister of sport, launched an agency called the Sport Marketing Council to facilitate the process. "The 1980s are signalling a change in amateur sport funding," proclaims the council's glossy brochure. "In the early 1970s, a more technocratic, 'production-driven' program was adopted for the development of elite athletes. With some financial security, provided by Sport Canada, coaches and administrators focused on their product (the athletes, their performance and developmental programs). Because of this emphasis Canadian sport overlooked the links between production, marketing, finance and administration."

It's all there in the language: sport is "product" and training is "production." In this universe, the "technocratic, production-driven" development of sport is a welcome but still insufficient condition for

sport's metamorphosis into a truly profitable corporate venture. In the same brochure Jelinek explains the motivation behind the founding of the Sport Marketing Council. "The time has come to take new initiatives that will enable both amateur sport bodies and corporate sponsors to come to the realization that viable marketing deals can be negotiated to their mutual benefit." The Council is housed in the National Sport and Recreation Centre, along with the national offices of the twenty-seven summer and ten winter Olympic sports, to enable "immediate communication with the professional staffs and quick response to marketing needs.... The basic techniques of successful, competitive marketing must become ingrained," admonishes the brochure. "Corporations want VALUE for their MONEY."

Olympic athletes and the associations that support them now face pressures identical to those on professional athletes. David Meggyesy played football for the St Louis Cardinals in the 1960s and is now the western director of the National Football League Players Association. When he talks about what has happened to amateur sport, he draws on his twenty-five years of experience as a player and player's representative in the NFL. "I think the capture of Olympic sport by commercial interests is the single most important factor in the creation of working conditions that promote drug use among athletes," he says. "When those big dollars are there, it puts a person, especially a poor person, in the position of being able to make it big financially through sport. The beauty of the play, the performance you give for your community, even decent wages and safe working conditions for everyone, they're all lost in the scramble for the prize money now associated with elite sport through endorsements and corporate sponsorships. Even in Olympic sport, the highest values are now monetary. That creates the context for steroids. I believe that if sport is going to turn around it needs protection from commercialization."

What the Johnson scandal has made publicly apparent is that elite sport is not about physical well-being but about the making of a body that can deliver extraordinary performances over a few short years. Increasingly, this means submitting the body to abusive practices. And this has happened, in the final analysis, because of something quite outside the control of governments and corporations: the natural limits of the human body. The most important indication that these have been reached lies in how little the records for men's Olympic events have changed, even with the phenomenal developments in athletic training during the last twenty years. The men's marathon record has been shortened by only two minutes, from 2:08 hours in 1969 to 2:06 in 1989. In the men's 100-metre dash, the 1968 record of 9.95 seconds has been cut down by only 3/100 of a second (taking Carl Lewis's, not Ben Johnson's, performance as the bench mark).

This does not mean that exceptionally talented and disciplined athletes cannot make some gains. But athletes will not be able to improve their times the way the Canadian hurdler Julie Rocheleau (caught using steroids by random testing in Switzerland and disqualified for two years) did, cutting her 100-metre hurdles time from 13.46 seconds in 1986 to 12.78 in 1988. Without drugs, many athletes may never reach those faster times at all. But as long as Olympic gold remains the only really important goal, coaches and athletes will use steroids in the same spirit in which they use cortisone, amphetamines, narcotics, and beta-blockers: to wrest ever-increasing feats of strength, speed, and endurance from bodies and psyches pushed past their natural capacities.

All performance-related drugs take their toll, but steroids are essentially gladiatorial, as football players will tell you, because athletes pay so heavily when they use them. Steve Courson, former NFL hotshot, is thirty-four years old today and awaiting a heart transplant. Courson is only one of many athletes who, to use the words of Terry Todd, a sports writer and former power lifter, travelled "in the Faust lane." But steroids are only a part of a much larger picture of drug use among football players, and one reason why, in David Meggyesy's estimation, NFL players have an average life expectancy almost fifteen years below the national average for American males. "It's like war out there," Bubba Paris, tackle for the 49ers, the 1989 Super Bowl champions, told *The Toronto Sun* last year. "We're like the gladiators in ancient Rome. And Pete Rozelle [then NFL commissioner] sits upstairs like Caesar."

"The debate over whether to officially condone steroid use or work to eradicate it in my mind is not about the level playing field as such," says David Meggyesy. "It's about the effect of the steroids on the athlete's life. And so far all the evidence points to those effects as deleterious, even deadly in some cases. What kind of a sick society would condone that destruction or premature death for a gold medal?"

"When I was training, I had to play with four stress fractures and I was on anti-inflammatories for extended periods," says Janet Borowy. "Though we field-hockey players didn't have to take them, I knew lots of women athletes, not only gymnasts, who were given birth control and other hormonal drugs, and couldn't refuse them because of fear of disfavour or because of contractual obligations with sports associations to follow an established training programme–despite what we know about the harm such drugs do. We trained intensively for sixty hours a week, the average for elite athletes, and far too much, in my opinion." Bruce Kidd puts it succinctly: "Everyone knows it's often unhealthy to be an Olympic athlete."

From our athletes, we have come to expect and reward machine-like performances. But we all pay for their physical and emotional sacrifices, because athletes serve as models of behaviour against which our own and our children's lives are measured. Are we tough enough, strong enough, big enough? Can *we* cut it? Are *we* winners? Whole coteries of young people are emulating Ben Johnson, regardless of the physical and personal consequences, because of the approval that "winning" gets. (As athletes across the country commented at the conclusion of the Dubin inquiry, its major accomplishment was to provide detailed schedules of Johnson's and other winners' drug programmes for eager athletes everywhere. Moral exhortations against cheating most athletes found simply laughable.) And in this sense David Steen is right: unless we change what we value in sport, the drug problem will persist. Even as steroids are detected and banned, the growing acceptance of the artificial boosting of athletes' performances means that other substances will be found to replace them. (Former steroids guru Dr. Robert Kerr suggested to the Dubin inquiry that nerve gas and strychnine have already been employed.)

As Olympic sport more and more becomes the business of politics and commerce, Olympic athletics inevitably follow much the same trajectory as commercial sport. But we have been very reluctant to admit this. "If we looked at the Olympics the way we do at the Super Bowl," Richard Gruneau says, "as a bald display of spectacle and hype, then we could examine our commitment of public resources to it. But we still want to believe that the Olympics are about brotherhood and international understanding and the celebration of health. I understand that, and I share that longing. But given the complete bankruptcy of the games as they really are, I think we have to frankly ask ourselves, are the Olympics a model or are they a cancer? And if they're a cancer, what do we do to heal our sport?" Canada has been praised by athletes and coaches around the world for having the guts to mount a public investigation. But if the Dubin inquiry is to be more than a soap opera, if it is to deliver what it promised, the real discussion about the conditions that promote the use of "banned practices" in sport must begin, not end, with its report.

For the past thirty years, the federal government has favoured elite athletics over community oriented sport, and justified this policy by appealing to ideals of physical and social well-being. (In 1987-1988, elite sport ate up 51.1 million public dollars, while community sport hobbled along at $7.4 million.) If the Johnson scandal has demonstrated anything, it is the dramatic disparity between those ideals and reality. In truth, Johnson is neither villain nor hero. Like the many other competitors at Seoul whose urine has subsequently been found to contain evidence of steroid use (rumour puts the number as high as fifty), he is simply a product of today's world of high-performance sport. His case is important not for the details of his personal story but for what those details reveal about the larger issue of "gladiatorialization." "As important as the steroid issue is, it's still only a part of the real issue," David Meggyesy concludes. "The real issue is designer drugs for athletes, drugs that reflect individualized fine-tuning and manipulation of every athlete's body. This raises the question of what kind of athletics we want to celebrate. Is our ideal a mechanically tuned killer cyborg coming down the track, or a full, vital, healthy human being?"

Source: Varda Burstyn is a writer and broadcaster living in Toronto. This article was originally published in *Saturday Night*, March 1990, pp. 42-49. Reproduced by permission of the author.

5.

Offering the Illusion of Reform on Drugs

John Hoberman

Failing to define doping out of existence, Samaranch tries an Olympic-size gesture

Last February, at a news conference held on the eve of the 1998 Olympic Winter Games, the president of the International Olympic Committee, Juan Antonio Samaranch, launched a pre-emptive strike against long-festering criticism of the I.O.C.'s campaign against doping in elite sport. "We are going to invest $50 million in the doping struggle," he proclaimed. "We have won many battles, but not the war. Yet that, too, we will win. I just don't know when."

Almost a year later, this now-forgotten public relations stunt can be appreciated as the desperate gesture it was. A month earlier, the world swimming championships in Perth, Australia, had been ruined by a doping scandal involving the Chinese athletes and officials Samaranch had long defended. And worse was yet to come. The Tour de France doping scandal that erupted in July exposed the underground drug culture of an entire sport that might well come back to haunt the 2000 Summer Olympic Games. A month later, the controversy over Mark McGwire's use of the hormonal "supplement" androstenedione made headlines around the world, thereby recruiting an international cohort of adolescent customers who place their drug orders on the Internet.

Alarmed by the spectacle of Tour riders being hauled off to jail on television, Samaranch weighed his options. Real reform would mean discrediting him and exposing to intolerable scrutiny his record of inaction, while recent events had shown that the I.O.C.'s standard public relations operation, which is long on rhetoric and short on funding and enforcement, was no longer viable.

The third option was to define the doping issue out of existence. That is why Samaranch proposed to a Spanish newspaper in late July that doping should be redefined to allow medically supervised (or "safe") doping for Olympic athletes. While this proposal was hailed by a few of the professional riders still struggling through the Tour, the I.O.C. president's publicity-conscious colleagues in the sports federations turned him down flat—a sure sign that his once-fabled power is waning and that new measures against the doping epidemic may now be possible if the initiative can be seized by antidoping activists unbeholden to the sports bureaucrats.

The I.O.C.-sponsored antidoping conference scheduled for Feb. 2-4 in Lausanne, Switzerland, is Samaranch's last chance to repair his legacy as a self-proclaimed opponent of the doping evil he once equated with death itself. Yet one look at the preconference agreement that has been embraced by the I.O.C. and the international federations makes it clear that the real purpose of this much-heralded meeting is to enable the people who created and tolerated the doping crisis to retain virtually all of their powers. It is yet another power play by a corrupt old guard.

The regressive core of this document is the provision for an "independent" anti-doping agency, situated like the I.O.C. in Lausanne, to be headed by the president of the I.O.C. and the chairman of the I.O.C. Medical Commission. Only the hopelessly naïve will accept this sort of Orwellian nonsense about "independence" from the authoritarian personalities who run the international sports fiefdoms. These men have never tolerated monitoring or the principle of accountability, and with this document they have reiterated their traditional autonomy from any standards of behavior apart from their own. So the I.O.C. and the international federations retain their authority to monitor doping offenses. Unmentioned are the stables of politically passive scientists who are kept busy devising drug testing procedures that, for various reasons, are never put into effect by the I.O.C.

Indeed, passive tolerance of doping has been part of Samaranch's political strategy for many years. Under his management, I.O.C. drug testing policy has made sure that no more than one-tenth of 1 percent of the athletes test positive at any given Olympiad. Another standard technique is to express confidence in corrupt federation colleagues. "Italian sport knows what to do," Samaranch said last September as the moral foundations of the country's sports establishment buckled under the weight of multiple doping

scandals that involved accusations against 700 doctors, the discrediting of Italy's drug-testing program and the resignation of the president of the Italian Olympic Committee. Remote from the ugly world of lying, cheating and covering up, Samaranch continues to affect the transcendent status of a pope.

An effective international antidoping campaign will not originate in the I.O.C., because such activism requires committed leadership based on ethical convictions the I.O.C. leadership does not possess. For Juan Antonio Samaranch and his closest associates, doping has always been a public relations problem that threatens the lucrative television and corporate contracts that have guaranteed their prestige and their privileges since Samaranch's accession to the presidency in 1980. "The public must be persuaded that something is being done," the head of the I.O.C. Medical Commission said in 1991 about the doping crisis. It is disheartening now to see the same cast of characters using the Lausanne conference to pursue the strategy of deception that has preserved their powers while damaging the credibility of Olympic sport.

Today the realistic alternative to I.O.C. mismanagement is the aggressive enforcement of laws that have been passed, not by the I.O.C. executive board, but by democratically elected parliamentarians. This is the lesson of the 1998 Tour de France, and it is the lesson of the Berlin trials of former East German doctors and coaches accused of administering male hormones to young girls. For the historic legal drama that has been unfolding in Berlin over the past several months was not catalyzed by the German sports federations, let alone by the I.O.C., but by a heroic antidoping crusader, the biologist Werner Franke, and a team of state prosecutors who were willing to take on a politically unpopular responsibility the sports federations should have handled but did not.

But which politicians will make the doping laws and enforce them? The records of the German, French and Italian governments over the last two decades show that, as a general rule, left-of-center politicians are willing to use the long arm of the law against doping while right-of-center politicians prefer inaction to legal action.

This political conflict has abetted the spread of doping practices and underlies last year's legal assaults on doping. It is no accident that the Tour prosecutions had to wait for a Socialist prime minister willing to appoint a Communist Minister of Youth and Sport, the redoubtable Marie-George Buffet. Nor is it by chance that the conservative regime of the recently deposed Chancellor Helmut Kohl killed every Social Democratic attempt to pass an antidoping law in the German Bundestag. Nor should we be surprised that Communists and Greens have been leaders in the campaign against corruption in the Italian National Olympic Committee.

A real antidoping program would require the following agenda:

The hiring of truly independent physician-informants to guarantee the "physiological transparency" of athletes by means of physical examinations as well as drug tests.

An intelligence operation to track the movements and contacts of former East German doping doctors and coaches as well as all medical personnel associated with athletes who show sudden improvements in performance. The I.O.C. has not lifted a finger to stop or even deplore the worldwide export of former East German doping experts into responsible positions in sports federations in at least 20 countries.

An independent prosecutor's office to pursue doping doctors, officials and athletes, unimpeded by national or federation politics.

The tragedy of modern sport is that drugs have made it a tainted and even sordid venue for the celebration of the human spirit. At this late date only the hardest measures can save it from perverse hormonal enhancements and the genetically engineered nightmares that await us.

Source: John Hoberman is a professor of Germanic studies at the University of Texas at Austin and the author of *Mortal Engines: The Science of Performance and the Dehumanization of Sport* (1992) and *Darwin's Athletes: How Sport Has Damaged Black America and Preserved the Myth of Race* (1997). This article was originally published in *The New York Times,* Sunday, January 10, 1999. Reproduced with the permission of the author.

6.

The Third Sex

Don Gillmor

Driven by the muscle imperative, female bodybuilders sculpt themselves to the point at which they are literally, hormonally male

In the lobby of the airport Howard Johnson hotel, Lynea Brehm looks like a cross between Scarlett O'Hara and Rambo, a sexual icon for the end of the millennium. She is tanned to the colour of a blood orange, wearing a sleeveless yellow dress and heels, carrying a purse. Her exposed biceps measure sixteen and a half inches and, even in repose, the striations twitch with every movement and veins snake along the exposed ridges. Her hair is dyed white blond and artfully piled in festive ringlets. Her face is gaunt from dieting and has the slight masculine frieze that is associated with steroid use. Brehm has flown in from Victoria for the amateur Canadian Bodybuilding Championships, and is considered one of the favourites. She is five feet two inches tall and weighs 140 1/2 pounds. In our march through the coffee shop, she attracts the buzz and stares of a captured alien.

Over coffee, we discuss her weight as if it were philosophy. She first competed at 104 1/2, then went to 114. A year later she competed at 133. This year she has added seven and a half pounds of shredded muscle. In the off-season she goes up to 170. Before this all began, she weighed 65 pounds.

"I'm an alcoholic. I was dying," she says, her voice resigned in the way of those trained to confess. When she left the treatment centre in July 1990, she joined a health club. "For the first three months, I just used the stationary bike; I didn't have enough confidence to even look up. It's surprising what bodybuilding has done for me. If you use it correctly, the power it gives you is unbelievable. Every day, I set myself a personal goal."

In the twenty weeks before an event, she works out four hours daily, beginning at 4:45 a.m. running stairs. She eats six bland, prescribed meals a day, works one muscle group and finishes with half an hour on the stationary bike. Her hands are square and masculine from moving millions of pounds of iron; the nails are long and painted white. I ask about drugs. "You have to be knowledgeable," she says. "There are certain drugs that women can use and certain drugs they can't. You get to a crossroads where you have to ask: Do I want this? And how bad do I want this?" She stares at her hands.

I mention a woman on the pro circuit whose face had come to resemble Fred MacMurray's, the barrage of testosterone reshaping the bone. Brehm says she saw the woman recently and she'd had the bone of her forehead, cheeks and chin shaved to reduce the masculinized density. "She was truly beautiful," Still, you have to be careful. Brehm says sweetly, "I want to have a family one day."

Tomorrow, the day before the event, she won't drink any water, flushing the liquid out of her system so that the skin is shrink-wrapped against the exaggerated musculature. Her confidence is vacillating wildly; she has seen pictures of Lisa Moore, her main rival. Some mornings she would like to sleep in rather than run stairs. "But I picture Lisa Moore up and running stairs," she says, "and I get up."

On the day of the national championships, Lisa Moore is backstage at Theatre Aquarius in Hamilton, wearing a bikini, waiting to be photographed. A former gymnast and swimmer, Moore has the foxlike beauty of a soap-opera villainess, a perfect steely smile, fine features and a pile of permed white hair. This is her fourth trip to the nationals. "Bodybuilding is everything," Moore says. "Hair, skin, colour, aesthetics. Everything is money. You have to be marketable. You need the complete package. I think I have the complete package. I'd like to go to the Arnold [Schwarzenegger] Classic and see where they place me."

Around us other competitors are applying instant tan and oil to one another in sweeping brushstrokes. The tanning product comes out almost black and is used to highlight their cuts under the lights. The smell is something like singed in fur. With a room full of faces etched from water loss and drugs, it looks like an audition for the opera *Othello*.

"In the off-season, I'm 170 pounds," Moore says. "The body has to go somewhere." It can't maintain this shape. Bodybuilding is an ephemeral suspension, that moment when the diet has reached its zenith, the muscles have inflated, the water has

been drained, and the drugs are humming to their logical conclusion. At the point of competition, the bodybuilder's health can be ravaged, the immune system compromised, the liver under assault. The fat can be gone from the soles of the feet, making it painful to stand. The competitors are dizzy and anxious and winnowed to a handsome exterior gloss. At a 1993 bodybuilding competition, the winner in the men's division, Mohammed Beneziza, died of heart failure backstage, believed to be the result of diuretic abuse, which can cause arrhythmia. Other competitors flocked around like crows, asking what he had taken. He had won, after all.

"It's a selfish sport," Moore says. "For twenty weeks before the event, everything is about your body. Everything is me me me me me." She cut out carbohydrates on Wednesday and Thursday and then sought refuge in them on Friday. Drugs, she says, are an inescapable part of bodybuilding; she is acutely aware of the masculinizing qualities of steroids. "You have to know what you can take," she says, "what package you want to present."

At eleven a.m., the heavyweight women take the stage, all fifteen dyed and shredded, ripped and cut. I am sitting with Laura Binetti, Canada's highest-ranked professional woman bodybuilder. She and her husband, Scott Abel, coached Brehm to this varnished sheen. They had once coached Moore, but she left their stable and now trains herself. Binetti quickly assesses the field. One girl is holding too much water, another doesn't know how to pose, a third lacks symmetry. In the 500-seat theatre, the mood has the intimacy of a twelve-step meeting, with calls of encouragement coming from the crowd as latissimi dorsi flare like cobras. Binetti says that Brehm has the density and the separation. Onstage, she and Lisa Moore are standing side by side in the centre of the line, two dark masses topped by halos of shining ringlets. From Row N they could be each other's evil twin. I think of what Scott Abel said earlier: "Bodybuilders believe that the more they deprive themselves, the more they deserve to win."

The women stand rigid, blinking into the lights, offering their packages. After going through the mandatory poses to highlight the basic muscle groups, they leave the stage, waiting for the finals at nine p.m.

After the prejudging, a few of the eleven judges stand outside the theatre and have a cigarette. I ask Jake Franceschini, a former bodybuilder himself, what they are looking for. "It's a saw-off between muscularity and femininity," he says. "We're looking for the total package. Looks are important. If she's had children, if she's got bad skin, pimples, it counts against her." He shrugs. It isn't fair, but...

Another of the smokers, Ron Haché, who also judges professional shows for the International Federation of Bodybuilders, the body that sanctions and judges competitions internationally, says that in the last pro show, the sexiest woman won, not the most muscular. "The Ms. Fitness shows are where it's at. That's where the money is," he says. The muscular women don't sell magazines. "They get caught up, it becomes an obsession," he says. "They go too far."

One of the competitors, Dayana Cadeau, has breast implants that cut quite a swath. "Now with the end of the century and everything, implants are okay," Franceschini says. "Five years ago, we frowned on them. But you lose your breasts when you train. You have to be marketable in the pros. As far as I'm concerned, in the pros, they all look like men."

Mark Baker, a Toronto lawyer who is the president of Bodybuilding Ontario, thinks Cadeau's implants are extreme. "They're too big," he says. "They detract. I want to have a feeling of a complete woman." And what is the complete woman? She is taut, hormonally undecided, tanned, almost naked and childless, an adolescent's wet dream. Contestants often ask judges what they are lacking, and several have been advised to get breast implants to recapture some feminine ground. "They come to us for direction," Franceschini says, lighting another du Maurier.

Some of the amateur competitors then go on to compete professionally. "It can take more of a commitment chemically," Baker says. "The competition is so severe, it can be a death sentence career-wise. They are tempted to quit their jobs and go to greater extremes. It's for people who want to become an icon, a symbol." A symbol of what, though? Of suffering and perfection, of what it means to be Promethean.

Drugs are tacitly accepted in bodybuilding. Competitors argue that most athletes are using them; *they* are simply being honest. Everyone's a freak now. Football players weigh 370 pounds. Female gymnasts are suspended in a never-never land of prepubescence. "You have juicers in *synchronized swimming*," Jake Franceschini says. "And you know why there are drugs at the Olympics? Because no one is going to pay to watch a man run the 100 metres in twelve seconds."

Between the prejudging of the morning and the evening event, Lisa Moore goes home and eats bananas. "The judges have me at number one right now," she says with a flash of that grim smile. She can sense it. Brehm goes back to the Sheraton hotel and has a steak and a piece of cheesecake, but no water. She takes a nap and wakes up and eats potatoes. "It's my show," Brehm says. They each feel that they are deserving, that they have suffered with greater zeal.

"Bodybuilders equate their worth as people with their bodies," says Scott Abel, himself a former competitive bodybuilder. "If you tell them they look good, they feel they are good people. If you say their pecs need work, they are bad. Their body is their moral universe." Abel has a reputation for chemical wizardry, an enviable knowledge of how drugs and diet affect the body. He now trains athletes, including his wife, who won the European Grand Prix in Prague last year and finished first or second in three other pro shows. Their Don Mills apartment is a mecca for the unformed. Local bodybuilders from the Pitbull Gym in Scarborough come for advice; others drive up from Buffalo or fly in from California to be tuned like an Indy car.

"Competing is a way of keeping reality at bay," Abel says. He and Binetti are critical of bodybuilding but are seduced by it themselves. Abel has maintained his wide, compact build since he quit nine years ago. He has a blond flat-top haircut and a soft voice. He and his wife condemn the subjective judging and thuggish mentality that pervades bodybuilding, but pursue a physical nirvana. They accept drug use as a reality but are critical of the uncontrolled abuse that is common in their sport. Binetti sees herself as an athlete, but one who is effectively without a sport. She is stranded between the masculine and feminine worlds, with a soft, pretty, doe-eyed face and the flayed musculature of an anatomy chart. Chemically she is stranded between a naive public that thinks Ben Johnson was an anomaly and the rampant, dangerous juicing in her sport.

"If you're against drugs, don't do them," Abel says. "But don't expect that you're going to be competing at a worthwhile level." You can't win without them. Not in bodybuilding, not in most sports. But bodybuilders tend to be the most flagrant abusers. "It's unbelievable. You've got people dying. It's becoming an arms race."

Steroids have been in use as an athletic training tool almost fifty years. Testosterone was first synthesized in 1935, when researchers Karoly Gyula David and Ernst Laqueur isolated the hormone. It was applied clinically to various ailments; in men it was used to treat hypogonadism and, occasionally, impotence. In women it was applied to menorrhagia and breast cancer, and to revive the female libido. In the 1940s, bodybuilders on the American West Coast began using steroids to build bulk, and by the 1960s steroid use had spread to track and football. Doctors now use it clinically to combat muscle wasting in AIDS patients and routinely prescribe it to men complaining of waning potency. In 1990 the World Health Organization oversaw a global clinical trial that used anabolic steroids as a male contraceptive. It established its efficacy, with minimal side effects, using a dose that exceeded the one measured in Ben Johnson's Seoul urine sample. If steroids are legitimized as contraceptives, it would conceivably weaken the medical argument against their use by athletes. At any rate, they are entrenched as training aids. The international black market in steroids is estimated by *Scientific American* to be one billion dollars a year.

And steroids are not the only performance-enhancing drugs. "The latest thing," says Abel, "is to combine HGH [human growth hormone] and insulin, which is anticatabolic—it prevents the breakdown of tissue. The drugs that are being taken aren't just for making muscles now, they're about making other drugs work better. So with insulin and growth hormone, they take thyroid, with steroids they take estrogen blockers."

Because most steroids are synthetic testosterone, the effect on women bodybuilders tends to be the most graphic in sport. Testosterone is the hormone that produces the androgenic, or masculinizing, aspects in male adolescents as well as the anabolic

(or tissue-building) properties. When women take steroids in sufficient quantities, they in effect go through male puberty: a deepening voice, growth of the reproductive tract, with the clitoris mimicking the lengthening of the penis, new facial and body hair and a quickened libido. Extended abuse ushers women further along the male continuum, into thinning hair and a shift in facial structure, the forehead, chin and cheekbones thickening, the skin coarsening—effects that are irreversible.

"There is definitely a problem with women taking so many hormones," Abel says. "They are literally, hormonally, men. They've upset their DHT [dihydrotestosterone] so much that they have to shave. The masculinization doesn't have to happen, but they don't care. There's no fear about drugs. Even if they know it's fake, they'll take it anyway and hope it's real. The women look like transvestites because they're making mistakes. There's no guidance. Bodybuilding is a drug subculture."

But the subculture is a reflection of the culture. In North America, an industry has grown up around the idea of metamorphosis. We continually search for ways to make ourselves well, or simply happier, or at least less like ourselves. Only a fool would remain the old you, the one that was fat, single, poor, spiritually null and addicted to bad relationships, the one who hasn't unleashed the power within, or sent their inner child to military school. Women's bodybuilding is the most complete metamorphosis obtainable; it literally produces a new you. It is not an isolated freak show, but the embodiment of one of the dominant cultural messages of the past thirty years—that you are not stuck with yourself. Man is something to be surpassed, Nietzsche wrote. "I teach you the Superman."

But how to market the new Superman? Especially if he's a woman. Women's bodybuilding evolved from the Miss Body Beautiful contest, which used to accompany the men's bodybuilding events in the late 1960s. The women posed in heels and bikinis to offset the static tedium of the men's competition. Wayne DeMilia, the head judge of the International Federation of Bodybuilders, says that sometimes the women were strippers from New York burlesque houses. "They'd enter the Miss Body Beautiful contest to win the hundred-dollar prize, then go back to the burlesque-house owner and say, Now you have to pay me more because I'm Miss Body Beautiful."

In 1979, Carla Dunlap, a contestant in the Best in the World contest, another swimsuit affair, removed her high heels and struck a double bicep pose in a parody of the male bodybuilders. The crowd, as they say, went wild. The following year, the first Ms. Olympia was staged. In 1985, the film *Pumping Iron II: The Women* was released, piquing interest partly because of the sexual allure of the champion, Rachel McLish. Since then, as the women have grown more muscular, attendance at such events as the Ms. Olympia contests has steadily declined. "Let's face it," DeMilia says, "when you get down to the nitty gritty, the fans want skin. And without fans, there's no sport." Whether there is a sport even with fans is arguable, but certainly without fans there is no business, a problem for those who control bodybuilding. They are paradoxically uneasy with women who follow the muscle-building imperative.

"Bodybuilding is autocratic," Scott Abel says. "The Weiders control the sport, period." Ben Weider, seventy-two, is the founder and president of the IFBB. His older brother, Joe, created the Mr. and Ms. Olympia contests, co-sponsors the Arnold Classic, and runs the lucrative publishing arm, which produces several slick muscle and fitness magazines each month. Ben Weider is still based in Montreal, where the brothers began their empire in 1940, selling weights and publishing *Your Physique.* Joe moved to Los Angeles in 1972 because that was where the bodybuilders were. The Weider empire is now worth an estimated $250 million. Many of the top bodybuilders are under contract to Weider, and are judged by IFBB judges in Weider-sponsored events covered by Weider magazines promoting Weider products, weights and food supplements with simple, Orwellian names: POWER, MASS, CUTS. The Weiders have cornered the market.

"The judges are judged," Jake Franceschini says. They have to toe the party line. "It's a pyramid where you have the IFBB and the Weiders at the top, then the Canadian Federation, then the provincial bodies."

The Weider empire was built on the idea that an improved physique had benefits beyond the aesthetic. The advertisements in comic books in the 1960s appealed to a male adolescent sense of doubt: "Pick out the body you want in place of your puny weakness." The thread of masculine accomplishment that ran through the Weiders' advertising is still evident, but there isn't a corresponding niche for women. At the Ms. Olympia, the winners are not always the most muscular, but the most marketable. It is essentially a trade show, with a predetermined winner.

Women's bodybuilding has simply followed the inevitable arc of sport—go further, go faster, do more. But the furthest in this case is somewhere deep into the gender frontier. The Weiders haven't been able to stop the inevitable muscular progress and are left trying to market the result. *Flex* magazine, a Weider publication, experimented with nude centrefolds of women bodybuilders, inching toward the idea of sexuality and female muscle. Laura Binetti has declined offers to star in nude videos and photo shoots, and she was advised by an IFBB judge to get breast implants. (She refused.)

Competitors are routinely advised to consider breast implants, collagen lips, hair extensions and fearsome nails. They are in the odd position of having to buy back the feminine qualities that they lost to testosterone. In a way, women's bodybuilding may be a fitting sport for the next millennium. It incorporates suffering, drugs and metamorphosis, and gives the illusion of glowing Californian health while masking inner decay.

In the Dofasco lobby of Theatre Aquarius, the crowd mills, waiting for the evening event. Tables are set up, selling Solid Mass powder in gallon jars, Promax Designer Protein and Body Language clothing. Men are wide and brilliantined, their upper bodies tapering to tiny waists. The women are in heels, sleeveless and tanned, the surgeon's breasts nestled into latex, faces chiselled. Everywhere there is that luxuriant walk, the slow Lipizzaner prance of the body-conscious. They discuss body parts as if they were offspring and dispute the probable winners. "His shit is *melting*," one man says. "But they're still going to give it to him." At six foot one and 190 pounds, I am a four-eyed, pencil-necked geek. I feel like the maypole in a Brueghel painting. I buy a Hard Body Amino Bar from a beautiful blond woman and eat it, and then a Steel Bar. A man offers me a protein shake out of pity and I wash down two thermogenic stimulator capsules. I finish up with a FiBar and take my seat, reading the list of ingredients from my dinner, waiting for the ephedrine to kick in.

For the finals, the top six finalists in each class do a sixty-second posing routine set to music. The top three then do a pose-down in front of the judges, snapping and locking their muscles in quick succession. Brehm does a conservative musical routine. Dayana Cadeau, of the breast implants, does a flirting, seductive dance, shimmying into a suspenseful split. Lisa Moore's music employs her own name and she coyly lipsynchs the words "It's not over yet" to the row of judges. She is confident and lithe.

They are, as expected, the three finalists in the heavyweight class. The crowd anticipates the judges' decision with their own interpretations, while the three women sweat under the lights, exhausted, their muscles locked into place, the packages inching toward their expiry date. When Lisa Moore's name is called as the third-place finisher, she looks as if she has been slapped. Her face freezes into a tribal mask of revenge and betrayal. Dayana Cadeau takes second. Lynea Brehm is judged heavyweight champion. The judges choose muscle today. She stands smiling, her confidence, tan and muscles all held in proud suspension.

Women trained by Scott Abel dominate the event, winning first and second in the women's middleweight category, first in the heavyweight and first overall. His rigid program of diet, weight training and what he describes as "ergogenic advice" has produced the desired effect. The girls have built flawless, sexually ambiguous, public husks. They have triumphed over themselves.

Source: Don Gillmor is a journalist covering the arts, politics and sports. He has received eight magazine awards, including three national magazine awards. Since 1989, he has been a contributing editor at *Saturday Night Magazine* and is a regular contributor to *Saturday Night*, *Toronto Life* and *The Globe and Mail*. This article was originally published in *Toronto Life*, January 1997. Reproduced with the permission of the author.

7.
Don't Cheat Your Body
Laura Robinson

When it comes to artificially enhancing human performance, sport is just the tip of the iceberg

In November, I started my search for snow. Ever since my cycling club decided to cross-country ski to stay in shape back in 1972, I have prayed impatiently for the white stuff. I don't compete as much as I once did, but I love to balance speed and technique to see whether I can still push the margins of my own mortality in some wonderful natural environment. That is why I recently found myself at Lake Louise in the Rocky Mountains with some colleagues from the Banff Centre for the Arts.

It was what we call a blue-wax day: a combination of new snow and temperatures below freezing to give good grip, but not so cold that one had to wear a tuque. These conditions couldn't be better for the novice skiers from Australia, Mexico and Brazil. They picked up the basic idea of kicking and gliding fairly quickly. (Especially the Latin Americans; I only needed to say, "Imagine kicking a soccer ball," and they were off.)

The gathering of friends and strangers on a part of Earth, whether it be a ski trail or soccer pitch, to converse in the universal language of sport is one of the most human experiences one can ever have. As a former competitive cyclist and skier, I have been with people from all over the world in such situations, and we've understood each other as dancers do—through the way in which our bodies and spirits move through space and time. It is both primitive and profound, and it is for this reason that I mourn not only what is happening to athletes and their bodies, but also the way in which sport has come to be a reflection of a set of very troubling and dehumanizing values in Western culture.

The International Olympic Committee has just announced a new program of reforms, including a four-point anti-drug program for athletes, and a world antidoping agency headed by Canadian

IOC member Dick Pound. While this may appear to smooth the rough ethical edges of international sport, I believe these measures will matter little. Sport was never the problem in the first place.

A certain percentage of athletes use performance-enhancing drugs because they know they can push the body further. Farther, faster and higher is what wins Olympic medals and million-dollar sponsorship contracts. The cyborg athlete–someone whose performance is dependent on various technologies–is a given today. Whether we rely on state-of-the-art bicycles, rowing shells, or performance-enhancing drugs, athletes are slaves, in one way or another, to artificial interventions. When competing, I ski on fluorocarbon wax on a graphite base, and use carbon fibre poles. Without question, my performance is improved. But what happens when the technology moves from the equipment and is internalized in the body? Where does technology end and the organic human being begin? Where does enhancement end and cheating begin?

In any case, athletes (myself included) are only mirroring a narcissistic society caught in ethical dilemmas involving the body, technology and money. Sport is just a bit player in these dramas. The central role goes to the Western world's belief that it should be able to have whatever it wants. The body has become a material good to be altered, bought or traded in a way that financially benefits someone. This dilemma is certainly worth thinking about while skiing to Kicking Horse Pass.

What's happening to sports is also happening to other human experiences: making ourselves physically attractive, having a child, living in an aging body. Consumer magazines carry pages of advertisements for cosmetic surgeons selling us new and improved bodies. Whether we want a child, a shot at the gold, or a sliced and tightened body for the unathletic, not only do we think we can buy it, we think we deserve it.

Earlier this fall, Maureen McTeer wrote of the ethics of reproductive technology on this page. She wrote of the female body as a commodified site: human eggs are for sale, wombs are for sale, some genetic futures are for sale, and will be saved and valued, while others will be terminated, all in the name of a better product. In order for this commerce to occur, what the body symbolizes must also change. Or perhaps we are simply regressing to the days when it was legal to sell a human being.

When the body becomes a site for commerce because of its reproductive capacity, value is determined not by innate humanity or the sacred nature of life but by the age and genetic potential of the person inhabiting it. Even though the parents of a child created through reproductive technology will no doubt love it whether or not it meets some standard of perfection, the very act of trying to create a better baby, or delivering a baby through a more perfect womb, may devalue the mystery of life.

The reasoning behind reproductive technology is that everyone who wants a child should be able to have one, as long as they have enough cash to pay for the procedures. That some bodies simply aren't supposed to have children–especially after a certain age–does not enter into this debate. When nature fails, technology delivers. You *can* always get what you want.

Like becoming a good parent, becoming a great athlete is a process that takes years. It's contrary to the notion of immediate gratification delivered through technology and money. But the kicking of a soccer ball or a ski, and the meeting of challenges–in other words, the process that makes sport real and wonderful–is of little consequence in a culture driven by the making and selling of products.

Since the time of the ancient Greeks, artists have paid tribute to the mystery and beauty of the athletic body. But in our secular age of money and technology and performance-enhancing drugs, that mystery is destroyed. Our new magic wand can change our dissatisfaction with ourselves and improve on what God, or nature, gave us. As they become consumed with becoming sport's version of the perfect body/machine product, athletes are just giving the public what it asked for.

The technology of medicine has delivered plenty of drugs that undoubtedly enhance athletic performance. But some, such as the blood-boosting erythropoietin (EPO), have caused coronary heart failure and death among

Dutch and Belgium cyclists earlier this decade. And we know now that steroids can affect the development of sex organs, especially in women. That certain athletes willingly alter the chemical composition of something as intimate as their own sexuality in quest of better performance surely indicates their devotion to the gods of narcissism, money and technology. Perhaps it is not coincidental that the ancient Greeks, who celebrated the perfection of the body through rituals such as the first Olympic Games, also developed several cautionary myths about body worship. They must have known that, for a culture to have any kind of perspective on itself, it must be able to reflect on more than just its physical image. Narcissus didn't have technology or an insatiable market for the perfect body to urge him on. Yet he still obsessed to death, staring at his own reflection in a pool of water.

Our modern myths are fixated on the need to acquire and keep an ageless, high-performing body. But being human is greater than that. Yes, it can be about great athletic effort and striving for excellence. But, at its roots, it is about experiencing one's humanity, not buying it. It is about a free body and spirit.

Anyone tempted by such 20th-century magic as cosmetic surgery or reproductive technology can hardly point the finger at athletes who practise their own version of getting what they want. Ultimately, athletes are simply giving society what it seems to demand from everyone: a body beyond what is humanly possible.

Source: Laura Robinson is a former national-level cyclist and cross-country ski racer. She is the author of two books about sport, *She Shoots, She Scores: Canadian Perspectives on Women and Sport* and *Crossing the Line: Violence and Sexual Assault in Canada's National Sport*. This article was originally published in *The Globe and Mail*, December 28, 1999, A13. Reproduced with the permission of the author.

Part 3
Olympics

The Olympic Movement celebrated its 100th anniversary in Paris in 1994 and 1996 (Atlanta) marked the 100th anniversary of the Olympic Games. The Games have always been just one part of the Movement– a Movement guided by the philosophy of Olympism.

The Olympic Movement was founded by Baron Pierre de Coubertin, who drew on the Victorian British sporting codes of fair play, amateurism, and the notion that sports could be used to develop character. In addition to these goals, Olympism emphasizes peace, international understanding, and the whole development (mental, physical, spiritual) of human beings. Most of those currently involved in the Olympic Movement will assert that, to a greater or lesser extent, these are still the aims of the Movement. However, to a growing number of people outside the Movement, the Olympics appear to be just a huge commercial sporting spectacular–a World Championship of World Championships. This has been the case particularly since 1984 (Los Angeles), with the first overtly commercialized Games and the first open appearance of professional athletes.

The first full public exposure of cheating around the bidding practices of potential Olympic cities–the Salt Lake City scandal in 1999–has now exposed corruption at the heart of Olympism. But anyone who cared to pay attention was well aware of these problems before 1999. Doug Booth and Colin Tatz take us through the bidding process that led up to the 1993 announcement that Sydney would host the "millennium" Olympics. They expose the corruption associated with the bidding process–a process that casts both the "lords of the rings" (see, Simson & Jennings [1992] and Jennings, [1996] for an even more in-depth exposé of corruption in the International Olympic Committee) and the organizing committees in a particularly bad light. They conclude by outlining some of the "costs" that Australians are likely to incur as a consequence of hosting the Games. (This article also relates well to the **Economics of Sport**.)

The International Olympic Committee, which decides on the location of future Olympic Games, has been a by-invite-only club. John Hoberman and Andrew Jennings suggest that the recent scandals are a direct consequence of the type of people that Juan Antonio Samaranch has invited to join this club. Angela Schneider and Robert Butcher report on the reforms put in place by the IOC as a result of corporate, political, and particularly athlete pressure. And Kevin Wamsley raises some important questions about social priorities in relation to bids for Olympic Games.

References

- Simson, V., & A. Jennings (1992). *The Lords of the Rings: Power, Money and Drugs in the Modern Olympics*. Toronto: Stoddart.

- Jennings, A. (1996). *The New Lords of the Rings: Olympic Corruption and How to Buy Gold Medals*. London: Simon & Schuster.

Additional Sources

Videos:

- *Lords of the Rings* is a British "World in Action" video exposing the corruption behind the Olympic Games. It has not been broadcast in North America.

- *Corporate Sponsorship of the Games*, HBO's "REALsports" series, focuses on modern sponsorship of the Olympics.

Print Resources:

- Hoffman, T. (1996). Munich 1972, Atlanta 1996. *Queen's Quarterly* 103(2), September, pp.477-486. [An insightful look at politics and terrorism at the Olympics from a former Canadian intelligence officer.]

- Beamish, R. (1996). Pierre de Coubertin's shattered dream. *Queen's Quarterly,* 103(2), September, pp.489-501. [An examination of the origins of Olympism and the way that the rules have been changed to permit the present professionalized and commercialized Games.]

- Brunt, S. (1998). And he told two friends ... and he told two friends. *Report on Business Magazine,* June, pp.47-52. [Looks at the jockeying for power and profits around Toronto's 2008 Olympic bid.]

8.

Swimming with the Big Boys?

Douglas Booth and Colin Tatz

Sydney's 2000 Olympic bid

The Olympics have, indeed, been what their founders wanted them to be: political.—Allen Guttmann[1]

On 23 September, 1993, the International Olympic Committee (IOC) met in Monte Carlo to decide which of five competing cities would host the 2000 Olympic Games. In the final round of voting, with three cities already eliminated and against the predictions of almost every observer and commentator, IOC members chose Sydney ahead of Beijing by forty-five votes to forty-three.[2] The decision raises two questions: how did Sydney win the vote and what opportunities will the Games offer black and white Australians?

The IOC's sporting politics

When Frenchman Baron Pierre de Coubertin revived the Olympic Games he said his aim was to create international respect and goodwill and help build a better and more peaceful world through a quadrennial festival of sport. The idea of Olympism as a peace movement has become a shibboleth. Even events in recent host countries and cities have failed to debunk de Coubertin's idea: disintegration of the Soviet Union, an attempted coup in Russia, insurrection in Moscow, race riots in Los Angeles, war in Sarajevo, bloody student demonstrations in Seoul, and secessionist politics in Spain. IOC president Juan Antonio Samaranch regularly cites the 1988 Games in Seoul as a success for Olympism and South Korea. While the Games were a catalyst for Soviet and Chinese reappraisal of South Korea, one could reasonably assume that this diplomatic thaw would have occurred the following year with the end of the Cold War. Certainly Seoul did not ease tensions between North and South Korea. In fact, North Korea, Cuba and Albania boycotted the Games.

Why does this myth survive? It endures because international sport contains an inherent political utility and because the IOC propagates sport as a *suprapolitical* project. Organised sport is a competitive relationship which emphasises prestige and superiority. Victors in sport—whether individual participants or collectives such as teams, supporters, communities, regions, nations—invariably make claims about their status in any number of areas. Countries seize victory in international sport to display national accomplishments in ideology, economics, politics, science, diplomacy, religion and race.[3] Indeed, this emerged amid the jubilation in Australia on 24 September. Prime Minister Keating said the victory put Australia "in the swim with the big boys": "I think a lot of hard-nosed international representatives made a judgement about that question tonight and decided in the affirmative."[4] Even ordinary Australians saw the decision in these terms: Sydney "is a victory for the right and just. Our beautiful city on the harbour, cosmopolitan, multiracial and free, will show the world what freedom really means at the dawn of the 21st century."[5] Such political utility has enabled the Olympic Games to become the premier international pageant.

Samaranch admits that the IOC practises politics which he says is necessary to protect the humanist ideals of sport. But the great sophistry of the IOC is that its sporting politics are the antithesis of Olympism. Yugoslavia's participation at Barcelona is a prime example.[6] Despite a United Nation's resolution banning it from Barcelona, and contrary to tradition, the IOC welcomed the Yugoslavs as "independent Olympic participants." It also chartered a plane to fly seventeen athletes from war-torn Bosnia-Herzegovina to Barcelona. Lest anyone needs reminding, civil war racks Bosnia-Herzegovina despite the IOC's carrot of Olympic participation.

By politics Samaranch means personal business, money, power, prestige, status. His own opportunism and ambition have been exposed.[7] Active lobbying for IOC observer status at the United Nations and for the Nobel Peace Prize reveal Samaranch's ambitions. He first publicly mooted the Nobel Prize in 1988 after Seoul, which he described as a major contribution to world peace. The North Korean boycott, however, remained a blemish and he resolved that every country would participate at Barcelona—hence Yugoslavia's presence in defiance of the United Nations. Still unrewarded, Samaranch hired a British-based public relations company to lobby on his behalf. Privately he told colleagues that "success will be measured on whether or not we win the Nobel Prize." After the Norwegian press exposed the plan and revived the IOC President's political background as an MP in General Franco's fascist regime, Samaranch conceded he was "not qualified." But, he said, "the IOC might be considered because it has fought for 100 years for youth, peace, sport and solidarity. It should not be for me but the IOC."[8] Of course, only Samaranch, as President, could accept the Nobel Prize.

Samaranch has overseen the commercialisation of the Olympic movement. Multinational companies now buy rights to the five-ring Olympic symbol and television rights give producers power to reschedule events and modify rules in the interests of advertisers. Samaranch's view is that "any sport that does not get television interested has no future."[9] Drugs, professionalism and bidding frenzies between cities vying to host the Games are further manifestations of commercialism which undermine the IOC's credibility.

The host city game: The politics of (stretched) credibility

The IOC's political credibility depends upon host cities conveying the humanist ideals of sport. This is the ultimate criterion by which the IOC *publicly* rewards Games. (While technical competence and financial viability are obvious selection criteria, neither is the determinant. For example, the IOC's Inquiry Commission, which assesses the suitability of bidding cities, ranked Beijing fourth).[10] Seizing the moment of Sydney's victory, Samaranch explained: "we have given the Games to a young country with young people and maybe they will set an example for the future."[11]

Beijing posed a dilemma: would it confirm or stretch IOC credibility? Samaranch argued that Beijing would open China to democratic values and rejected criticism of its human rights' record. The IOC employed Peter Knight, prominent Washington lawyer and former Vice-Presidential aide, to lobby against U.S. Congress opposition to Beijing. It ignored the text of Congress resolutions which identified Chen Xitong, the Chairman of the Beijing Bid Committee, as the Mayor who had signed the martial law decree before the violent suppression of the Chinese democracy movement

in Tiananmen Square.[12] Samaranch repeated the hackneyed position that politics should not influence IOC decisions, although he admitted some members would reject Beijing on human rights' grounds. But he stressed his personal view: the Games "could help to open up a country and change many things the way it did in Seoul."[13]

Two conditions constrained the Sydney Olympic Bid Committee (SOBC) from officially criticising China's human rights' record. Firstly, SOBC's own campaign was built around the premise that sport brings people together and unites them above all other considerations. Secondly, Australia's human rights' record introduced the problem of logical consistency.[14] Fearing that black groups would campaign against Sydney, SOBC employed prominent Aborigines, including Charles Perkins, David Clark, Cleonie Quayle, Justine Saunders and Ricky Walford. The media, of course, felt no qualms about disparaging and reproaching China while at the same time reporting the views of sympathetic Aborigines such as Bill Naird, former Chairman of the National Aboriginal Conference. He said that "the 2000 Olympics would provide a perfect focal point for reconciliation" and offer "a showcase" for Aboriginal culture.[15] Sadly, no correlation exists between cultural displays and racial harmony. In the week before the vote, SOBC flooded Monaco with black dancers and performers, but as Aboriginal Commissioner Sol Bellear reminded us, they were "tourist curios–like koalas and kangaroos."[16]

Mired in the government's intended legislative response to the High Court's Mabo decision, Aborigines took little interest in Sydney's Olympic bid. Only the Aboriginal Legal Service in Redfern intervened. In a letter to the IOC it said that "mistreatment" of Aborigines—including police harassment, drug and alcohol dependency, high rates of imprisonment, unemployment and infant mortality, and racism in sporting institutions—"disqualified" Sydney.[17] The IOC never replied. Aboriginal leaders made a tactical error. Australian sports officials and the New South Wales (NSW) Government desperately wanted the Games: when NSW Premier John Fahey suspended the NSW Treasury's financial risk analysis until after the IOC's decision,[18] he signalled that literally no cost was too high. Such desperation afforded Aborigines space in which they could have wrung social justice packages from the Fahey Government; the Premier may have even repaired the acknowledged disgrace of Toomelah township.[19] Australians took fright when Aborigines threatened to mount a black nation boycott of the 1982 Commonwealth Games in Brisbane. Under the force of public pressure, including intense foreign media investigations, even Queensland Premier Joh Bjelke-Petersen was moved to allow two hitherto banned street marches.

Commercialisation has complicated the IOC's political objectives in choosing the host city and has undermined its credibility. Firstly, it gives major IOC sponsors–who pay $US40m each for worldwide rights to the Olympic symbol–vast influence. Many of the IOC's sponsors supported Beijing in the belief that it would assist their profiles and marketing efforts in China.[20] Secondly, commercialisation has given cities new incentives to bid for the Games. After Montreal incurred a $US1bn debt (largely for an accompanying urban infrastructure program), other cities began balking at the Games for fear of the financial consequences. But Los Angeles, which made a $US215m profit, showed that the Games offered cities potentially massive economic rewards and it launched bidding frenzies.[21]

Profit transformed the lobbying landscape. New, non-sporting interests were suddenly attracted to the Games and manoeuvred themselves onto bid committees. The vanguard of SOBC comprised leaders of the transport, construction, hotel and tourism industries, the financial sector and the commercial media. Members of SOBC included Peter Abeles (TNT), Kevan Gosper (Shell), John Ward (Qantas), Eric Neal (Westpac), Kerry Packer (Consolidated Press), John Alexander (Fairfax) and Kenneth Cowley (News Limited).

Bid committees traditionally shy from public scrutiny and the only constraints on their lobbying appear to be the consciences and mores of IOC members. But they are answerable and responsible only to the IOC President who appoints them. Samaranch personally selected more than half of the current ninety-three members who will hold their positions until retirement at seventy-two. The IOC President is accountable to no one and wields total power. He appoints members to the organisation's all-important working committees and has the authority to settle all procedural questions at IOC sessions. In its quest for the 2000 Games,

China presented the IOC museum with a 2200-year-old terracotta soldier from the Ch'in tomb.[22] Explaining the donation of priceless Chinese heritage, Chen Xitong, Chairman of the Beijing Bid Committee, said, "We look upon the IOC as God–their wish is our command."[23] In their desire to satisfy the "Gods," bid committees laud, indulge, coddle and pamper IOC members. Dossiers identifying IOC members' personal wants and tastes are mandatory bid committee tools. Bob Scott, Chief Executive of Manchester's Bid Committees for the 1996 and 2000 Games, once boasted: "I even know the shoe size of the second daughter of one particular IOC member!"[24] Early in its campaign for the 2000 Games, Berlin's committee apologised for investigating IOC members' sexual preferences.[25]

While the style and intensity of lobbying is antithetical to the noble sporting ideal of fair competition, some IOC members happily exploit this deferential treatment. They fashion opulent lifestyles from all-expenses-paid "investigations" of cities bidding for (summer and winter) Games, and from the pilgrimages of gift-and-favour-bearing delegations who arrive at IOC meetings and even members' homes. An official of the Barcelona Organising Committee summed up the behaviour of IOC members: "They're used to getting what they want, to having their demands met–their motto is 'we all want more'."[26]

After its meeting in Birmingham in 1991, the IOC introduced strict rules to curtail the obvious and acknowledged corruption and to repair its image as a rapacious family. It introduced a $US200 limit on gifts to IOC members: IOC headquarters must issue air tickets (nonrefundable to the individual) to members visiting bid cities which then reimburse the IOC: bidding cities cannot hold receptions or cocktail parties for IOC members or arrange exhibitions or demonstrations; meetings between bid city committees and IOC members can only take place in a single room or suite; and delegations from bidding cities which visit IOC sessions are limited to six members.[27] But no structures exist to enforce the rules. Just two months after they were introduced, the Berlin committee invited the IOC executive to "a soirée at the beautiful Witshaus Schildhorn [Berlin]."[28]

IOC members oppose changes to the way they choose host cities. Samaranch recommended that the eleven-member executive select host cities, but this would remove the only power ordinary IOC members possess. Nor would it guarantee a fairer selection process. The only way to cleanse this sordid game is to dispense with lobbying and compel members to publicly rank cities according to strict, unambiguous criteria.

Buying the 2000 Games: Inside the Sydney bid

Failed bids by Brisbane and Melbourne, both of which received favourable Inquiry Commission assessments, point to the biggest obstacle that faced SOBC: systematic cajoling and flattering of IOC members.[29] (Of course, there were also other factors including southern hemisphere seasons and distances, and the fact that Melbourne hosted the 1956 Games). Notwithstanding the dangers of "packaging and labelling national character," cultural historian John Rickard has identified and described an Australian psyche characterised by "irreverence and at times an almost surreal mordancy."[30] In short, obsequiousness is not an Australian trait.

Yet, contrary to the "national character," SOBC consciously fawned upon IOC members to acquire their votes. Its lobbying program, modelled on the successful Atlanta 1996 bid and euphemistically referred to as the "let's be friends" campaign, consisted of bestowing royal treatment on visiting IOC members and, particularly in the case of Third World members, building their profile and status in their own countries. Visitors flew first class to Australia, were cleared through customs before the plane "docked," and were driven by limousine to a five-star hotel. According to Perry Crosswhite, Secretary General of the Australian Olympic Committee (AOC), they were given free rein to structure their itinerary and "nominate anything special that they, or their wives, wanted to see or do. We encouraged them to do what they were interested in; some were interested in art, some were interested in jewellery, particularly opals." IOC visitors dined at the best restaurants and were entertained at the Opera House. Every effort was made "to get as many IOC people [to Sydney] as often as possible." For example, SOBC paid $A300,000 towards the cost of staging the 1993 World Youth Soccer Cup in Australia. Thirteen IOC members visited Sydney for that tournament. SOBC also introduced scores of members of the extended Olympic family to Sydney by hosting the General Assembly of International Sporting Federations in 1991.

SOBC lobbied IOC members around the world. It divided the earth into five regions and assigned a senior official to each. For example, Phil Coles, a member of SOBC, Director General of the AOC and an IOC member, lived in Paris for several months in 1993. A SOBC team, which co-opted former Prime Minister Gough Whitlam, also trekked through sub-Saharan Africa in July and August 1993. Africans revere Whitlam: he ordered an Australian boycott of South African sport in 1972 and thirteen years later, as ambassador to UNESCO, he chaired a world conference on apartheid sport. His mere presence in their countries conferred prestige on IOC delegates.[31]

Several cases of vote-buying surfaced during and in the aftermath of the bid, although precisely how deep into the murky water individual officials dived will probably remain unknown. The AOC and the NSW Government offered each African IOC member one-year scholarships to the Australian Institute of Sport for two of their country's athletes. They were promised that these would be extended to seven years if Sydney won.[32] John Coates, a Vice-President of SOBC and President of the AOC, arranged a place at the International Catering Institute (Sydney) for Nomsa Sibandze, daughter of Swazi IOC member David Sibandze.[33] SOBC also invited another, unnamed, IOC member and his family to spend Christmas 1992 in Australia. According to Coles

> it was quite an experience for [the IOC member]. When he went back home we got feedback from the people he mixes with and he hasn't stopped talking about Sydney. He said "my decision's very easy for me. I know where I'm going with my vote for the city to host the 2000 Games."[34]

The most underhand example of vote-buying was the employment of Nick Voinov, son-in-law of Romanian IOC member Alexandru Siperco, at the NSW State Rail Authority. The most extravagant case was the inclusion in the Games' staging budget of travelling costs for 10,000 athletes (and their equipment) and 5000 officials at a cost of $35 million.

Justifying the favoured treatment given Sibandze, Coates said that he had "known her father for 10 years":

He is president of Swaziland's National Olympic Committee as well as being the country's IOC member. I am the father of six children and I hope that one day my contribution to the Olympic movement can be acknowledged by one of my kids studying overseas.

Coates concluded with a rhetorical rejoinder: "Isn't this what the Olympic family is all about?"[35] No. Such behaviour breaches the spirit of Olympism which espouses meritocratic principles based on fair and equal competition. It also contravenes the IOC's own rules which, somewhat ironically, Coates applauded.[36] The notion that assisting African countries to field competitive teams at Olympic Games constitutes development aid trivialises the socio-economic plight of hundreds of millions of people and misconstrues what amounts to preferential exchange between social elites.

Consistent with the "Australian character," some SOBC delegates confessed that they found the lobbying process offensive and demeaning. Vice-President of SOBC and Sydney Lord Mayor Frank Sartor said that during the week before the decision, we "prostituted ourselves to try to get one more vote for Sydney." Sartor described the Hotel de Paris in Monaco, where IOC members stayed, as the "Brothel de Paris."[37] But the rewards assuaged the act. As one official put it: "You shut your eyes and think of Sydney in 2000. We decided that as we had to do it, we would be the best whores you could find between Rome and Marseilles."[38]

In Monte Carlo the contest to host the 2000 Games was between Beijing and Sydney. Tactically, SOBC focused on surviving the first ballot and then drawing the preferences of eliminated cities. As Chief Executive of Atlanta's bid committee, Billy Payne, advised, "If you are everyone's second choice [after the first ballot] you will win."[39] Survival in the first round depended upon support from Third World members, some of whom viewed Beijing as their ideological representative while others were under government instruction to repay China for longstanding military and economic aid. Jean-Claude Ganga, an IOC member, President of the Association of National Olympic Committees of Africa and a former Congo ambassador to China, was an important Chinese ally in Africa along with the French Government and French IOC member Maurice Herzog. Chinese-French

relations had cooled after France sold fighter planes to Taiwan. As part of the process of restoring relations, and to induce China to buy a consignment of its trains, France lobbied Africa for Beijing.[40] The Whitlam safari appears to have negated China's influence in Africa although the exact number of African votes is not known. However, according to one Chinese official, "Beijing lost the bid in Africa."[41] SOBC also successfully countered Beijing's lobbying in Latin America, despite IOC power broker and President of the Federation of International Football Associations João Havelange's support for China.[42] Elizabeth Fox, a former Colombian émigré and honourary consul, and now naturalised Australian, lobbied for Sydney in Central and South America and observers credit her with five votes.[43]

Sydney trailed Beijing by just two votes after the first ballot (see note 2). But in the second round, China received five of the seven votes from Istanbul supporters and Australia fell seven votes behind. Sydney thus required maximum support from members whose first preference was Berlin and Manchester. SOBC lobbied European members intensely and more similarities in cultural values presumably favoured Sydney. But Sydney also benefited from its twin themes: environmental responsibility and the "athletes' Games." The former resonated well in Europe, particularly environmentally conscious Scandinavia, and lobbying by the Chief Executive Officer of Greenpeace International, Australian Paul Gilding, helped.[44] Beijing led by three votes in the third ballot which saw Manchester eliminated. In the deciding round, eight of Manchester's eleven votes flowed to Sydney; both bid committees had employed the "athletes' Games" theme.[45]

"Our crawlers were even more effective than Beijing's bribes," political journalist Alan Ramsey wrote in his satirical letter from "Prime Minister Keating" to Sydney.[46] Ramsey's words capture the essence of the lobbying game. Yet Sydney's win may ultimately have been due more to Beijing's strategic blunder. Chinese officials believed they would win on the first or second ballot. Perhaps they confused pledges with actual votes, but irrespective they paid insufficient attention to second preferences. Lastly, if IOC members cared little about human rights' issues,[47] or even about China's threat to boycott Atlanta,[48] the medium term stability of the Deng Xiaoping regime posed concern.

Mobilising support and silencing criticism: The politics of deception

Throughout its campaign SOBC claimed that virtually all Sydneysiders supported the bid. It feared any dissension, which is anathema to the IOC. The experiences of the 1996 Games competitors, Toronto and Atlanta, are illustrative here. When Toronto launched its bid in the mid-1980s, it too claimed overwhelming public support and by 1989 believed that it had already secured most IOC votes. But from that point on it was "thrust into a bitter public consultation process, fuelled by mounting media criticism,"[49] Atlanta, led by African-American Mayor Andrew Young, campaigned as a racially harmonious and progressive city and defused potential dissent.

According to Rod McGeoch, Chief Executive of SOBC, "90 percent of people want the Games and this is backed up by support from government, business, ethnic groups, unions and Aborigines."[50] Indeed, there was genuine support; but support was also engineered. Much "grassroots community support" came from school children. SOBC enlisted the NSW Department of Education and they devised some twenty tactics, the most important of which were the "Sign for Sydney" petitions and the "twinning" project. A total of 160,000 pupils signed petitions supporting Sydney and the Department collected and presented them to IOC members. Under the twinning project, schools applied through the Department of Education to lobby individual IOC members. The Department selected 120 schools from about 450 applications on the basis of the ethnic background of pupils, academic and sporting programs, and pupils' and teachers' cultural interests. IOC members who visited Sydney were taken to "their" school and presented with scrapbooks containing pupils' messages supporting Sydney.[51]

As an exercise in teaching cultural diversity and understanding, the twinning project may have had merits; it may also have given some pupils insights into political lobbying, although we suspect that was not an objective. But the Olympics embody a tension between practice and ideal, between international political rivalry and goodwill. The Curriculum Directorate studiously avoided this contradiction in its lists of suggested Olympic teaching activities.[52] Similarly, did principals give their pupils all the facts and allow them to make their own decision about the petition?

Given that it may reap the kudos of hosting the Games and given high levels of support in opinion polls, the Opposition not surprisingly endorsed the NSW Government's sponsorship of the bid. Nonetheless, one could have expected more critical support. For example, Bob Carr, the leader of the Opposition, refused to pursue Voinov's State Rail appointment.[53] The union movement, motivated by prospects of jobs for its members, also rallied behind the bid. The NSW Labor Council secretary, Michael Easson, guaranteed total support when he addressed the IOC's Inquiry Commission. But how many jobs will the Games create? According to a report produced by KPMG Peat Marwick for SOBC, the Games will generate 156,000 jobs over fourteen years between 1991 and 2004 and only 34,000 jobs in 2000. Most will be temporary, low paid, unskilled jobs in construction and hospitality.

The commercial media was an integral element of Sydney's bid. In addition to the high profile media representatives on SOBC and the communications subcommittee, a number of outlets, including 2UE, 2GB, AAP, Australian Television International, Media Monitors, News Limited, *Sun-Herald* and *Time Magazine*, sponsored the bid. As expected, few journalists bothered to question either the politics of the bidding process or the social impact and the economic costs of hosting the Games. Whenever journalists or commentators ventured to explore the issues, SOBC quickly responded. Just before a *Four Corners'* investigation into the bidding process went to air in July 1993, Bruce Baird, the NSW Minister for Transport and the Olympic Bid bellowed his now famous warning, "If anybody gets in the way of the bid, then all I can say is watch out."[54] Baird attempted to stop the *Sydney Morning Herald* from publishing details about Voinov's appointment[55] and McGeoch successfully blocked a request by *Four Corners* under freedom of information legislation to obtain NSW Treasury cost analyses. He argued the information would breach the confidentiality of a registered private company–SOBC![56] SOBC angrily denounced economics commentator Max Walsh who challenged revenue estimates and expenditure on infrastructure. Compared with Atlanta, Walsh said, Sydney's revenue targets were "outrageously optimistic" and that "there are potential shortfalls of hundreds of millions of dollars."[57] SOBC estimates $US813 million revenue from television rights, but Atlanta received only $US706 million for American ($US456 million) and European ($US250 million) rights. Although the American rights increased by $US55 million over that paid for Barcelona, it was still $US100 million less than expected. (It should be noted that 40 percent of television revenue goes directly to the IOC.) The time difference between Australia and North America, which will make it difficult to broadcast premier events in the latter's prime viewing time, is just one reason why Walsh is correct.

The NSW Government learned well the lesson from Toronto; taxpayers oppose governments which spend money on circuses. Indeed, while 86 percent of Australians are happy that Sydney is hosting the Games, 64 percent oppose new taxes to meet the costs.[58] Throughout the bid, the government maintained that the cost of *staging* the Games was $1.697 billion. Yet, after Sydney won, it admitted that the total cost, including essential infrastructure (principally at the main site of Homebush Bay), was $3.232 billion.[59] Fahey initially said that redevelopment of Homebush Bay was part of a capital works program "independent" of the 2000 Games decision. But he misled taxpayers because Sydney's victory condensed and converted a twenty-year *discretionary* project into a seven-year *essential* project. Redevelopment of Homebush Bay will not provide an economic return and it will compete with other capital works programs associated with health, education, housing and roads. Coincidentally, the same day that Sydney won the hosting rights, the NSW Government announced the closure of the Prince Henry, Royal South Sydney and Royal Women's hospitals at a cost of 225 beds and 800 jobs.

In the end, there was no organised criticism of Sydney's bid. Two factors defused potential criticism: scepticism and hope. On the one hand many people dismissed Sydney's chances: failed bids by Brisbane and Melbourne, Australia's geographic isolation, limited domestic markets for sponsors, and active lobbying for Beijing by prominent IOC members, all seemed to conspire against Sydney. On the other hand, deceived about the full costs of the Games, SOBC's seductive promise of a Games-led economic recovery engendered hope.

An Australian victory?

The IOC awarded Sydney the 2000 Games because of politics–not despite them. This is more than a simple axiom: the IOC's politics, played so successfully by SOBC, expose the contradictory nature of Olympism, the sectional interests it represents, and the opportunities it affords. The IOC's politics are the very antithesis of de Coubertin's Olympic philosophy which it purports to represent. The IOC represents business, money, power, prestige and status; it employs deceit, hype, threat, surreptitiousness and manipulation in their service. SOBC, too, adopted these tactics. It wanted Australians to suspend their critical faculties. We anticipate that the grand coalition of Games' interests will maintain this tradition over the next six years–for, they want us to believe, the betterment of sport.

A few days after the IOC's announcement, the *Age* publicly endorsed Prime Minister Keating's strategy of using the Games "as an impetus to Australia becoming a republic." Sydney's success, the paper said, focused attention on the "sort of country Australia will be at the turn of the century."[60] But there are definite limits. The same day, Aboriginal leaders, including Social Justice Commissioner Mick Dodson and lawyer Michael Mansell, said they would organise a boycott of the Games to force the government to rewrite its draft Mabo response legislation.[61] Howls of outrage greeted the threat. The tabloid television current affairs program *Real Life* described Mansell as "the man who will destroy Australia's dream"; the *Sydney Morning Herald* called it a "stunt."[62] Later, Mansell said "his group" would support the Games and make no moves towards a boycott, provided Aborigines were allowed to enter a separate team in the Games. No one replied. Obviously the lack of rights which Australians afford Aborigines are not criteria by which they care to judge themselves as a nation.

As 2000 approaches, Aborigines should consider highlighting social inequalities, especially in sport. In terms of politics and sport, Aboriginal leaders lost an ideal opportunity prior to Monaco. Olympic history is replete with precedents, including the Catalans at Barcelona in 1992.[63] Similarly, the Commonwealth Games in Brisbane was a good example of sport being used for political advantage.

Aborigines should reject the inane view that making noises at international sporting festivals "isn't cricket"–the 206-year history of the Aboriginal experience has been anything but cricket. However, their strategy will need careful and considerate thought: it will have to be more sensible than the suggestions to date. The Olympics are not holy or sacrosanct; nor are they immune from the political or social issues of the day.

The NSW Government will involve harsh measures if Aborigines use the Games for "extraneous" objectives. SOBC has assured the IOC that there will be "no disruptions."[64] The NSW Government has numerous precedents. Russia cleared Moscow of its Jews in 1980, and in 1982 the Queensland government passed the *Commonwealth Games Act* to keep Brisbane "clean" of Aboriginal "dissidents" during the Commonwealth Games. The Act empowered police (rather than government) to declare a "situation of emergency," to seize persons and property, and to take toe-, foot-, palm-, finger-, and voice-prints of suspected persons. It designated notified areas in which only accredited persons could assemble, and it imposed fines of $2000, or sentences of two years' jail, or both, for offences under the Act. The purported objective was "good conduct and order." But the Act was not about law. Rather, it was about Bjelke-Petersen's sense of political order.

Will the Games be an economic boon? No. KPMG Peat Marwick's "most likely" economic scenario predicts a total injection of $A7.3 billion into the national economy over fourteen years. This represents a minuscule average annual increase in national output of $A500 million–one-eighth of 1 percent of an Australian economy worth $A400 billion per annum. Max Walsh put this figure in perspective by noting that the fall in the value of the dollar in the second and third quarters of 1993 and the consequent rise in foreign debt had wiped out the projected benefits of the Games.[65] Barcelona had a minimal effect on Spain's economy. Despite an intense advertising campaign in Europe, Japan and the U.S., foreign visitors increased by only 7 percent over the depressed levels of 1991. After the Games, unemployment soared to 21 percent and in 1992 the economy grew by just 1.5 percent. Twice that year the government devalued the peseta.[66]

NSW Treasury officials estimate that local taxpayers will face a $1 billion debt for Games' related infrastructure.[67] Fahey dismissed all criticism of costing: he denigrated Treasury officials as "bean counters" and labelled a belatedly more critical NSW Labor Party "anti-Games." His admonishing tones insinuate that critical analysis of the Sydney Games is un-Australian and that those who don't want to be "on the team" must be anti-Australian.

Hype-masters and flag wavers are already building expectations. The Games may foster a sense of pride and initial voluntary efforts that are construed as "common purpose" in the lead up to, and during, the Games. But what happens after the ceremonies? In the mid-1970s Prime Minister Whitlam urged Australians to forge an independent national identity. He successfully encouraged the development of Australian art, music, dance, literature, even a new civic culture. These constitute the substance of culture. Two decades later our politicians, backed by outstandingly unqualified sports spruikers in the profit-motivated media, contend that the 2000 Games will launch, in the words of SOBC's theme song, "a golden age." It is prattle: sport is an "expensive form" which "survives only in its own present–the one it itself creates."[68] Whatever shadows or shudders of memories individuals retain from the Games, of the dramatic, beautiful, tearful, dastardly, mean or disdainful, or whatever the Olympics add to social history, they cannot change fundamental Australian economics, politics, sociology or anthropology; they are not a foundation on which a nation can build. Fading memories, vacant hotel rooms, underutilised stadia and a $1 billion debt are a high price for seventeen million people to try and "swim with the big boys."

Footnotes: The notes to this article are to be found at the end of the book.

Source: Douglas Booth teaches at the University of Otago, New Zealand. Colin Tatz teaches at Macquarie University, Australia. This article was originally published in *Sporting Traditions*, 11(1), 1994, pp.3-23. Reprinted with permission of The Australian Society for Sports History.

9.

Olympic Scandal Extends Far Beyond Economic Boundaries

John Hoberman

Where are the real reformers?

After weeks of damaging revelations about corruption inside the Intentional Olympic Committee, the official line out of Lausanne, Switzerland, is that the IOC is reforming itself. The "Olympic family," top officials say, is expelling its "bad apples" and shutting down the vote-peddling opportunists who have exploited the bidding process for Olympic sites. Olympic corruption, they say, amounts to no more than a limited number of financial transactions that, according to the IOC report issued Jan. 23, are merely violations of the Olympic oath rather than criminal acts of bribery.

Media coverage of the Olympic scandal has almost invariably endorsed this version of what is wrong inside the IOC. And by defining Olympic sleaze as exclusively financial in nature, the IOC's beleaguered power elite is on the verge of securing an important propaganda victory it does not deserve but that it will need to survive the current crisis. For the fact is that financial improprieties constitute only one dimension of the unseemly racket that presents IOC members to tile world as earnest idealists dedicated only to serving the fraternity of man.

Given unprecedented public interest in the integrity of the IOC membership, now is the time to examine some of the characters IOC President Juan Antonio Samaranch has picked to preside over what he calls the Olympic "movement."

Independent scrutiny of this group is essential, since Samaranch has shown himself to be an intransigent megalomaniac who remains blind to his own shortcomings. In typical fashion, he has defied recent calls for his resignation by asserting that he is accountable only to the IOC membership that elected him. But this is circular logic because Samaranch himself "elected" about 80 percent of the voting members since he assumed the presidency in 1980.

One of the marginal figures in the corruption scandal is the Ugandan member of the IOC, Major General Francis Nyangweso, who was elected in 1988 after being nominated by Samaranch. Norm Seagram, a vice president of the Toronto Olympic Organizing Committee, admitted last month that he bought Nyangweso a new wardrobe when the Ugandan came to Toronto on an official visit in 1990 and reported that his luggage had been stolen. On Sept. 22, 1993, on the eve of the vote for the 2000 Games, Nyangweso was offered $35,000 by John Coates, an Australian member of the IOC who was supporting Sydney's bid. Though the money was supposedly earmarked for sports programs in Uganda, the current climate of suspicion has made Nyangweso a target of the IOC's investigation of its own members.

The investigation of Nyangweso should extend far beyond the question of whether a friendly Canadian once bought him a suit. Indeed, his presence on the IOC raises questions about moral standards that are much more serious than the bribery allegations that have come to light.

Nyangweso served the murderous dictator Idi Amin throughout the eight years of his regime (1971-79) as Army commander, minister of culture and ambassador. In early 1973 he went on the radio to warn the people of the Bugisu district that any village found to be sheltering "guerrillas" would be "destroyed completely." This threat was made in the context of a centrally organized terror campaign that was "orchestrated to produce a maximum sense of fear among any community suspected of helping the regime's opponents," as the Africa Contemporary Record (1974) put it.

The barbarities of Amin's rule, including a body count estimated at 300,000, produced a series of resignations from the government during the terror of 1973. The defectors included Edward Rugumayo, Uganda's minister of education; John Batigye, ambassador to West Germany; and Wanume Kibedi, foreign minister and Amin's own son-in-law, who described himself as "a man of honor" who could no longer associate himself with the "continual disappearance of innocent people without any adequate investigation. " For whatever reasons, Nyangweso did not join this exodus from the killing grounds of Uganda.

So how did this man get onto the IOC? As a former Ugandan heavyweight boxing champion, Nyangweso's climb through the international sports bureaucracy was facilitated by his appointment as a vice president of the International Amateur Boxing Federation. This is the corrupt organization that presided over the 1988 Seoul Olympic boxing scandal marked by absurd decisions handed down by bribed judges. The IOC should ask Nyangweso whether he knew about these payoffs, which are confirmed by an East German secret police report.

More important, Nyangweso must have been "packaged" for IOC president Samaranch's approval by senior African members such as Jean-Claude Ganga of Republic of Congo, who has been marked for expulsion from the IOC, and Keba Mbaye of Senegal, an IOC member since 1973 and a vice president of the International Court of Justice since 1987. Over the past several weeks Mbaye has been playing the role of Mr. Clean for the IOC, serving both on the six-man committee that recommended the expulsions and on the three-man IOC working group that will propose an ethics commission of distinguished outsiders whose task will be to restore the IOC's battered reputation.

It is hard to believe that Mbaye was unaware of Nyangweso's role as an accomplice of Idi Amin, since an Amnesty International document released in June 1978 shows that Mbaye had been appointed by the International Commission of Jurists to head an investigation of human rights violations in Uganda. Now it is time for someone to ask Mbaye what he knew about Nyangweso, and when he knew it.

For Samaranch, who has conferred Olympic Orders on the Romanian dictator Nicolae Ceausescu and the architects of the East German doping program, Nyangweso's past may well have had no political resonance at all. We can only guess whether the old Spanish fascist knew or cared about a remote and buffoonish despot such as Amin. What we do know is that receiving one

of his generals into the IOC appears not to have ruffled a single Olympic feather.

This is the deeper scandal that pollutes the "Olympic family" Samaranch likes to coat in a veneer of pseudoaristocratic dignity. Three of the other starry-eyed idealists he has brought on board are Kim Un-Yong, the Korean CIA spook exposed during the 1978 Koreagate hearings who has served every South Korean dictator since the military coup of 1961; Mohamad "Bob" Hasan, the Suharto crony who became a billionaire logging the Indonesian rainforest; and Shamil Tarpischev, the Russian sports minister who was fired by his former tennis pupil, Boris Yeltsin, for corruption.

Now is the time to shut down this offshore enterprise zone for unsavory opportunists. Samaranch & Co. should move out of the Chateau de Vidy, so that real reformers can move in.

Source: John Hoberman is a professor of Germanic studies at the University of Texas at Austin and the author of *Mortal Engines: The Science of Performance and the Dehumanization of Sport* (1992) and *Darwin's Athletes: How Sport Has Damaged Black America and Preserved the Myth of Race* (1997). This article was originally published in *The Atlanta Journal*, Sunday, February 7, 1999, F1. Reproduced with the permission of the author.

10.

Olympic Money Medalists

Andrew Jennings

The behind-the-scenes truth of the Nagano Olympic Games

As living standards collapse in the Pacific's former "Tiger" economies, three of Asia's leading billionaires will be beaming triumphantly into the cameras throughout the Winter Olympics this month in Nagano, Japan. The national financial systems they have managed (and benefited from immensely) may be crashing down, overwhelming many of their less fortunate countrymen, but these moguls are medal winners in the international order where sports, politics, corporatism and cronyism overlap. And in Japan they are collecting congratulations as members of the secretive and autocratic Olympic establishment.

When the TV cameras pan across the V.I.P. section, you might be able to spot Mohamad "Bob" Hasan, one of Indonesian President Suharto's closest confidants and an International Olympic Committee member. Hasan fronts businesses owned by the presidential family and symbolizes the crony capitalism that has brought sweatshop Indonesia to its knees. One of the conditions of the I.M.F.'s $43 billion bailout is the dismantling of Hasan's plywood monopoly (Indonesia is one of the world's major suppliers). Hasan is one of the world's largest rainforest loggers, and his companies have been accused of contributing to the smoke haze that settled over Southeast Asia last autumn, a result of the massive burning of undergrowth. In January, as the rupiah went into a free fall, Hasan laid off 2,500 workers from his timber businesses. But losing the plywood concession won't bankrupt him. The government recently gave him a large chunk of the country's growing cell-phone monopoly.

While honest reporters are jailed in Indonesia for seeking to disclose government corruption, Hasan publishes a weekly newsmagazine that takes a benign view of the cartels that have enriched the ruling family and its protected friends—like him. And what is Hasan's contribution to sports? A round of golf every week with Suharto and sponsorship of long-distance road races with fabulous prize money. He's significantly wealthier than any of Suharto's pampered offspring.

At the various lavish I.O.C. receptions, Hasan will be able to relax with Lee Kun-Hee, chairman of Samsung, South Korea's second-largest conglomerate. Lee joined the I.O.C. in July 1996. Five weeks later, in a Seoul courtroom, he admitted contributing suitcases of cash to a $652 million slush fund run by two former presidents and was given a suspended two-year jail sentence. Last fall, as the won was about to plummet, Samsung pledged $45 million in sponsorship to the I.O.C., a deal the company may find hard to honor as it scrabbles for its share of the I.M.F's $57 billion bailout of Korea. Lee, who draws a salary of $6.5 million, is reluctant to accept the blame heaped on him and other *chaebol* leaders by the I.M.F. "I repent having not fully performed my duty to head off the economic catastrophe," was all he would concede.

Lee and Hasan were invited onto the I.O.C. by its president, Juan Antonio Samaranch, a 78-year-old former official of the mid-century fascist regime in Spain and a fellow who has recruited into the Olympic community a number of disreputable people. Samaranch's favorite crony of the moment must be Yoshiaki Tsutsumi, 63, the world's richest man before the collapse of Japan's bubble economy and the principal architect and beneficiary of the Nagano Olympics. Tsutsumi's Seibu Group is one of Japan's biggest landowners, and it also controls railways, hotels, sports franchises, golf courses and ski resorts. He became president of Japan's Olympic committee in 1989 and led the campaign to secure the Games for Nagano. This lobbying included $20 million in donations from Japan's leading companies to Samaranch's much-cherished Olympic museum in Switzerland. And I.O.C. members visiting Nagano were entertained in hot tubs by fawning geishas.

The Olympics have become an efficient machine for transferring wealth from the public to the private sector, providing welfare for a small number of rich corporations [see Jennings, "How Olympic Insiders Betray Public Trust," July 29/August 5, 1996]. The facilities required for Olympic competitions are usually publicly funded, but the Games' immense profits are diverted to the accounts of the I.O.C., their sponsors and the TV networks. This time around, the Japanese government spent $19 billion on venues, new roads and a new bullet train that stops, conveniently, where Tsutsumi owns a holiday complex. Tsutsumi's companies have carved dozens of ski runs out of the mountains near Nagano. Before the snows fell and turned the area into a picturesque sight, anti-Olympic activists posted pictures on the Internet showing hills scraped clean of forest—bare, grassless slopes remodeled for skiers. These runs look more like freeways than the average ski slope.

On the opposite side of the story stands Masao Ezawa, a 47-year-old weaver who leads an anti-Olympics group in Nagano. Ezawa predicts tax bills of up to $40,000 over two decades for families in the Nagano region. "We're impoverishing ourselves for 20 years to pay for a two-week event," he says. Perhaps it's fitting that these winter games are being held in Japan: The behind-the-scenes truth of these Olympics reflects the Asia crisis—the people with the best seats do not have to pay the real costs.

Source: Andrew Jennings is author of *The New Lord of the Rings: Olympic Corruption and How To Buy Gold Medals.* This article was originally published in *The Nation.* February 23, 1998, pp.6-7.

11.
Faster, Higher, Stronger

Angela Schneider and Robert Butcher

Canada's Olympic reformers say the IOC is still far from the finish line

The international Olympic Committee took a significant step this week toward putting its discredited house in order, but those who believe in the ideals and dreams of the Olympic movement cannot breathe a collective sigh of relief just yet.

The proposed IOC reforms announced Sunday, and underscored by the appearance of IOC president Juan Antonio Samaranch before the U.S. Congress on Wednesday, go a long way to addressing concerns over bribery and doping. But the struggle to clean up the Games and all they stand for is more a marathon than a sprint.

Mr. Samaranch promised an Olympic committee that would be "more transparent, more accountable and more responsive." The reforms he and his representatives have proposed, however, will leave it far short of that.

Our organization, OATH (Olympic Advocates Together Honourably), was formed by people who love (and in many cases have lived) the Olympic dream. Supported by athletes around the world, we offered proposals for constructive reform and produced a report with 50 recommendations, everything from adding athlete members to the IOC and increasing the number of women members to the creation of an international doping agency and a formal commitment to transparency in choosing Olympic sites.

How do the IOC reforms measure up?

The IOC has proposed the creation of 15 positions for athletes on its central committee and has suggested ways to increase the effectiveness of the IOC Athletes' Commission—two good moves. Athletes are at the heart of the Olympic movement and are the soul of the Games. Having athletes on the IOC presents the current face of Olympic sport.

For athlete representation to be effective, however, the athletes who serve must be accountable to their peers. Candidates need to be independently selected by their fellow athletes, and must be allowed to campaign and present platforms. How this will be done in the context of the competition of the Olympic Games is yet to be worked out.

We must avoid letting the athlete positions become another form of patronage, nominated by the power brokers in the IOC.

The IOC made its first tentative steps toward gender equity. Before this past weekend, only 11 of the IOC's 105 members were women. Three more were added with the appointment of the first 10 athlete members, including Canada's Charmaine Crooks. In future, half of the athlete positions are to be filled by women.

But if equity is important for athletes, then it should be important for the IOC as a whole, and there are as yet no similar provisions for balancing the broader IOC membership.

The IOC has established a new ethics commission, and many hopes are pinned on it. This commission is chaired by an IOC vice-president, Judge Keba Mbaye of Kenya, and Ms. Crooks is one of its eight members. Others include former United Nations secretary-general Haviar Perez de Cuellar, former U.S. Senate majority leader Howard Baker and former Swiss president Kurt Furgler. But there are no ethicists or members with formal education in ethics.

Of more concern, this commission reports to the IOC executive board and appears to lack both the power and ability to act independently.

The IOC is appointing a "special representative" who may turn out to be an ombudsperson, as called for in the OATH Report. If this person is independent with the powers of investigation, it would constitute a major change in the right direction.

If not, this would indicate that the IOC still does not recognize the seriousness of the crisis in ethics and values it faces.

Instead of moving toward such transparency in its institutions, the IOC opted for public relations ploys. It banned visits by IOC members to cities bidding for the Games, and limited to eight years the term of IOC members.

But visits to cities that want to play host to the Games was never the problem; it was members accepting bribes from such cities that was the concern. It is difficult to see how members can properly judge applicants without seeing the site of prospective facilities. The ban on visits means that the IOC cannot trust its members sufficiently to be sure that they will not accept bribes.

As well, the vaunted term limits are of questionable impact since the eight-year limit remains renewable until the mandatory retirement age of 70.

The IOC has started to move on the critical issue of doping, committing $25 million (U.S.) to its new World Anti-Doping Agency intended to govern all anti-doping efforts. Headed by Canadian Richard Pound, WADA is beginning to talk with the agencies around the world that have provided good, credible and effective anti-doping programs for years. This is a major step forward, but the organization still has a long way to go before it is seen as truly open, independent and accountable.

A big cause for concern, however, is the IOC's apparent emphasis on public relations. Some of Mr. Samaranch's recent statements indicate that the IOC sees itself as having an image problem more than a crisis in values. The real issue is not that the public does not know enough about the IOC, but that what it does know, it does not like. A crisis in ethics and values requires a solution based in ethics and values, not a public relations campaign.

Genuine openness to public scrutiny, a real commitment to accountable decision making, election and selection procedures that exhibit the very best practices are the routes to improving the Olympic movement and ultimately enhancing the image of the IOC, not the employment of more and better public relations staff and spin doctors.

Finally, without a process for continuing reform, it will be impossible to monitor the effectiveness of the changes made. These reforms are a first step, but just that. What is required is ongoing, independent and public scrutiny.

Source: Angela Schneider teaches ethics in sport at the University of Western Ontario and is a silver medallist in rowing. Robert Butcher teaches philosophy at Brescia College at the University of Western Ontario and is an ethicist for Foundations: Consultants on Ethics and Values. They are co-authors of the OATH Report. This article was originally published in *The Globe and Mail*, Friday, December 17, 1999, A23. Reprinted with permission of the authors.

12.

Hosting the Olympic Games: What Price for World Class?

Kevin B. Wamsley

Why are millions of dollars being doled out for just a sniff at the Olympic Games?

During the pre-Olympic scandal era, before any decisions were made by the International Olympic Committee (IOC) as to who would host the Olympic Games almost a decade from now, the bidding teams from Toronto and Vancouver-Whistler prepared to spend in excess of $50 million. For groups opposed to hosting the Olympic Games, such as Toronto's Bread Not Circuses, it becomes a question of who will benefit, who will pay, and why are millions of dollars being doled out for just a sniff at the Olympic Games when some Canadians have no food or shelter? The first line of defense is a "trickle down" argument: Canadians will benefit from the international prestige, the local and national pride, and the economic spinoffs. Cities will benefit, the bidding committees suggest, from a legacy of facilities, a boost in tourism, and from becoming "world class." But how could Canadians possibly forget the financial debacle of Montreal? Or Mayor Jean Drapeau's boast that the "Games could no more have a deficit than a man could have a baby"? Perhaps the more recent positive association with 1988 lingers in the Canadian psyche, tweaked whenever a foreign winter Games site is in trouble and the city of Calgary rallies to offer its services.

In spite (or maybe because) of the political roller coaster that is the Olympic Games—the scandals, the unbridled commercialism, the drug-taking-Canadians of all ilks are still fascinated by them. Community groups and corporations are still willing to risk spending large sums of money and hundreds of volunteer hours for no guaranteed return, just a slim chance to host, and when it comes to hosting hallmark events, neither money nor social conscience seems to be an issue for organizers and city boosters.

Canada's participation in the Olympic Games goes back one hundred years; top Canadian runners, who attended universities in the U.S., participated in the Paris Olympics of 1900 under the American flag. Recently, hundreds of thousands of Canadians tuned in during the middle of the night to watch the Canadian men's hockey team play at the Nagano Olympics. International sport competition has always been part of Canadian foreign policy and an important aspect of Canadian identity. Indeed, the Olympic Games, particularly the winter hockey tournaments, have played a significant role in Canada's sporting reputation: so much so, in fact, that a national sport system was established to improve Canada's international performance, and hundreds of millions of dollars have been spent to support elite sport programs and the hosting of sport festivals since the 1970s. With recent government cutbacks to health care, education, and welfare, can such spending be justified? Does Canada need more elite sport facilities?

There are few Canadian cities structurally capable of hosting a summer Olympic Games. The Olympics are so massive that only Toronto, Montreal, and Vancouver could meet the IOC minimum requirements for bidding cities. How many bobsleigh and luge tracks, 90-metre ski jumps, and speed skating ovals does Canada need? It is a reasonable argument that Quebec City derives no benefits from the Calgary facilities and that other "non-Olympic" cities wish to reap the benefits of government-funded facilities. Winnipeg, for example, is in its final stages of preparation to host the Pan American Games this year, and London is beginning to prepare for the Canada Games of 2001. Part of the justification for these bids is that some of the facilities will be used by local citizens, for tourism, and for future national and world competitions. Studies have shown, however, that the economic spin-offs and tourism that stem from such events, particularly the Olympics, tend to fall off significantly when they are finished. Many of the large summer Olympic facilities, moreover, such as stadiums and velodromes, are not used by average citizens or tourists. Calgarians receive some benefits from the Games facilities, and some are available for tourists, but for the most part they are used by elite athletes. Would it not make more sense to upgrade the Calgary facilities, if hosting the winter Games is a good thing for Canadians? The appeal for boosters and local organizers, however, goes far beyond facilities and tourism.

Changing the Olympic schedule from every four years to every two has essentially doubled the coverage of events, news, and issues in the popular press. The lucrative, exclusive corporate sponsorship programs and the revenues from television have provided the IOC with financing well beyond the imaginations of even the sport leaders of the 1980s. The IOC and the Olympic caravan is reaching more and more people around the world every year. In spite of boycotts, massacres, political blunders, scandals, shifts to explicit professionalism, and a glamorous program that borders at times along the ridiculous, people are still tuning in to the Games and corporations are paying millions to be official Olympic sponsors. If anything, the competition among cities around the globe to host the Games has increased. The so-called Olympic Movement has always appeared to draw strength, at least in terms of public visibility, from every crisis. The recent Salt Lake City scandal has done more to enhance the notoriety of Olympic leaders than to raise questions about the Games themselves. Bidding city organizers in Osaka, Beijing, and Toronto are waiting anxiously for the IOC to inform them of the next step in the bidding process.

The claim from Toronto is that no public money will be spent on the Games. Even if tax rates, access to land, and housing remain unaffected somehow, the fact is that millions of dollars which could be used to provide basic needs for Torontonians will be spent on elite sport and entertainment. Accessible, practical recreation and sport facilities for families and all citizens would undoubtedly serve the greater population. True, business requires a tangible return on its "investments," but well-conceived corporate donations and private funding could go a long way to solving some of Toronto's social problems. Why have there not been movements of such

creative magnitude and volunteer participation to provide basic necessities for people, before entertainment and spectacle are even considered? It seems that in a socially just society, a right to a decent quality of life, including daily access to recreation and physical activity, would define a "world class" city much better than hosting the Olympic Games.

Source: Kevin B. Wamsley is director of the International Centre for Olympic Studies at the University of Western Ontario. This article was originally published in *Canadian Issues/Themes Canadiens* (CITC), Autumn 1999, pp.14-16. Reproduced with the permission of the author.

Part 4
Health, Fitness, and Injury

Most physical education/kinesiology students I have talked to agree that "sport participation is healthy" and "exercise is good for you." In fact, they usually accept such statements uncritically. Most are puzzled by the contradiction that I then pose to them: "Why are so many of you planning a career in the field of 'sports medicine'?" Many have experienced illness or injury as a result of sport and exercise. A growing number of students report having had an eating or exercise compulsion disorder (associated with their body image) and most report injuries ranging from the traumatic to the overuse variety. Still, they accept the relationship between exercise, fitness, and health without qualification or reservation.

In the first article in this section, Philip White and Kevin Young directly challenge the notion that this relationship is simple by showing that exercise is not always related to fitness and fitness, in turn, is not always related to health. They explore the politics of health and fitness and outline the moral, rather than the biological, imperative behind the "fitness boom." In a related article, White examines the issue of employee fitness. White is not concerned about the actual activity, nor does he deny that health benefits may result from exercise. However, he does question the motives behind it, who benefits, and the meaning behind the programs. Is employee fitness just another way of controlling, disciplining, and attaining higher productivity from workers? Do the workers have any say? Do they exercise for the pleasure of exercise?

The next two articles are concerned with illness and injury. Studies in the sociology and psychology of sport have tended to focus on eating disorders among athletes, while the exercise sciences have tended to focus on the problems of obesity. Critser's controversial article suggests that obesity is a far more serious problem than anorexia or bulimia nervosa, and he draws attention to the issues of social class and exercise and their relationship to obesity—a reminder of the even more powerful and consistent relationship between social class and health. (See also Article No. 20.)

Some sports produce injury rates (even among children) that, if they occurred in schools or industry, would be considered a major cause for concern. Studies are beginning to show that sport and exercise injuries represent a significant proportion of emergency room usage. And one British economic analysis suggests that, up to the age of 45, participation in sport and exercise actually costs the health care system far more than it would if people did not participate. But sport injuries are not just an economic and medical problem; they are also a social problem. And Stephen Brunt's article on boxing and head injuries again implicates social class in the relationship. (See also the following section on **Violence and Masculinity**.)

Additional Sources

Videos:

- *Gymnastics and Eating Disorders*, an "On Your Mark" broadcast from the Women's Television Network (see also *The Famine Within* from TV Ontario for a broader view of eating disorders and health).

- *Playing Hurt*, TSN "For the Love of the Game" series, provides an interesting insight into sport injuries (see also, *Fighting Injuries*, TSN "Inside Sports," which shows that injuries actually do occur in hockey fights). Both are also useful for the following section, **Violence and Masculinity**.

- *FIT: Episodes in the History of the Body* is available in many university and college libraries.

Print Resources:

- Simonds, M. (1995). Who's fit? Who's fat? *Equinox*, May/June, pp.38-50. [An examination of recent research on obesity and health, showing the cultural and biological complexities of the notion of "overweight."]

- McDougall, D. (1994). Young men most likely to be hurt in sports: study. *Montreal Gazette*, 16 September, p.B16. [Report of research showing the death and traumatic injury rates of young males and females in sports.]

- Nocera, J. (1995). Bitter medicine. *Sports Illustrated*, 6 November, pp.74-88. [Special Report on professional sport team doctors, and the tendency of some to withhold crucial information from injured athletes in the "best interests of the team."]

13.

Health and the New Age Ascetic

Philip White and Kevin Young

The contemporary fitness boom

In recent times, the parameters of what is popularly considered healthful behaviour have expanded dramatically. Whether the definition of "healthy" is seen to include regular "workouts," giving up smoking, using unleaded gasoline and avoiding other pollutants in the environment, preferring herbal or other alternative medicines, or cutting cholesterol and fat from our diets, it is clear that a new health consciousness has dawned (Labonte, 1982). Such changes in lifestyle also suggest that the idea of health has shifted from something that is viewed as the result of luck or biological inheritance to something that has to be achieved through volition. In other words, health has changed dramatically from being a passive to an active status. Nowadays, we achieve or work at health, and are bombarded by messages celebrating ascetic attitudes to it. The media, health educators, celebrities, employers, and even politicians constantly prevail upon us to monitor our bodies and to embark on lifestyle modifications that will enhance our "wellness" (Crawford, 1984; Gillick, 1984; Vertinsky, 1985).

Academe has not been untouched by these changes. For instance, in the physical education/kinesiology profession there has been a concomitant move toward health-oriented activities, as may be witnessed in the widespread relabelling of departments to indicate more inclusive concentrations on elements of lifestyle such as dance, recreation and leisure, as well as health itself. Indeed, many professors have begun to make the traditionally implicit baggage of their trade *explicit*, and now see themselves as being in the business of helping people improve their physical quality of life. They have become modern-day evangelists leading the masses toward the good life. Other proponents of the fitness movement, such as the proprietors of commercial fitness clubs, also reinforce the notion that along with other health promoting activities, exercise produces fitness which enhances health (Hall, 1990). This belief, often viewed as self-evident, is a simplistic summation of a far more complex issue.

Behind popular wisdom about the generally unquestioned merits of exercise also lie moral imperatives: that people *should* exercise; that people *should* control their weight (Edgley & Brisset, 1990). After all, it is argued, the slackers and the slothful are failing society by burdening the health care system with largely preventable illnesses (Crawford, 1984). What is ignored in this rather cursory approach is that fitness-oriented people also get sick—often, ironically, as a result of their fitness regimes themselves—and that the financial and psycho-emotional costs of exercise-related injuries can be as disabling as the injuries themselves (Young, White and McTeer, 1994). Indeed, the cost-benefit effects of exercise on the public purse have yet to be established (Vertinsky, 1985; Wagner, 1987).

Much of this critique has been prompted by the emergence of health as a key political issue in contemporary Western societies. Recent analyses on the body written from a social scientific perspective have critically examined the previously dominant biomedical model which regards the body as a kind of a machine, an object to be worked on (Gillick, 1984). Of course, the ascendance of health and health consciousness as a public issue did not "just happen." Rather, it can be traced to a marked shift in values since the early 1970s when health became reconceptualized as being sustainable through effort, discipline, and self-control (Rader, 1991). With this shift in values, ill health has increasingly come to be associated with moral laxity. In this view, some people are viewed as unhealthy "on purpose"; they have insufficient resolve to exercise more, to quit smoking, and so forth. Remarkably, the sick have come more often than before to be blamed for being ill (Shilling, 1993). Frank (1991) demonstrates this clearly in his reflexive study of cancer, as does Sontag (1979) in her brilliant critique of social attitudes towards disease in general. But perhaps the most graphic example of "victim-blaming" in the connection of illness is to be seen in the ongoing AIDS crisis, and in the ultra-conservative ideologies that refuse to understand HIV as a disease affecting both gays and heterosexuals.

A key component of this way of thinking is the coupling of health with body shape. Despite widespread problems with anorexia, bulimia, and other eating disorders in contemporary society, the slender (particularly female) body has come to be a metaphor for health (Kirk & Colquhoun, 1989). Obversely, fat people (particularly women, again) are said to lack discipline and self-control despite the fact that body shape is primarily determined genetically (which explains why diet regimens are notoriously unsuccessful). Such has been the significance of slenderness as a symbol of upright living that even those who are heavy but healthy elicit moral reproof: "s/he could afford to lose a few pounds!" Cultural fanaticism for the socially trim body leads to guilt among those who don't, quite literally, "shape up."

During times of economic and political upheaval, of which the recessionary late 1980s and early 1990s are examples for Canadians, themes of self-control, willpower, and personal restraint move forward on the cultural agenda (Glassner, 1989; Stein, 1982). Contemplating reasons for our collective problems we look to the body as a metaphor for moral character and societal well-being. This type of thinking is typical of those who hope to exorcize the evils of modern society by a return to an ascetic lifestyle (Carlyon, 1984). Under conditions of fiscal retrenchment, unemployment crisis, and other forms of socio-cultural exigency, all of which elicit a degree of panic in society (Kroker et al., 1989), the body emerges as one of the last sites over which even disempowered individuals can maintain control. But the struggle for meaningful control over bodies sometimes becomes distorted such as when people undergo cosmetic surgery without adequate counselling on its long-term health consequences. When the body moves forward on the cultural agenda people become more vulnerable to cynical and profit-oriented media campaigns which play on their physical and sexual insecurities. As a result, dominant notions of masculinity and femininity become narrower and more rigid, even physically hazardous. Health risks associated with extreme body ideals all too often include eating disorders for women and illnesses linked to violence, steroids, and other drugs for men.

This seems particularly the case for the current generation of young people for whom the future appears less promising than it did for their "baby boomer" parents. If current predicaments and projections are accurate, this so-called "lost generation" has a smaller chance of getting a secure job, of being able to own their own home, and an eroding sense of the future as holding good things. For them, there is an even greater need to devote themselves to ascetic values: hard work, self-restraint, and discipline. But as critics of youth culture have indicated, this may be much more of a short-run rather than a long-run effect of social crisis. Among other things, increasing pressures to do well educationally in a hostile economy are just as likely to precipitate among youngsters a return to the hedonistic joys of drug and alcohol abuse, smoking, unsafe sex, and other "unhealthy" deviances.

The proposition that health is primarily determined by the volitional behaviour of individuals is a good example of the inadequacy of offering simple solutions for complex problems. Since body shape has become a metaphor for health and moral worth, the person who does not conform to prevailing norms for fitness tends to be given universalistic advice for self-improvement. For instance, women perceived to be overweight are told, "Just eat less and exercise more–it's simple." So, those who for reasons beyond their control don't have the time or the resources to apply to health management and body sculpting (single mothers, shift workers, the poor) tend to be blamed for their failure to live up to their social responsibility to their own bodies (Labonte, 1982). Ironically, the strongly middle-class bias of the fitness movement is vividly exposed by the practical reality that for the working class and other disempowered groups who labour at physically demanding jobs, meaningful leisure is often built around liberation from physical effort.

All of this is not to deny that there is a relationship between exercise and health. Certain types of exercise clearly have health benefits for some people. Our concern is to indicate that this relationship is neither equally available nor without costs. The taken-for-granted assumption that physical activity is a major contribution to health is seldom, if ever, challenged. Take, for example, the common assumption that body type is connected in a simple way with health. Slim and muscular people are assumed to be healthier than other less culturally valued body types. The truth is far more complex. It is possible, for example, to be heavy and healthy (Ritenbaugh, 1982) and it is also possible to be healthy without undue exercise (Nichter & Nichter, 1991). Further, complicating the "body-image-equals-health" stereotype is the fact that intense exercise clearly has its own associated disadvantages including high injury rates and body image disorders (Edgley & Brisset, 1990; Young, White & McTeer, 1994).

We certainly endorse the equitable provision of opportunities to pursue health and fitness for all regardless of social background. But we are also concerned that current social pressures to increase ascetic styles of living have had the effect of escalating a victim-blaming approach to body image, illness, and health, and have re-energized the view that individuals, not institutions, are entirely responsible for their health. There are often good reasons why some people may seem less attentive to health issues even though they may seem irrational to the middle-class moralizer. These reasons may clash with the conservative values that are woven into a health ethic tilted favourably toward middle-class experiences and that obfuscate the limited opportunities for large sections of the population to work at their health. And this view also ignores or diverts attention away from structural factors such as mass unemployment, chronic poverty, and dangerous work conditions which compromise the health of many and render bourgeois notions of health and fitness (becoming vegetarian, giving up cigarettes, joining a health club) either materially unachievable or culturally unappealing.

In closing, it has been our goal to show that a relationship popularly believed to be simple—that exercise leads to fitness which leads to health—is, in fact, complex, multi-faceted, and deeply political. Clearly, while people do have some responsibility for their own health, choices and opportunities around fitness are neither equally available nor meaningful to all people. As sociologists, we have also wanted to emphasize that an adequate etiology of either illness or health requires an examination of both biomedical and sociocultural factors. Such an approach is not only useful in understanding the place of cancer, AIDS, anorexia, obesity, athleticism, muscularity, slimness, slothfulness, and a range of other bodily states and predicaments, but also goes some way in uncovering the ascetic agendas of, and contradictions in, the contemporary health revolution.

References
- Carlyon, W. (1984). Disease prevention/health promotion: Bridging the gap to wellness. *Health Values: Achieving High Level Wellness*, 8, 27-30.
- Crawford, R. (1984). A cultural account of "health": Control, release, and the social body. In J. McKinlay (ed.), *Contemporary Issues in Health, Medicine and Social Policy*, pp. 60-103. New York: Tavistock.
- Edgley, C. & Brisset, D. (1990). Health nazis and the cult of the perfect body: Some polemical observations. *Symbolic Interaction*, 13, 257.
- Frank, A. (1991). *At The Will of The Body: Reflections on Illness*. Boston: Houghton Mifflin.
- Gillett, J., & White, P. (1992). Male bodybuilding and the reassertion of hegemonic masculinity: A critical feminist perspective. *Play and Culture*, 5, 358-369.
- Gillick, M. (1984). Health promotion, jogging and the pursuit of moral life. *Journal of Health, Politics, Policy and Law*, 9, 369-387.
- Glassner, B. (1989). Fitness and the postmodern self. *Journal of Health and Social Behavior*, 30, 180-191.
- Hall, A. (1990, May). Gender, body practices and power. Presented to the Frauen Forschen in der Sportwissenschaft-Frauenforschung, Munster, FRG.
- Kroker, A., Kroker, M., and Cook, D. (1989). *Panic Encyclopedia: The Definitive Guide to the Postmodern Scene*. Montreal: New World Perspectives CultureTexts Series.
- Labonte, R. (1982). Half-truths about health. *Policy Options*, 3, 54-55.
- Nichter, M., & Nichter, M. (1991). Hype and weight. *Medical Anthropology*, 13, 249-284.
- Rader, B. (1991). The quest for self-sufficiency and the new strenuosity: Reflections on the strenuous life of the 1970s and the 1980s. *Journal of Sport History*, 18, 255-266.
- Ritenbaugh, C. (1982). Obesity as a culture-bound syndrome. *Culture, Medicine and Psychiatry*, 6, 347-361.
- Rojeck, C. (1992). "The eye of power": Moral regulation and the professionalization of leisure management from the 1830s to the 1950s. *Loisir et Societe*, 15, 355-373.
- Shilling, C. (1991). Educating the body. *Sociology*, 25, 653-672.
- Shilling, C. (1993). *The Body and Social Theory*. London: Sage.
- Sontag, S. (1979) *Illness as Metaphor*. New York: Vintage Books.
- Stein, H. (1982). Neo-Darwinism and survival through fitness in "Reagan's" America. *Journal of Psychohistory*, 10, 163-187.
- Vertinsky, P. (1985). Risk benefit analysis of health promotion: Opportunities and threats to physical education. *Quest*, 37, 71-83.
- Wagner, G. (1987). Sport as a Means for Reducing the Cost of Illness—Some Theoretical, Statistical, and Empirical Remarks. *International Review for the Sociology of Sport*, 22(3), 217-227.
- Young, K., White, P., and McTeer, W. (1994). Body Talk: Male Athletes Reflect on Sport, Injury, and Pain. *Sociology of Sport Journal*, 11(2). Forthcoming.

Source: Philip White is a professor in the Department of Kinesiology at McMaster University. Kevin Young is an associate professor in the Department of Sociology at the University of Calgary. This article was originally published in *Social Problems in Canada Reader*, E.D. Nelson and A. Fleuras (Eds.), Scarborough, ON: Prentice Hall, 1995, pp.432-437. Reprinted by permission.

14.

Employee Fitness

Philip G. White

Can we take the "work" out of working out?

ose weight, feel great!" "Buns of steel!" We have become obsessed with bodies that are lean, fit, tight, toned, and supposedly less burdensome on healthcare costs. As individuals we are made to feel personally responsible for the maintenance of our health. It's as if those who don't exercise, monitor their diet, or quit smoking are unhealthy on purpose. But why? Where did this obsession come from? And how has it become such a powerful orthodoxy?

Here I will play the devil's advocate and take a peek at the fitness movement from a somewhat removed position. As I will argue, it is naive to think that we are all free agents in the world of fitness and health. Rather we are all subject to forces that shape and contour how we think about these things.

It was back in the middle of the 1970s that Canadian business, following some American examples, began taking a renewed interest in employee fitness. Since then, there has been a steady growth of an industry whose product is health and productivity via physical fitness. At around the same time, our provincial and federal governments also got into the act of promoting behaviour more consistent with corporate profitability. To carry forth the crusade for fitness, a new cadre of fitness and physical productivity technicians emerged. Physical educators became "kinesiologists," all the better to tune up the body with a dash of scientific know-how.

Now, employee fitness programs start from a legitimate position. Physical activity is, in principle, related to health (even though the strength of the relationship is often exaggerated). But enough of physiological outcomes for the moment. What are the social and moral ramifications of work-related fitness? Historically, one thing is quite clear and that is that employee fitness programs are not usually expressions of largesse by employers toward employees. As long ago as the first decade of this century the Canadian Manufacturers Association suggested in their journal, *Industrial Canada*, that the intelligent manufacturer be advised that "wholesome food, and wise recreation are as necessary for the efficiency of the individuals in his (sic) employ as are the oil and brush for the machinery."

One has to take a look at how the fitness industry has become structured over the last decade or so to conclude that contemporary physical activity has perhaps become even more focused on preparation for work than for leisure, on fitness more than fun, on the grim pursuit of health than the sheer enjoyment of bodily movement. Somewhere along the way, the idea on non-work time as an opportunity for recreation, for escape from the demands of the daily grind, has been subsumed, at least to some extent, by the necessity of making a more productive body. Why else in the spirit of the times would we, automaton like, mimic those ever-cheerful aerobics leaders or spend hours lifting metal weights? Whatever happened to the spontaneous levity of fun and games?

What this means is that moral issues related to employee fitness programs are, in general, underappreciated. Employee fitness programs communicate moral imperatives—that people should exercise; that people should control their weight. After all, it is argued, the slackers and the slothful are letting the rest of us down by burdening corporations and the healthcare system with their preventable diseases.

Employee fitness programs rest on the assumption that, among the Canadian population, health and fitness depends on the degree of the health of the individual. As a Bell Canada newsletter once proclaimed—"one gets the heart one deserves." Ignored in the line of argument is the reality that the causes of illness often originate in the workplace. Absenteeism and low productivity become identified as a lifestyle problem of the employee rather than as a consequence of, say, job dissatisfaction or job-related stress. More research attention should be given over to assessing whether employee fitness programs should pay greater heed to the possibility that work itself could be better organized to help avoid the onset of disease.

Interestingly, the symbolic links between exercise/diet and self-control, willpower and personal restraint tend to be promoted more in times of economic hardship. It seems as though the out-of-shape body becomes a metaphor for an out-of-shape economy. This type of thinking is prevalent among those who hope to exorcise the evils of modern society by a return to good clean living.

Again, this is not to say that physical activity does not have many benefits for many people. However, the issue is more complex than is widely believed; for some working people (single mothers, the working poor) leisure may ideally involve liberation from physical effort and pressure to exercise can have negative effects—high injury rates and body image disorders to name two.

I write this, of course, at the risk of being castigated as a traitor among the ranks—after all, I teach in a department of kinesiology. To the faithful, criticism is anathema and is sometimes taken as being wholly negative rather than determinedly constructive. Let me clarify, therefore, that I am not calling for an end to employee fitness programs. Rather, I would like to see them created with more attention to the needs and desires of employees for joyful recreation and less to the demands of productivity.

Source: Philip White is a professor in the Department of Kinesiology at McMaster University, Hamilton, Ontario. This article was originally published in the Spring 1995 issue of *Canadian Healthcare Manager*. Reprinted with the permission of the author.

15.
Let Them Eat Fat
Greg Critser

The heavy truths about American obesity

Not long ago, a group of doctors, nurses, and medical technicians wheeled a young man into the intensive care unit of Los Angeles County-USC Medical Center, hooked him to a ganglia of life-support systems—pulse and respiration monitors, a breathing apparatus, and an IV line—then stood back and collectively stared. I was there visiting an ailing relative, and I stared, too.

Here, in the ghastly white light of modern American medicine, writhed a real-life epidemiological specter: a 500-pound twenty-two-year-old. The man, whom I'll call Carl, was propped up at a 45-degree angle, the better to be fed air through a tube, and lay there nude, save for a small patch of blood-spotted gauze stuck to his lower abdomen, where surgeons had just labored to save his life. His eyes darted about in abject fear. "Second time in three months," his mother blurted out to me as she stood watching in horror. "He had two stomach staplings, and they both came apart. Oh my God, my boy…" Her boy was suffocating in his own fat.

I was struck not just by the spectacle but by the truth of the mother's comment. This *was* a boy—one buried in years of bad health, relative poverty, a sedentary lifestyle, and a high-fat diet, to be sure, but a boy nonetheless. Yet how surprised should I have been? That obesity, particularly among the young and the poor, is spinning out of control is hardly a secret. It is, in fact, something that most Americans can agree upon. Along with depression, heart disease, and cancer, obesity is yet another chew in our daily rumination about health and fitness, morbidity and mortality. Still, even in dot-com America, where statistics fly like arrows, the numbers are astonishing. Consider:

- Today, one-fifth of all Americans are obese, meaning that they have a body mass index, or BMI, of more than 30. (BMI is a universally recognized cross-measure of weight for height and stature.) The epidemiological figures on chronic corpulence are so unequivocal that even the normally reticent dean of American obesity studies, the University of Colorado's James O. Hill, says that if obesity is left unchecked almost all Americans will be overweight within a few generations. "Becoming obese," he told the *Arizona Republic*, "is a normal response to the American environment."

- Children are most at risk. At least 25 percent of all Americans now under age nineteen are overweight or obese. In 1998, Dr. David Satcher, the new U.S. surgeon general, was moved to declare childhood obesity to be epidemic. "Today," he told a group of federal bureaucrats and policymakers, "we see a nation of young people seriously at risk of starting out obese and dooming themselves to the difficult task of overcoming a tough illness."

- Even among the most careful researchers these days, "epidemic" is the term of choice when it comes to talk of fat, particularly fat children. As William Dietz, the director of nutrition at the Centers for Disease Control, said last year, "This is an epidemic in the U.S. the likes of which we have not had before in chronic disease." The cost to the general public health budget by 2020 will run into the hundreds of billions, making HIV look, economically, like a bad case of the flu.

Yet standing that day in the intensive care unit, among the beepers and buzzers and pumps, epidemic was the last thing on my mind. Instead I felt heartbreak, revulsion, fear, sadness—and then curiosity: Where did this boy come from? Who and what had made him? How is it that we Americans, perhaps the most health-conscious of any people in the history of the world, and certainly the richest, have come to preside over the deadly fattening of our youth?

The beginning of an answer came one day last fall, in the same week that the Spanish language newspaper La Opinión ran a story headlined "Diabetes epidemia en latinos," when I attended the opening of the newest Krispy Kreme doughnut store in Los Angeles. It was, as they say in marketing circles, a "resonant" event, replete with around-the-block lines, celebrity news anchors, and stern cops directing traffic. The store, located

in the heart of the San Fernando Valley's burgeoning Latino population, pulsed with excitement. In one corner stood the new store's manager, a young Anglo fellow, accompanied by a Krispy Kreme publicity director. Why had Krispy Kreme decided to locate here? I asked.

"See," the manager said, brushing a crumb of choco-glaze from his fingers, "the idea is simple—accessible but not convenient. The idea is to make the store accessible—easy to get into and out of from the street—but just a tad away from the—eh, mainstream so as to make sure that the customers are presold and very intent before they get here," he said, betraying no doubts about the company's marketing formula. "We want them intent to get at least a dozen before they even think of coming in."

But why this slightly non-mainstream place?

"Because it's obvious..." He gestured to the stout Mayan doñas queuing around the building. "We're looking for all the bigger families."

Bigger in size?

"Yeah." His eyes rolled, like little glazed crullers. "*Bigger in size.*"

Of course, fast-food and national restaurant chains like Krispy Kreme that serve it have long been the object of criticism by nutritionists and dietitians. Despite the attention, however, fast-food companies, most of them publicly owned and sprinkled into the stock portfolios of many striving Americans (including mine and perhaps yours), have grown more aggressive in their targeting of poor inner-city communities. One of every four hamburgers sold by the good folks at McDonald's, for example, is now purchased by inner-city consumers who, disproportionately, are young black men.

In fact, it was the poor, and their increasing need for cheap meals consumed outside the home, that fueled the development of what may well be the most important fast-food innovation of the past twenty years, the sales gimmick known as "supersizing." At my local McDonald's, located in a lower-middle-income area of Pasadena, California, the supersize bacchanal goes into high gear at about five p.m., when the various urban caballeros, drywalleros, and jardineros get off work and head for a quick bite. Mixed in is a sizable element of young black kids traveling between school and home, their economic status apparent by the fact that they've walked instead of driven. Customers are cheerfully encouraged to "supersize your meal!" by signs saying, "If we don't recommend a supersize, the supersize is free!" For an extra seventy-nine cents, a kid ordering a cheeseburger, small fries, and a small Coke will get said cheeseburger plus a supersize Coke (42 fluid ounces versus 16, with free refills) and a supersize order of french fries (more than double the weight of a regular order). Suffice it to say that consumption of said meals is fast and, in almost every instance I observed, very complete.

But what, metabolically speaking, has taken place? The total caloric content of the meal has been jacked up from 680 calories to more than 1,340 calories. According to the very generous U.S. dietary guidelines, 1,340 calories represent more than half of a teenager's recommended daily caloric consumption, and the added calories themselves are protein-poor but fat- and carbohydrate-rich. Completing this jumbo dietetic horror is the fact that the easy availability of such huge meals arrives in the same years in which physical activity among teenage boys and girls drops by about half.

Now consider the endocrine warfare that follows. The constant bombing of the pancreas by such a huge hit of sugars and fats can eventually wear out the organ's insulin-producing "islets," leading to diabetes and its inevitable dirge of woes: kidney, eye, and nerve damage; increased risk of heart disease; even stroke. The resulting sugar-induced hyperglycemia in many of the obese wreaks its own havoc in the form of glucose toxicity, further debilitating nerve endings and arterial walls. For the obese and soon to be obese, it is no overstatement to say that after supersized teen years the pancreas may never be the same. Some 16 million Americans suffer from Type 2 diabetes, a third of them unaware of their condition. Today's giggly teen burp may well be tomorrow's aching neuropathic limb.

Diabetes, by the way, is just the beginning of what's possible. If childhood obesity truly is "an epidemic in the U.S. the likes of which we have not had before in chronic disease," then places like McDonald's and Winchell's Donut stores, with their endless racks of glazed and creamy goodies, are the San Francisco bathhouses of said epidemic, the places where the high-risk population indulges in high-risk behavior. Although open around the clock, the Winchell's near my house doesn't get rolling until seven in the morning, the Spanish-language talk shows frothing in the background while an ambulance light whirls atop the Coke dispenser. Inside, Mami placates Miguelito with a giant apple fritter. Papi tells a joke and pours ounce upon ounce of sugar and cream into his 20-ounce coffee. Viewed through the lens of obesity, as I am inclined to do, the scene is not so *feliz.* The obesity rate for Mexican-American children is shocking. Between the ages of five and eleven, the rate for girls is 27 percent; for boys, 23 percent. By fourth grade the rate for girls peaks at 32 percent, while boys top out at 43 percent. Not surprisingly, obesity-related disorders are everywhere on display at Winchell's, right before my eyes—including fat kids who limp, which can be a symptom of Blount's disease (a deformity of the tibia) or a sign of slipped capital femoral epiphysis (an orthopedic abnormality brought about by weight-induced dislocation of the femur bone). Both conditions are progressive, often requiring surgery.

The chubby boy nodding in the corner, waiting for his Papi to finish his *café,* is likely suffering from some form of steep apnea; a recent study of forty-one children with severe obesity revealed that a third had the condition and that another third presented with clinically abnormal sleep patterns. Another recent study indicated that "obese children with obstructive sleep apnea demonstrate clinically significant decrements in learning and memory function." And the lovely but very chubby little girl tending to her schoolbooks? Chances are she will begin puberty before the age of ten, launching her into a lifetime of endocrine bizarreness that not only will be costly to treat but will be emotionally devastating as well. Research also suggests that weight gain can lead to the development of pseudotumor cerebri, a brain tumor most common in females. A recent review of 57 patients with the tumor revealed that 90 percent were obese. This little girl's chances of developing other neurological illnesses are profound as well. And she may already have gallstones: obesity accounts for up to 33 percent of all gallstones observed in children. She is ten times more likely than her non-obese peers to develop high blood pressure, and she is increasingly likely to contract

Type 2 diabetes, obesity being that disease's number-one risk factor.

Of course, if she is really lucky, that little girl could just be having a choco-sprinkles doughnut on her way to school.

What about poor rural whites? Studying children in an elementary school in a low-income town in eastern Kentucky, the anthropologist Deborah Crooks was astonished to find stunting and obesity not just present but prevalent. Among her subjects, 13 percent of girls exhibited notable stunting; 33 percent of all kids were significantly overweight; and 13 percent of the children were obese—21 percent of boys and 9 percent of girls. A sensitive, elegant writer, Crooks drew from her work three important conclusions: One, that poor kids in the United States often face the same evolutionary nutritional pressures as those in newly industrializing nations, where traditional diets are replaced by high-fat diets and where labor-saving technology reduces physical activity. Second, Crooks found that "height and weight are cumulative measures of growth ... reflecting a sum total of environmental experience over time." Last, and perhaps most important, Crooks concluded that while stunting can be partially explained by individual household conditions—income, illness, education, and marital status—obesity "may be more of a community-related phenomenon." Here the economic infrastructure—safe playgrounds, access to high-quality, low-cost food, and transportation to play areas—was the key determinant of physical-activity levels.

Awareness of these national patterns of destruction, of course, is a key reason why Eli Lilly & Co., the $75 billion pharmaceutical company, is now building the largest factory dedicated to the production of a single drug in industry history. That drug is insulin. Lilly's sales of insulin products totaled $357 million in the third quarter of 1999, a 24 percent increase over the previous third quarter. Almost every leading pharmaceutical conglomerate has like-minded ventures under way, with special emphasis on pill-form treatments for non-insulin-dependent forms of the disease. Pharmaceutical companies that are not seeking to capture some portion of the burgeoning market are bordering on fiduciary mismanagement. Said James Kappel of Eli Lilly, "You've got to be in diabetes."

Wandering home from my outing, the wondrous smells of frying foods wafting in the air, I wondered why, given affluent America's outright fetishism about diet and health, those whose business it is to care—the media, the academy, public-health workers, and the government—do almost nothing. The answer, I suggest, is that in almost every public-health arena, the need to address obesity as a class issue—one that transcends the inevitable divisiveness of race and gender—has been blunted by bad logic, vested interests, academic cant, and ideological chauvinism.

Consider a story last year in the *New York Times* detailing the rise in delivery-room mortality among young African-American mothers. The increases were attributed to a number of factors—diabetes, hypertension, drug and alcohol abuse—but the primary factor of obesity, which can foster both diabetes and hypertension, was mentioned only in passing. Moreover, efforts to understand and publicize the socioeconomic factors of the deaths have been thwarted. When Dr. Janet Mitchell, a New York obstetrician charged with reviewing several recent maternal mortality studies, insisted that socioeconomics were the issue in understanding the "racial gap" in maternal mortality, she was unable to get government funding for the work. "We need to back away from the medical causes," she told the *Times*, clearly exasperated, "and begin to take a much more ethnographic, anthropological approach to this tragic outcome."

In another example, a 1995 University of Arizona study reported that young black girls, who are more inclined toward obesity than white girls, were also far less likely to hold "bad body images" about themselves. The slew of news articles and TV reports that followed were nothing short of jubilant, proclaiming the "good news." As one commentator I watched late one evening announced, "Here is one group of girls who couldn't care less about looking like Kate Moss!" Yet no one mentioned the long-term effects of unchecked weight gain. Apparently, when it comes to poor black girls the media would rather that they risk diabetes than try to look like models.

"That's the big conundrum, as they always say," Richard MacKenzie, a physician who treats overweight and obese girls in downtown L.A., told me recently. "No one wants to overemphasize the problems of being fat to these girls, for fear of creating body-image problems that might lead to anorexia and bulimia." Speaking anecdotally, he said that "the problem is that for every one affluent white anorexic you create by 'overemphasizing' obesity, you foster ten obese poor girls by downplaying the severity of the issue." Judith Stem, a professor of nutrition and internal medicine at UC Davis, is more blunt. "The number of kids with eating disorders is positively dwarfed by the number with obesity. It sidesteps the whole class issue. We've got to stop that and get on with the real problem."

Moreover, such sidestepping denies poor minority girls a principal, if sometimes unpleasant, psychological incentive to lose weight: that of social stigma. Only recently has the academy come to grapple with this. Writing in a recent issue of the *International Journal of Obesity*, the scholar Susan Averett looked at the hard numbers: 44 percent of African-American women weigh more than 120 percent of their recommended body weight yet are less likely than whites to perceive themselves as overweight.[1] Anglo women, poor and otherwise, registered higher anxiety about fatness and experienced far fewer cases of chronic obesity. "Social stigma may serve to control obesity among white women," Averett reluctantly concluded. "If so, physical and emotional effects of greater pressure to be thin must be weighed against reduced health risks associated with overweight and obesity." In other words, maybe a few more black Kate Mosses might not be such a bad thing.

While the so-called fat acceptance movement, a very vocal minority of super-obese female activists, has certainly played a role in the tendency to deny the need to promote healthy thinness, the real culprits have been those with true cultural power, those in the academy and the publishing industry who have the ability to shape public opinion. Behind much of their reluctance to face facts is the lingering influence of the 1978 bestseller, *Fat Is a Feminist Issue*, in which Susie Orbach presented a nuanced, passionate look at female compulsive eating and its roots in patriarchal culture. But although Orbach's observations were keen, her conclusions were often wishful, narcissistic, and sometimes just wrong. "Fat is a social disease, and fat is a feminist issue," Orbach wrote. "Fat is not about self-control or lack of will power…. It is a response to the inequality of the sexes."[2]

Perhaps so, if one is a feminist, and if one is struggling with an eating disorder, and if one is, for the most part, affluent, well-educated, and politically aware. But obesity itself is preeminently an issue of class, not of ethnicity, and certainly not of gender. True, the disease may be refracted though its concentrations in various demographic subgroupings–in Native Americans, in Latinos, in African Americans, and even in some Pacific Island Americans–but in study after study, the key adjective is *poor*: poor African Americans, poor Latinos, poor whites, poor women, poor children, poor Latino children, etc. From the definitive *Handbook of Obesity*: "In heterogeneous and affluent societies like the United States, there is a strong inverse correlation of social class and obesity, particularly for females." From *Annals of Epidemiology*: "In white girls … both TV viewing and obesity were strongly inversely associated with household income as well as with parental education."

Yet class seems to be the last thing on the minds of some of our better social thinkers. Instead, the tendency of many in the academy is to fetishize or "postmodernize" the problem. Cornell University professor Richard Klein, for example, proposed in his 1996 book, *Eat Fat*, "Try this for six weeks: Eat fat." (Klein's mother did and almost died from sleep apnea, causing Klein to reverse himself in his epilogue, advising readers: "Eat rice.") The identity politics of fat, incidentally, can cut the other way. To the French, the childhood diet has long been understood as a serious medical issue directly affecting the future of the nation. The concern grew directly from late-nineteenth-century health issues in French cities and the countryside, where tuberculosis had winnowed the nation's birth rate below that of the other European powers. To deal with the problem, a new science known as puériculture emerged to educate young mothers about basic health and nutrition practices. Long before Americans and the British roused themselves from the torpor of Victorian chub, the French undertook research into proper dietary and weight controls for the entire birth-to-adolescence growth period. By the early 1900s, with birth rates (and birth weights) picking up, the puériculture movement turned its attention to childhood obesity. Feeding times were to be strictly maintained; random snacks were unhealthy for the child, regardless of how "natural" it felt for a mother to indulge her young. Kids were weighed once a week. All meals were to be supervised by an adult. As a result, portion control—perhaps the one thing that modern obesity experts can agree upon as a reasonable way to prevent the condition—very early became institutionalized in modern France. The message that too much food is bad still resounds in French child rearing, and as a result France has a largely lean populace.

What about the so-called Obesity Establishment, that web of researchers, clinicians, academics, and government health officials charged with finding ways to prevent the disease? Although there are many committed individuals in this group, one wonders just how independently minded they are. Among the sponsors for the 1997 annual conference of the North American Association for the Study of Obesity, the premier medical think tank on the subject, were the following: the Coca-Cola Company, Hershey Foods, Kraft Foods, and, never to be left out, Slim Fast Foods. Another sponsor was Knoll Pharmaceuticals, maker of the new diet drug Meridia. Of course, in a society where until recently tobacco companies sponsored fitness pageants and Olympic games, sponsorship hardly denotes corruption in the most traditional sense. One would be hard-pressed to prove any kind of censorship, but such underwriting effectively defines the parameters of public discussion. Everybody winks or blinks at the proper moment, then goes on his or her way.

Once upon a time, however, the United States possessed visionary leadership in the realm of childhood fitness. Founded in 1956, the President's Council on Youth Fitness successfully laid down broad-based fitness goals for all youth and established a series of awards for those who excelled in the effort. The council spoke about obesity with a forthrightness that would be political suicide today, with such pointed slogans as "There's no such thing as stylishly stout" and "Hey kid, if you see yourself in this picture, you need help."

By the late 1980s and early 1990s, however, new trends converged to undercut the council's powers of moral and cultural suasion. The ascendancy of cultural relativism led to a growing reluctance to be blunt about fatness, and, aided and abetted by the fashion industry's focus on baggy, hip-hop-style clothes, it became possible to be "stylishly stout." Fatness, as celebrated on rap videos, was now equated with wealth and power, with identity and agency, not with clogging the heart or being unable to reach one's toes. But fat inner-city black kids and the suburban kids copying them are even more disabled by their obesity. The only people who benefit from kids being "fat" are the ones running and owning the clothing, media, food, and drug companies. In upscale corporate America, meanwhile, being fat is taboo, a surefire career-killer. If you can't control your own contours, goes the logic, how can you control a budget or a staff? Look at the glossy business and money magazines with their cooing profiles of the latest genius entrepreneurs: to the man, and the occasional woman, no one, I mean *no one*, is fat.

Related to the coolification of homeboyish fat—perhaps forcing its new status—is the simple fact that it's hard for poor children to find opportunities to exercise. Despite our obsession with professional sports, many of today's disadvantaged youth have fewer opportunities than ever to simply shoot baskets or kick a soccer ball. Various measures to limit state spending and taxing, among them California's debilitating Proposition 13, have gutted school-based physical-education classes. Currently, only one state, Illinois, requires daily physical education for all grades K-12, and only 19 percent of high school students nationwide are active for twenty minutes a day, five days a week, in physical education. Add to this the fact that, among the poor, television, the workingman's baby sitter, is now viewed at least thirty-two hours a week. Participation in sports has always required an investment, but with the children of the affluent tucked away either in private schools or green suburbias, buying basketballs for the poor is not on the public agenda.

Human nature and its lazy inclinations aside, what do America's affluent *get* out of keeping the poor so fat? The reasons, I'd suggest, are many. An unreconstructed Marxist might invoke simple class warfare, exploitation fought through stock ownership in giant fast-food firms. The affluent know that the stuff will kill them but need someone (else) to eat it so as to keep growing that retirement portfolio. A practitioner of vulgar social psychology might argue for "our" need for the "identifiable outsider." An economist would say that in a society as overly competitive as our own, the affluent have found a way to slow down the striving poor from inevitable nipping at their heels. A French semiotician might even say that with the poor the affluent have erected their own walking and talking "empire of signs." This last notion is perhaps not so far-fetched. For what do the fat, darker, exploited poor, with their unbridled primal appetites, have to offer us but a chance for we diet- and shape-conscious folk to live vicariously? Call it boundary envy. Or, rather, boundary-free envy. And yet, by living outside their boundaries, the poor live within ours; fat people do not threaten our way of life; their angers entombed in flesh, they are slowed, they are softened, they are *fed*.

Meanwhile, in the City of Fat Angels, we lounge through a slow-motion epidemic. Mami buys another apple fritter. Papi slams his second sugar and cream. Another young Carl supersizes and double supersizes, then supersizes again. Waistlines surge. Any minute now, the belt will run out of holes.

Endnotes:

[1] Certainly culture plays a role in the behavior of any subpopulation. Among black women, for example, obesity rates persist despite increases in income. A recent study by the National Heart, Lung, and Blood Institute concludes that obesity in black girls may be "a reflection of a differential social development in our society, wherein a certain lag period may need to elapse between an era when food availability is a concern to an era of affluence with no such concern." Other observers might assert that black women find affirmation for being heavy from black men, or believe themselves to be "naturally" heavier. Such assertions do not change mortality statistics.

[2] At the edges of the culture, the inheritors of Susie Orbach's politics have created Web sites called FaT GIRL and Largesse: the Network for Size Esteem, which claim that "dieting kills" and instruct how to induce vomiting in diet centers as protest.

Source: Greg Critser is a regular contributor to *Harper's Magazine*.This article was originally published in *Harper's Magazine*, March 2000, pp.41-47.

16.

Boxing Is Not To Blame

Stephen Brunt

A fighter died of his injuries, but the culprit isn't pugilism, it's poverty

Almost no one fights for a living because they want to. That is the case now, and that has been the case almost since boxing for money first became an option nearly 300 years ago. It can be easy to pretend otherwise, watching the fresh-faced amateurs at the Olympic Games, or because of the temporarily fashionable "boxercise," "executive" boxing clubs, women's boxing, Tae Bo and the like, all of which can make it seem like a game, like play, like any other sport.

But the truth is that becoming a professional fighter has always been the last resort of the poor, that boxing's talent has always been drawn primarily from among the desperate. It is the only sport in which, without working your way through a minor-league system or playing in college, you can get paid tomorrow—not much, but something—just so long as you can pass a physical.

That's why any survey of the sport's dominant participants over time is like a survey of the changing (or unchanging) face of the North American underclass: the Jews and the Irish in the first decades of this century, the Italians in the middle, Hispanics now, blacks always.

And that's why Stephan Johnson stepped into the ring on Nov. 20 in Atlantic City, N.J., for a fight he perhaps understood he couldn't win, but one that he surely didn't think could cost him his life.

Mr. Johnson, who died on Sunday from brain injuries suffered when he was knocked out by Paul Vaden, had told friends that he would keep fighting until he raised enough money to move his mother out of the housing project in which she lived in New York. His purse for the Vaden fight was reported as $10,000. And anyone who is familiar with boxing's standard, exploitative accounting practices understands that only a fraction of that amount would have found its way into his pocket in any case.

Still, it was real money, which is why boxers rarely quit of their own volition, why there's no dignified wind-down for even the best and most famous. One big win, one big payday, always lies just beyond the horizon, whereas the loss that's the end of the road always comes as a surprise. That's the case for the lowly pug just as it was the case for the two fighters recently judged the greatest of this century, Sugar Ray Robinson and Muhammad Ali.

As happens each time there is a ring death, ethical debate has ensued about whether the sport ought to be allowed to exist. This time, there is the added evidence that Mr. Johnson had been knocked out in a fight last April in Toronto, had been taken to hospital afterward, and had been suspended by the Ontario Athletics Commission for 60 days–a suspension that was ignored by at least one U.S. state commission, which allowed Mr. Johnson back in the ring before the prohibition had expired.

Although it worked like that for years–fighters moving from one jurisdiction to another, sometimes using aliases, seeking out the places where the sport was all but unregulated in order to keep their meagre incomes flowing–it's not supposed to work like that any more. Record keeping has never been better in boxing, and there are few if any rogue territories remaining. The commissions talk to each other and are bound to honour each other's suspensions. Boxing has never been more tightly monitored by government than it is right now.

Still, Mr. Johnson slipped through. But by the time he fought his final fight in Atlantic City, the suspension had long passed, and he had undergone at least one of the medical tests mandatory for relicensing, a CAT scan.

Had he undergone the others–an EEG, and a psychometric examination–would the tragedy have been prevented?

Perhaps, but probably not. Others fighters who have died (so many of their names remain familiar: Benny Paret, Duk Koo Kim, Johnny Owen, Jimmy Garcia…) were deemed fit before they stepped into the ring, to the limits of the testing of the time.

And they weren't career losers who might have been weeded out. They hadn't taken beating after beating. Those kind of fighters–used to pad other boxers' winning records–know when it's time to quit, understand their role and surrender in order

to be able to lose another day. Invariably, the boxers who die are involved in tough, competitive bouts, and it's their bravery, their willingness to persevere, that gets them into trouble.

The fact is, it almost never happens. Boxing apologists will point out, quite accurately, that in terms of fatalities, many other, more socially acceptable sports (football, for one) are far more dangerous. A ring death is a terrible fluke, impossible to anticipate, and nearly impossible to prevent without outlawing all fights at all times. Understanding why one fighter is susceptible to traumatic brain injury at a given moment has so far proved to be beyond the powers of the doctors who examine boxers, and the regulators who empower them. (Non-fatal brain damage is far more common, and a far greater indictment against boxing: injured fighters continue to deteriorate for 10 or 15 years after they've absorbed their last blow. The brain doesn't completely heal–something hockey and football players who've suffered multiple concussions understand as well as fighters.)

But ring deaths do provide a simple, stark image for the abolitionists to hang their arguments on, dramatic and to the point and then forgotten until the next one comes along, likely years later.

Easily ignored by both sides of the debate is the sport's economic underpinning, the reason most fighters decide to fight in the first place, the real crime.

Of course that's a little more complicated, a little more difficult to sum up in a broadside. A boxer's life is difficult, but without boxing so many lives would have been so much more difficult. In a better world, the supply of fighters would immediately dry up, and there would be no need to crusade against boxing.

But Stephan Johnson didn't live in a better world, and he didn't have much of a choice.

Source: Stephen Brunt is a sports writer with *The Globe and Mail*. This article was originally published in *The Globe and Mail*, Friday, December 10, 1999, A23. Reproduced by permission of *The Globe and Mail*.

Part 5
Violence and Masculinity

Shortly before the 1995 boxing match in which Gerald McClellan suffered from brain damage, he was quoted as saying: "It's a great feeling for me to knock a man unconscious. It's better than sex."

In the past few years, gender studies have developed the notion of multiple masculinities and femininities—that there are many different ways in which to be male and female. The masculinity that is held up for our example is pain tolerant, risk taking, and sometimes violent. And, while most males are not like these images, there are a number of consequences of this dominant form of masculinity. It is young males who experience the vast majority of sports injuries (and auto accidents). It is also young males who engage in the majority of violent behaviour, in society and in sport.

Fan violence, player violence, and occasional violence between fans and players seem to be an integral part of the modern sport scene. But the questions that are now being asked more frequently concern violence against women. Are males involved in violent sports more likely to act in violent ways against women. Is there a connection between the two? Are male athletes more likely to be punished for such violence? Anecdotal evidence suggests that violence against women increases at the time of events such as the Super Bowl. There is some (admittedly controversial) evidence from the U.S. that suggests that male university athletes in major sports are more likely to be sexually violent against women (Crosset et al., 1995; Koss & Gaines, 1993). This can be added to the anecdotal evidence of sexual and physical assault of women by celebrity athletes. And a recent study indicates that while celebrity athletes in the U.S. are more likely than non-athletes to be arrested and indicted for sexual assault, they are far less likely to be convicted (Benedict & Klein, 1997).

In the first article in this section, journalist Laura Robinson looks at the effects of the more general messages about masculinity. In a disturbing counterpoint to the previous section on health and injury, she asserts that "male athletes are far safer on the playing fields than the women and girls of this world are on the street or in their homes." In an article written shortly after the Columbine High School massacre in Littleton, Colorado, Robert Lipsyte notes that elitist and bullying athletes were implicated in the event and asks a series of disturbing questions about "jock culture" in North America. And, finally, Susan McClelland notes that body image issues are now just as likely to influence the behaviour of men as the behaviour of women. [See the section on **Drugs and Sport**.]

References

- Benedict, J., & A. Klein (1997). Arrest and conviction rates for athletes accused of sexual assault. *Sociology of Sport Journal*, 14(1), 86-94.
- Crosset, T., J. Benedict & M. MacDonald (1995). Male student-athletes reported for sexual assault: Survey of campus police departments and judicial affairs. *Journal of Sport and Social Issues*, 19(2), 126-140.
- Koss, M., & J. Gaines (1993). The prediction of sexual aggression by alcohol use, athletic participation, and fraternity affiliation. *Journal of Interpersonal Violence*, 8(1), 23-39.

Additional Sources

Videos:

- *Disposable Heroes?* TSN "Name of the Game" series, deals in part with violent and career-ending injuries to male athletes (see also *Disposable Heroes,* an HBO video).
- *Crossing the Line*, from CBC's "The Fifth Estate," deals with male coach sexual abuse of female athletes.

Print Resources:

- Burton Nelson, M. (1994). Jock violence hits home. *The Globe & Mail*, 23 June, p.A19. [An examination of male athletes' involvement in domestic violence that again questions the relationship between the two.]
- Nack, W., & L. Munson (1995). Sport's dirty secret. *Sports Illustrated*, 31 July, pp.63-74. [Special Report on domestic violence and professional athletes.]
- Brunt, S. (1995). Mike Tyson: He's back. And he's not sorry. *The Globe and Mail*, 19 August, pp.D1, D5. [Examination of Tyson after his release from prison.]
- Barfoot, J. (2000). Boys will be boys will be … criminals. *London Free Press*, 6 February, p.A7. [Looks at the John Rocker incident and other recent examples of abuse by pro athletes.]

17.

All-Male Sports Fit All Too Well into Our Culture of Violence

Laura Robinson

The great paradox

I'm sitting on a plane with a male colleague from the CBC, flipping through the *Globe and Mail*, and come upon coverage of the United Nations' Fourth World Conference on Women. "Violence stalks world's women," the headline reads. Abuse in the form of rape, battery and murder is increasing in what some call the silent crisis of the century.

"It's about time these issues get some real coverage," I say.

There is silence.

"Can you pass me the sports section?" my seatmate finally replies.

And so it goes. Like a wart hog burrowing into the ground until a perceived danger has passed, another man takes shelter from a woman wanting a conversation about her world. By escaping to the world of male-only sports, men are not only reassured that things are proceeding as they should, but also that women are not a part of the real world—so we don't count.

I always want to ask these men whether they think there is any relationship between the worshipping of male athletes who play violent and confrontational sports and men who commit violence against women to assert a sense of masculinity and power.

Great paradox

It is a great paradox that sport is perceived to be a place where risks are taken and danger lurks behind every helmet. It is even more ironic that men imagine that, simply by watching sports, they are part of the risk-taking, sharing the challenges of the playing field and scoring the goals.

In truth, it is women who lead dangerous and risky lives—simply because we are women and must share the Earth with men. Male athletes are far safer on the playing field than the women and girls of this world are on the street or in their homes.

So athletes remain gods. Team gang rapes don't happen, spouses aren't abused, the locker-room diatribes against women—sluts and pigs in jock talk—go unspoken and the relegation of women to the role of hostess, cheerleader or groupie in stadiums and arenas is somehow normal.

Although male sports fans might like to think so, it's not as though you can become more of a man by knowing all the statistics of yards won and lost, home runs, batting averages, salaries, injuries and trades. Yet I get the impression that many fans base their own sexuality on precisely these stats, which means their identities are staked on someone else's performance.

It is a world that not only doesn't include women, but pretends the world exists without us.

Not surprisingly, when women challenge this culture, there is violence. For example, Canada's Justine Blainey fought the Ontario Hockey Association for the right to play the sport and endured death threats, mass ostracism in the hockey community and pornography about her in locker rooms.

Consider Algeria's Hassiba Boulmerka, the 1991 world champion and 1992 Olympic champion in the 1,500-metre race. While some compatriots congratulated her, fundamentalist Muslims hurled obscenities while she tried to work out in her home country. She could end up with her throat slit—the popular punishment by extremists of Algerian women who try to pursue their dreams.

Their experiences mirror the international relationship between the worship of masculinity—whether it be through sport or religion—and violence and contempt against women.

Men are unaware on a conscious level of the relationship between male-only sport and violence against women. They don't see the link between the worshipping of professional male sport, which by definition disallows women the right to play, and their culture's same propensity to allow men to use violence as a vocabulary in their relationships with women.

Stay ignorant

Some men want to stay ignorant. But I don't believe most do. I believe most men want their daughters, sisters, mothers and partners to live in a world that embraces, affirms and protects them. I believe most men think women have every right to play the sport they wish to the very best of their ability. But there is a big gap between what they would like and how they behave.

In order to live up to these beliefs, men would have to give up on what they perceive as masculinity. They would have to accept that men are men only because of their biology and not because they play sports or watch sports, or because they violate women. To realize what they say are their aspirations for women, they would have to care more about women—way more—than they do about professional sports.

They would have to understand that the freedom of women to dream big dreams and work hard to obtain them does not detract from their sexuality. On the contrary, a world where dreams are possible for all human beings enhances everyone's life.

Julie Croteau put it perfectly earlier this year. She's a professional baseball player with the Colorado Silver Bullets who took her high school to court when they cut her from the boys' baseball team.

"Sports isn't inherently gendered. There's nothing masculine about baseball. Sports is about freedom, not categories."

Source: Laura Robinson is a former national-level cyclist and cross-country ski racer. She is the author of two books about sport, *She Shoots, She Scores: Canadian Perspectives on Women and Sport* and *Crossing the Line: Violence and Sexual Assault in Canada's National Sport*. This article was orginally published in *Now*, September 14-20, 1995, pp.34-35. Reproduced with the permission of the author.

18.

The Jock Culture: Time to Debate the Questions

Robert Lipsyte

As family rituals fade, sporting events become our national campfires

Yelling, "Sports, sports, don't you get it, everything in Glen Ridge is sports," a teen-age Jeremiah runs through a forgettable television movie tomorrow night with an inescapable message: love it, hate it or try to ignore it, jock culture haunts our national daydreams.

It may be as seemingly benign as renaming a New York highway after Joe DiMaggio, who last played here almost 50 years ago and afterward contributed little to the life of the city. It may be as threatening and damaging as Little League parents, the corruption of higher education by "revenue-producing" intercollegiate sports or the patterns of violence by individual athletes and by teams.

In recent weeks, in the frantic attempts to box and examine the high school massacre in Littleton, Colo., jockcult became a hot topic again. The teen-age killers were quoted as shouting: "All jocks stand up. We're going to kill every one of you." To some, this marked the two former Little Leaguers as bitter athletic failures, which is probably not accurate. (Alternately, a hero of the massacre, Dave Sanders, who saved lives at the sacrifice of his own, has tended to be characterized by his after-school job as a girls' sports coach rather than his full-time job as a business teacher.)

Some commentators saw in the murders-suicides the ultimate pathological response of outsiders to a world from which they had been excluded. Within these theories were other assumptions: that jockhood was a golden goal, or at least an expression of mainstream values, and that perhaps the athletes had brought this upon themselves with their postures of entitlement and their drive to domination inside and outside the white lines.

The worship of high school athletes is hardly a new story and certainly never surprising. Why wouldn't you idolize—or resent—peers who are bigger, better and more confident at the time of life when it seems to matter most, adolescence. Furthermore, the school and the community often afford athletes special privileges, including relief from many rules.

This, of course, goes beyond high school. The greatest defensive football player of the century, the troubled Lawrence Taylor, caused havoc in the hallways of his high school and college and then went on to up the ante on the streets as a pro or, more recently, as a jock out of water. Felony arrests among pro and college athletes may or may not be rising, but better reporting makes it clear that many of them cannot turn off their aggressive behavior at the buzzer.

Meanwhile, the nice jocks, the ones we assume never trashed bars, raped dates or even made fun of fat boys—Michael Jordan, Wayne Gretzky, John Elway—were justifiably eulogized at retirement. In this time of fading family and community rituals, when major sports events have become our national campfires, who wants to cheer for clay feet?

Local campfires tend to afford more warmth, which is why the Glen Ridge rape story of 1989 was such a sensation. High school football players were accused of sexually molesting a mildly retarded female classmate while teammates watched. Glen Ridge, N.J., was seen as a bland, self-satisfied, mainly white Protestant suburb. Picture-book America. The football team was not particularly good, but the young athletes were regarded as the pride and extension of the community. Covering the story at the time, I was surprised at the fury of some residents toward the news media for "bothering" them, the annoyance of others that for so long we had bought into the myth of the Glen Ridges as exempt from class, race and gender problems. As with Littleton, Glen Ridge became a long-lasting symbol, somewhat unfairly, of the American dream come apart at the seams.

In his fine, absorbing 1997 book, "Our Boys," Bernard Lefkowitz raised the level of discourse. He suggested that as individuals the pack of Glen Ridge football players and wrestlers were not as confident as they seemed. He wrote: "A compelling argument can be made that the hyper-masculine style they were asked to assume by parents and brothers and sports enthusiasts was a heavy burden for a kid to carry through adolescence."

Lefkowitz added: "The swagger they affected—the jock swagger—was a handy way to camouflage their doubts."

It would be a long time, if ever, before the nerds, blacks, greasers, geeks, burnouts and non-"Jockette" girls that the "Ridgers" terrorized would figure that out.

The book has been made into a flat, disappointing movie that airs tomorrow night on ABC. But it will hopefully reinvigorate explorations of sports' role in American society. And by focusing on Glen Ridge and Littleton, where most of the athletes were white, it may be possible to discuss some of the bio-anthropological theories of violence.

In their 1996 book, "Demonic Males: Apes and the Origins of Human Violence," Richard Wrangham and Dale Peterson trace patterns of imperialistic behavior in male gorilla and chimpanzee groups that are recapitulated in prestate warrior societies and urban gangs.

They write: "The psychology engaged may be hardly different from that expressed in predominantly male team sports—American football and hockey, for example. Demonic males gather in small, self-perpetuating, self-aggrandizing bands.

"What matters is the opportunity to engage in the vast and compelling drama of belonging to the gang, identifying the enemy, going on the patrol, participating in the attack."

And we, of course, are caught up in that compelling, relentlessly promoted drama. The noted Rutgers anthropologist Lionel Tiger offers his own jeremiad. In his new book, "The Decline of Males" (Golden Books), he writes: "Television sport is to male personal achievement as videocassette pornography is to love."

Tiger, best known for his exploration of male bonding in his famous "Men in Groups," has taken a controversial tack in his current work. He asserts that the power given to women through effective contraception has made men feel "obsolete and out of control." Men have turned to drugs, porn and obsessive sports fandom which "may reveal a turbulent male preoccupation with competition and physical assertiveness that is no longer available to ordinary men."

Some of these issues deserve national forums, although such airings-out seem less and less likely as media conglomerates invest in sports programming that promotes athletes as soap opera stars, if not icons. Their excuse—the fans want it!—is true. A mildly critical look at Joe DiMaggio here several weeks ago brought a flood of negative mail, some of it abusive. The angriest were those who felt that sympathy toward a supposedly treacherous ingrate like Darryl Strawberry was somehow an oil spill on the Clipper's memory.

All the more reason to press on. In future columns, perhaps with the help of forward-thinking psychiatrists, psychologists, anthropologists, sociologists, historians, philosophers and, yes, even fans, we will try to open our own jockcult forum.

Some early, first-draft questions:

- What is the role of sports beyond health and entertainment, as moral crucible, as national campfire?

- Is there a thread of pathology among certain athletes that fuels their achievement? Do the psycho-scouts know and look for it?

- Is the emotional neediness of some fans a pathology, and, if so, is it satisfied or exacerbated by their fandom?

- How has the national struggle with matters of race, class and gender been affected by sports?

- Has the media's promotion of violent, abusive sports heroes affected our definitions of masculinity?

- Will female athletes change the game, or be changed?

Your thoughts are welcomed. Requested.

Source: Robert Lipsyte is a columnist for *The New York Times*. This article was originally published in *The New York Times*, Sunday, May 9, 1999, SP11. Reproduced by permission of *The New York Times*.

19.

The Lure of the Body Image

Susan McClelland

In their quest for the beefcake look, some men try extreme measures

The year Ralph Heighton of Pictou, N.S., turned 30, he decided to lose some weight. At five-foot-nine, pushing 210 lb., Heighton says when he stood in front of the mirror, he knew something wasn't working. He joined the YMCA in the nearby town of New Glasgow, started taking nightly walks and altered his diet, cutting out the late-night pizzas and pitas with spiced beef, onions and sauce. Now, at 34, Heighton fluctuates around the 185-lb. mark, and has converted one of the three bedrooms in his new two-storey home into a gym, complete with weights and a tattered heavy bag bound by duct tape. Heighton, a wildlife technician with Nova Scotia's department of fisheries, says he has achieved his goal of feeling better. Though still single, he says bashfully that he thinks he has never looked as good—which was one of his key reasons for getting in shape. "The magazines sort of force this body image on you of what it means to be a physically fit person," says Heighton. "Whether we want to admit it or not, this image is what we want to look like."

The idealized male body image nowadays is beefy and muscled, as epitomized in the Calvin Klein underwear advertisements showcasing the bulging pecs and rippling abdomen of Antonio Sabato Jr. And like Heighton, hundreds of thousands of men in Canada are flocking to gyms and health clubs in the quest to look buffed and toned. There are signs, however, that some men are taking the image to extremes. Statistics on steroid use show an alarming number of male teenagers across the country are using the substance illegally simply to put on muscle. Men are increasingly being diagnosed with eating disorders. And plastic surgeons report a general increase in men seeking their services to improve their appearance. "This is an early warning," said New York City author Michelangelo Signorile, whose book *Life Outside* chronicles the history of body image among homosexual men.

"This 'cult of masculinity' isn't just in gay culture as so many like to believe. It envelops the entire culture. It is an obsessive devotion to an ideal."

Although worshipping the body is hardly new, the emphasis on the beefcake look has evolved gradually in North America over the past 100 years. Both Signorile and Brian Pronger, a philosopher in the faculty of physical education at the University of Toronto, say that many men, straight and gay, adopted a more masculine appearance after the Oscar Wilde trials in the 1890s associated effeminate behaviour with homosexuality in the popular mind. Pronger and Signorile also say that women's suffrage and, later, the modern feminist movement caused men to covet a larger appearance as a means of defending men's status. "As women take up more space in traditionally masculine places," says Pronger, "some men feel compelled to take up more in order to maintain their position."

It takes a lot of sweating and spending to achieve a hard-body look. According to a 1995 report published by the Canadian Fitness and Lifestyle Research Institute, men spend more than twice as much as women in all categories related to fitness, including clothing, exercise equipment, membership fees and instruction. Brad Whitehead, who works for one of the largest distributors of creatine, a controversial supplement that increases the energy capacity in muscles, says sales have increased 130 percent since 1997.

Calvin Klein and other underwear merchants are not alone in using men with buffed bodies to sell products. Other advertisers include Coca-Cola, Nike and Marlboro, which has introduced a bulkier version of its original "Marlboro Man." As well, magazine stands now offer dozens of titles devoted to health, fitness and muscle, tantalizing readers with snappy headlines like "Great abs in eight weeks." Their pages are adorned with ads featuring big, bulky men selling muscle-building supplements.

One of the sad consequences of the push towards a hyper-masculine image is that it can rarely be obtained without the use of potentially harmful drugs. A 1993 study conducted for the Canadian Centre for Ethics in Sport concluded that 4 percent of males aged 11 to 18—as many as 83,000 young Canadians—used anabolic steroids in 1992 and 1993. In the study, which involved 16,169 high-school and elementary students, one in five reported that they knew someone who was taking anabolic steroids. Among the reasons given for their use, nearly half said it was to change their physical appearance. That contrasted starkly with previously held notions that steroids were used mostly to increase athletic performance, says Paul Melia, the centre's director of education. "The reality is for most of these young men, even if they do get on a regimen of weight training, they are not going to look like these picture boys," said Melia. "And sustaining that look is a full-time job."

In a downtown Toronto gym, Mike, a 32-year-old former bodybuilder and weight lifter and a longtime user of anabolic steroids, says as many as four out of five of the 18- to 25-year-old men using the facility are on the illegal drugs. When he started using steroids 16 years ago, Mike says, he was part of an elite group of men who took them for competitive reasons. "Today it is for the body image," he says. "And these kids stack—they add steroid upon steroid, thinking they are going to get a certain look. They take this stuff, go out to night clubs, get drunk and mix everything together. It's all for image."

Mike says one result of working out seriously can be that, no matter how big their muscles get, men start thinking they are still not big enough. It is a phenomenon disturbingly similar to cases of eating disorders among women who believe they are too big, no matter how thin they get. Maintaining a hard body takes not only a regimen of heavy workouts, but also a dedication to eating right and at times dieting to avoid gaining fat, says Mike. And psychologists across the country say one result of those self-imposed pressures is an increased incidence of eating disorders among men. According to Dr. Howard Steiger, a clinical psychologist and director of the eating disorder program at Douglas Hospital in Montreal, surveys have shown that 5 to 10 percent of eating disorder sufferers are men. He says most people with eating disorders have unstable self-esteem. He also says there are increasing sociocultural pressures on men to connect their self-esteem to body image. While there are no new national figures, specialists in many centres say that bulimia nervosa, characterized by binge eating and vomiting, is on the rise in men. "What you find," says Steiger, "are people who diet too much, who condition too much, and what you are doing is setting up this pressure of hunger—a constant state of undernutrition that eventually leads to bulimic-type eating patterns."

In addition to steroid use and erratic eating behaviour, John Semple, secretary treasurer of the Canadian Society of Plastic Surgeons, says he believes men are increasingly having plastic surgery to alter their body image. Dr. Bill Papanastasiou, a plastic surgeon in Montreal, estimates that only 10 percent of his patients were male when he opened his practice 13 years ago. Today, it is as high as 15 to 20 percent. In Halifax, plastic surgeon Dr. Kenneth Wilson says one of the most common surgeries he does for men is liposuction. For Nathan Estep, a 27-year-old from Detroit who spent $1,800 in Pontiac, Mich., in 1997 to have liposuction done on his waistline, the surgery has transformed his life. Since he was 10, Estep was a constant dieter, at times bulimic, and for many years tried to control his weight using diet drugs including Dexedrine, ephedrine and laxatives. Today, Estep says he can walk proudly, with his shirt off and with no hint of any fat from his childhood returning. "I was a fat kid—I had fat in the wrong places," he says. "The first thing I did after the liposuction was go to the beach, take my shirt off and eat a pint of Häagen-Dazs. I feel like a new man."

According to Pronger, who has been studying the philosophy of physical fitness for five years, a person with a hard, fit body considers it a signal of discipline and a capacity for hard work. "When you see somebody who is overweight," he says, "often the response is how did they let themselves get like that." The mistaken presumption, he adds, is that the person doesn't have the discipline to be a productive citizen. One of the solutions, says Pronger, is to teach children to look at body images in the same critical way they are told to consider art and literature—to be able to recognize what has merit. "If we were doing the same with physical education, people could learn to have a different reaction to these extreme body images," he says. "They would say, 'Hey, I don't want to be part of this pressure to fall in love with a highly commercialized image.'"

Source: Susan McClelland is an associate editor at *Macleans*. This article was originally published in *Macleans*, February 22, 1999, pp.38-39. Reproduced by permission of *Macleans*.

Part 6
Women

"There is an obvious truth that if the Olympic Games removed the Men-Women distinction, there would be Women only in the graceful events" (extract from the English translation of the Marc Lépine suicide letter). [Marc Lépine murdered 14 female engineering students at University of Montréal's Ecole Polytechnique on December 6, 1989 before committing suicide.]

Just as we have seen that there are numerous ways to be masculine, there are also numerous ways to be feminine. And just as Stallone and Schwarzenegger represent the dominant form of masculinity, it is the "supermodels" who seem to represent the dominant form of femininity. While they are "clothes-horses" whose bodies are clearly the result of diet and exercise, they are not necessarily "athletic." Yet, while female athletes may not yet represent the *dominant* form of femininity, being female and being athletic no longer represents the kind of contradiction that people believed it did even 20 years ago.

Sport participation is far more acceptable for girls and women, not only in the so-called "feminine" sports (gymnastics, figure skating, swimming, tennis, etc.), but also in soccer, rugby, ice hockey, wrestling, rock climbing, and many other sports formerly closed to females or only engaged in previously by those women brave enough to step outside the mainstream. There are many more females participating in this greater variety of sports, and there are also moves towards, and demands for, greater equity and opportunity for participation everywhere from high schools to the Olympics.

But, there are still costs associated with being female and an athlete—costs not incurred by most male athletes. Kari Fasting, in a speech first made at the Centennial Olympic Congress in Paris (1994), identifies one of the costs that has been recognized recently. The female athlete "triad" is that insidious cluster of related conditions that afflicts far too many—eating disorders (and compulsive exercise), amenorrhoea, and osteoporosis. (The latter was a condition thought only to affect older women, but young female athletes are now being found with bone densities characteristic of much older women.) She suggests several steps that must be taken to resolve this problem.

Next, Laura Robinson, in an article that is extremely critical of the Canadian Hockey Association, looks at what can happen in formerly male-dominated sport organizations as women become more involved in the sport. Rachel Giese then looks at the growth of women's sport, and how some men (and women) are beginning to point to the culture and ethics of women's sports as salvation from the corruption and violence of men's sports. She pointedly asks whether this is a responsibility that belongs to women. And, finally, another piece by Laura Robinson shows how the Canadian Human Rights Act can be used to achieve gender equity in sport, especially in situations where a traditional status quo in terms of financial support and facility use favours male participation.

Additional Sources

Videos:

- *Baseball Girls* is a National Film Board production documenting the history of women's involvement in baseball and softball.
- *Le Tour cycliste féminin* is the CBC's *Adrienne Clarkson Presents* video on the Canadian cycling team in the women's Tour de France.
- *Thin Ice*, available from the CBC, looks at the sexual exploitation of young women (and young male players) by players and others in ice hockey.

Print Resources:

- Davidson, J. (1994). Ottawa women play hardball to get recognition for soccer team. *The Globe and Mail*, 5 October, p.A20. [The University of Ottawa women's soccer team had to threaten a human rights' suit before they were promoted from club to varsity status.]
- Lamb, L. and Kane, M.J. (2000). Can women save sports? *UTNE Reader*, February, pp.56-57. [Looks at the popularity of and problems in women's sports today.]
- Robinson, L. (1997). *She Shoots, She Scores: Canadian Perspectives on Women and Sport*. Toronto: Thompson Educational Publishing, Inc.

20.

The Female Athlete Triad

Kari Fasting

Eating disorders, amenorrhoea, and osteoporosis

On July 26, 1994, Christy Henrich, a member of the 1989 United States gymnastics team, died from complete organ failure as a result of anorexia and bulimia. Under intense pressure from coaches, parents, teammates, and often even from themselves to lose weight, many young athletes slip into disordered eating which can lead to menstrual irregularities and bone loss, affecting their health and placing them at risk for premature osteoporosis.

Based on the latest studies, the number of female athletes with serious eating disorders is estimated to range from 15 to 62 percent, depending on the sport. Research has also shown that the spinal bone density of some of these young athletes is similar to that of women in their seventies and eighties, and may never return to normal. To prevent this situation:

- educate the athletes, coaches, parents, health professionals, sport-governing bodies, and athletic administrators about the seriousness of the problem and how to recognize the warning signs;

- establish and enforce appropriate standards of conduct for those responsible for coaching and training athletes;

- examine the rules governing each sport to see if changes in the rules might discourage the type of behaviour which leads to eating disorders.

To prevent the serious medical and psychological consequences resulting from the Triad requires the cooperation of all bodies involved in the Olympic movement. Education is extremely important, but it is not enough. Some of the rules and judging procedures must also be changed.

The world of sport and the Olympic movement cannot stand by while young female athletes suffer the medical consequences of the Triad and even risk death for their sport. The Olympic movement has the power to change this situation and should use this power to start this challenging and difficult process immediately. With respect to the scientific knowledge of today and the values embedded in the Olympic Charter, I can't see that you can delay such changes any longer.

Source: Kari Fasting is at the Norwegian University of Sport and Physical Education. She was a speaker at the IOC Centennial Congress in Paris. This article was originally published in *Action*, Spring 1995, p.2. Reprinted with permission of the Canadian Association for the Advancement of Women and Sport and Physical Activity.

21.

Games Boys Play

Laura Robinson

The off-ice antics of the men who run women's hockey

The receptionist at the Canadian Hockey Association's office in Calgary says she doesn't know Melody Davidson's phone number. Why should she? Davidson is only the coach of the Canadian women's national team, the current world champions. The third women's coach in as many years does not have an office at the hockey centre, though her male counterpart, Tom Rennie, does. But Rennie has a full-time job as a CHA vice-president and as the senior men's national coach. Davidson's position is part-time.

The CHA's other office in Ottawa doesn't have Davidson's number either—in fact, they've never heard of her. "Sorry, I have no idea who she is," replies the receptionist, suggesting that I call the Calgary office. When I phone Calgary again, I am told they have passed my message on to Davidson. So they did have her number. "She asked me not to give it out," the receptionist says.

This little Monty Pythonesque exchange is just one of many ways in which the CHA doesn't quite tell the truth when it comes to the women's side of the game. The CHA believes it is doing all it can to promote women's hockey, but that's not what the women inside the sport say. If there ever were two Canadian solitudes, they exist on the ice where the national dream appears to come in only one sex.

Of course, women's hockey has come a long way since the first world championships in 1990 when the players were forced to wear pink and white uniforms so they wouldn't be offensive when they took to the ice. Exactly who would be offended if they wore the same jerseys as the men's team was never articulated. The uniform has been replaced, but the attitudes that put it there remain intact.

From her hockey school in her home town of Stettler, Alberta, Melody Davidson returns my phone call. In its fifth year, the school hosts 140 boys and 175 girls. Davidson is a busy woman. She runs the hockey school and the national women's team, and coaches women's hockey and volleyball at Connecticut College, a small Division III team in the United States where she lives for nine months of the year. She tells me,

I would love to coach just hockey for a living, and down the road I have quite a few goals to achieve with the Olympics. Whether there'll be an opportunity with the CHA as a paid coach, I can't say. Opportunities are limited, and that's because opportunities for women haven't expanded in hockey the way they have for men.

Davidson spends a huge amount of time and energy jumping time zones and rink boards so that she has enough money to continue working for next to nothing in a sport she feels passionately about. She has coached for all of her adult life, from the chilly Steffler arena to the international level, and gave her oral defence to obtain Level V under the National Coaching Certification Program, the highest level possible. "Pardon," says Davidson when I ask her when she last had a vacation. Then she laughs. Like her predecessors as head coach, Shannon Miller and Danièle Sauvageau, she spends her vacations rinkside.

In preparation for the upcoming season, 500 players have already been evaluated at the 1999 Canada Winter Games, the national championships and four camps. Davidson must narrow that number down to 20 by the time the World Championships roll around in the spring. She is hosting a camp in Ontario in October, will take a pared-down roster of players to compete in the Three Nations Cup tournament in Quebec in November, has a tentative four-game series with the Americans in January, and then winds up with the World Championships in Mississauga in April. In between tournaments and camps she is on call as Canada's head coach while coaching in the U.S. For this, the CHA pays her $8,000 annually.

Is there another coach of Davidson's stature who would be paid what many coaches make in one month? Is there any other sport where a coach could come home with an Olympic silver medal only to find she no longer had a job? Is there another sport that would replace this coach with her assistant and then fire the new coach after she came home from the World Championships with a gold medal and a 14-0-1 season? Welcome to the CHA's version of fair play.

Shannon Miller, the first full-time coach of the Canadian women's hockey team, lasted all of one year in a paid position before the CHA decided it wanted to "give other coaches the opportunity to coach at that level," didn't renew her contract, and made the position part-time. Miller had volunteered thousands of hours over the years and spent two years coaching the team for a $6,000 annual honorarium from the CHA before she was finally given a 12-month contract to coach the Olympic team for the 1997-98 season. No one will reveal her salary as full-time coach during that year, but she says her $70,000 starting salary as coach at the University of Minnesota Duluth campus was more than the CHA paid her.

During the 1997-98 season, assistant coach Danièle Sauvageau took a six-month unpaid leave of absence from her job as a Montreal police officer, moved to Calgary where the pre-Olympic training camp was being held, paid her own room and board, and continued to pay for her place in Montreal. For this she was paid slightly more than $6,000–neither Sauvageau nor the CHA will reveal the exact figure. For years she has worked overtime as a cop and taken her vacations during hockey season so that she could coach.

During the 1998-99 season, she continued to work full-time for the Montreal force and averaged 25 to 30 hours of coaching per week. She was again paid a little over $6,000. "In September I worked every day of the entire month," Sauvageau said after she wasn't rehired:

> Some of those days were 16 hours long, but I gave up all my days off so I could coach the team during the hockey season. I imagined I would be the coach next year, but they told me they wanted to give a chance to Melody Davidson to develop at that [international] level. But this is at the cost of my development. I'm not bitter or mad, but I am disappointed. My career in women's hockey is not over, but when there is something else, I don't know.

This is as critical as Sauvageau will be of the CHA. Miller is equally guarded, saying only that working with the CHA was, on occasion, "like locking horns with raging bull." Neither of them has ruled out coaching the team for the 2002 Olympics, so they won't criticize the organization responsible for choosing the coach. That the CHA has turned the coaching position into a contest among three people who were once colleagues united in their fight for better hockey for women is an unspoken fact of life. The CHA is committed to women's hockey and to "giving top women coaches the chance to coach at the highest level," says Denis Hinault, the CHA's director of high-performance. "There are sports where the same person stays on as the national team coach for ten years, and when he or she retires, there is no one there to take the place." Hinault's argument has validity. The Canadian women's team is the top team in the world and, except for its second place at the Nagano Olympics, has won every world championship since 1960. Coaching this team is a great opportunity for women in a sport where opportunities for them are rare. It makes sense to develop as many high-level women coaches as possible.

However, this creates an unpredictable, volatile environment for women who have dedicated years to the sport, and pits the select few who have obtained a Level V coaching designation against one another in a contest called "Don't Upset the CHA." How can a coach speak up about job security and sexism if she thinks a more compliant colleague will replace her?

It is not coincidental in most critics' minds that Shannon Miller was let go, and at the same time was the target of a homophobic slur campaign. Before the 1998 Olympics veteran player Angela James had a meeting with Murray Costello, then the CHA's president, and Bob Nicholson, its vice-president of operations, to appeal Miller's decision to cut her from the team For days afterward, sports pages were filled with allegations and innuendoes that Miller was having an affair with an athlete. James repeatedly declared she made no such claims, and maintains the meeting was supposed to be in confidence. It was the CHA that leaked the details of the meeting to the press. Miller still bristles when the subject of her coaching integrity is brought up:

> I told Bob I would take a lie detector test to prove that I did not have an inappropriate relationship with a team member. He kept brushing it off, but it was someone in the CHA who floated those rumours to the press in the first place, and that person should have taken the test with me, because what they said was completely false.

If any woman on the team was contemplating coming out, this little media exercise taught her what might be in store. Players talk about HP and LP athletes—that's high-profile and low-profile. "The high-profile ones are usually the pretty ones," says one who does not want to be identified. "They get most of the contracts and sponsorship."

The CHA used the image of player Cassie Campbell, a former fashion model, to promote the 1997 World Championships in Kitchener, and again on their anti-harassment posters. She appeared on the cover of *Elm Street* and *Chatelaine* before the Olympics. As the public became more familiar with her image, Campbell received more sponsorships while the less conventionally heterosexually appealing women went without. If the Miller-James fiasco silenced lesbians, allowing commercial sponsors to call the shots makes them invisible in a sport where a significantly high percentage of players are gay.

No one acknowledges that the more "dykey"-looking women remain "low-profile," not because they're not great players, but because they're not straight. Decision-makers believe parents won't send their girls into a sport that has lesbians in it, and sponsors won't back gay women. The coach of a top women's team says he would lose their sponsor who pours hundreds of thousands of dollars into the sport if the women on his team came out. A national team member who would not be named says not receiving sponsorship money is a given for the lesbians who, she says, comprise 30 percent of the team: "It's just something you live with if you want to play."

The CHA also manipulated the Olympic team into signing contracts that worked against the financial best interests of the women. At a press conference in February 1997, the CHA said it would "pay the women what the men were receiving, $15,000 to $20,000," for attending the six-month pre-Olympic training camp in Calgary:

As federally carded athletes, the national team members currently receive between $300 and $810 a month depending on their carding status. Canadian Hockey will augment that with a stipend that will make their compensation comparable to the $15,000-$20,000.

What the CHA said it was going to do and what it did do aren't quite the same. First of all, the $15,000 to $20,000 figure the CHA cited isn't what the coach of the men's team at the time, Andy Murray, believed his players were making. In 1997 he said players were being paid between $12,000 and $25,000 for the eight-month season, "depending on their level of experience." The CHA thus overlooked a $5,000 difference at the upper end.

In addition, while CHA representatives mentioned that they were figuring in the monthly payments Sport Canada pays to the athletes as part of the CHA salary, they failed to note that they were also including the $5,000 each woman who played on the 1997 team that won the World Championships received from the Canadian Olympic Association. (Since the men are replaced by NHL players for the Olympics, they don't qualify for a COA grant.) Mark Lowry, executive director of sports programs at the COA, says hockey is the only sport he knows of that counted the COA's financial contribution as its own: "All funds are supposed to go to the athletes, unless they make a decision to enter into an agreement with their sports federation."

No one on the 1997 team imagined that she would have to give her $5,000 to the CHA to play on the Olympic team. It was like working two part-time jobs and being told by one employer that he was counting the salary from the other job as his. The CHA also failed to mention that the $15,000 to $20,000 it bragged about was what the women would have earned if they had been paid for eight months instead of the six for which they were actually paid.

CHA Vice President Nicholson managed to stall the signing of the team contract until the day before the Olympic training camp was to commence in September 1997. If they didn't sign, the women weren't allowed on the ice. Reluctantly, and in some instances angrily, they all signed, fearing reprisals if they protested. While the CHA continues to maintain that it paid the women the equivalent of $15,000, two veteran players say they received $237 a month from the CHA, or $1,422 for the six months. When their Sport Canada carding money and COA grant are added in, the total for the entire training camp was $11,282. Players were expected either to quit or to take a leave of absence from jobs or school. They had to pay their own room and board in Calgary, and were responsible for maintaining mortgages or rental payments in their home towns at the same time.

The CHA says that while it won't use the same system again, it wanted things "to be fair." Veteran players would have received more money than rookies at the training camp if the COA contributions hadn't been counted. Fair for whom? Only six athletes at the camp hadn't played in the 1997 world championships. There were two other options: either the rookie wages could simply have been topped up, or the women could have been treated like the men's team, with increments in salary "based on experience." But rookie or veteran, top male hockey players and coaches don't live on the poverty-level wages paid to Canada's national women's team and their coaches.

The CHA won't reveal the current salaries of the two full-time senior men's coaches, but in 1997 the positions paid $70,000 each. The fact that these coaches come home from the Olympics and World Championships empty-handed doesn't appear to jeopardize their jobs. Male coaches stay with the CHA until something bigger comes along in the NHL. There has been a lot of noise lately about cutting the men's team. Replaced by NHL players for big games, it is a remnant of past dreams when Canada thought it could win simply by fielding a hockey team filled with Canadians who had their skates on. A men's national team that is replaced by better players who still can't win is an expensive luxury, and a glance at the composition of the CHA may give us a hint as to why this team still exists.

If administrative assistants are excluded, of the 50 employees of the CHA, six are women. One coordinates domestic programs for female athletes, one coordinates CHA travel plans, two manage accounting offices, and two more manage merchandising and advertising. When a new position was created to manage the women's high-performance program, which includes all international competitions, it went to a man.

The CHA board of officers is an executive of eight men. The 35-member board of directors includes two women: athlete rep Thérèse Brisson, who doesn't have a vote, and Florence Rempel from the Centre for Excellence, Research and Development. Seven of the 15 members of the CHA Female Council are male, including its representative on the Board of Directors, Bryon Stephen.

The gender bias found at the CHA level is also found at the local level where, with a few exceptions, arena directors and their boards are male. Ice time is still the determining factor deciding whether girls and women can play. Normally ice time is allotted through the first-come-first-serve method. Guess who comes first at the hockey rink? Recently in Vancouver a girl's family settled out of court after alleging that municipally run community centres were giving an inordinate proportion of facilities and services to male hockey players. A study showed that of the 207 hours of available ice time, 200 went to males. The same can be said for female coaches and general managers—breaking into the male ranks is next to impossible.

Denis Hinault says the CHA's hands are tied. It can't determine ice time and who gets to coach. Except that it does. Anyone who want to coach a CHA-registered team must take an anti-harassment workshop. Why couldn't gender equity be added to this program? It is men, not women, who are responsible for the vast majority of assaults on children. The presence of trained women would substantially decrease the risk children face in hockey. The CHA could also withhold insurance coverage and registration to leagues that play in arenas that don't share the ice equitably.

The CHA points to women's hockey in the Olympics, a women's national team advisory committee, the creation of a full-time position at the CHA that looks after elite-level women's hockey, and the general increase in teams, tournaments and championships for women as signs of its commitment to the women's game. Hinault says the budget for the national women's team has grown from $100,000 five years ago to $600,000 to $700,000 in the 1998-99 season. (Melody

Davidson says she has no idea what the budget is for this year—this sort of information isn't shared with the women's coach.)

But the CHA hasn't even begun to recognize the discrimination, both overt and systemic, that women face, ensuring that female participation will remain marginal. The men who run Canadian hockey seem to imagine that the game will magically change without a change in the rules that favour male players, and think that after women have been excluded from the national dream for a hundred years, allowing them on ice and letting a few coach is a great, magnanimous, sensitive-guy step. For these men hockey, even women's hockey, is still a boys' game.

Source: Laura Robinson is a former national-level cyclist and cross-country ski racer. She is the author of two books about sport, *She Shoots, She Scores: Canadian Perspectives on Women and Sport* and *Crossing the Line: Violence and Sexual Assault in Canada's National Sport*. This article was originally published in *The Canadian Forum*, October 1999, pp.18-21. Reproduced with the permission of the author.

22.
She Got Game
Rachel Giese

Female athletes can't escape the classic doublebind

The Nike Air Swoopes basketball shoe, which hit the market in 1995, comes in black with a white stripe and a red logo for winter, white with a black stripe and red logo for spring. ("Black is a symbol of toughness to me," the shoe's namesake, former Texas Tech all-American guard Sheryl Swoopes, told *The New York Times*.) The sneaker is designed specially to support Swoopes's narrow size 10 1/2 feet and weak ankles and has a basketball encircled by an "S" at the top of the tongue. When the wearer goes up for a slam dunk, another big "S" on the sole is visible to the mortals left earthbound on the hardwood. Swoopes, there it is.

But what's really newsworthy about the Air Swoopes is that it's the first sneaker to be named in honour of a woman. And what a woman. Swoopes is one of the greatest female college basketball players of all time—she once scored 47 points in a National Collegiate Athletic Association final. These days, she plays forward for the Houston Comets of the year-old, professional Women's National Basketball Association (WNBA). She appeared on the cover of the première spring 1997 issue of *Sports Illustrated Women Sport*—a basketball in one hand, the other resting on her pregnant belly (the birth of her son last June forced the 27-year-old to sit out most of the WNBA's first season).

But it's really the shoe that counts. In the money-crazed, corporate world of sports, it's the endorsements that prove an athlete has really arrived. In fact, the future of female athletes depends as much on how well they can sell themselves as it does on how well they play. And aggressive, media savvy women like Swoopes—along with a handful of others, such as Mia Hamm, the humble star of the U.S. Olympic soccer team, and Hayley Wickenheiser, the golden girl of women's hockey and a member of Canada's 1998 Olympic team—are rising to the challenge.

Although it doesn't yet even approach male sports in terms of status, opportunity and cash, women's athletics are thriving–developing its own heroes, culture and fan base. The past five years have seen the development of two professional women's basketball leagues, tremendous viewership of women's events in the 1996 Atlanta and 1998 Nagano Olympic Games, and a subsequent surge of media interest. In fact, there are a half-dozen new magazines devoted to women's sports and fitness alone.

But underneath the new opportunities and hype, the playing field is far from even. Sports programs for women on an amateur and collegiate level remain vastly underfunded compared with men's. And outside of the Olympics, women's sports are barely covered by the media. Female athletes continue to struggle against homophobic and sexist notions that they are either too fluffy or too butch. In order to be viable, women's sports have to be as aggressive, exciting and, well, masculine as men's sports; but in order to be accepted, women have to prove that playing sports doesn't compromise their femininity. It's the woman's classic double-bind: act like a man, but don't ever forget that you're a girl.

Despite long-held fears that sports cause every affliction from shriveled ovaries to rampant lesbianism, there have been prominent female athletes since the turn of the century, renowned not only for their talents, but also for their ground-breaking endeavours. In the 1920s and 1930s, American Mildred "Babe" Didrickson was an international star, a three-time Olympic medal winner in track-and-field, an accomplished golfer and co-founder of the Ladies Professional Golf Association (LPGA). Another American, Althea Gibson, broke the racial barrier in women's tennis in the 1950s, winning multiple Wimbledon and U.S. Open championships–despite being barred from most whites-only clubs and tournaments.

But it was the 1970s feminist movement and its modern attitudes about women and their bodies that really boosted women's and girls' involvement in sports. In Canada, Abby Hoffman–who'd been infamously booted off a boys' hockey team in the late 1950s when it was discovered she was a girl–rose to prominence again in the 1960s and 1970s as a track athlete. The 1972 passage of Title IX in the U.S., a federal law legislating equality in funding, opportunities and resources for female athletic programs, gave girls a leg up in that country. And the legitimacy of female athletics was sealed by Billie Jean King when she wiped the sexist smirk off self-proclaimed "male chauvinist" Bobbie Riggs's face and solidly trounced him in their famous tennis match in 1973.

Throughout the 1980s, women's involvement in physical fitness and sports continued to rise. The aerobics craze popularized a new ideal for women's bodies–strong, toned and fit. Olympic heroines such as track star and heptathlete Jackie Joyner-Kersee and gymnast Mary Lou Retton became celebrities, garnering major endorsements. And more recently, rower Silken Laumann became a global hero for her grit and tenacity when she won a bronze medal in the 1992 Olympics only two months after she almost destroyed her leg in an accident.

But despite these achievements, women have had very few opportunities to enjoy the usual spoils of athletic success. Until recently, the Olympics and collegiate sports were the pinnacle of achievement. Outside the fields of golf, tennis and figure skating, few women were actually able to make a career out of sports. No one figured that women could be taken seriously as professional athletes–let alone draw an audience.

Atlanta and Nagano put those myths to rest. Some of the Games' greatest buzz centred on women's tremendous showing in rowing, soccer, softball and hockey. Not only did these athletes show they could play, they demonstrated that women's sports provide as much drama, personality and flair as men's.

The boys with the big bucks were paying attention. Both the WNBA and its poorer, less promoted rival, the American Basketball League (ABL), debuted within the last two years with much fanfare. And rumours are flying that professional soccer and hockey leagues are on the way. Corporations have also become interested in female athletes as a way to reach a growing market of active women. At its peril, Nike ignored women during the fitness boom of the 1980s–leaving Reebok to scoop up the lucrative market. Today, Nike has become a huge sponsor of *Sports Illustrated For Kids'* special "Girls and Sports Extra" supplement–which appears about six times a year–and has launched an ad campaign, titled, "If You Let Me Play," which points out that, among other benefits, involvement in sports bolsters girls' self esteem and makes them less likely to contract breast cancer. But this ain't just about boosting girl power. A media kit for "Girls and Sports Extra" pointed out that "supporting girls in sports yields tremendous marketing benefits for advertisers [because] the women's sports market is currently a $10-billion market and growing."

As spokespeople for their sport and its products, these new female jocks are undeniably appealing. They are an untapped source of entertainment for an almost insatiable sports audience, as well as a surefire draw for female viewers.

Physically, these Amazonian athletes are a far cry from the most familiar athletic women's bodies: the muscley, munchkin forms of prepubescent figure skaters such as Nagano gold medallist Tara Lipinsky. Canadian hockey dynamo Hayley Wickenheiser (5'9" and 170 pounds) and beach volleyball star Gabrielle Reece (6'3" and 172 pounds) provide a liberating challenge to the asparagus stalk female body ideal. Even pregnancy is proving to no longer be a hindrance to an athletic career. Last year, golfer Laura Baugh continued on the LPGA tour until she was almost nine months' pregnant. In 1995, U.S. ultramarathoner Sue Olsen gave birth only 30 hours after she finished a 24-hour-long race.

Which isn't to say that concerns about being too masculine don't still dog female athletes. The people who cover women's sports are obsessed with the issue. While personal profiles and sentimental human interest stories have always been a part of sports reporting, you aren't likely to see Michael Jordan on the cover of *Sports Illustrated* cradling his kids in his arms, discussing how fatherhood changed his game, the way coverage of Swoopes and her new motherhood eclipsed discussions of her athletic prowess. Nor do we—as Megan K. Williams and Elizabeth point out in their 1996 book, *On the Edge: Women Making Hockey History*—hear Eric Lindros being described primarily in terms of his looks. When Quebec goalie Manon Rhéaume became the first woman to play professional hockey on a men's team in 1992, journalists harped endlessly about her delicate prettiness. In a *Toronto Star* column, Rosic DiManno described Rhéaume as "a comely nubile with hazel eyes, a glowing complexion, and a decidedly feminine grace. There is no hint of testosterone in her nature."

Some of this new breed of female athlete even play into the glamour trap. At least three prominent athletes—Gabricile Reece, French track gold medalist Marie-José Pérec and the WNBA's Lisa Leslie—moonlight as fashion models. That these women can still be beautiful and strong eases all those penis-shrinking fears, the same way that the endless contextualizing of female athletes as daughters, girlfriends, mothers and wives demonstrates that they would never be so foolish or selfish as to put their career first. During the Nagano Olympics, the CBC ran a human interest profile on the Canadian women's curling team, focusing on their husbands and children. The whole gushing story seemed designed to allay concerns that these mannish-looking women were not "that way."

In fact, if you believe all of the stories, very few female jocks are that way. Lesbian athletes are deeply closeted—and have good reason to be. A 1994 U.S. survey found that 53 percent of women's college athletes, coaches and administrators were concerned that their involvement in sports would lead others to assume they were gay. And 49 percent of female athletes and 51 percent of female coaches said they felt homophobia was a hindrance to attracting and retaining women in athletic careers. Tennis great and out lesbian Martina Navratilova, with 50-odd Grand Slam titles, earned far less in endorsements than her less successful heterosexual rivals such as Steffi Graf.

In golf, one of the most female-friendly sports, CBS golf commentator Ben Wright stuck both feet and a couple of limbs in his mouth back in 1995 when he told a reporter that lesbians on the LPGA tour hurt corporate sponsorship and that women were hampered in their golf swings by their "boobs." Wright, who recently apologized for his remarks, was suspended by CBS in 1996.

When Canada's Shannon Miller made history as the only full-time, female head coach of a national women's hockey team at the Nagano Games, she was under fire right from the beginning for her coaching choices. But when her critics set their sights on her sexual orientation, the attacks became downright ugly—including a *Frank* magazine exposé titled "Bettys On Blades," which accused Miller of sleeping with her players and playing a game of lesbo-favourites with her rookies.

On the flip side of these negative attitudes about female athletes being too masculine, there's the expectation that women's "feminine" approach will clean up the professional sports industry. Since most women's sports are still played on an amateur level and the pro sports are still in their infancy, the thinking goes, they provide the perfect antidote to the increasingly bloated and bratty—but high-paying—world of men's sports. Women's athletics —with its numerous stories of defeating the odds, playing for no money and training in near obscurity—conjure up all kinds of romantic ideas of playing for the sheer love of the game. But increasingly, female athletes are less interested in purity and more interested in making a decent living. So the big question remains: can women's sports stand on its own and create its own culture and ethic, or will it be overwhelmed by the style and attitude of men's competition? In hockey, there are concerns that if the women's game does go pro, it'll have to go more macho—incorporating tougher play and body-checking. Female basketball players are in their own peculiar bind. The ABL has a reputation for better players, friendlier management and a longer season (October through February), but has a much lower profile, smaller game attendances and fewer endorsement possibilities. The WNBA has all of the loot and marketing savvy of the NBA behind it, but the players get a shorter season (June through August) to accommodate the men's games.

Female athletes are themselves divided on the direction of women's sports. Some see themselves as part of a greater movement that will affect opportunities for all women, others just want to play their sport, politics be damned. Many female hockey players were less than thrilled over the hype that ensued when Manon Rhéaume joined a professional, men's hockey team in 1992. There were concerns that Rhéaume's move diverted attention and support away from women's hockey and demonstrated that women's professional aspirations could be met by playing with men.

In an even less traditional sport, boxer Christy Martin has earned herself few allies for her grand-standing and me-first attitude. A member of Don King's stable who has fought on a Mike Tyson undercard and earned upwards of $75,000 for a fight, Martin is a thug of a fighter. She trains only with men, smears other female boxers with dyke-baiting comments, and plays up her femininity by fighting decked out in pink trunks, boots and tank top, her long hair loose.

When it comes to being tough and ambitious, some women are already on par with male athletes. In hockey, Hayley Wickenheiser has been known to throw down her gloves and start slugging. As for trash talk, the WNBA is as guilty of it as the men's league. And in terms of sheer ambition and money-making opportunities, women are jumping right in—shilling for everything from shoes to shampoo. WNBA hoopster Lisa Leslie has called the ubiquitous basketball player/rapper/movie star Shaquille O'Neal her "entrepreneurial role model."

But even if they wanted to, it's still unclear how much power women have to change sports institutions. How do you undo the "Dream Teams," the commercialism, the need to win and the money-grubbing agents that characterize men's sports? And, secondly, why should it be up to female athletes to do so?

In fact, it's both demeaning and infantilizing to assign women's sports the chore of cleaning up the industry. Why, just as women are coming into their own as athletes, should they be held back from earning even a fraction of the cash and a small part of the fame of their male counterparts? It's not that women's athletic competition should turn into a blood sport, or that it's wrong to value cleaner, fairer, more principled play. But rather, women shouldn't be relegated to the ladies' auxiliary of men's sports—making less money and getting less attention, but proud in the knowledge that their play is uncorrupt.

As female athletes take over the courts, the rinks and the playing fields, they should play because they're talented, ambitious and exciting to watch. They should be able to be as gracious as Mia Hamm or as cocky and attitudinous as tennis star Venus Williams. Women should play and be watched because they've worked hard and earned our attention.

Source: Rachel Giese is presently the Executive Director of the Toronto Lesbian and Gay Film and Video Festival and a regular columnist for *The Toronto Star*. This article was originally published in *This Magazine*, July/August 1998, pp.10-12. Reproduced with the permission of the author.

23.
Level the Playing Field

Laura Robinson

The NHL whines about a lack of government support; it should try playing with girls' rules

Something can be worked out. That's what Ontario Premier Mike Harris said last week when asked if property tax breaks could be given to Ontario-based National Hockey League teams that just can't seem to make a profit any more. Something can always be worked out when it comes to male professional team sport, but perhaps parents of girls who aspire to be athletes—professional, Olympic, or simply recreational—should be questioning why even more money should go to the already favoured sex.

Much as some people would like to think that sport should have its own rules outside of the law, it is part of Canadian culture and not exempt from human rights violations. It is, after all, the Canadian culture argument that is used by those who support the government subsidization of professional hockey in the first place.

The Canadian Human Rights Act states: It is a discriminatory practice in the provision of goods, services, facilities or accommodation customarily available to the general public (a) to deny, or to deny access to, any such good, service, facility or accommodation to any individual, or (b) to differentiate adversely in relation to any individual, on a prohibited ground of discrimination.

In British Columbia this year, David Morrison, the father of gymnast Katie Morrison, won a sex discrimination case after he took his municipality to the provincial Human Rights Commission. He showed under Section 8 of the B.C. Code, which is similar to the Canadian section stated above, that girls were clearly not given equal access to sport and recreation services and facilities.

His daughter's gymnastics club, which was non-profit and privately owned, had requested financial assistance on several occasions from the City of Coquitlam. They argued that other non-profit sport groups had received municipal grants, but despite their pleas, the city chose not to assist the club. It was at this point, on Feb. 14, 1994,

when Katie was 9, that Mr. Morrison lodged his sex-discrimination complaint.

Initial investigations by the HRC showed grounds for the issue to move forward. The complainants had argued that a disproportionate amount of public funds subsidized male-only sport, and that within this group, the sport of hockey dominated. The City argued back that if all recreation services and programs were factored in, funding would be proportional. However, the HRC said the case was about similar activities available in sport and physical activity programs—not arts and crafts. Within these parameters, the funding was unfair.

"The issue for us is equity," says Deputy Chief Commissioner, Harinder Mahil, who eventually became a co-complainant with Mr. Morrison. "It has been recognized by all levels of government that there is inequity. There [have] to be systemic changes in order to provide opportunities for females in sport."

But, says Commissioner Mahil, even though governments are aware of this human rights violation, they generally don't do anything about it. "They should not keep providing services and facilities to male-only sport. Female sport has to be encouraged. There are many barriers for girls and women in sport."

Governments should consider passing legislation similar to a law in the United States (Title IX) that makes it illegal for institutions that receive public funds to discriminate. Title IX has been in existence since 1972 and is the single biggest reason for the surge in women's sports in the U.S.

Parents, aunts, uncles, grandparents, and those of us who believe the world should hold as many dreams and promises for girls as it does for boys, might think about the message girls receive when public funds are seamlessly piled on top of private ones so male-only hockey can flourish. They should ask themselves how the self-worth of girls is affected when they live in communities that heavily favour boys and boys' teams.

And for those who don't care about girls, but do care about bottom lines, the settlement agreed upon in the Morrison case might act as a wake-up call.

On March 24, 1999, when Katie was 14, the City of Coquitlam finally agreed to a five-part Gender Equity Program. The Gender Equity Fund, which begins at $50,000 per year for a minimum of five years, will be used to kick-start the increases in female sport and recreation programs. If a group would like to rent or lease a City facility, they must have a Gender Equity Policy.

Coquitlam may be the only municipality in Canada that will monitor the subsidization of sport and physical activity by gender. In a preliminary monitoring process of one arena, it was found that of the 207 hours of available ice time, 200 of them went to males. Over the next five years this type of discrepancy is to be decreased by 50 percent, with a proportional increase in female participation rates.

They have also created a Gender Equity Committee that would keep City Council informed on the program and make implementation recommendations, and a Gender Equity Coordinator who will do the groundwork for the Committee.

The Chief Commissioner of the B.C. Human Rights Commission wrote, he was "hopeful that the establishment and implementation of this Program will not only effect both attitudinal and systemic changes but will also serve as a model for other municipal governments to follow in the future."

Such sentiments seem to be much more in line with the kinds of values with which we want children to grow up.

Let's put aside the gratuitous and sanctioned violence in NHL hockey and the values it instills for a second. Do we want kids to learn that one privileged group gets to play while the less fortunate group can only watch, because right now that's how hockey—with the exception of a very few programs—is organized, whether it is a local house-league game or in professional leagues. It is ridiculous that girls are held hostage while their parents must fight for years just so their daughters have the right to play.

While owners, public commentators, and journalists whine about a vanishing national dream, let's remember that more than half the population has not had the opportunity to live their athletic dreams to their fullest. Until that happens, I hope there are plenty of David Morrisons out there who care more about human rights than they do about an imagined and romanticized past.

Source: Laura Robinson is a former national-level cyclist and cross-country ski racer. She is the author of two books about sport, *She Shoots, She Scores: Canadian Perspectives on Women and Sport* and *Crossing the Line: Violence and Sexual Assault in Canada's National Sport*. This article was originally published in *The Globe and Mail*, November 1, 1999, A17. Reproduced with the permission of the author.

Part 7
Sexual Orientation

The various derogatory words referring to gays and lesbians have been common in sport for some time. Terms that question their gender or sexual orientation have been used by coaches (and sometimes other athletes) to motivate male athletes, or to berate them for what is perceived to be a less than adequate performance in terms of skill, risk taking, or effort. Terms that question gender or sexual orientation have been used by males (perhaps males who feel insecure or threatened) to insult talented female athletes, especially those in sports not traditionally associated with "femininity."

However, the question of whether athletes were actually gay or lesbian rarely came up in sport before the 1990s. Like the ostrich burying it's head in the sand, "sport" did not want to know. While there is no reason to expect that the proportions of homosexuals and heterosexuals in sport will be any different from the proportions in the larger society, there has been an assumption at work in sport that all athletes are heterosexual. In fact, this assumption has been so powerful—and the environment it has created has been so clearly hostile to gay and lesbian athletes—that it has been referred to as "compulsory heterosexuality." The articles in this section address the difficulties of being a gay or lesbian athlete, the need to hide one's true identity, and the costs (and sometimes rewards) associated with "coming out of the closet."

Brian Pronger raises some intriguing questions about the establishment of gender differences in sport through the establishment of all-male and all-female environments, and about the assumption of heterosexuality in those environments. Using the example of a men's football game, he reveals the homoeroticism of men's sport and demonstrates the complexity of the relationships between sport and sexuality. Caroline Fusco reports the results of a small research project examining the experiences of lesbian athletes in team sports at the university or elite level in Canada. These experiences describe the costs and fears of declaring one's sexual identity, particularly in the hostile environment created by "compulsory heterosexuality," but also note the empowerment that results from being able to "be yourself."

Additional Sources

Videos:

- *Out for a Change; Addressing Homophobia in Women's Sports* (from A Woman's Place Productions, San Francisco), a film involving Pat Griffin's programme against homophobia in sport.
- Gay Boxer, *Jocks in Paradox, and Lesbian Athletes*, TSN's "Name of the Game" three-part series on gay athletes.

Print Resources:

- Rubenstein, L. (1996). CBS drops controversial Wright as golf announcer. *The Globe and Mail,* 10 January, p.C5. [Report on Ben Wright's firing from LPGA commentary after claiming that lesbians were hurting women's golf, and that women could not swing the club properly because of their breasts.]
- Smith, G. (1994). Review of Brian Pronger's, The Arena of Masculinity. *Labour/ Le Travail,* 34, pp.372-374. [Informative review of the only major study of gays in sport.]

24.

The Unspoken Sexuality of Sport

Brian Pronger

Men seek out men and women, women, in sport

The assumptions people make are interesting. Italian soccer coach Azeglio Vicini, thinking that sexual abstinence would bring athletic victory at the recent World Cup, supposed that if the men on his team were separated from women, sexual activity would be circumvented. With the same logic it was thought that celibacy was somehow guaranteed by the fact that the 1964 Japanese women's volleyball team went a whole year without intimate contact with men. Surely by 1990 it should be obvious to all but the most naive that sexuality is not confined to relations between men and women.

Lesbianism in all-women environments, especially sports, is a "secret" known by many women. Perhaps the advantage the Japanese women had over other teams, which led them to an Olympic gold, was not that they abstained from sex, but that by spending more than a year without the company of men, some were free to be themselves, free to develop emotional and sexual ties with other women without the interference of men.

There's an assumption that if there are no members of the other sex present, sex doesn't happen. But it doesn't follow that just because the Italian men's soccer team was segregated from women they didn't engage in sex. They did, after all, have each other, or at least themselves. It's well known that men in exclusively male environments, especially highly charged ones, will find sexual satisfaction by themselves or by engaging homosexually with others; witness prisons and the military. Why should sport be any different?

Perhaps not as well known, or at least as easily admitted, is that male homoeroticism is not confined to the bedrooms of gay men; it is also an important dimension of men's sports and competitions, an often deeply hidden subtext of masculine life, an inevitable corollary to the fact that men like playing sports with men.

Sport does not exist in a social vacuum; it plays an important role in creating and reflecting the beliefs, values and power struggles of our society. One of the most important of those struggles is sexism, the polarization of men and women. Women are excluded from most men's sports. Generally speaking, men don't want women on their hockey teams, in their rugby scrums, on their wrestling mats, in their locker rooms. And so they have cultivated sporting styles, rules and regulations that make it virtually impossible for women to join them.

Rather than taking advantage of the many similarities of male and female physical capacities, sports have developed to emphasize the differences, reproducing in that athletic sphere the social discourse of gender difference.

That emphasis on the difference on men and women has isolated them—we even speak of them as "opposite sexes." This is the opposition between social superiors and their subordinates, an opposition that makes it difficult for most men to see women as their fellows.

Because women are made subordinate in sexist culture, men seek social and erotic satisfaction in their "equals," that is, one another. One of the ways they do so is in sports. Now it might seem that this is not erotic satisfaction in the usual sense; after all it doesn't usually, or at least publicly, proceed to genital expression. But if you consider the wide range of experiences one finds erotic, it's clear that for most of us eroticism is not a strictly genital phenomenon.

Consider this popular, indeed legendary, scene. A group of men get together in what are usually the rather close quarters of a locker room and take off their clothes. In various states of undress, they stand around talking to each other, preparing themselves for what is to follow.

Ritual garments are donned. A coalition of pads and suspenders come together to dramatize and accentuate the much revered masculine form. The men work themselves into a psychic frenzy of masculine unity and run out on the playing field to get the other team.

One man bends over, while another from behind puts his hands between the inclined man's legs, grasps a ball that's shaped like a large testicle and attempts to throw it to another man.

Everybody wants the ball. Men along the line of scrimmage press themselves against each other enthusiastically. Then, as a man on the field runs with the ball, many others run after him, trying to grab him. The play climaxes with men lying on top of each other, the testicle-shaped ball forming the nucleus of this masculine clutch. When the time is tip, the boys go back to the locker room, take their clothes off again and shower together.

The homoerotic ecstasy of man-to-man struggle, disguised by the orthodox masculinity of sport, is a deep secret whispered incomprehensibly in the grunts, groans and moans of athletes straining their bodies against each other. For some men that is frightening; for others it's exciting, and for still others it's both.

I am not saying that men who like sports are necessarily gay, or that their deepest *personal* sense of themselves is essentially homosexual. The homoeroticism of sport is a *structural* manifestation of our sexist culture, a culture that has made men and women unequal, thereby making truly egalitarian relations between them virtually impossible. And men seek out men and women, women. One of the ways they do that is in sport.

In our culture, the presence of homosexuality in notable families, the military or clergy has traditionally been denied by a conspiracy of silence: "Don't say anything about it and no one will think it exists." So too in the homophilic/phobic culture of sport, we see every day in newspapers and on television men playing sports with each other exclusively, even choosing to segregate themselves from women, and not a word is said. Do people really just assume that sport is a completely heterosexual world? Or are they just very good at denying, by their silence, what they deeply and secretly already know?

Source: Brian Pronger is the author of *The Arena of Masculinity: Sport, Homosexuality and the Meaning of Sex* and Assistant Professor in the Faculty of Physical Education and Health at the University of Toronto. This article was originally published in *The Globe and Mail*, Monday, July 30, 1990. Reproduced with the permission of the author.

25.
Lesbians and Locker Rooms
Caroline Fusco

Challenging lesbophobia

There isn't a political force to say "it's okay to be a lesbian and be a woman in sport." And because that wasn't there people were hiding. And when you see people hiding, they're afraid. And you know, it's because it's so damn homophobic. (Research Participant)

Lesbians in sport do not escape the discrimination which reflects the systemic intolerance of sexual diversity in our heterosexist culture. The institution of sport is a microcosm of society, "a dynamic social space where dominant ideologies are perpetuated" (Messner, 198) and contributes to the perpetuation of values that sustain "heteronormativity" (Hennessy). Sports associations and governing bodies rarely address or acknowledge the existence of lesbian athletes. Indeed there seems to be an unwritten yet understood agreement among associations, governing bodies, and athletes to avoid direct discussion on lesbian issues (Peper).

Bennett labelled this avoidance of addressing lesbianism in women's sport "a silence so loud it screams" (quoted in Nelson, 139). Although lesbians have not overtly been denied access to participation in sports or active living, the heterosexual image of women in sports persists and is encouraged. The lesbian label is still used to intimidate lesbians and undermine attempts by all women to challenge constructed gender relations in sport. Griffin states:

> Women's athletics is, in fact, held hostage to fear of the "L-word." As long as women's athletics continues to deny that there are lesbians in sport [...] we will never control our sporting lives and will be forced to waste energy defending a counterfeit heterosexual-only image that we all know is a lie (Quoted in Nelson, 142).

The purpose of my research was to give a small sample of Canadian lesbian athletes the opportunity to talk about their experiences in sport, and how the challenge to reject and resist "compulsory heterosexuality" (Rich) affects their lives. I specifically addressed the experiences of elite lesbian athletes and explored how lesbian athletes construct and describe their realities in sport.

All the athletes in the research identified themselves as lesbian. Only two of the participants acknowledged that they were totally "out" in their sports and other environments; yet all had disclosed their lesbian sexuality at some point in their lives as athletes, students, teachers, and workers to at least one other team member, colleague, family member or friend. The study was limited to lesbian athletes who participated in team sports at an inter-varsity or elite level of competition and who participated on teams that are *not* all lesbian. I conducted in-depth interviews with eight lesbian athletes in the following team sports: basketball, field hockey, ice hockey, lacrosse, and water-polo. Their ages ranged from 18 to 35 years old. All of the participants were white.

All the participants spoke about the centrality of sport in their lives:

> My athletic career started when I was seven. I was a jock, I was completely immersed in sport, lived and breathed sport. Thinking about it in some ways, I knew nothing else. I was good at it. I liked it, I loved the camaraderie, the team. I loved being physically active and being able to push my body farther, that's still something I enjoy doing...

Sports represented the "biggest and best" part of the participants' lives and none of them wanted to "jeopardize [their] sport career in any way." This affected their lives as lesbians in their sports and provided a context for their experiences.

> You would think a lot of teams would be a kind of haven. That there would be a lot more people accepting of that kind of thing. But, you know, it could have been way better for us, it really could've. It could've been a much more positive experience for us. You would think that it would have been. I know people must look at it and say, "Oh it's ideal, you're on a sports team. Isn't that what you guys like?" But it just wasn't as positive as it could've been. And I say that at the same time as saying it was one of the best times that I ever had. It was wonderful. But it could have been more positive...

The athletes reported that lesbianism rarely received positive acknowledgment in their sporting environments. From an early age many knew that talking about "homosexuality" was "taboo" and persistent questions about "boyfriends" conveyed the expectation of heterosexuality.

> The straightness of [my university], it was always there. Always in your face, especially on the team. Everyone talked about boyfriends. And laughed and joked, and teased when a new fellow appeared at the game. No one ever did that when a woman came to watch me. Even though they knew exactly what she was there for...

One woman recalled how heterosexuality was valorized by her team's motto: "If you're straight, you can skate..." Another remembered being told that lesbianism was "abnormal and unnatural." Many had overheard conversations where lesbianism was referred to as "sick" and "such a disgusting thing." Often the "topic of the day" was "who was and who wasn't [lesbian]" which generally precipitated a "rolling of eyes" and "groans of disgust." One athlete talked about her best friend's reaction to her disclosure:

> It was a really hard time for me and I thought she would be there for me. And I said, "You know, I'm lesbian." And she said, "What did you say?" I said, "I'm gay, I'm lesbian." And she said "Oh! I'm shocked! I'm horrified! Oh my god, I can't believe it!" Her head was in her hands and she just kind of got up and walked away. She said, "Well, you can't justify yourself, you can't explain this, can you? It's all mental..."

Lesbophobia was manifested when people were "not as comfortable with lesbians as they were with heterosexuals." Lesbian athletes were often physically avoided when in close quarters, hotels, or locker rooms with other team members. One athlete remembered that "people were really reluctant to be in the same room alone with [her]" when they heard that she was a lesbian. She labelled this "the locker room effect." Disassociation from lesbians was exhibited by both heterosexual and lesbian individuals. In fact, lesbian teammates often used other lesbians as "scapegoats" to deflect suspicion from themselves:

> There were a core of women who were very protective of their own identity, sexual identity, to a point where they would blurt out on many occasions, "Gosh, she looks so gay! Look at the hair cut, look at the size of her, look at the way she walks"...

In addition, lesbian issues were verbally avoided. Discomfort with lesbianism was often reflected when "something was not said" or in an "unspoken tension." There was rarely "openness" or "massive discussions" about lesbians. One athlete figured that "*enough* of [the team] knew [she was lesbian] just because of conversations they *didn't* have!" and spreading rumours about "who was and who wasn't lesbian" was "rife." Rumours were spread maliciously without any recognition of the consequences for the "suspects":

> I was told right off the bat, as soon as I made the provincial team—I think it's something that all the new little people get told. Like "so and so's a dyke, so and so's a dyke. And so is she, and so is she. And she's living with her." I got all this information and some of it was lies. Total gossip...

This kind of speculation may have persisted because lesbians were physically and behaviourally stereotyped. "[The] lesbian stereotype, as perceived by straight people ... [is someone with] short hair, doc's [shoes], softball player, aggressive, not attractive to men, no make-up..." Many derogatory comments were directed at "what lesbians do!" The perception was that lesbians were sexual maniacs, waiting to pounce on unsuspecting heterosexuals at every moment. "People used to make comments about our coach. Their first response was 'I think you'd better watch your step around this coach...'" Many athletes stated that "suspected" lesbians were ostracized, their social lives rarely validated, and treated differently from heterosexuals.

Incidences of verbal bashing, whisper campaigns, homophobic jokes, slurs, and derogatory comments were identified. Many of these athletes had overheard "condescending comments" about lesbians which they described as "anti-gay" and "destructive."

> I had a jean jacket on over top of a white T-shirt and my track pants. And I think I was wearing a baseball cap. And I came into [my coach's] vicinity. And she said, "Oh, you look like those [lesbians] over there. Take your jacket and your hat off, and spruce yourself up a bit." The assistant was very good and she said to the coach, "I hardly think that's appropriate to say something like that." And the coach said, "Well they look like hell, and I don't want that type of woman reflected on our team"...

Athletes were cognizant that lesbianism should not be "flaunted" or "talked about." The often explicit animosity resulted in, as one participant described, a "pretty poisonous environment" for lesbians in sport.

> It was the time when there was that big earthquake in San Francisco. We were in the changing rooms. It was after practice. And someone was saying, "Oh yeah! Did you hear about the earthquake? It cut out the base-

ball game." And [another player] turned to whoever was talking and said, "Do you know what I really wish? I really wish there was a whole bunch of fags underneath that bridge. And it came crashing down and killed them all..."

One strategy for coping was to mask their lesbian identities. Athletes talked about physically withdrawing from hostile environments, remaining silent and secretive about their lesbian lives, passing as heterosexuals, and normalizing their lesbian identities. However, many also chose to ignore the risks involved in being stereotyped or identified as lesbian, deliberately challenging "heteronormativity" and notions of femininity. For these athletes in particular challenging stereotypes was an important way to assert their identities as strong and independent sportswomen. Others chose to confront discriminatory attitudes towards minority groups, attempting to promote knowledge of diversity. One athlete was viewed as the "language police" on her team:

> I was strongly opinionated when it came to things that were sexist, racist or homophobic. And that's something that, although I wasn't out, I would not put up with. I would not listen to someone say the "blonde jokes." If someone said "Hey, you, fag!" I would call people on that. And even though I wasn't out, I would call people on language. And I would use the excuse—not the excuse—I'd use the reasoning "why say this, when there are so many other words to describe how you are feeling..."

Some of the athletes disclosed their lesbian sexuality. The desire to let others know "what was going on in their lives" was inexorably tied to their confidence in themselves and their sexuality.

> I've developed an "in-your-face" attitude that I've never had before and things don't affect me the way they used to. I think the most important thing that I've learned to develop is my self-assurance and confidence. And the knowledge that I'm just as good as everybody else. I think that is so important. You want to learn that...

Identifying with a lesbian community is an essential part of their coping mechanisms.

> I've surrounded myself with a lot of gay and lesbian friends. So it's really easy to be out, and hang out, and go to all sorts of gay establishments, restaurants and bookstores. You can become kind of exclusive in who you hang out with...

All the athletes, at some point in their lives, socialized at lesbian bars, participated in all-lesbian/gay events, or joined teams where the majority of the players were lesbians. Three athletes had competed at the Gay Games in 1990, and 1994. Although these events do not gain extensive exposure outside the lesbian and gay community it was often difficult for them to conceal what they were doing because, as one woman said, in elite sport "everybody knows every intimate detail of what you're doing and if they're not asking, they're too afraid to ask." "Finding a niche" in a lesbian community allowed them to confirm and celebrate their lesbian identities.

> Now that I'm in the community more, and I feel more comfortable about it [being lesbian], I realize, "Yeah! That this is what I am and this is what I like. And I don't think I'm going to change..."

If they played on all-lesbian teams, "it was such a release," and "a wonderful relief." They could talk openly about their lives and "wave at [their] honey without having to worry about what people think."

> It was wonderful, the first time I was ever exposed to a community of lesbians when I realized there were other gay women out there. It was incredible. It was like a huge load had been lifted off my shoulders because now I could enjoy the sport and love it, and play to my hearts content. And also know that I didn't have to cover everything anymore...

Reversing the discrimination helped to offset some of the consequences of lesbophobia.

> It would help if [my coach and teammates] were more tolerating of the way I was. But you know, I don't really care anymore. They are going to have to tolerate me because I am here. And, you know, I'm putting up with them, so they'll have to put up with me...

> Oh, people just have the most hilarious perceptions. It's so funny. And they say, "Oh, we accept you." And that's wonderful. But, well, too bad, "I don't accept you..."

Sport is not free from heterosexism and homophobia. Lesbians have been silenced and discredited on their teams while heterosexuality has been vehemently upheld as the "norm." As a decade of studies have demonstrated there is a price, in terms of emotional energy and self-esteem, for having to be silent about one's lesbian sexuality (Woods and Harbeck). However, despite the systemic harassment that these athletes experienced their love of sport was evident. They all succeeded in their sports, some achieving honours at the highest level possible. There is room,

therefore, for lesbian athletes to resist patriarchal and heterosexual gender relations in sport and to use sport as a means of empowerment. These lesbian athletes have refused to be victimized in sport.

The lesbian athletes' experiences articulated here are subjective, not representative or generic. This research acknowledges that we are all differently positioned and privileged, therefore, conclusions cannot be generalized. However, the research recognizes that these lesbian athletes' experiences constitute legitimate knowledge and provide a vital commentary on our understanding of the sports world as a heterosexist institution in which lesbianism challenges the status quo of the inter-relations between sport and sexuality. This research is committed to a vision of a more equitable and affirming sports world and recognizes that all individuals are entitled to the privileges which are controlled by a dominant white, heterosexual society. Lesbian athletes and other marginalized peoples should not be denied either access to active living or the celebration of their empowerment through sport.

References

- Hennessy, R. "Queer Theory: A Review of the *differences* Special Issue and Wittig's The Straight Mind." *Signs Journal of Women and Culture in Society* 18 (1993): 964-973.
- Messner, M.A. "Sports and Male Domination: The Female Athlete as Contested Ideological Terrain." *Sociology of Sport Journal* 5 (1988): 197-211.
- Nelson, M.B. "A Silence so Loud it Screams." *Are We Winning Yet? How Women are Changing Sports and Sports are Changing Women.* M.B. Nelson, ed. New York: Random House, 1991.
- Peper, K. "Female Athlete = Lesbian: A Myth Constructed from Gender Role Expectations and Lesbiphobia." *Queer Words, Queer Images: Communication and the Construction of Homosexuality.* R.J. Ringer, ed. New York: New York University Press, 1994.
- Rich, A. "Compulsory Heterosexuality and Lesbian Existence." *Blood, Bread and Poetry. Selected Prose 1979-1985.* A. Rich, ed. New York: W.W. Norton & Co, 1986.
- Woods, S.E., and K.M. Harbeck. "Living in Two Worlds: The Identity Strategies Used by Lesbian Physical Educators." *Coming Out of the Classroom Closet. Gay and Lesbian Students, Teachers and Curricula.* K. Harbeck, ed. New York: Harrington Park Press, 1992.

Source: Caroline Fusco was an international field hockey player for Ireland. She is currently studying for her Ph.D. in the Faculty of Physical Education and Health at the University of Toronto. From "Lesbians and Locker Rooms: Challenging Lesbophobia" by C. Fusco, 1995, *Canadian Woman Studies*, 15(4), pp.67-70. © 1995 by Inanna Publications and Education Inc. Reprinted with the permission of the author.

Part 8
Youth

For most young people, involvement in sport is a generally positive experience. It is social, it is fun, it can result in self-confidence derived from physical accomplishment, and it may help to develop other life and social skills as well as physical health. But this should not detract us from exploring the dark side of youth sport and, by exposing it to the light, helping to resolve some of the problems.

The dark side is not an automatic consequence of children's sport. Rather it is primarily a result of adult involvement in children's sport. Since the late 1940s, adults in North America have been organizing community sport programs for children and, while bringing safety and supervision for children, they have also far too often brought their adult ambitions and sense of cut-throat competition into those programs. The development of house-leagues in Canada went a long way toward resolving some of the concerns for at least the less athletically gifted children. However, at the elite levels, especially since lucrative professional careers in sport have been available (and even more so since the symbolic and economic values of Olympic medals have become so significant), the situation has deteriorated. This has been magnified since the 1970s by attempts to imitate the former Soviet and East German systems of early talent identification and specialization. More recently, these problems have begun to appear in school sport programs in Canada—programs that were in the past generally more oriented to education than outcome.

In the first reading, Jay Teitel argues that our emphasis on and concerns about children's sports have had an unintended consequence—now adults (particularly baby boomers) play and children do not. He goes on to state that "abducting play is only the first part of our crime; holding play hostage, and then returning it to kids in an adulterated form, is the second part."

In my own article, I look at the serious costs of children's involvement in the high-performance sport system in a study based on interviews with retired high-performance athletes. I suggest that the threat of a dramatic solution (protection of young high-performance athletes under the child labour laws) will lead to policies of more concern and care for the development of the whole child. In the following piece, Robert Butcher calls for a return to "the spirit of sport" in youth sports. And, finally, an article by myself and Robert Sparks examines the most recent problem to have caused widespread concern in youth sport—child sexual abuse. The article points to the growing body of evidence for its existence in sport, suggests reasons why it might be both more prevalent and less reported than we might imagine, and proposes some solutions based in changing the culture of youth sport.

Additional Sources

Videos:

- *Kids 'n' Sports*, a 1990 NBC News Special, is slightly dated now, but still deals with some useful themes.

- *The Good, the Bad, and the Ugly*, TSN's "For the Love of the Game" series, deals with problems in youth hockey.

Print Resources:

- Donnelly, P. (1993). Problems associated with youth involvement in high performance sport. In B. Cahill & A. Pearl (eds.), *Intensive Participation in Children's Sports*, Champaign, IL: Human Kinetics, pp.95-126. [Full report of the research presented in the second reading.]

- Nock, W. and Yaeger, D. (1999). Every parent's nightmare. *Sports Illustrated*, 13 September, pp.40-53. [Exposes child sexual abuse by coaches in U.S. sport.]

- Swift, E.M. (1994). Give young athletes a fair shake. *Sports Illustrated*, 2 May, p.76. [Article suggests that eliminating the post-game handshakes in youth sports, because they occasionally lead to trouble, cops out on the lessons that children are supposed to be learning from sport.]

26.

The Kidnapping of Play

Jay Teitel

Adults now play and kids don't. What went wrong?

When I was eleven my father played handball, which at the time was a game fathers played. He played at the Y, with a group of guys his age, forty and older, who were all bald—or so it seemed to me. Baldness was apparently a prerequisite to playing handball in 1960, along with the handball shape, squat and earth-hugging and powerful. If you were a little less bald, a little less stocky, you played squash or possibly racquetball, more exotic versions of handball, but equally mature. They were all wall games, shot with a satisfying nihilism. You hit the ball, and it came right back to where you hit it from. Handball was sport as eternal recurrence, and my father played it recurringly. The only other sport he played—usually on Saturdays when the Y (a Jewish one) was closed—was golf.

He did not, that is, play hockey, or baseball, or soccer, or football, or basketball. He played with us, sure, tossing a ball on the street or on Visitors' Day at camp (the same way he played catch with me in the backyard or the park, with a nicely classic hitch to his throw, a succession of cricky windups that became more pronounced as he grew older); but he would no more have considered calling up a group of his friends for a pickup hockey game than he would have thought to hold a pee-sword-fight-competition with them in someone's basement bathroom. Team games were for kids, as were most games. Fathers flooded backyards to make skating rinks, but rarely skated on them themselves (or if they did, like Wayne Gretzky's dad, Walter, it was to teach their kids). Adult games were a restricted few: handball, golf, maybe tennis or skiing if you were WASP, or had grown up around some. To be an adult in 1960 was generally to abjure play as an art form that was no longer befitting your dignity, the way you abjured dungarees for houndstooth slacks and Banlon shirts. My old man, dapper as he was (cool as he would turn out to be), did this as a matter of course. As a schoolboy he'd been a small, quick baseball player, so canny at laying down a bunt that he was actually called "Bunty." But that was in the past. Play—real play, serious play—was the province of children.

Today, half a decade older than my father was in his handball heyday, I play pickup hockey twice a week. I would be playing pickup basketball as well, with some squash, touch football, and slow-pitch softball thrown in if I did not have encroaching arthritis in one hip; I played *real* baseball, with a hardball, well into my thirties. And I'm not alone. All around me adults, younger and older, graced by varying degrees of fitness or decrepitude, are playing the games children alone used to play. This would be strange enough, but what's stranger still is the corollary. As play in our waning century has become more the province of adults, it's become increasingly terra *incognita* to kids. This may be the ultimate inverted baby-boom insult to the natural order, one that's twice as insidious as a terminal addiction to blue jeans: today we play, and our kids do not. We have stolen play from them.

In his quirky but illuminating classic, *Homo Ludens (Man at Play)*, the Dutch historian Johan Huizinga lists as one of the main characteristics of play that it is "distinct from 'ordinary' life as to locality and duration." Play, like crime, requires both opportunity and motive.

Consider opportunity first. The case of adult hockey in this country alone is a good place to start. In the early 1970s, men's hockey was largely a pickup sport, a pastime for never-say-die jocks who were willing to play at ungodly hours of the morning. The whole recreational mood was captured by a cheesy Molson's ad that quickly became a Canadian classic: "For years Eddie and the guys have been getting in a little hockey…." Back then, "industrial-league" hockey really was industrial league—teams sponsored by companies for their employees—and adult hockey comprised only a small percentage of the ice-rental time across the country. By the early eighties, though, according to some estimates, men's hockey accounted for over 30 percent of rental time in privately owned arenas. Today, many of the biggest multiplexes, like the six-rink Beatrice Ice Gardens in Toronto, are built primarily for adult hockey, both men's and women's, servicing pickup and shinny hockey, as well as literally hundreds of adult leagues, many of which are run as profit-making, private businesses. According to Larry Marson, the general manager of the Ice Gardens, the split in ice-time rental at his facility, adult to child, is 80 percent to 20.

And the same thing is happening in almost any other sport you can name. At Soccer City in west Toronto, an indoor soccer facility, adults, a large percentage in their forties and fifties, have cornered the majority of rental time. "If we had the space and the time," says Phil Seward, owner of Soccer City, "the kids would get more opportunity. As it is, we have adults playing not just weeknights but weekdays too." Soccer City runs a ball-hockey league as well during the summer that, up to this year, has been for adults only. In 1995, the city of Toronto had to legislate a 70 to 30 percent split of its recreational facilities–children to adult–to make sure that kids would have somewhere to play. Slow-pitch softball, fifteen years ago a purely recreational, almost bucolic game, now has an estimated ten million North American adults playing the sport. (The game even has its own resident Mark McGwire, the legendary Mike Macenko, of Steele's Silver Bullets in Brook Park, Ohio, who in 1987 hit 844 home runs.) And these team-sport evolutions are all in addition to the parallel boom in individual-sport patronage among grown-ups: fringe activities that include paintball, laser tag, and Frisbee golf, as well as adult video arcades and bars, and the more mainstream items–squash, cycling, in-line skating–that fall under the rubric "fitness." (In the fifties and sixties, the only adults who were into fitness were Swedes. Today, we're all Swedes.)

In general, the "games" we play as adults seem indistinguishable from the games children play. But spiritually, there's a world of difference. Abducting play is only the first part of our crime; holding play hostage, and then returning it to its owners in adulterated form is part two. Not only do kids play less these days than they used to; they also play differently.

Five minutes from where I live, there's a park. It's a typical neighbourhood park, typical at least for the suburbs, a big, flat square of grass, bounded by a street along one side, and the backyards of houses along the other three. A jungle-gym apparatus sits in one corner, beside a swing set, just across the pathway from a baseball diamond with a gravel infield. A little gazebo-roofed shelter with a picnic table underneath it provides the only shade.

One Saturday morning not long ago I sat in the park and watched the people coming into it. It was a late fall day, but unseasonably warm, the kind of day when you'd expect to see people flocking pale and squinty-eyed to parks, kids suddenly proliferating outside on bicycles. But the traffic in my park was surprisingly light. In the space of two hours I saw half a dozen little kids with their parents, and a couple of sets of eight- and nine-year-olds, also supervised. Two teenagers, maybe fifteen, rode through on bikes, did some desultory dangerous things on the swings, then left. No one used the baseball field, except a woman with a dog and a Frisbee. Dogs, in fact, were as numerous in the park as people. And adults were as numerous as children. More important, the youngest kid I saw without an adult was fourteen, possibly thirteen years old, no less. Chances were if I'd been sitting in any park in my neighbourhood that day, even a more crowded one, I would have noticed the same ratio. (And received the same number of suspicious stares, a solitary man taking notes at a table in a park.)

Another of the characteristics on Johan Huizinga's "true play" list is the stipulation that real play is "free, is in fact freedom." By "free" Huizinga means without compulsion, but he also means without constraints, with the spur-of-the-moment spontaneity that most of us can remember. Supervised, organized play, for Huiziriga, is "play to order," lesser play at best; at worst, not really play at all.

But more and more, supervised play is exactly what our kids are getting. It's evident if you visit parks and neighbourhoods across this country, in urban and suburban settings alike. It's become so commonplace–the way bicycle helmets for children have become commonplace–that we don't even think about it any more. The mean age of kids allowed outside alone, even with friends, has risen to the point where, in many cases, it excludes the traditional definition of "kids." The chances of seeing a child riding a bike on the street without adult supervision (F. Scott Fitzgerald's definition of freedom) are even smaller; indeed, the absolute number of kids riding bikes on many streets these days is a fraction of the number of adult riders. When we were children, an adult riding a bike was an odd enough sight to be a marvel.

During one of the years when my father was playing handball, I turned six, and my parents moved our family from downtown Toronto to the suburbs. The day after we moved into our new house I went bike-riding to explore our new territory, with two older kids for supervision—my sister and a friend named Albert Michaels, both aged eight. It was fitting that Albert was there, because he'd been my chaperone a year earlier on our downtown street, when he was seven and I was five, and we'd walked alone on a Saturday morning to a natural rink at a nearby schoolyard where he spent four hours showing me how to skate. Neither situation was deemed unnatural at the time.

When I reminded my mother of this story recently she was assailed by revisionist guilt, and claimed she should have been "put in jail." Today parents guilty of such "laxness" *could* be put in jail. The idea of young kids running around alone on the streets, through a neighbourhood, evokes alarm—even in kids themselves. A woman I know who lives in a large Canadian city recently took her daughter to visit relatives in a small rural town. The first day they were there her daughter looked out her bedroom window and said, "Mummy, there are kids playing out there, and they're by themselves. What's wrong?"

Not just the characters have changed; the vocabulary has too. Kids used to "call on" people. Calling on people was the precursor of play, its starter button. You called on your friends—on Judy; on Marshall—to see what they were up to. Were they lying around, were they grounded, were they as bored as you? The possibilities were all open, the outcome unknown. The same was true of the timeless statement, "I'm going out to play." Play what, with who? The lack of precision wasn't accidental, but intentional and all-pervasive. The same dialogue pattern continued when a kid actually did go out and call on someone. "Can _____ come out to play?" Not to play three-on-three, but simply to play. When was the last time the average parent heard that line from a supplicant at the door? It's a phrase that today exists mainly in the hyperspace

of pop culture, in a *Simpsons* episode or a McDonald's commercial starring Charles Barkley, Larry Bird, and Michael Jordan.

What, on the other hand, is the staple vocabulary for today's kids at play? Making plans. Making arrangements. We encourage our children to do both—or we do it for them—so they won't be bored after school or on the weekends. The "free time" of children has taken on a social formality that would have done a Victorian matron proud, kids asking other kids to come over, or being taken to someone else's house, where, in an enclosed backyard or basement, they will then play. But over-planned play, like over-supervised play, can easily turn into work. One of the brilliant side effects of the Orthodox Jewish Sabbath is that it's against the spirit of the day for kids to make plans during the week to play on Saturday. Kids can play on the Sabbath, but that play has to maintain an element of spontaneity. Arranging the Thursday before to meet Susan in the park is frowned on, but bumping into Susan in the park on Saturday is fine. This is the essence of free play. What you want when you play are very definite limits in time and space (what Johan Huizinga calls "secludedness") to separate your simulation from ordinary life, but no limitations in impulse or vision. What you want is not to know.

Of course, there are still people out there who are independent agents, who can call up their friends and find out what they're doing, and without knowing precise outcomes, meet them at the park to play: adults.

My nine-year-old daughter has a dream: she wants to live close enough to a school to walk to it. I've always considered it a laudable goal (I walked to both elementary and high school), but the other day something happened that convinced me it was a true fantasy after all. The crucial piece of evidence was a flyer my daughter brought home in her knapsack from school, promoting an innovation called "The Walking School Bus." What is the Walking School Bus? The flyer answers the question. The Walking School Bus is a plan to encourage parents to walk their kids to school, preferably picking up other kids on the way, instead of driving them, and so to avoid the classic line-up of cars (dangerous and polluting) you now see in front of every school. It's a primer, in other words, on how to walk to school. There's even a number to call to help you get started. It turns out my daughter was labouring under a romantic misconception: these days *nobody* lives close enough to walk to school, at least not without supervision.

The car is what you'll hear most often implicated as the villain when people talk about the devolution of kids' play. People blame cars, and by extension the suburban mindset that makes cars necessary; we have to drive because things are farther apart, goes the argument, and our kids have become inordinately lazy because of it. Consequently, they end up monopolizing our time and controlling our lives.

But the car is a red herring, effect camouflaged as cause. While we may complain about the indolence of our children and its corollary—our need to function as chauffeurs and social convenors—those facts don't bother us quite as much as they should. This may be because in letting our kids assume dominion over our lives we've managed, with a judo sensei's sleight of hand, to gain control of theirs. We have two very good reasons for coveting this victory: fear and perfection.

In a way, play as we once knew it—at least play in urban North America—can be said to have ended during the early 1980s. It was at this time that a number of highly publicized child kidnapping and murder cases hit the headlines, in what appeared to be an unprecedented flurry. It was this ostensible "epidemic" of the worst crime most people can imagine that went a long way toward convincing our generation of parents that we were living in a "different world." "Things are different today," went the mantra. "It was simpler when we were kids." The overprotectiveness of baby-boom parents was largely justified as a necessary response to the hostility of this new world, a world where people put razor blades in apples and arsenic in Tylenol, where snuff films were made, pedophiles inhabited half the cube vans on the road, and children killed children.

It should be commonplace by now to point out that this was an exaggeration, fuelled in no small part by the insecurity and guilt of parents who were both, for the first time in modern history, working outside the home. An article that appeared in *Maclean's* in 1990 captured the paranoid doublespeak perfectly. Entitled "The Mounting Toll of Missing Children," the article concludes, "...in the

end, constant vigilance and care on the part of parents may be the only way of safeguarding children in an increasingly dangerous society." Meanwhile, buried in the middle of the piece, are the following statistics: in 1989 in Canada, 574 children were abducted by one of their parents; only four were kidnapped by strangers. (All four were eventually found.) A 1988 U.S. Justice Department study described similar findings: the ratio of abductions by parents to abductions by non-family members was almost 100:1. Today, the rate of serious violent crime in Canada has fallen to the level of the late 1960s. The world has changed, but not nearly as much as we think. What has changed is us. What has changed is the attitude of parents toward the power of their children.

Why was my mother sanguine about letting me ride around my neighbourhood with my eight-year-old sister in 1960, whereas I would never consider doing the same with my own children? Why did she let my pee-wee baseball coach pick me up three times a week in a rusted-out Volkswagen bus along with twenty other eleven-year-olds and take us to practice, not to mention to Detroit on the weekend to see the Tigers play? Because of a fundamental philosophical difference of faith. She was convinced that whatever the world could throw at her children on a Saturday afternoon they could probably handle; I am not. My mother's children's power was a thing so natural to her she almost never thought about it; the power of my children for me is a nice notion, but I wouldn't stake their safety on it.

It's hard to believe that there has ever been a generation of parents more intense about their children than ours, who actively thought about their children more than we think about ours. But at the same time it's hard to imagine parents who think *less* of their kids than we do—at least when it comes to their ability to fend off the slings and arrows of the world. We cast them as potential victims as opposed to survivors. And we're so concerned about our children's emotional safety, their "feeling good about themselves," that on at least a certain middle-class level, we've gutted play by taking the risk out of it.

We have created a vogue for games without winners, games closely supervised to make sure there is no gloating or bullying—a moratorium on competition in general. These might seem like laudable innovations, but they have a developmental downside. Spontaneous play goes to places, sometimes dark ones, where made-to-order play fears to tread.

If spontaneous play is unavoidably about winning and losing, it's also not about an excess of either. If play exposes a child to the existence of a bully, it also offers him the gratification of learning to deal with one. By cocooning our children we've taken away their opportunity to educate themselves in the ways of the world, as we did as kids. (Children who were treated badly by their playmates used to have the option of saying "I'm going home," a tactic that's tough to pull off when home is a five-mile drive away and your father's not picking you up for another two hours.) Our overprotective madness has a method to it, but forgotten in the process is the fact that powerful play requires powerful and independent players. To play without power is like trying to light a concert hall with a flashlight.

Last summer, when I was in Los Angeles researching an article on roller hockey in California, I happened to catch an adult roller-hockey game one night in a complex called Coast 2 Coast. The game in question was a championship game; just before it started the lights dimmed, and while dramatic music played and a spotlight rotated at centre ice the players were introduced. The rink owner later told me that the adults really liked the professional feel of the "extras," which is why he'd invested in sound and light equipment. At the time, the "extras" seemed funny, but when I remembered the game later they seemed primarily weird. For one thing, while the adults were playing their championship game, an uptempo practice was being held with no fanfare at all on the adjacent rink, involving a team of twelve-year-olds who skated as naturally as fish swim in water. And secondly, the big-league fantasy came ready-made for the adults enjoying it; it was part of the package they'd paid for, like the uncomfortable, ready-made "family" enthusiasm drummed up by a DJ at a bar mitzvah. The creativity was all external and complete, not internal and open-ended. The result wasn't real make-believe; it was ersatz make-believe; it was pretend let's pretend.

In *Homo Ludens* Johan Huizinga identifies seriousness as one of the most important characteristics of real play. Children at play know perfectly well that they're "only pretending," Huizinga says, but "the consciousness of play being 'only a pretend' does not by any means prevent it from proceeding with the utmost seriousness, with an absorption, a devotion that passes rapture...." As an illustration, Huizinga tells the story of a four-year-old boy he knew, who was sitting in front of a row of chairs playing trains, when his father came into the room and hugged him. "Don't kiss the engine, Daddy," the little boy, obviously pissed off, said, "or the carriages won't think it's real." The four-year-old was right. Simulative universes should never drift too close to the original. This imperative can apply to something as simple as size. Life-size does not mean life-like. This was why Torquil Norman, the legendary founder of Britain's Bluebird Toys and the visionary past president of the British Toy Association, spent a part of his career trying to restore toy soldiers to what they had been when he was young: not the current twelve-inch-high action figures, but tiny inch-and-a-half men children could organize in ranks on their bedroom carpet.

As adults playing, on the other hand, we tend to act like the grown-up roller-hockey players I saw in California. Our simulations aim at too-precise imitations. Although we have the freedom to call up our friends—play's first prerequisite—we've forgotten how to be free when we finally get together with them.

If this formulaic style of play affected only us it would be unfortunate—but the trickle-down effects are eerie. The result is as close as your rec room. Too often, if you watch kids at play, what you'll see is a slick simulacrum of what adults think play should be, a store-bought story. Play has become a consumer product, a packaging tale told with too much expression and the wrong kinds of detail. As Nancy Carlsson-Paige and Diane E. Levin point out in their book *Who's Calling the Shots?* ("Dramatic Play, an Endangered Species?" is one section heading), the play of kids today is usually derived from TV shows or movies. The toys children buy—that we buy for them—come with scripts as well, usually tied to TV, with their own ready-made stories and simulations, heroes and villains, most of which are the products of middle-aged (baby-boom) minds. Kids have been playing at adult popular culture since the invention of mass media, but never before have the stories adults told been aimed so shamelessly at them, and never before have they been so stilted and unsupple, and ultimately self-serving.

A couple of months ago my nine-year-old became infatuated with the latest toy craze to hit her set, something called "Crazy Bones." Based on the ancient Greek and Roman game *tabas*, in which children played with painted sheep's knuckles, Crazy Bones appears at first glance to be an exemplary, if insanely priced, toy: chunky little inch-high plastic totems with faces that can be traded, collected, and knocked over. They look like marbles for the nineties. But where Greek kids once painted the knuckles themselves and undoubtedly named their own characters, Crazy Bones comes ready-coloured and identified, complete with a checklist giving the names and descriptions of the forty "bones" and sixteen "power bombers" in Series 1 (another forty in Series 2). And where kids playing marbles used to store theirs in Seagram's Crown Royal bags, mixing their own simulation with the thrill of adult dissipation, Crazy Bones comes with an official plastic coffin for storage, just $9.99, including the official Crazy Bones sticker-book. We're not simply content to intrude on the packaging of our kids' play, but on its sole: imagination. Our parents' generation included adult hucksters who peddled marbles to kids, sure, but somehow (by design, through a sense of proportion, through having lives of their own) they managed to avoid including a booklet that named every marble and described every variation of game you could play with it. But then again, our parents knew when to stop playing. They knew when to take off their short-shorts and put on Bermudas; they knew when to take up bridge and mah-jong. In fact, in their embracing of "social" games, games designed to provoke conversation that was usually as freewheeling as the games were structured, our parents may have come close to a truly adult incarnation of children's play.

We haven't. What we fear, I suspect, isn't so much what the external world might do to our kids if they engaged in truly free play, as what their own internal world might do to us. Or more exactly, what that world might reveal about us. The danger is that our children's story, and the story of their profound play, might implicate the profound artificiality of our own.

"The spoil-sport is not the same as the false player, the cheat," Johan Huizinga writes, "for the latter pretends to be playing the game and, on the face of it still acknowledges the magic circle. It is curious to note how much more lenient society is to the cheat than to the spoil-sport. This is because the spoil-sport shatters the play-world itself.... He robs play of its *illusion*–a pregnant word which means literally 'in-play' (from *inclusio*, *illudere*, or *inludere*). Therefore he must be cast out, for he threatens the existence of the play-community."

Maybe casting out is a bit harsh. But stepping aside might be called for, a graceful retreat to the wings. If letting our own kids play means we have to stop playing ourselves, it's a risk we should consider taking. As Jean Piaget believed, to know something truly, you have to invent it for yourself. Or, as any kid will tell you, eventually everyone has to come in for dinner.

In my father's handball-playing days there was one team sport grown-up men played: fastball. The fastball players, not car-poolers but serious jocks in their twenties and thirties, as skilled as semi-pros, wore gaudy-coloured T-shirts: they had barrel-arms and thick legs; the game they played, all whip wind-ups and reflex explosions of bat and glove, was like pinball writ large. Invariably, they played at night, under the lights, in parks across from strip plazas, truncated circles of light illuminating painfully green grass and tan infields. And invariably, just beyond the arc of lights in the outfield, in the penumbral shadow, there was a group of kids, racing their bikes, or playing touch football, or just assing around, sliding theatrically across the grass, plucking momentous plays out of a dozen sports histories, just waiting for the game to be over, so they could charge into the real light for a brief and dazzling moment of their own celebrity, before the field went black, and someone told them to get home fast, in the thrilling dark, before they got murdered or at least grounded.

The men are still there, with women dotting the field too now; there are more adults than you can count. But the kids are ghosts, already home, safer in every way, and smaller too, waiting for their chance to play.

Source: Jay Teitel is a writer and games inventor who lives in Toronto. He has won twelve national magazine awards. This article was originally published in *Saturday Night*, April 1999, pp.55-60. Reproduced with the permission of the author.

27.

Young Athletes Need Child Law Protection

Peter Donnelly

The costs that the children pay

I want to begin by arguing that, in some ways, we in Western society attach far too much importance to athletic talent or athletic giftedness—but—in far too many ways we do not attach enough importance to it. It is this latter point that probably results in many of the problems that we find in high-performance sport for children.

Arguments about sport being too important are familiar to us—we all see the amount of media attention, time and money that is concerned with sport; and we can all think of numerous good causes that deserve more media attention, time and money.

At the same time, we do not attach enough importantance to sport. If we think back to, say, our high-school days, the most admired individual was the all rounder—the individual gifted with multiple intelligences—he or she achieved academically and athletically, could play at least one instrument, draw, tell jokes, etc. But if we separate the aspects of intelligence we find that there is a hierarchy, with kinesthetic intelligence/athletic giftedness ranking lowest. Otherwise we would not find it so easy to refer in derogatory terms to the *dumb jock*—the individual who is only blessed with athletic talent. (I always remind my physical education students that, if they become teachers, their status in the teacher's room is likely to rank below that of even the "shop" teachers; and if you consider the length of the lines for consultations with various teachers at a high-school open house, parents demonstrate their perception of the importance of sport by leaving the shortest line for the physical education teacher.)

This low status or lack of importance has a number of serious consequences. It appears to permit us to behave toward talented people in ways that would never be permitted in other areas of life. It has allowed us to turn a blind eye to anorexia, bulimia, and steroid use among young athletes for far too long. It permits us to encourage young athletes to engage in physical acts that have a high likelihood of leaving them with chronic arthritis when they are in their 30s and 40s.

Let me give an example that may be close to home for some of you. I know parents who interview babysitters, employ certified nannies, and make frequent appointments with their childrens' school teachers. I have seen these same parents drive into the parking lot next to a soccer field, drop their child off for practice, and leave until the practice is over, or even later. Their children are left in the care of an unqualified, or uncertified, volunteer coach who they may have never met. Why? Perhaps because it is only sport!

My interest in this area began when I met a woman who had been a nationally ranked figure skater. She drew a direct connection between her career as a figure skater and her recent divorce, attaching most blame to the fact that her skating involvement had caused her to miss out on childhood and adolescence. If I had asked her about her career at age 18, she would not have had the time to reflect on the consequences; thus, my subsequent research was concerned with retired and successful high-performance athletes. The research received further impetus from the drafting of the United Nations Convention on the Rights of the Child (1989), and from a growing number of observations that, while recreational sports for children were continuing to improve in Canada (with house leagues and increasing education for volunteer coaches), the situation of young high-performance athletes was deteriorating. For example:

- Young athletes are involved in an increasing number of competitions—10-year-old hockey players may play 90 games in a season (as many as adult professionals); and some 11-year-old rugby players in the U.K. have played more games than international players twice their age.

- Young athletes are involved in increasing numbers of hours of training—20-25 hours per week is normal; 35 hours per week is not unusual; and I interviewed one figure skater who trained almost 60 hours per week in preparation for the national championships.

- Some young athletes are experiencing deteriorating parental behavior—one 12-year-old girl in the U.S. National Junior Tennis Championships lost in the quarter finals, and was dragged off the court by her ponytail by her 90-kilogram father and slapped across the face. Mary Pierce's father has been banned from all of her tournaments.

- Some young athletes are experiencing deteriorating coach behavior—Todd Crossett (University of Massachusetts) conducted research on male coach-female athlete relationships and concluded that, "Tactics employed by abusive coaches are clearly similar to those employed by wife beaters, incestuous fathers, and pimps."

Extensive interviews were conducted with 45 retired high-performance athletes regarding both the positive and negative aspects of their sport experiences, particularly during their childhood and adolescence, and their recommendations for improving the situation.

Although the subjects were given every opportunity to dwell on the positive aspects of their experiences, they devoted very little of the interview time to that aspect. All had enjoyed the opportunity to travel, and they frequently mentioned the prestige and resulting attention from family, friends and the media. The subjects were generally confident and self-assured individuals, characteristics that they attributed to their sport involvement; and they also mentioned the friendships they had made, and the pleasure they experienced in being able to do something very well. The athletes spent a great deal more time talking about the negative aspects of their experiences. These may be summarized as follows:

- **Family concerns**. Many of the athletes had experienced problems such as sibling rivalry and parental pressure as a consequence of their sport involvement. Rivalry resulted from the athletes receiving an inordinate amount of the family resources (time, money, attention) in comparison to their siblings, and many felt guilty about the amount of money that was spent on their involvement. Parental pressure often took subtle forms. One subject who had been thinking of quitting her sport noted that her mother had driven her two hours each way, each day to practice, and asked, "Who wanted it more?"

- **Social relationships**. Almost all the athletes had "regrets" about how much they had missed during their childhood and adolescence—parties, holidays, dances, etc. One swimmer who, preparing to compete at a meet, defied the demands of his club officials in order to attend his high-school graduation formal was ostracized for the remainder of his career. Others pointed to their feeling of inadequacy during social occasions that involved pick-up games of basketball or softball—their specialized sport experiences had left them with no other athletic skills.

- **Athlete-coach relationships**. Although we took an extremely conservative approach to data presentation, not using sensational items of data that we could not substantiate, there were clearly many examples of abusive relationships between coaches and athletes—emotional, physical and sexual. Male coach-female athlete relationships were particularly problematic, and resulted in problems ranging from dieting to unhealthy dependency relationships. Some female athletes gave every indication that they were just beginning to "name" their experiences as a result of the interviews, particularly in terms of the controlling nature of the relationship with their coaches.

- **Educational problems**. All of the subjects had successfully completed high school and many were in, or had completed, university; however, many indicated that they had achieved their success in spite of, rather than because of, the school system.

- **Physical and psychological problems**. Psychological and developmental problems included burnout, fear of the increasingly dangerous "tricks" that were being performed by gymnasts and skaters, and fatigue; almost all of the athletes had suffered from a variety of over-training injuries.

- **Excessive behavior**. A number of the subjects reported on the excessive or "binge" type behavior that followed major competitions or marked the end of a season. This behavior, which involved "eating, popping, drinking, injecting, and sniffing everything that wasn't nailed down," and some vandalism, seemed to go beyond even that which is expected as a part of adolescent development.

- **Performance-enhancing drugs**. Most interviews occurred before the Dubin Commission revelations and, while many acknowledged knowing about drug use in their sports, few admitted to personal use.

- **Dietary problems**. As noted previously, dietary problems were a major issue for the female athletes. All except the hockey player had experienced dietary and body-image problems and were very conscious of the widespread existence of such problems in their sports.

- **Politics**. A number of the athletes felt that they had been victimized by the internal politics of their sports and noted issues such as funding, team selection, subjective judging and poorly trained coaches that resulted from administrators making political rather than objective decisions.

- **Retirement**. Retirements tended to follow the patterns widely reported in the literature; some of the athletes had satisfactory retirements and left "when they were ready" but others reported adjustment difficulties or engaged in excessive behavior. Some felt isolated and lost, others felt bored or bitter, and some just missed the physical routine.

Three issues appear to be involved in the degree of difficulty experienced by athletes:

- **Organizational structure of the sport.** Athletes experiencing the most difficulties appeared to be in the sports that had Olympic or adult professional levels, well-developed levels of youth competition, and were individual in nature (frequently involving one-on-one time spent with a coach).

- **Major time commitments at an early age.** The data show a very considerable relationship between time committed to a sport and the number of negative experiences reported; this is particularly true of time commitments at younger ages.

- **Gender.** In almost all cases the problems for female athletes were more serious than the problems for male athletes, and in the case of dietary problems they are almost exclusively female. When the experiences of males and females are contrasted it seems that:
  - whereas girls fight natural growth, and sometimes retire when the post-pubertal curves inevitably appear, boys embrace their natural growth;
  - whereas girls deny themselves food in order to conform to some artificial standard, boys eat in order to grow bigger and stronger;
  - whereas girls appear to cram their careers into a few short years, retiring in their teens in a number of sports, boys mature at a slower and more relaxed pace in order to peak at a later age;
  - whereas female athletes may be subject to questions about their sexual preference, male athletes may be seen as desirably heterosexual.

Extended careers as professional athletes, coaches, or administrators are also far more available to male than to female athletes.

When the athletes were asked if they would repeat their careers, and if they would put their children in the same sport, a significant number answered either in the negative or with a qualified positive (i.e., "knowing what I know now, I would not make the same mistakes, and I could make it a better experience for my children"). Two factors appear to be involved in the creation of these negative experiences, even for athletes who define their careers as having been "successful" (we have not even begun to consider what the case might be for those athletes who consider that they had "failed" or "disappointing" careers):

- **Rationalization of sport.** As success (i.e., winning, sometimes euphemized as "excellence") has come to be the ultimate goal of high-performance sport, the focus has been far more on performance rather than the person who is producing the performance. Detachment of the body and its performance from the person legitimizes the use of drugs and other techniques, even violation and abuse, in the name of improved performance. The "body's education," social and family relationships, safety, and future well-being do not have to be considered–if "it" is having problems, call in the physician or the sport psychologist to fix "it."

- **Disappearance of childhood.** Our original thesis about the disappearance of childhood or adolescence for these athletes was not supported. Despite having been in an adult-dominated and quite authoritarian setting, many of these athletes had found ways to act like children and adolescents; thus, their childhood experiences were of a very different order than the "stolen childhoods" of modern child slaves and labourers or the "lost childhoods" of concentration camp and ghetto children in World War II. But these athletes clearly experienced modified childhoods, and this is a matter for concern.

When the athletes were asked for their recommendations for improving the experiences of young athletes, a number of the recommendations were utopian while most were concerned with fine-tuning the present system rather than changing it in any radical manner. They did not feel that there should be any externally imposed constraints on such things as training time; but there was widespread agreement that young athletes should be treated as children first, and that training programs should be adjusted to meet the social, physiological and psychological capabilities of the children.

In general, I agree with these recommendations and my preference would be to see sport put its own house in order. It is appropriate that parents, and society, should want to see talented (and less talented) children in whatever field achieve their fullest potential. In the case of sport, the "ideal" would be a child-centred system in which parents, coaches, physicians, administrators and teachers worked together in the best interests of the child under the auspices of the sport-governing body. Such changes are unlikely, however, because too many vested interests and ingrained ways of thinking are embodied in sport institutions, and because funding and sponsorship of sport-governing bodies will likely continue to be based on the achievement of international success. Given this situation, even minor changes will likely be re-interpreted to maintain as nearly as possible the status quo.

Given this, it may be appropriate to consider some externally imposed changes for the structure of children's high-performance sport. To this end, I would like to propose an extension of the child labour laws in order to protect such children. This proposal may not be as radical as it first sounds. The fundamental problem now stems from the fact that adult careers and incomes may be contingent on the performance of children. Apart from the illegal use of child labour in advanced societies, the only other area of social life where this is the case is in the entertainment and advertising industries where special laws have been introduced to protect children. Because of the scandalous behavior of some parents and Hollywood executives during the 1940s and 1950s, laws were introduced to determine the number of hours and days the children may work or rehearse, the maximum amount of time that they work each day, the amount of time that must elapse between performances and the conditions that must be established to ensure that a child received an education. Income is protected from parents and agents in trust funds, and government health and safety regulations are in force in the places of employment.

Sport seems to fall between the cracks of the legal system. It is not covered by the general child labour laws, nor the ones developed for the entertainment industry. Yet young athletes who receive Sport Canada funding meet all of the criteria to be considered as employees of the federal government, and some young athletes receive lucrative rewards and sponsorship money. (Jennifer Capriati, the American tennis player, signed a deal for $3 to $5 million with a sportswear manufacturer at age 13).

It is appropriate that some costs should be incurred in order to achieve in high-performance sport (e.g., reduced social life, longer time required to complete education), but these should not be disproportionate. It is time for both parents and children to be aware of the risks and problems associated with high-performance sport so that they may give a more valid informed consent. Such consent would be consistent with knowing that children would be protected by a carefully considered set of regulations that negate many of the problems identified in this study.

Serious advocacy of the protection of young athletes under child labour laws may lead to more focused research and may encourage a change in the policies and structure of high-performance sport, creating less emphasis on early performance. The current system of high-performance sport for children has a great many good points but it also has far too many bad points and even some ugly and shameful aspects. It is time to consider a change.

Source: Peter Donnelly is a professor and Director of the Centre for Sport Policy Studies in the Faculty of Physical Education and Health at the University of Toronto. This paper was presented to the 10th World Congress on Gifted and Talented Education, Toronto, August 10, 1993, and published in *Canadian Speeches: Issues of the Day,* 7(10), March 1994, pp.47-51. Reproduced with the permission of the author.

28.

What Has Gone Wrong with Athletics Today?

Robert Butcher

We lost when we forgot that sport, at every level, is still a game

What, if anything, does non-tyke soccer (five and under) have in common with pro sports? And, perhaps more interesting, what should it have in common?

Recently, I attended the grandly titled International Summit on Ethics in Sport, held at the University of South Florida. It featured keynote addresses by sports heavyweights Kareem Abdul-Jabbar, and Walter Payton, a cast of well-known U.S. journalists and writers, plus a sprinkling of academics.

The program consisted of panel sessions on violence, drug use, child abuse, stereotyping, the influence of the media and so on.

The picture that emerged was unremittingly awful. In the drug-use panel the focus was not, as one might expect, on the use of performance-enhancing drugs (although they were mentioned) but rather on the practices of team physicians, particularly in football, in drugging and treating injured athletes so that they can continue to play through pain.

In the session on violence, the theme was violent acts committed by athletes not on, but rather off, the field. There is apparently a major problem of athletes perpetrating acts of violence unrelated to their sports performance. (There was no discussion of any possible connection between violent and aggressive sports or highly competitive training regimes and violence by athletes off the field.)

In another session, the story was of college athletic programs that systematically failed to graduate any of their athletes.

Overtraining, pushing

The problem of child abuse in sport was not that of the rogue sexual predator preying on vulnerable young athletes but rather the systematic abuse that arises through consistent overtraining and the constant pushing of young children, often by their parents, to work and work to achieve competitive success. One prominent psychologist spoke of her research, which shows that competitive athletes consistently show lower scores on scales of moral development than do their non-athlete peers.

If there was one message that came through loud and clear, consistently from session to session, it was that the sports system has gone horribly wrong. The picture was that somehow sport had lost its way. None of the participants in the system being described seemed to have any fun. Sports was work, and brutal work at that. And athletes were the tools for that work. Athlete's bodies were expendable, there is always another one waiting, always another one that can be used.

But where did sports go wrong, why, and what can we do to stop it?

I had another significant moment in sports shortly after this conference The kids I coach in mini-tyke soccer had their first game. For 40 minutes these four- and five-year-olds buzzed around the ball like flies. They ran from end to end (and often from side to side), they did headstands and spent time staring into space. Every now and again, one would break from the pack and go tearing down the pitch, trailed by a cloud of other children. And, at the end, they stood tired and flushed and happy.

Working the way it should

Not only did those kids have fun, but their parents did, too. Here was sport working the way it should. The kids were trying their best and learning all sorts of new things. For now, they are learning how to be a team and co-operate, they are learning basic soccer skills—how to kick—and they are experiencing the pure joy of having a body and running. Later will come other skills and the pleasures and rewards of pushing oneself and competing with others in a shared enterprise, a game.

Sports works when it brings communities together, too. Our local soccer association is a network of volunteers and parents, who organize, prepare pitches, raise funds, coach, ferry kids around and cheer. What brings us all together is a shared love of sport and the desire that our children should be able to include sports and physical activity as a rewarding part of their lives—for the rest of their lives.

What went wrong?

So what went wrong? I'm sure the elite athletes that I heard about in Florida started their sporting lives in just the same way as the little kids who buzzed around the pitch last week. They too had shining smiling faces; they too had fun.

We lost our way when we forgot that sports at every level is still a game. That doesn't mean just a game, for we can treat a game with the utmost seriousness, but it does mean that the outcome of winning is necessarily tied to the process of playing. To win a game, I have to agree to limit the possible means I might use to achieve some arbitrarily created goal. I have to play by the rules, or I don't play at all.

The goal of golf is to drop a ball into a little cup. The easiest way to do that would be to pick the ball up and place it in the cup. But no, the game of golf requires that we get the ball into the cup by whacking it with a stick—and we must whack the ball from wherever it happens to lie. That's crazy—but fun—and it only makes sense if you follow the rules. The same is true for other games: we lost our way when we forgot that you cannot win without playing.

We lost our way when we forgot that athletes are people. In kids' sports, the purpose has to be to create an experience that helps the child to grow and develop as a person. Sports should contribute to a person's life and be a source of joy, not a trial that crushes self-esteem and alienates the child from his or her body. And that is as true of the highly paid professionals as it is of the little kid. We cannot simply use athletes' bodies for our pleasure and then discard them like toys when they are broken.

So what can we do? We start with those little kids and we do our best to keep their joy alive, for that, from minitykes to pro, is the true spirit of sport.

Source: Robert Butcher teaches philosophy at Brescia College at the University of Western Ontario and is an ethicist for Foundations: Consultants on Ethics and Values. This article was originally published in *The London Free Press*, July 4, 1998. Reproduced with the permission of the author.

29.

Child Sexual Abuse in Sport

Peter Donnelly and Robert Sparks

Moral panic

Recent revelations about the sexual abuse of children, ranging from native residential schools and Christian brothers' homes to daycare centres, primary schools and suburban neighbourhoods, and culminating in the recent Graham James and Maple Leafs Gardens cases in hockey, have apparently created a moral panic around the issue of paedophilia. Moral panics attract a great deal of media and public interest and generate righteous moral indignation, but they rarely result in sound long-term policies. Rather, they often result in repressive measures such as the recent proposal for suspending bail and parole for convicted paedophiles, attempts to extend the "dangerous offenders" provisions and proposals to publish lists and the whereabouts of "known" paedophiles and institute police checks for coaches.

Sexual harassment refers to any unwanted sexual advances or attention, physical or verbal, including "leering." The term is also increasingly being applied to apparently consensual sexual contact where one individual is in a position of power over another (e.g., teacher-student, employer-employee, coach-athlete). The term sexual abuse tends to be reserved for the more severe, ongoing and/or coercive cases of sexual harassment. The usual victims of sexual harassment and abuse are women and children (including youth). This is not to imply that men are not sexually harassed. Clearly, some men are stalked or are subject to unwanted sexual advances, yet evidence to date suggests this is a relatively infrequent occurrence in comparison with harassment of women and children.

Awareness and concern about sexual harassment has increased in the last 25 years in response to the women's and subsequently the children's rights movements. This has led to growing concerns and revelations about the types of sexual abuse that can occur in family and institutional settings. Schools, and other institutional settings for children, have been more closely monitored for sexual harassment, and there has been increased encouragement to report such incidents.

Youth groups such as the Big Brothers organization and the Boy Scouts have instituted policies to guard against those seeking sexual access to children. But sport and other recreational settings have been very slow to respond to these changes. Sport organizations have, in general, continued to act as if such things could not occur in the pristine world of sport and, as in the case of fighting other forms of violence, behaved as if the laws of society were suspended in the world of sport. After all, adults touching children and adults touching each other is a necessary part of the training and practice of many sports. The erotic elements of such touching have always been denied, as has recognition of the opportunities for private encounters and coercion that readily exist in sport.

There were increasing rumours during the 1980s about cases of male coaches sexually harassing female athletes, and there were occasional newspaper reports of coaches charged with molesting young athletes. But these charges were always dismissed as unfortunate aberrations having nothing to do with sport. In 1989, however, Todd Crosset found that there were recurrent features of coach-athlete abuse in sport. In fact, the strategies of abusive coaches were very similar to incestuous fathers, abusive husbands and child molesters. Crosset documented the hyper-controlling aspects of the relationships between such coaches and their athletes, and he noted the ways in which young athletes were disempowered by, for example, the coach befriending her parents.

During the 1990s there has been a slight increase in research with some work on university athletes by Helen Lenskyj, and Celia Brackenridge's work on young athletes and child sexual abuse. However, media attention to the topic has shown a marked increase. For example, The *Shirley Show* in April 1993 had retired athletes talking about their experiences; the *Fifth Estate* in

November 1993 featured four separate cases of coaches and female athletes; and *Dateline* NBC in March 1994 dealt with a California track coach and one of his female athletes.

Increasing attention has resulted in an increasing number of court cases. In 1994, an Edmonton track coach was convicted of having sexual relations with a number of female athletes in his club ranging in age from 12-20. Last year the national cycling team coach was charged with harassing a number of athletes, but the chain of evidence was contaminated and he was acquitted reluctantly by the judge. However, the case of the cycling coach was only one of a number of 1996 events in which the issue of sexual harassment in sport came to the forefront:

- During the summer of 1996, Sport Canada announced that, from 1997, funding to sport governing bodies would be tied to having a policy on sexual harassment and a designated sexual harassment officer in place. A training program for harassment officers was held in November.

- A Professional Coaches Association was formed with a very clear set of ethical guidelines concerning harassment; but membership is not mandatory, most coaches are not professionals, and again the enforcement/penalty guidelines are not clear.

- A survey of Canadian national team athletes found that 20 percent had had sexual intercourse with a coach or authority figure; 8.6 percent had experienced forced sexual intercourse (20 percent of these under the age of 16); and that most incidents occurred on team trips.

- A 1995 doctoral thesis by Marge Holman at the University of Windsor received publicity; the study showed that 57 percent of Canadian university athletes had experienced sexual harassment.

- Another *Fifth Estate* program in October documented the sexual abuse of young women by Junior hockey players, but it also looked at hazing practices on teams, one incident of which clearly involved the sexual harassment of boys by adult males.

Around the time of this broadcast another rumour was confirmed. Graham James, the coach of an IHL team in Calgary, was charged with sexually abusing players between 1984 and 1994 when he was coach of the Western Hockey League Junior teams in Moose Jaw and Swift Current.

It is worth commenting at this point about how surprising this level of activity is in regard to sexual harassment and sport. All cases of sexual harassment and abuse are problematic—there are difficulties in making the charges and lining up the evidence, victims are victimized in court; cases often come down to one (often subordinate) person's word against another's; and convictions are relatively rare—therefore most cases go unreported, for a variety of reasons. For example:

- Shame—all children feel shame after such incidents, but the lower reporting rate among boys suggests that the level of shame may be higher for them, especially in tough, contact sports because of the feeling that they should have been able to prevent what happened to them. There is another increment of shame associated with homosexual abuse—in the world of macho sports it is easy to feel that one's peers would believe that one should have been able to prevent it, and that if one did not, it must have been consensual.

- Guilt—guilt is associated with shame, and in the case of children there are many reports suggesting that they feel responsible for what happened to them.

- Normalization—there was the sense among female athletes that this was somehow the way things were, at least in the 1980s and earlier.

- Fear—abusers rely on their power, and the fear of the athlete that his/her future career in the sport may be jeopardized by refusing sexual approaches.

Evidence suggests that the following conditions have prevailed in sport sexual abuse cases. Athletes who fall prey to sexually predatory coaches were:

- under their coaches' direct control;

- often lonely and isolated (e.g., away from home);

- sometimes, especially in adolescent female heterosexual cases, "romantically" attached to the coach;

- threatened and/or bribed with regard to their future in the sport;

- generally unable to report what was happening to them to their parents, the police, sport administrators, etc., because: (a) they would not be believed (e.g., in a case where the coach had befriended the athlete's parents, or where the coach was well known locally or nationally); (b) because there were no procedures in place for athletes to make such reports; (c) because it was quite clear to athletes that no one in their sport wanted to deal with such issues; and (d) because if the coach was successful, it was quite clear that team owners, administrators, and sometimes even parents were prepared to turn a blind eye to rumours of misbehaviour.

It is because of this absence of anyone to turn to that Sport Canada introduced the system of sexual harassment officers—however, since these are appointed by the sport administrators, even that policy is open to abuse.

Graham James pleaded guilty on January 3 of this year. In an obvious plea bargain, he was sentenced to 3.5 years in prison. A court-ordered ban on publication kept the names of the two victims who had come forward secret, but it was revealed that James was guilty of 300 incidents of abuse of one victim and 50 of the other. Rumours were flying, including a suggestion that one of the victims was a current NHL player and that other high-profile players had been victims.

A few days later, Sheldon Kennedy, who plays for the NHL Boston Bruins, held a press conference to announce that he was the victim of the 300 cases of abuse. He had been identified as a "problem" player during his NHL career, with drug and alcohol abuse problems, and their cause was now apparent. Going public may have been recommended by his therapist as a way of dealing with the issues, but it is also likely that the U.S. media—who are not subject to Canadian court orders—were about to announce his name as a victim. However, his stated reason was that he wanted to make it easier for other victims of sexual abuse in sport to come forward, and it has certainly had that effect. Charges are pending against other hockey coaches in Calgary and Winnipeg; another Western Hockey League owner and league official—Brian Shaw of Portland, who had died of an AIDS-related cancer—was reported to have been abusing players; sexual abuse crisis centres have reported a significant increase in calls from young males; and the Maple Leaf Gardens "sex ring" of the 1970s and early 1980s became public. The CHA has appointed a lawyer to examine the issue in hockey (where there are 75,000 minor coaches), and to recommend sexual harassment policies to be implemented in time for next season.

The effect has also gone well beyond hockey to Canadian sport in general, and there were a number of calls for a Royal Commission to study sexual harassment in sport. However, it was also clear that no one in sport wanted another Dubin Commission, since the laundry to be washed in public this time would have been even dirtier than that associated with the abuse of performance-enhancing drugs. In a clear attempt to curtail such an inquiry, sports have become pro-active on the issue. It was reported on January 23 that the Canadian Association for the Advancement of Women and Sport brought together representatives of 14 national sport organizations to develop a position paper and policy on the issue. By January 31 there were 25 organizations involved. Research for the position paper turned up a Web site for paedophiles which advocated involvement in youth sport because of the lack of checks and controls. It is clear that both the CHA and Sport Canada will be implementing sexual harassment policies in the near future.

The most obvious, and knee-jerk, policy recommendation to emerge so far has been to implement police checks of all coaches of children's sports. More cautious voices have suggested that the task would overwhelm police forces, particularly in large urban centres, and that such a policy would not have revealed Graham James because he did not have a police record. A more reasonable approach to policy would be to examine the culture of youth sport, and sport in general, to determine the circumstances that have led to the present situation. Among the most obvious issues of concern are:

- Children leaving home to participate —whether it is the "midget" draft for junior hockey, or other highly talented young athletes moving to work with the best coach available, the procedures and circumstances surrounding such moves need careful consideration.

- Related to the above, the circumstances around athletes traveling for competitions also need to be considered. Coaches and administrators have tended to turn a blind eye to post-competition excesses, including those involving under-age drinking. It is under these circumstance that many cases of abuse have occurred.

- While it is clear that the moral panic will sensitize many parents to be more vigilant, there is a clear need for more parental education and empowerment. Parents need to be empowered to ask any questions they feel necessary concerning the circumstances of their child's participation in a sport, to observe practices and competitions, and to be assured that the sport organization has the best interests of the whole child in mind (not just successful athletic performance).

- Both parents and children need to know that they can "blow the whistle" on any behaviours that they feel are inappropriate without the fear that they may be jeopardizing the child's future in the sport.

- Private meetings, and private training or therapy sessions, have been common in sport—coaches have closed their office or gymnasium doors in order to offer support or criticism to athletes. They have visited athletes' rooms when on road trips, spent time in locker rooms and showers, given athletes a lift home, and had them over to their house. Such private time has been important, and most athletes will recount positive stories of nurturing and mentoring coaches who provided support in a variety of ways at vulnerable times in athletes' lives. However, such time is also open to abuse. Perhaps the culture of coaches could learn from the culture of school teachers, who are supposed to have had a no-touching, no private meetings policy for some 10 years. It became quite obvious to teachers, particularly in primary schools, that a no-touching policy was inhuman—a small child who is hurt or upset clearly needs some contact. So, teachers have developed a culture whereby they look out for each other, do not put themselves in private one-on-one situations with children, leave office and classroom doors open, and have clear guidelines for extra-curricular activities and trips. Such a culture would have some costs—both teachers and coaches recognize, for example, the problem of having an upset student or athlete in one's office, with the door open, while others are walking past outside. But such a culture is also more likely to lead to coaches and others associated with young athletes intervening and reporting problematic incidents, rather than engaging in the type of cover-up that has clearly been the norm in sport.

The key problem is going to be to initiate such policies and cultural changes while maintaining the positive aspects of the coach-athlete relationship.

Source: Peter Donnelly is a professor and Director of the Centre for Sport Policy Studies in the Faculty of Physical Education and Health at the University of Toronto. Robert Sparks is an associate professor in the Department of Human Kinetics at the University of British Columbia. This article was originally published in *Policy Options/Options Politiques*, 18(3), May 1997, pp.3-6. Reproduced with the permission of the authors.

Part 9
Heritage

The term "heritage" is used to refer to the racial/ethnic background of Canadians. As a largely immigrant society we all lay claim to a "heritage," usually African, Asian, European, or Native American (aboriginal). But heritage is frequently far more complicated since it is often shared—our heritage might be French and Irish, or it might be African and Native Canadian.

The vast majority of research on heritage in sport has been concerned with African Americans, and since we share athletes and a border with the United States, these concerns are evident in Canada (see Hoberman [1997] for the myth of "black" athletic superiority). There is some historical and anthropological research on Native North Americans, and a very small amount of research on individuals with Asian and Hispanic heritages in North America. Minority (i.e., non-European) heritage appears to be related, in many cases, to restricted access to physical activity opportunities or to a channeling of these opportunities into a few sport opportunities (Harvey & Donnelly, 1997). In Canada, for example, we are aware of the limited number of individuals with other than European heritage who are involved in hockey. The limited opportunities appear to be a result of either overt or covert discrimination (cf., Christie, 1997) and, when combined with the restrictions that result from social class and gender, can be a powerful barrier to involvement in physical activity.

The four articles in this section deal with the complexities of discrimination based on heritage. Laura Robinson compares the lack of financial support for Native youth sports in Manitoba with the campaign to "Save the Jets." (Note the sections on the **Economics of Sport**, and the **Crisis in Hockey**.) Robinson particularly focuses on the effect of restricted funding on Faith McDonald, a Grade 8 student and talented athlete from Nelson House. In the following article, Dallaire addresses the issue of multiculturalism in Canada, focusing on the Alberta Francophone Games as an attempt to sustain French language and culture in Canada outside Quebec. Her study focuses on the difference between the organizers and the participants in the ways in which they expressed their Francophone realities.

David Shields uses the character of Vince Carter, star player on the Toronto Raptors basketball team, to explore the complexities of black-white relationships in North America. And, in another piece, Laura Robinson explores the subtleties of discrimination in questioning whether Angela James was cut from the Canadian women's ice hockey team at the Nagano Olympics because she is black. (See also the sections on **Women** and **Sexual Orientation**.)

References

- Christie, J. (1997). Colour bar shattered one Canadian's NHL dream. *The Globe and Mail,* 5 April, pp.A1, A20.
- Harvey, J., & P. Donnelly (1997). L'accès à l'activité physique et au sport: Un impératif politique? *Policy Options,* 18(4), May.
- Hoberman, J. (1997). *Darwin's Athletes: How Sport has Damaged Black America and Preserved the Myth of Race.* Boston: Houghton Mifflin.

Additional Sources

Videos:

- *Black Athletes—Fact and Fiction* (and the follow-up studio discussion), a 1989 NBC Special, is dated and controversial, but it still provides a good basis for discussion.
- *Pride and Prejudice,* CBC Prime Time News (1 February, 1996), documentary on racism and the men's national basketball team.

Print Resources:

- Rubenstein, L. (1993). Fuhr matter a nasty reminder of games old boys play. *The Globe and Mail,* 5 June, p.A16. [A timely reminder, in the year of Tiger Woods, of a Buffalo golf club's refusal to admit Grant Fuhr as a member.]
- Campbell, N. (1995). Tense clash of cultures surrounds Mann Cup. *The Globe and Mail,* 14 September, p.C8. [Report on the violence between a Native (Six Nations) and a non-Native (New Westminster) team at the Senior A lacrosse championships.]
- Rogan, M. (1997). Great expectations. *Toronto Life,* December, pp.85-95. [Close-up look at the life of a young African-heritage basketball star.]

30.

Prairie Priorities on Thin Ice

Laura Robinson

Aboriginal athletes given the back seat

Hockey in Winnipeg is in a state of crisis. The Jets are losing money and have almost died several times. Hearts have been broken. People retreated to their favourite watering hole to lament.

But then they rallied, painted their faces in team colours and sang and danced at Portage and Main. The team must stay, otherwise how will they get through the cold Prairie winter? A new stadium must be built to save the team, or the Americans will buy them.

Grown men break down in tears as they try to explain what the loss of the Jets means to them. This is a Canadian catastrophe.

First Nations youth are in a state of crisis. They have a suicide rate six times greater than non-native youth in Canada.

Many hearts have been broken. Faces are painted in grief and pain. No one is singing or dancing. Children give up hope and decide not to stay in this world. What will their family and friends do without them? How will they get through the long Prairie winter? Something must be done.

Grown men break down in tears as they try to explain their loss. This is a Canadian catastrophe.

In the case of the Jets, it was a matter of days before all three levels of government found $94 million to save the team.

No one seemed to know exactly how this money would be accounted for, or if more cash and a new stadium would actually save the team. There are examples of taxpayers being stuck paying a giant tab so a privately owned team could profit and play–Toronto's SkyDome and Montreal's Olympic Stadium are two.

Team boosters say the Jets provide Winnipeg youth with positive role models. But many of the free agents will be kissing Winnipeg goodbye as soon as their contracts are up. Other players will be traded mid-season when teams start to slump.

No one has explained why players, who only come in one sex and almost always in one colour, and fight at the drop of a glove, are considered role models at all.

Winnipeg seems like a million miles away for Faith McDonald, a 15-year-old hockey player from Nelson House, Manitoba. She starred this winter as centre forward for the Bantam boys' team in Nelson House and played for the Thompson girls' team when she could find someone who would drive the hour to the town.

She also made the Northern Manitoba team at the 1995 Manitoba Winter Games. The team won a bronze medal in a semi-final game that ended 9 to 1. McDonald scored five of those goals.

"I dream of playing in the Canada Games," says McDonald, from Otetiskiwin School (the name means "footprint" in Cree). She is one of the top academic students in Grade 8.

"I dream of making the women's national team some day, but it's hard because you have to travel out of town, and we have money problems. There's four kids in our family…. The band office gives me money for travel and accommodation to go to games, but I have to pay it back when I can."

Physical education teacher Cory Churchmuch says McDonald is one of the most talented hockey players he's ever seen.

"She skates circles around the guys, even a lot of the high-school players. She knows how to take the puck hard to the net, she's not afraid to mix it up with the guys, and she's smart around the net. The only thing she's missing right now is top-end speed.

"But her opportunities are so limited, it's frustrating. She's not being held back by talent. She's held back by economics."

David Moose is a school employee and a member of Otetiskiwin's tragic events team, set up after three suicides and three attempted suicides by young people in the community. He says the arena is the only place people can go for recreation.

"You need a pair of skates to use the arena, and a lot of people can't afford them. You also have to pay, and some people can't afford to do that, either," says Moose from his office.

"We used to have beautiful beaches and islands here and everyone swam and canoed. This is what we have always done. We want to give an outlet of any kind that's not harmful. But ever since Hydro put the dam in at South Indian Lake, the water and rocks are gray and polluted. No one can swim. It's very dangerous to canoe, too. The dam flooded everything, and there (are) deadheads everywhere."

The stories from Nelson House sound only too familiar to those working in aboriginal sport. Talented athletes come along, but as soon as they want to move beyond their community, financial constraints, in the majority of cases, prove prohibitive. Outlets for traditional sports lose ground as people's lives become displaced by non-native values and culture.

In McDonald's case, lack of athletic opportunity occurs year-round. She competed recently in the track and field zone championships in Leaf Rapids in the 800 and 400 metres, the 4x100 relay, and the discus. The relay team qualified to go on to the Rural School Championships in Stonewall, a five- to seven-hour drive.

If she tries to move past these isolated local competitions, she meets an economic stone wall.

Tryouts for the track and field athletes for the Manitoba team to the North American Indigenous Games took place in Peguis on the Victoria Day weekend. McDonald didn't know they were being held, but would have had no way of getting to them anyway. The two communities are about 600 kilometres apart.

Morris Sutherland, spokesperson for the Manitoba team, says there is no money to advertise the tryouts, no money to transport athletes to them, and no money if the kids do make the team and have to travel to Blaine Lake, Minnesota, to take part in the games.

"One of the problems is, kids have to rely on their communities to get them to the track meets," says Sutherland. "We have absolutely no money. It's ironic (the Jets) got money. As soon as a crisis comes up, there's money. I've been in aboriginal sports for over 30 years. Nothing surprises me any

more. Every time we approach the government for our sports, it's nothing."

McDonald says her experiences in sport have shaped how she sees the world.

"When I score a goal, I feel good, really happy. It gives you confidence when you score. It makes me try harder in school, too. But the others who don't play, they think everything's boring. They get mad when they think they might lose."

Studies have shown that children who have positive experiences in sport tend to have more self-esteem and confidence and higher achievement scholastically, and they learn how to work on a team and set and obtain goals.

The provinces and the federal government have an opportunity to contribute to something positive that is happening in the native community.

Sutherland says they have asked the province for $300,000 to send 1,000 athletes to the North American games. A pittance, compared to the Jets.

But when it comes to sport in Manitoba, no one seems to be talking about anything except how the Prairie sky will fall if the Jets die.

Source: Laura Robinson is a former national-level cyclist and cross-country ski racer. She is the author of two books about sport, *She Shoots, She Scores: Canadian Perspectives on Women and Sport* and *Crossing the Line: Violence and Sexual Assault in Canada's National Sport*. This article was originally published in *The Toronto Star*, June 3, 1995, B5. Reprinted with the permission of the author.

31.

At the Alberta Francophone Games

Christine Dallaire

Countering assimilation and retaining teenagers in francophone ranks

The Alberta Francophone Games (AFG) were established in 1992 to provide, like other sport events in the country for francophone youth, a context that was French-speaking and a cultural environment where youths could enjoy themselves. Open to all 12-to-18-year-old Albertans who can speak French, the Games are a means to counter assimilation and retain teenagers in francophone ranks, thereby ensuring a lasting francophone community in Alberta. However, they have been bedeviled by debates. Who, for example, counts as a francophone? And how much can organizers, for whom the real purpose of the Games is to promote a francophone agenda, insist that participants speak French during the weekend-long event? The issues discussed below are extracted from my doctoral research, entitled The Alberta Francophone Games: A question of identity in which the reproduction of francophone identities among young people is examined in the context of this sport and cultural event.

When I asked participants what they thought of the fact that many of the youths at the AFG spoke English, two teenagers—both of whom spoke French as a first language and attended francophone schools—clearly stated, in two separate interviews, that staging a large event—even if it included participants who would inevitably speak English at some point during the weekend—was more important than holding it completely in French.

> Je pense qu'on parlait de si c'est correct qu'il y a des personnes qui parlent en anglais [aux JFA]. Bien moi je trouve que ça serait mieux si les personnes parlaient plutôt en français. Mais j'aimerais mieux avoir beaucoup de personnes qui sont là, et il y en a qui parlent en anglais, que d'en avoir pas beaucoup, tout le monde parle en français. (Edmonton/E, 1997).

> Aprés une secousse, tu veux juste du monde qui vient. Qu'ils parlent quatre mots de français, ça ne fait rien. […] On veut qu'il y ait du monde qui vient. (Jean Côté/E, 1997).

They argued that the greater the number of participants, the more enjoyable and interesting the Games would be, and that, according to them, was better than restricting the event to youths who would speak French throughout the weekend. The performance of the French language was preferable, but certainly not a priority for these participants.

AFG founders and organizers viewed sport as a lure to attract youths, and it was indeed sport that drew participants. Questionnaire and interview results demonstrated that participants were aware of the requirement to speak French throughout the weekend, and they agreed, in principle, with the purpose of the Games to promote "francophoneness." However, they attended the AFG primarily to practice sports and to have fun. In most cases, the francophoneness of the event was incidental to their motivation to participate.[1] Furthermore, participants expected the AFG to be similar to modern organized sport. Their expectations concerning organizational and sporting know-how were clearly stated in their evaluations of the Games. For instance, they complained about incompetent officials and referees, long waiting periods, the taste and lack of food, poorly organized transportation, the damaged running track, the volleyball courts being too small, poorly organized track and field competitions, early bedtimes and early mornings, and the need for medals.

The results of the participant evaluations conducted by organizers were certainly not all negative. Some youths were evidently satisfied and enjoyed their experience at the AFG. What is significant here is that the majority of their comments, positive or negative, pointed to sport and organizational considerations. Evaluations and interviews revealed that participants were more concerned with having fun and enjoying the sport competitions in an organized setting than with living an experience entirely in French. Indeed, the particular configuration of sport and francophone discourses at the AFG produced a situation where youths acknowledged the francophone agenda of the Games, but were attracted by their sporting character and did not necessarily comply with the official requirement to speak French. Much interaction between participants was, in fact, conducted in English–to the point that it is not at all obvious that the Games provided youths with a weekend "in French." Teenagers did speak French, or tried to, when they communicated with organizers, volunteers, chefs de mission, sports officials[2] and coaches. However, many of them used English widely in their informal conversations–in other words for most communication. Thus, at this very basic level, the francophoneness of AFG participants was a fact much more complicated than might appear.

Bernard (1998) observed that minority francophone youths in Canada wished to retain their francophone language and culture and wanted to pass it on to their children. One of the AFG participants clearly expressed this wish in a written statement produced at the end of the interview: "J'espère garder ma langue pour enfin la montrer à mes enfants. Ma langue est IMPORTANTE[3] pour moi." (Drawing/statement #26, AFG/E8, 1997).[4] The paradox, Bernard (1998) noted, was that these youths primarily lived their life in English. This, I argue, is what fundamentally set AFG participants apart from organizers. French-speaking youths' spontaneous use of English to converse with each other was a discursive practice that contributed to the construction of their distinct hybrid identity, merging francophone and anglophone identities.

> A: Comme nous autres on n'est pas, on parle toujours comme un peu des deux langues. On va dire un peu en franqais…
>
> B: On mélange les deux.
>
> A: Mais, on ne va jamais avoir une conversation complètement en français. Il va toujours y avoir des mots en anglais. (Edmonton/E, 1997).

These young people considered it "normal" for them to mix the two languages, since French and English were ultimately part of who they were.

> C'est dure de ne pas parler anglais. Parce qu'on parle anglais tout le temps.
>
> Oui. C'est notre environnement parce qu'on parle anglais tout le temps.

> C'est drôle parler en français.[…]
>
> Oui, c'est naturel de parler l'anglais.
>
> Mais, je sais pas. On essaie.
>
> Des fois. (AFG/E3,1997).

Organizers lived a larger part of their own francophoneness routinely. The strategic dimension of their francophone identity was manifested in their concern for the community, in the importance they placed on supporting community institutions and activities. For example, rather than listening to an English-speaking radio station, they would tune in to CHFA, even if they were not necessarily satisfied with its programming. AFG participants, on the contrary, experienced their personal francophoneness as a project that constantly required work. Speaking French was, for them, a rehearsed and conscious exercise; they viewed the Games as a context where they could "practice" their French. Still, many of them evidently did not think that it was necessary to speak French at all times to identify as a francophone, nor did they all consider the performance of French at the Games a priority; for them, the presence of English was not an issue.

What distinguished participants from organizers was that participants, for the most part, explained their francophoneness in terms of a conscious and strategic project. Youth francophone identities were not lived unproblematically at the individual level. Even if some participants expressed an emotional and essentializing attachment to the French language and/or francophone culture, the majority of them stressed that they had to make a conscious effort to maintain their ability to communicate in French. Whereas for organizers, who were from older generations, speaking French was more of a spontaneous practice, for the youths that participated in the Games it was an intentional undertaking–whether they claimed it as their first language or not. Organizers had referred to the strategic dimension of francophone identity in terms of the necessity to contribute to community building and participate in francophone institutions. Conversely, teenagers lived their francophoneness as a responsibility, and had to constantly work at its production, quite apart from thinking about their obligations towards the collectivity.

References

Bernard, R. (1998). Le Canada français: entre mythe et utopie. Ottawa: Le Nordir.

Field notes and interview

Dallaire, C. (1996-1997). Research journal. Field notes from March 4, 1996 to August 23, 1997.

Alberta Francophone Games (AFG)/E3. (1997, May 17). Third participant interview with six girls from the Peace River region.

Alberta Francophone Games (AFG)/E8. (1997, May 19). Eighth participant interview with two boys and one girl from the Centralta region.

Echnonton/E. (1997, April 15). Interview with three girls, former participants.

Endnotes

[1.] The francophoneness of the AFG did not necessarily attract the youths who took part in the event, but neither did it deter them from participating. Conversely, it appears to have been a reason other French speaking youths refused to participate. At a General Council meeting, some chefs de mission reported that the francophoneness of the Games did bother some teenagers, mostly French immersion students. These potential participants refused to attend because they did not consider francophone events "cool" (Dallaire, 1996-1997). For these youths, then, the francophoneness of the AFG was more significant than their sporting character. At any rate, these were not really the teenagers that organizers wished to attract.

[2.] Except, of course, when addressing English-speaking officials who could not communicate in French, such as the volleyball officials at the 1996 AFG.

[3.] In capital letters in the original.

[4.] The fact that at fifteen years old, this young French speaker was already consciously articulating the desire to transmit her language to her future children points to the problematic character of her francophoneness. If her language, i.e., her own fluency, or the political and social status of French in Alberta and Canada had not been weakened or threatened, she would not have thought about it: that her children would have spoken French would have been a given.

Source: Christine Dallaire is a lecturer at the School of Human Kinetics, University of Ottawa, Ontario. This article was originally published in *Canadian Issues/Themes Canadiens (CITC)*, Autumn 1999, pp.25-26.

32.

Vince Carter as African-American

David Shields

The best three seconds in sports

Behold the agony of the white NBA fan as he contemplates the imminent apotheosis of Vince Carter. For if I join the Hallelujah Chorus concerning his "work ethic" and deference to his older teammates, his absence of jewellery and tattoos and showboating, his desire to "do things the right way," his post-game ritual of calling his mom and then playing video games rather than going to bars and clubs, his contentment in Toronto, I feel as if I've been unwittingly enlisted in a neo-con crusade against rebellious players like Allen Iverson and Latrell Sprewell and in service of the old (supposed) verities—civility, humility, niceness.

Still, it's hardly Carter's fault that his mother is a schoolteacher and his stepfather was a high-school band director; that after leaving the University of North Carolina a year early he went back last summer (per the contract he signed with his mother) to get his degree in Afro-American Studies; that a childhood friend was quoted saying, "Whenever I need advice, I call Vince. He's the best listener I know." What's so bad about being good? Isn't our romance with evil getting a bit boring in its own way? Why must Iago always get the best lines? Isn't it sweet that Carter's teammate, Dell Curry, says, "Vince is definitely the man I'd like to see my sons grow up to be," and his coach Butch Carter complains, "He lacks a mean streak," and Raptors general manager Glen Grunwald says, "Everybody [every team] needs someone like him"?

And yet, as one of my favourite bumper stickers has it, "If you're not angry, you're not paying attention." Television traffics exclusively in images. Images magnify the body. The NBA traffics, almost exclusively, in African-American bodies, and from the time the first slave ship pulled into the harbour, African-American bodies have been big sellers. "I propose," as Ralph Ellison says in *Shadow and Act*, "that we view the whole of American life as a drama acted out upon the body of a Negro giant." It's a strange strip-tease, the way the NBA markets itself—on the one hand, relentlessly selling the erotic appeal of "outlaws" like Iverson, and, on the other, never acknowledging that the NBA is a place where white fans and black players enact and quietly explode virtually every racial issue and tension in the culture at large. So is the NBA a sport, a business, or Reparation Theatre? To what extent are players interested in such questions? To what extent can one insist that players be interested in such questions?

Who am I to dictate to Vince Carter how he feels about his own life? What's that fantasy all about—the self-congratulatory yet masochistic liberal white dream about black men and their perpetual down-ness? For Carter didn't grow up impoverished; nor has he publicly said he was ever the victim of any particularly overt racism. He's been treated as a deity since high school, when, beginning his junior year, ticket scalpers gathered outside the gym two hours before his games.

So perhaps the best and only thing to do is to concentrate on Vince Carter the Basketball Player, specifically Vince Carter the Dunker, since that's why he's been anointed, in his own words, "the next 'man.'" Those other two conspicuously "nice" superstars, Tim Duncan and Grant Hill, have nothing especially spectacular about their games; there's nothing about their bodies begging to be fetishized. Carter, by contrast, has what Woody Allen once called "thrill capacity": George C. Scott is a great actor but Marlon Brando rearranges our neurons. After Carter dismantled the Lakers, Shaquille O'Neal called him "half man, half amazing." In a game against Dallas, Carter took off from the free-throw line, spun 360 degrees in the air, carrying the ball in his right hand as a waiter would carry a tray; then switched to his left hand before jamming the ball through the hoop. Afterwards, Dallas's Steve Nash said, "He's one of those guys who might do something you never see again." If you're a basketball fan, this particular play is one you're exceedingly

unlikely never to see again: it's replayed so often on ESPN that it threatens to overtake the Rodney King video in the Reification Sweepstakes.

And, well, that's the thing. It's not possible to talk about Vince Carter in the context of no context, not when *ESPN The Magazine* just named him "Next Athlete 2000" because "we can't take our eyes off of him in or out of uniform" and because he "delivers the best three seconds in sports." How long does an orgasm last, anyway? I've come not to praise Carter but to hijack him for my own purposes, only what exactly are those purposes? Why, no matter how I frame him, do I inevitably need to simplify him, reduce him to an allegory, stick a black hat or a white hat on his shaved head? Why can't I internalize him? Why can't I make him mine? How twisted is my impulse to even want to?

Source: David Shield's most recent book, *Black Planet: Facing Race During an NBA Season*, was a finalist for the U.S. National Book Critics Circle Award. This article was originally published in *Saturday Night*, March 2000, p.34. Reproduced with the permission of the author.

33.
Shutout
Laura Robinson

No one in women's hockey has as impressive a CV as Angela James. So why is the Canadian Hockey Association keeping her out of the game?

She hops over the boards at York University's Ice Palace and flies across the rink, her blades dancing with deft familiarity. She pivots near centre ice and charges after the puck. She has an intensity that can't be coached. While she assumes a jockish, intimidating posture, she is graceful on the ice. If Angela James hadn't become a four-time hockey world champion, she could have made it as a figure skater.

The girls beside me in the stands—twelve- and thirteen-year-olds from the North York Storm Pee-wee Hockey Club—are screaming her name. Angela James, now thirty-four and a recreational co-ordinator at Seneca College, is also their coach. And although she says she doesn't hear her fans once she's on the ice, a smile under her face guard suggests otherwise. In the end, her team, the Beatrice Aeros, wins 2-0. With one assist and one goal, James, as usual, comes through.

Marc Ouellette, statistician for the Central Ontario Women's Hockey League, says that on December 6, James stood second in the league with twenty-two goals and thirteen assists in eighteen games. It's an important date to note, because shortly afterward, fourteen Canadian women and two Americans from the league headed off to Finland for the Three Nations Cup. "She was ahead of all the women who were chosen from our league," says Ouellette, "and many of those played in Nagano." The same thing happened a little over a year ago, when James was dropped from the Olympic team: somehow the Canadian Hockey Association managed to leave her at home.

At Nagano, our team sobbed when Olympic officials draped the second-place medal around their necks. They had been working for gold since the first World Championship in 1990, which also happened to be the first of four World Championships in which James competed. The relationship between her absence on the Olympic rink and the absence of a gold medal was noted by many. As Cathy Phillips, who played for the 1990 Worlds, put it, "When Angela steps on the ice, the Americans say, 'Oh-oh, A.J.'s playing.' When those rookies stepped out in Nagano, they said, 'Oh good. A rookie.'"

How could Canada send a women's hockey team anywhere and not include Angela James—the Wayne Gretzky of women's hockey? And how could they do it again this season?

The answers can't be found in the statistics—this story is more complicated than numbers. It's about a girl growing up in public housing in Flemingdon Park in a single-parent household and becoming the top female hockey player in the world. It's also about an Old Boys' Club called the CHA, which sees women players as "a thorn in their side," according to one national team member, and "has absolutely no respect for women," according to another. The CHA doesn't tolerate women who question its decisions, and that's why the two players asked that their names not be printed. But James has lived a life that challenges the white, male traditions in which hockey has invested so deeply.

She started playing pickup in Flemingdon Park's parking lot at seven, graduating to league hockey at eight, skating as the lone girl the whole time. This was in the 1970s, well before Justine Blainey challenged the Supreme Court on co-ed play. At fourteen, James turned to women's hockey, and eight years later, in 1987, she played at the first international tournament for women, again breaking ground as the first black woman in international play.

No one in the history of women's hockey has as impressive a CV. She made the Central Ontario All-Star Team and was leading scorer for at least a dozen years. She made the World All-Star Team in 1990 and 1992 and was named top team player at the 1994 World Championships. By the 1997 Worlds (which Canada won, beating the U.S. 4-3 in the final), James was one of five women who had played in and won every World

Championship. She managed to be first in a sport that has an ugly reputation for putting women last.

Getting cut from the first Canadian women's Olympic hockey team seared through James like a bullet. On a cold December morning, she closed up her basement apartment in Calgary, cleared three months' worth of hockey equipment from her locker at Father David Bauer Arena, climbed into her car and started the lonely four-day drive across the wintry prairies.

Shannon Miller, the former national team coach, had called James a defensive liability. "All the veteran players knew they had to be in incredibly good shape," Miller told me later. "The other veterans trained really hard to reach that level of conditioning, and Angela didn't." It was a difficult decision, not arrived at lightly, but Miller had warned her that she was "in the grey area."

James wasn't ready to give up. She met with Murray Costello, then president of the CHA, and Bob Nicholson, vice-president of operations, to request an appeal. "We talked for three hours," James says. "It was supposed to be confidential. The next day, I expected a breakdown of exactly how I got cut, and instead the media is all over us talking about lesbians." The coverage stretched far and wide: "A lesbian scandal is shaking the famous Canadian women's team," read the lead in *Blick*, Switzerland's largest daily. "The question is, does the coach … sleep with the team captain ….?" The papers also suggested it was James who leaked the rumour.

"I couldn't believe it," she says. "So many lies were told."

When the CHA left her at home again this year, James didn't bother appealing. "I thought they were wrong, and I told them so, but obviously they don't want me."

The official reason: "We had an evaluation camp in May," says Denis Hainault, the CHA's director of high performance, "and the evaluation she received, combined with her performance the season before, didn't qualify her for our final selection camp for the Three Nations Cup."

Hainault is right—last season wasn't James's best. She had been feeling unusually fatigued and had lost considerable weight. Just before the evaluation camp, she had a complete physical and was diagnosed with Graves' disease, a condition of hyperthyroidism that affects hormone levels and energy production. It's not uncommon among athletes. Biathlete and double-Olympic gold medallist Myriam Bedard found out she had it when her results bottomed out a couple of years before Nagano. So far, Bedard hasn't come close to matching her past performances. James, on the other hand, has been on medication since mid-summer, and this season's results suggest a recovery.

Hainault claims the CHA takes medical conditions into consideration before evaluating players, but that doesn't seem to have been the case with James.

The decision-makers knew she had Graves' and that she had just started medication for it. Still, they chose not to give her another chance at the final camp in October. They did, however, put Natalie Rivard on the team. The former national team player was returning after more than two years away from the game. She hadn't attended the May or October training camps.

"It's their loss," James says as she finishes off a postgame caesar salad at the Ice Palace bar. "They should be putting the best product on the ice, and as far as I'm concerned, they're not."

Almost every corner of York University reflects the cultural composition of Toronto. But walk through the front doors of the Ice Palace, and you could be at an arena in Barrie. Or Calgary, for that matter, where the women's team trained for the six months leading up to Nagano. James wasn't *directly* discriminated against. If anything, Shannon Miller and the other women involved in the elite women's hockey program have gone out of their way to include women of colour. But systemic discrimination works in hidden ways. Throughout her career, James has been adamant that racism is not an issue. When she returned to Toronto after being cut, however, she seemed a little less certain. "You get these vibes," she told me. "It's not something you can put your finger on." Which is why it's so difficult to prove.

Jason Payne plays in the United Hockey League for the Flint Generals. But he grew up in North York, playing for the Metro Toronto Hockey League, and remembers when racial slurs were a regular part of the game. Whenever he was bumped from a team or league, he wondered whether his race had influenced the decision. "They're not going to come out and tell you they don't like you," he says. "It's not necessarily one person. It doesn't have to be the coach. It could be management, and that's all it will take to get you out."

The Colour of Democracy: Racism in Society is the bible on the ways in which racism permeates our institutions. Its author, Frances Henry, is a social anthropologist and professor emerita at York University. "Any person of colour who has tried to crack the colour barrier, particularly in a sport where there are so many structural barriers, is going to experience racism," she says. "For a black player from Toronto to have to go to Calgary is an example of a structural barrier. They don't have equal opportunity to the perks that white players are going to have in a mainly white city."

White middle-class kids possess the keys to a culture that's defined by their parents. James says she felt comfortable in Calgary, but she also says players from the inner circle had an advantage. Jennifer Botterill, a rookie who made the final cut, is a good example. Her father, Cal Botterill, is the team psychologist for the Calgary Flames and was the women's team psychologist until his daughter's arrival. He is also a professor at the University of Calgary, where the team trained. Her mother was an Olympic speed skater, and her brother is a three-time Junior World Champion who now plays in the NHL. No one's suggesting Botterill isn't a good hockey player. It's just that, for her, Calgary's hockey world worked seamlessly.

James was on her own. "I've always been willing to make the sacrifices," she says, "whatever they may be." Still, it couldn't have been easy leaving her job at Seneca and living in a $350-a-month basement apartment while trying to keep up mortgage payments back home. When Graves' began affecting her performance, her coaches assumed she wasn't bothering to give it her all. "They asked me if I was emptying the tank," she says. Maybe with a support system like Botterill's, her condition would have been diagnosed earlier. Maybe not. What seems clear is the lesson many Toronto kids are gleaning from her experience.

In the spring of 1998, I worked with the National Film Board on *The Game of Her Life*, a documentary on the women's team. Ninety-four minutes long, it had to be shortened for classroom use, so I took it around to schools and asked teachers and students in the Toronto area what they thought could be edited out. In the film, there's some emotionally charged footage of James being cut from the team. Some of the kids who viewed it cried, all felt it was unfair, and almost all–white and black–believed she was cut because she was black. Even after I explained that I felt the coaches wouldn't make decisions based on race, many students–especially those at the high school level–were unconvinced.

Right or wrong, their perception is fraught with repercussions. At the Ontario hockey training camps for the 1999 Canada Winter Games there wasn't a single black girl in attendance. Does James think they're getting the message that if you're black, you don't play hockey? "I'm not sure whether they think it's race or gender," she says, "but they can see politics at work, and that's probably enough."

Source: Laura Robinson is a former national-level cyclist and cross-country ski racer. She is the author of two books about sport, *She Shoots, She Scores: Canadian Perspectives on Women and Sport* and *Crossing the Line: Violence and Sexual Assault in Canada's National Sport*. This article was originally published in *Toronto Life*, March 1999, pp.59-62. Reproduced with the permission of the author.

Part 10
Economics of Sport

This is one of the largest sections of the collection—a result of the rapid commercialization and professionalization of sport in the last 20 years and the attention paid to sport in the media. While issues of labour relations have been less evident in the last few years, relationships between cities and professional teams and cities and sports stadia, government funding for professional sports, and financial support of Canadian national team athletes have all been prominent in the news headlines.

David Whitson opens the section by examining the league/franchise system and demonstrating the economics of professional sport in terms of the ways in which franchise owners make money. Gare Joyce, in two sidebars to an article on the Toronto Raptors, looks at the myths that are promoted in order to win, or retain, a franchise. Andrew Zimbalist, an economist specializing in the economics of professional sports, uses the case of the Miami Dolphins baseball team to show how owners can claim to be losing money while in fact they are making healthy profits.

Turning next to the issue of cities, teams, and stadia, Neil deMause tells the sorry story of the Toronto SkyDome and the bilking of Ontario tax payers. Laura Robinson continues this theme, drawing a contrast between professional sports stadia and regular sport participation and noting the gender inequities involved in taxpayer support for sports facilties used primarily by men. And White, Donnelly, and Nauright take the relationship one step further by considering alternative forms of ownership of professional teams. They note that fans "would delight in owning a share of their team," but the strength of the corporate franchise ownership system, and its media partners, appears to close off any discussion of community ownership. Mark Lowes then takes an alternative view of the private use of public space in his analysis of the Vancouver Indy.

Marketing and sponsorship are key to modern sport. Individual athletes, teams, organizations, and sports events all seek corporate sponsors, often without concern for the products that are endorsed (e.g., tobacco). Corporations seek to attach themselves to what they perceive to be the lifestyle and other dimensions of sport. Shoe companies are predominant in this type of promotion (see Article No. 49) and Cynthia Enloe reminds us where those shoes come from—usually Asia, and usually made by women (and sometimes children) for extremely low wages, who work long hours in conditions that are unsafe and unhealthy. Since the first edition of this collection, campus activism in North America is forcing many universities to ensure that all products (mostly sportswear) that carry university logos are produced under fair conditions.

The last three articles concern federal government spending. John Palmer provides an argument against spending tax dollars to maintain NHL franchises in Canada. (See also the section on the **Crisis in Hockey**.) James Christie argues that part of the federal surplus should be used to support Canada's national team athletes. And Mark Tewksbury, also addressing underfunding, notes that he can understand why athletes would leave Canada to take up citizenship where there is more financial support.

Additional Sources
Videos:
- *That's Entertainment*, PBS "Power Plays" series, deals with marketing the NHL and the NBA.
- *Be Like Mike*, PBS "Power Plays" series, on marketing, corporate sponsorship, and Michael Jordan.

Print Resources:
- Campbell, N. (1995). Hockey arenas skating into the lap of luxury. *The Globe and Mail*, 23 September, pp. A1, A16. [Report on GM Place in Vancouver, changes that are taking place in arenas and their sponsorship, and the growing difference between wealthy and poorer NHL teams.]
- Cluett, R. (1994). A solution to those sport strikes. *The Globe and Mail*, 7 October, p.A21. [A proposal to resolve labour unrest in sport by removing the tax perks available to owners.]
- Solomon, J. (1999). Whose game is it, anyway? *The Washington Monthly*, December, pp.31-34. [Makes a case for fan ownership of pro teams.]

34.

Pro Sports: Who Pays the Price?

David Whitson

Towards 2000: The integrated circus

In April 1994, city councils in Calgary and Edmonton narrowly approved controversial arrangements in which millions of dollars of federal infrastructure funding were allocated to refit the Saddledome and the Northlands Coliseum. The background to these deals, as any follower of Canadian sports will know, is the well-publicized threats by team owners that the National Hockey League (NHL) can no longer survive in smaller Canadian cities unless owners obtain more revenue from their publicly financed arenas. The additional "revenue streams" that hockey owners demand typically include the income from arena advertising, income from other (i.e. non-hockey) events, and—most important because it is this which requires structural refit—more income from luxury boxes, restaurants, and concession facilities.

"Hip" sport of the 21st century?

Yet April 1994 saw both *Macleans* and *The Globe and Mail's* "Report on Business" running upbeat stories about the economics of hockey. These articles depicted the NHL as poised on the brink of unprecedented visibility and prosperity as new commissioner Gary Bettman's game plan to sell NHL hockey in the United States begins to take effect. Tangible evidence that the marketing of hockey is working can be found in the large audiences for the league's newest franchises in Anaheim and Miami, and in the Canadian-style enthusiasm for playoff hockey generated this spring in San Jose. Other signs of hockey's new fashionability can be found in the instant box office success of the Disney hockey film *Mighty Ducks II*, in an April 10 *New York Times* feature asking whether hockey will be the "hip" sport of the 21st century, and most of all in the phenomenal growth in the market for NHL licensed apparel (team

sweaters and caps) from less than $100 million five years ago to more than $1 billion in the 1993-94 season.

How is it possible that NHL franchises are struggling in traditional hockey hotbeds like Edmonton and Quebec, at the very moment the game is making dramatic inroads into American popular culture while privately financed arenas are under construction in Vancouver and Montreal? What should the smaller Canadian cities do, if anything, to keep their NHL teams? Can they afford to spend the amounts of public money required to provide sports entrepreneurs with the facilities needed to pay what are now celebrity salaries?

Beginnings

In the early 1920s, there were several thriving professional hockey leagues involving the major centres on the Canadian prairies and on the west coast, as well as in the St. Lawrence basin. These leagues competed for players and for status in the public mind as the best league; their champions faced off for the Stanley Cup.

But as the culture of mass entertainment developed in North America, and arenas seating over fifteen thousand people were constructed in New York, Boston, Chicago and Detroit, it was soon obvious that the future of hockey as a business lay in these big-city markets. Canadian-based teams playing in smaller cities and markedly smaller arenas could not hope to compete for the best players. Entrepreneurs in Montreal and Toronto built the Forum and Maple Leaf Gardens, while owners in the smaller western cities seized the chance to sell their players to the new American clubs before the players themselves simply jumped.

As a result, the NHL moved into the 1930s as the only serious buyer of hockey talent and, therefore, hockey's recognized major league. Its presence in the major metropolitan centres of that era also assured a place for NHL news and gossip in an American popular culture increasingly dominated by the metropolitan media.

In Canada, the weekly radio broadcasts from Maple Leaf Gardens and the Montreal Forum became a rhythm of Canadian winter life. *Hockey Night in Canada* attracted regular audiences in every part of the country and helped to construct the now familiar place of NHL hockey in our emerging national consciousness. The broadcasts made NHL players into household names and NHL stars into national heroes. They made the Stanley Cup playoffs into an important national event. Most importantly, they made the NHL itself seem like a Canadian institution, even when it was a cartel already based substantially in the United States.

The pro-sports business

There are several features of the professional sports industry that are pertinent to the current situation.

The first is simply that the major leagues in all pro sports are best understood as combines of team owners whose perspective on the "good of the game" has less to do with national or civic traditions than with the prospects of their businesses, individually and collectively.

Also, major league status is best understood as a promotional description whose credibility with the public depends upon a league maintaining its monopoly position with respect to player talent. Status as a major league sport also depends upon that sport's presence in the biggest and most important cities and on media coverage that makes these big city entertainment events into objects of popular attention around North America.

Lucrative television industry

In the prosperity of the early postwar boom, the owners of the established teams were in a cozy position. Their teams had achieved the status of civic institutions, and they played mostly to capacity crowds in buildings long since paid off. Profits were comfortable and the prevailing attitude was captured in the cliché—"if it ain't broke, don't fix it." Yet the economy of professional sports was about to be transformed by television, by an explosion in player salaries and by a steady shift of population and wealth from the older industrial regions of North America to the west and south.

Television, of course, dramatically increased the amounts of money circulating within professional sports. At first, television money came primarily from contracts between a major league and a major national network for exclusive rights to a season of games; such as *Hockey Night in Canada* on CBC, or the National Football League's (NFL) *Monday Night Football.* These payments were initially small but rapidly escalated, as the television industry discovered that live sportscasts fetched large and reliable audiences and subsequent lucrative advertising dollars. This fueled competitive bidding among the networks for exclusive rights to popular sports "properties." The leagues split the money among member teams, and television revenues quickly became an integral part of the financial equation for every professional team.

Beyond these direct broadcast revenues, television created the potential for many more sources of revenue. It created the publicity that established the now-familiar link between sports sponsorship and public relations. It multiplied the value of billboard advertising in arenas and stadiums. It turned sports stars who were only household names into nationally recognized celebrities. Most of all, it vastly increased the visibility of professional sport and its presence in the rhythms of popular life.

Players demand greater share

Players wanted a share of all this new money. Salaries had remained low throughout the 1950s because the major leagues were monopolies and followed contract practices that gave owners effective control over a player's sports career. In the 1960s, major league monopolies were challenged by smaller leagues like the World Hockey Association and the American Football League. This introduced salary competition in these sports on a scale not seen since the 1920s.

Both the NHL and the NFL were able to restore their monopoly positions within a few years by incorporating some of their rivals into expanded major leagues. This would have only a temporary effect in containing players' salaries.

The formation of player unions and the institutionalization of collective bargaining were, as one would expect, big steps in improving player remuneration. The most important single factor, though, was the overturning of the legality of the reserve clause in sports contracts.

These clauses, which had their counterparts in every team sport, gave the teams perpetually renewable options on a player's services and effectively prohibited a player from seeking a higher salary from another team. Owners argued that free agency would destroy the game and pointed to the 1920s, when players freely moved to big-city clubs, as evidence. Once the courts ruled that reserve clauses were an unwarranted restraint on labour mobility, all the major leagues moved to make the conditions of free agency the subject of collective agreements. Free agency has had a profound effect, both on salaries and on the viability of small city teams.

Eager for a piece of the big league

Up until the 1950s the major leagues, in hockey and other sports, had been entirely situated in the Great Lakes region and the American northeast. With faster and cheaper air travel, pressure grew from the booming cities of the west and the sunbelt. Cities there wanted in on what television was making into national institutions.

The first departure from the traditional geography of professional sport occurred in baseball, with the moves of the Giants and Dodgers from New York to California, and of the Boston Braves to a new publicly financed stadium in Milwaukee.

Teams that had been thought of as civic institutions, part of local culture and of the social history of their communities, were abruptly moved to other communities for business reasons. What Milwaukee and Los Angeles also demonstrated was that other cities were anxious to get major league sport and that local governments were prepared to offer land and even a stadium to get them. These moves drew strong criticism from those who believed in the traditional and organic ties between teams and their fans.

It quickly became obvious that the interest in major league sport could not be satisfied by the transfer of established teams. As a result, most of the major leagues moved into expansions, creating new franchises in major cities where their sport was not yet represented: Toronto and Montreal in baseball, St. Louis and Philadelphia in hockey. Franchising created immediate revenues (franchise fees) for existing partners, at the same time that it added to the national presence of their product.

Franchising in professional sports involves exactly the same economic transactions it does in other businesses: namely, selling the rights to offer a nationally recognized product or service (NHL hockey or NBA basketball) in a given market area.

In fact, expansion in pro sports coincided with the growth of franchising in other businesses and the eclipse of many kinds of local businesses at the hands of nationally promoted, brand-name products.

Public money was usually part of the equation that brought major league franchises to cities like Calgary and Edmonton, like Denver and Seattle. Although local entrepreneurs paid the franchise fees, most expansion teams have played in publicly financed facilities, which socialized one of their major costs while creating opportunities for private profit.

Through the prosperous postwar years, though, the rhetoric of civic boosterism spoke to publics which were eager both for big-league sport itself and for the civic status and national visibility that were widely believed to be attached to big-league teams.

Towards 2000: The integrated circus

In the 1990s, television, higher players' salaries, and further transformations in the North American economy contribute to a new equation. Some of the same cities that gained major league franchises between 1960 and 1980 are now threatened with losing them. The threat is most acute in those mid-sized cities whose manufacturing base has been undercut, or whose traditional economic role was a commercial and cultural centre for a less than populous hinterland. Both kinds of cities must find new niches in an increasingly continental economy.

While this has affected U.S. cities such as Buffalo and Minneapolis, Canadian cities like Edmonton and Winnipeg are smaller, more peripheral and more vulnerable to marginalization. This is the context in which the corporate and civic elites of these cities, and indeed many fans, are desperate to hang on to their sports teams, both for the economic activity claimed to be generated and for the visibility and status that is attached to a big-league city.

Making it more difficult for the small-market franchises to survive is the continuing explosion in players' salaries. Easier free agency has made it increasingly normal for established stars to sell their services to the highest bidders. But when it became clear that even players of the stature of

Gretzky and Messier could not win championships without the right supporting cast, teams like the Kings and the Rangers (and, of course, the Toronto Blue Jays) were able and willing to pay whatever it cost for the "character" and role players who might make the difference between winning and losing.

The Kings and the Red Wings continue to demonstrate that high player budgets do not necessarily produce championships. Nonetheless, free agency has meant that salaries for even reliable journeymen in professional sports have risen beyond senior executive levels, while the stars are paid like the show-business celebrities they now are.

In hockey, the average NHL salary has tripled since 1989, from $180,000 to over $500,000. This means that while a team like the Edmonton Oilers succeeded in the mid-1980s with a total player budget under four million dollars, it cannot survive in an environment where team budgets must exceed twelve million dollars. Such teams find themselves losing their better players as free agents. Owners in Edmonton and Winnipeg claim that they can no longer ice competitive teams unless they gain access to new forms of revenue and they are right. Nevertheless, salaries are rising precisely because owners in Vancouver and Toronto, as well as New York and Los Angeles, are making lots of money out of hockey.

Cable business creates disparity

The most important developments, however, follow from changes in the television industry. The basic source of television revenue for major league sports has traditionally been network contracts.

For most of the last thirty years, this has provided dependable and rising revenues that have been divided on a fairly equal basis among the member clubs. However, the major networks have faced sharply increased demands from the major sports leagues at a time when their own dominance of television is threatened by the new reach of cable and satellite, which offers new options for cost-conscious advertisers.

This is a complex and rapidly evolving situation in which cable networks like Fox may outbid the traditional networks for national rights, as they recently did with NFL football. On the other hand, baseball is faced with accepting a sharply lower network contract and the NHL is still seeking its first U.S. network contract in many years.

The rapid development of the cable business and the concentrated market penetration that advertising on cable offers have together produced a new situation. Sports events on local cable stations offer cost-effective advertising to local and regional businesses. This means a lucrative revenue source for some major league teams, not least because local media revenue does not have to be shared with other teams in the way that revenue from national media coverage does.

This produces great disparities because the value of advertising on the New England Sports Network, for example, or the Madison Square Garden Network, is commensurate with the size and affluence of the audiences that they reach. Teams like the Bruins and Rangers get significantly more income from local media than do the Oilers or the Jets.

Beyond direct revenues, the visibility that regular television gives to a major league team opens the door to all sorts of other revenues. Television audiences are what make rink board messages and in-ice corporate logos attractive to advertisers. It is television's attention that makes it possible to sell the names of arenas to major corporate sponsors (United Airlines in Chicago, General Motors in Vancouver). It is television exposure that fuels the booming market in insignia merchandise, by making team logos and colours part of a widely shared repertoire of popular symbols and meanings. It is television that has made figures like Michael Jordan and Wayne Gretzky into popular icons, whose familiar images translate into multi-million dollar marketing contracts.

Corporate entertainment

Luxury boxes for corporate entertaining have also become an important factor in the new economy of professional sports. This is not entirely new; company tickets have long constituted an important portion of season subscriptions in most NHL rinks. However, what the Skybox phenomenon demonstrates is that once this form of corporate entertaining is established as a norm in the local business sector, luxury suites can bring in much more revenue than the bleacher seating they typically replace. Because the revenue from luxury seating is not shared in any way, it affords significant competitive advantages to franchises that can afford it. This is why otherwise fine arenas are being replaced in Montreal and Chicago, and why teams like Calgary's are demanding that what was a state-of-the-art facility less than ten years ago be reconfigured with more luxury seating. The effect of replacing cheaper seats with seating geared to corporate entertaining is to move the game increasingly upmarket and out of the reach of even middle-income fans. At the same time, costs of business entertaining remain tax deductible, and therefore it is the public who is subsidizing sky-suite patrons (both hosts and guests), as well as contributing to the salary explosion in professional sports.

Cross-ownership has been around for some time: in the links between Molson's, the Canadiens and *Hockey Night in Canada*; between Labatt's, TSN, and the Blue Jays; between the Kings and the Prime Network, the Braves and the Turner Network; and the Vancouver Canucks and BCTV.

Cross-ownership is increasing, and what it means beyond the normal effects of wealth and power is the strategic use of the various entertainment products in a corporate empire to promote and give visibility to one another. The Disney Corporation has been a pioneer of this kind of cross-marketing (of toys, films, souvenirs, and theme parks) and its acquisition of an NHL franchise and subsequent promotion of the film *Mighty Ducks II* may signify a further integration of hockey into the larger North American market for entertainment and leisure goods, with consequences for its Canadian meanings and roots.

Strategic marketing increases competition

This emphasis on strategic marketing, in which sweaters, videos and the game itself are all simply "product," needs to be recognized as a new stage in the economy of pro hockey; one in which the smaller Canadian cities may no longer matter. Today, all the major sports seek to demonstrate to transnational advertisers that they can reach out to new audiences, and the stakes are such that the demographics of these audiences matter more than national tradition. In these circumstances, it is difficult to remain confident that hockey can remain for long in Edmonton, Winnipeg, or Quebec, without

the highly problematic levels of public subsidy. This is because all these new sources of revenue tend to widen the gaps between small-market teams and large ones. In the 1970s, when the most important source of revenues was gate receipts, teams from good hockey towns in Canada could compete financially—and therefore on the ice—with teams from larger cities where hockey wasn't part of the local culture. In the 1990s, though, when big-league sport has less to do with cultural traditions than with marketing, the size and affluence of target markets make all kinds of difference.

The size of the regional television markets will mean that San Jose and St. Louis will get more revenues from local media, and also from rink board advertising, than will Winnipeg and Edmonton. The relative size of the local markets means that players like Eric Lindros are worth more as a marketing vehicle in Philadelphia than in Quebec. The size and composition of the local corporate communities means far more potential revenues from luxury boxes in Chicago and even Calgary (with its oil-related head offices) than in any of the three smaller cities.

Club owners in each of these cities continue to pursue deals which would give them more revenue streams in publicly financed facilities. Yet without both a salary cap and far-reaching revenue sharing, it is clear that player costs will continue to rise, while the ancillary revenue sources that make hockey an attractive marketing vehicle in populous American regions will be of much less value to the small-market Canadian teams.

So far, the players are refusing to consider a salary cap, while owners who are financing their own new rinks—in Vancouver and Montreal, as well as Chicago and Boston—say they cannot share their revenues with their small-market brethren.

If you build it ...?

That cities like Winnipeg and Edmonton may no longer be able to afford NHL hockey is difficult for many Canadians who have always thought of hockey as our game to accept. It is particularly unpalatable for fans in these cities who have loyally supported their teams and who, in Edmonton, have identified with the City of Champions version of civic pride. Yet the public debate about the possible loss of an NHL team often confuses a legitimate concern for the health of the city with some more speculative arguments about economic benefits and civic image.

Professional sports boosters routinely claim that public subsidies that attract or keep big-league teams in town need to be seen as investments in the local economy. They cite studies commissioned by the teams themselves that purport to show that the Nordiques, for example, are worth $75 million annually to the local economy. These studies vary somewhat in what they include in these estimates; but they typically add the team's revenues to its total expenditures and use a multiplier to capture the effects of the original expenditures being re-spent by local contractors, workers, etc.

Although professional sports undoubtedly generate some activity in the civic economy, critics of these studies raise three important questions about them. First, how much of the money the team takes in is new money, as opposed to local money that would otherwise have been spent on theatre, other sports or restaurants in other parts of the city? Secondly, how much of the team's expenditures stay in the community? Here the issue is that superstar athletes seldom live year round in the cities they play in, so that their salaries are less likely to be spent in the community than the salaries of more normal earners. Finally, although an arena is always a major building project, when public money is involved one has to compare its impact with the effects of public funding of other kinds of projects and programs. This is especially true when arenas are being proposed while other kinds of public expenditures are being cut back.

Chicago economist Robert Baade has undertaken the most systematic study of the economic impact of major league sports. He looked at the subsequent effects on wage levels, property values, and retail spending in more than twenty-five U.S. cities and concluded that the economic benefits were negligible.

If this is so, we are left with more intangible questions. Can we put a value on civic image, on being on the map, as boosters like to put it? It is remarkable how many of those who support public spending to keep major league sports teams in town appear to feel that being in the same league as New York or Los Angeles does confer status on a city. Yet it is difficult to find any evidence that the presence or absence of professional sports franchises has anything other than an imaginary influence on business relocation decisions.

The more difficult question here is whether we can put a value on civic pride and on the enthusiasm locals feel for their home town. The recent successes of the Toronto Blue Jays and Vancouver Canucks serve to remind us of the continuing power of professional sport to mobilize civic identifications. Yet again, it is legitimate to ask how many of the fans that celebrate in the streets ever get to attend games, and what differences the departure of a team would make in their lives.

Here it is worth reporting that a recent Winnipeg survey showed majority support for public subsidies for the Jets only among those earning over $60,000 per year. Three-quarters of those surveyed were opposed to the use of public funds to build a new arena for the Jets or to continue subsidizing their financial losses.

It is important for citizens in the smaller cities to understand that having a major league team will be an ongoing expense. It is not a matter of writing a cheque once for a new arena, after which the small-market teams will be profitable and competitive. Small-city teams will continually lose their good young players, and their owners will need regular infusions of public money to stay in the game. Community ownership will also mean regular losses, without the benefits of cross-marketing.

Some people may decide they want to pay this price in order to keep the NHL in town. However, if fans understood that the money spent on a new arena would add $400 to their taxes every year, how many would say it was worth it? The challenge is to create a genuine political debate in which these issues are clearly laid out, so that people are offered a real choice between their interests as consumers and their interests as citizens. Such a debate could cut through the boosterist rhetoric which too often protects professional sport from serious examination.

Source: David Whitson teaches Canadian Studies at the University of Alberta and is co-author, with Rick Gruneau, of *Hockey Night in Canada*. This article was originally published in *Canadian Dimension*, October-November, 1994, pp.9-14. Reprinted with the permission of the author.

35.

Ball Control

Gare Joyce

Myths—just how much can a city really expect to benefit from a sports franchise?

During its battle over the Pro-Line sports lottery, the Toronto Raptors' principals frequently proclaimed the benefits of a National Basketball Association franchise to the Toronto and Ontario economies. Club president John Bitove Jr. and former Ontario premier David Peterson boasted about the jobs that a franchise would create and the income tax that would be paid by their millionaire dunkmasters. Their arguments sounded like the songs sung by an owner threatening to move his team out of town and relocate in a lucrative market. That's because, for both the promised expansion team and the franchise purportedly on the move, events follow a predictable pattern. To illustrate this, we present a chronological array of headlines touting the arrival of a mythical team—the Fat City Zircons—as well as the real story behind the hype.

Expansion Zircons to be a boom to Fat City's economy

A franchise rarely has an indisputable effect on a city's economy. During the early '90s the NBA champion Bulls were Chicago's biggest tourist attraction; rumour had it that the Bulls brought into the city's economy between US$100 million and US$300 million. But the retirement of superstar Michael Jordan precipitated a falloff of interest and loss of cachet. It also demonstrated the fragility of a team's contribution to a city's economy.

One study showed that, in 1984, before their move to Indianapolis, the impact of the NFL's Baltimore Colts on the city's economy was a scant US$200,000. The previous year, a published estimate of the economic clout of Philadelphia's four pro teams was a staggering US$500 million. "In the face of these widely varying estimates of expenditure benefits, the correct attitude is one of skepticism," says James Quirk, retired professor of economics at the California Institute of Technology.

Mostly, these number games have been the plaything of partisans, those arguing for public subsidization of a stadium or tax breaks for a team. But in the late '80s Chicago's Heartland Institute conducted a study of nine cities before and after acquiring a new team and/or a new stadium. In four cities the rate of growth of income increased after the arrival of a franchise or construction of the stadium; in five cities there was no discernible change. To add further perspective, the study compared these cities' income growth to that of the states in which they were situated. In seven of nine cases, the city's share in the state's income actually fell.

Expansion Zircons will create jobs in Fat City

Pro sports teams are slimly staffed compared to other businesses generating similar revenues. For teams building an arena, the argument strengthens; but again, the jobs are not permanent. Though 2,000 jobs might be created, they last only for the duration of construction. Jobs within the stadium tend to be part-time and seasonal.

Zircons' income taxes to help balance budget

With the NBA franchiser coming to Vancouver and Toronto, be mindful of the models provided by the Toronto Blue Jays and the Montreal Expos. Those teams' highest-paid employees, the players, do not pay Canadian income tax on their entire salaries. In fact, less than half their salaries are subject to our income tax. A bit more than half their salaries are subject to U.S. income tax because more than half the teams' games are played in the U.S.

Zircons break even first year, show loss in second

Owners of pro sports teams frequently claim hardship when it suits them; bookkeepers can make the numbers jump through hoops. "Anyone who quotes profits of a baseball team is missing the point," says Paul Beeston of the Toronto Blue

Jays. "Under generally accepted accounting principles I could turn a $4-million profit into a $2-million loss and get every national accounting firm to agree with me." Earl Weaver, the legendary former manager of baseball's Baltimore Orioles, doesn't buy it either. "I get sick of hearing about poor owners. Baseball owners today are happier than pigs in slop. They're making money hand-over-fist."

John Smith to buy Zircons and move team from Fat City

Sports valuator Timothy Mueller explains why the price of the Toronto and Vancouver NBA franchiser exceeds the going rate for many established teams: "Though it seems easy, moving a sports franchise from one city to another is incredibly complicated. Buying a team to move it is injudicious unless the purchaser has guarantees from all parties, including league officials."

Mayor cuts new deal for Fat City arena, keeps Zircons in town

As Tom Wilson, CEO of the Palace, home of the NBA's Detroit Pistons, puts it: "There's been a holdup."

Source: Gare Joyce is a Toronto freelancer who frequently writes about sports and business. The articles "Ball Control" and "Vancouver Hoops" are extracts from "Ball Control" which was originally published in *enRoute*, July 1994, pp.28-39. Reproduced with the permission of the author.

36.
Vancouver Hoops
Gare Joyce

The ambitions of Toronto's Professional Basketball Franchise Inc. are in some ways outstripped by those of Arthur Griffiths, the majority owner of the expansion franchise, going to Vancouver. His father, the late Frank Griffiths, a broadcast-media mogul who founded Western International Communications, purchased controlling interests in the NHL's Vancouver Canucks back in the mid-'70s. Frank's youngest son, Arthur, came aboard in the team's management while still in his twenties. Today he is vice the Cannucks' vice chairman and governor.

In an age when revenues from executive suites, concessions and parking are paramount, the Canucks' home, the publicly owned Pacific Coliseum, was woefully inadequate—15,600 seats and only 14 suites. A new arena was necessary, but the revenues from the Canucks alone could not drive the financing of a playhouse at a cost of $150 million. Thus began the drive to acquire another attraction, an NBA expansion team. Though a team name had not been selected at press time, "the Mounties" had long been bandied about, but ownership of the name was in dispute and the NBA, which has final approval on all such matters, probably wasn't too keen on such a benign name. Griffiths might consider "The Girders," for his team will figuratively and financially support the building it will play in.

Though the NBA's approval for Griffiths' group, Vancouver Basketball Management Inc., came a few months after the league gave the go-ahead for Toronto, the West Coast's expansion franchise is ahead of its eastern counterpart in one department. Construction is already under way for GM Place, a 20,000-seat stadium named for its corporate sponsor. Like Toronto, the Vancouver team figures to struggle on the court for a few seasons. But there are a few indicators that the franchise might do well on the business side: Griffiths' team already has orders for 7,000 season tickets.

37.

A Miami Fish Story

Andrew Zimbalist

Far from losing $30 million in '97, the Marlins made a hefty profit. So why did their owner destroy the team?

How could a baseball team in a major media market win the World Series and lose $34 million? The owner of the Florida Marlins, H. Wayne Huizenga, claims that's just what his team did last year. He hoped that his proclamation of penury would shame Broward and Miami-Dade Counties into building him a new, retractable-roof ball park. When it didn't, he went ballistic. Putatively to stop the team's financial bleeding, he conducted the most radical fire sale of players in baseball history, lowering the Marlins' payroll from $53 million in 1997 to $13 million in mid-July 1998 and leaving many baseball fans wondering exactly what Bud Selig was doing in the commissioner's office. At the same time, Huizenga tried to arrange a sale of the Marlins to his longstanding associate and team president, Don Smiley, for $169 million.

As the Marlins stumbled through this season, losing 108 games, Huizenga refused to provide any details about the team's 1997 finances. However, Smiley issued a confidential report on the team to prospective partners in his effort to complete the purchase. Smiley's "Private Placement Memorandum" reports a variety of financial information for 1997 as well as projections for 1998 and beyond. Based on these projections, payroll figures from Major League Baseball and my own calculation of ticket sales (actual attendance multiplied by the average ticket price), the picture for 1997 is presented in the chart on the following page.

These numbers suggest an operating loss of $29.3 million. Quibbling over a few million dollars aside, what's the problem? Did Huizenga's Marlins really lose around $30 million? Of course not. Huizenga is employing an accounting trick as familiar to sports franchise owners as Mark McGwire's home runs are to viewers of ESPN's SportsCenter.

Huizenga owns Pro Player Stadium and the team's cablecaster, Sportschannel Florida. Pro Player was built in 1987 and is amply stocked with all the revenue-generating accouterments of a modern sports facility. Yet there is no mention in the team's reported revenues of income from luxury boxes, even though Pro Player Stadium has 195 suites that rent for between $55,000 and $150,000 a year. Nor is there mention of income from club seats, although the stadium has 10,209 club seats selling for between $900 and $3,500 a year.

Bob Kramm, president of the stadium corporation, estimates that in 1997 an average of 65 luxury suites and 5,000 club seats per game were sold. Assuming that the average suite rented for $100,000 and the average club seat sold for $2,000, the gross revenue from these two sources would be $16.5 million. Huizenga attributes none of this revenue to the Marlins and all of it to his separate business entity, Pro Player Stadium.

Similarly, Huizenga sells naming rights to the stadium, worth by conservative estimates about $2 million a year. Since the stadium is shared with the N.F.L. Dolphins (also owned by Huizenga), let us attribute half of this value to the Marlins. Parking for approximately 788,000 cars during the baseball season at $5 a car in 1997 brought an estimated $3.9 million. Sales of signs and advertising at the park and in the team program produced an estimated $6 million. (The Cleveland Indians' signage and ad sales at Jacobs Field yielded $8.8 million in 1997 on an average attendance of about 44,000.) Sales of merchandise brought in something like $3 million in net income. (The Indians' figure was $4.5 million.) All told, that's $13.9 million in ball-park revenue attributed to the stadium company, not the Marlins.

Further, the revenue from concessions appears to be substantially understated. Fans spend an average of $10 on concessions, with about 40 percent of that going to the team. With total 1997 attendance of 2.4 million, the Marlmis' net concessions income should have been around $9.4 million. Yet the team is credited with only $1.8 million, a discrepancy of $7.6 million. In all, $38 million in revenues are credited to the stadium rather than the Marlins ($16.5 million from luxury and club seating, $7.6 million from concessions, $6 million from signage, $3.9 million from parking, $3 million from merchandise and $1 million from naming rights).

Even though the Marlins receive only a small portion of stadium revenue, they still are charged $5 million to cover "stadium expenses." These expenses presumably are used to pay off Huizenga's debt service on the county industrial bonds that he assumed when he purchased the park. The yearly service on this debt has been estimated at around $5 million, but since the stadium is also the home facility of the Dolphins and the site of special events throughout the year, the Marlins' share of this debt should be no more than half.

Huizenga plays the same game with Sportschannel. According to Smiley's prospectus, an independent appraiser estimated that the Marlins' contract with the cable station is undervalued by more than $2.1 million a year. Herein lies a powerful reason why Huizenga wanted to sell his team to Don Smiley. Huizenga's deal with Smiley included an extension of the Sportschannel contract through 2024. Under that contract, the Marlins were to receive rights fees well below market value. While that didn't help the Marlins, it increased the station's value from an estimated $85 million to $125 million.

Unfortunately for Huizenga, the deal fell through when Smiley's fund-raising efforts came up $50 million short. So in August Huizenga began to talk to John Henry, a Boca Raton commodities trader and minority owner of the New York Yankees. They reportedly have reached a deal for $150 million plus other considerations worth, by my calculations, about $50 million. But all is not lost. Apparently, Henry acceded to a 10-year extension of the Sportschannel contract.

Adding the $2.1 million in lost cable revenues to the $38 million in lost stadium revenues brings the total earned by–but not credited to–the Marlins in 1997 to $40.1 million. But that's not the end of it. Smiley's prospectus suggests "other" revenues of $10 million. No details are provided. In 1997 the Marlins beat the Indians in the seventh game of the World Series. The Indians reported net postseason ticket revenues of $6.8 million. Presumably this is part of the "other" $10 million for the Marlins.

Then there is roughly $2 million that comes from Major League Baseball Properties as licensing

	REVENUES *In millions*	COSTS *In millions*
Ticket sales	$23.9	
Payroll		$53.5
Broadcasting	$23.2	
Team Operations		$18.9
Concessions	$1.8	
Player Development		$5.1
Other	$10.0	
Scouting		$5.1
Latin American Operations		$0.6
Stadium Expenses		$5.0
TOTALS	**$58.9**	**$88.2**

and sponsorship income. This leaves only $1.2 million for all "other" sources of revenue: roughly 15 preseason games at the Marlins' publicly financed spring training ball park; special functions; net income from the team store in Fort Lauderdale (since closed) and so on. Finally, in the "Private Placement Memorandum" Smiley reports that he intends to lower general and administrative expenses by $3 million a year, suggesting there is that much padding in the current budget.

In short, if the Marlins financial statement is adjusted for related-party transactions and bloated costs, what appears to be a $29.3 million operating loss in 1997 becomes instead an operating profit of $13.8 million (adding $40.1 million in additional revenues and $3 million of bloated costs). Why else would Don Smiley, who as team president knows its financial predicament as well as anyone, have wanted to buy the team?

Why does Huizenga want to sell a profitable team? Perhaps the same reason he sold Blockbuster to Viacom: he can get a good price for it with a nice capital gain and he can control the terms of the deal to benefit his other holdings, including Sportschannel and the Pro Player Stadium corporation. Further, Huizenga has owned the Marlins since 1993 and by now has used up his player amortization allowance (a tax benefit that allows an owner to set aside up to 50 percent of franchise value and then depreciate this sum, usually over five years). Thus, the substantial tax-shelter value of the club is exhausted.

Meanwhile, the team finished the 1998 season with a payroll of $13 million. Seven million of this was from the insured contract of pitcher Alex Fernandez, who was on the disabled list all season. As such, the insurance company was responsible for at least 70 percent of the $7 million. So the actual payroll disbursements for the 1998 Marlins were probably below $10 million.

With average attendance at Pro Player down from 29,555 in 1997 to 22,157 in 1998, ticket revenue fell by around $6 million. Auxiliary stadium income also took a proportional hit, but the player payroll was down by more than $40 million—more than offsetting lower stadium income. Thus, Huizenga's Marlins were even more profitable losing in 1998 than they were winning in 1997.

Source: Andrew Zimbalist is Robert Woods Professor of Economics at Smith College in Northampton, Massachusetts. He has published 12 books and dozens of articles in the areas of sports and comparative systems economics and has consulted extensively in the sports industry. His latest book is *Unpaid Professionals: Commercialism and Conflict in Big-Time College Sports*, Princeton University Press, Fall 1999. This article was originally published in *The New York Times Magazine*, November 18, 1998, pp.26-30. Reproduced with the permission of the author.

38.

Can a Ballpark Figure?

Neil DeMause

The truth about public money and sports

It was the final indignity for "the World's Greatest Entertainment Centre." Last October, after a roller-coaster 10-year history that included a delayed opening, millions of dollars of debt, and a cut-rate sale by the Ontario government to private investors, the Toronto SkyDome had come to this: the Blue Jays, the baseball team that just five years earlier had celebrated a World Series Championship beneath SkyDome's retractable roof, were threatening to move out. They were taking tens of thousands of fans (and dollars) and going, not just anywhere, but to their old, unloved home, "the Ex." Exhibition Stadium: a stadium with no roof. No luxury boxes. With no seats, in fact, since it was targeted for demolition before the year was out. The Jays actually paid the city, which owns the Ex, $50,000 to stay the wrecking ball.

It was the unmistakable sign of the end of an era. But like so many sports teams' recent threats to move across town or across the continent, the Jays' threatened Ex-odus was a ploy—one that paid off in $72 million in lease concessions for the team a few weeks later. The revised lease would keep the team in the Dome for the next 10 years. But for SkyDome, at that point run by a private consortium that included the Jays' owner, Interbrew S.A., it also removed the last hope of paying its own bills, and the building's owners promptly filed for bankruptcy protection.

The decline and fall of the World's Greatest Entertainment Centre is an ironic cautionary tale of the excesses of 80's development, to be sure. But the current wrangling over the Dome—the Jays' move threats, the bankruptcy filing and subsequent sale at auction—is something more. In the 10 years since SkyDome opened, public subsidies to the sports industry have exploded, to the point where Ontario's $600-million retractable-roofed gift to the Blue Jays looks like a cheap stocking stuffer. Cities as large as New York and as small as

Mesa, Arizona, are contemplating stadium complexes priced at upwards of a billion dollars apiece. Seattle is already building a pair of stadiums totaling a billion dollars. And in Canada, even Victoria, British Columbia, has been the target of stadium demands, with the owner of a bankrupt minor-league hockey team demanding government loan guarantees for a $125-million, 12,500-seat arena as a condition of moving his franchise there.

And in Toronto, as the Dome's erstwhile bidders and new owners circle around the Dome's bankrupt body, there are signs that the looting of the public purse may not have ended.

At SkyDome's opening in June 1989, bankruptcy was the furthest thing from anyone's mind. The stands were filled, the start of a streak that would see hardly an empty seat for the next five years. Even better, the roof—three enormous panels of steel and plastic—opened and closed as advertised.

When city planners had first dreamed up what would become SkyDome in the early '80s, they had a clear vision of what they didn't want. It sat 300 miles to the northeast, in downtown Montreal: Olympic Stadium, Canada's monument to mismanagement. Its retractable roof (the world's first) was 12 years late in being installed, then promptly jammed shut. Meanwhile, in the push to ready the stadium for the 1976 Olympics, cost overruns and rush charges drove the building's cost to an astonishing $1 billion—a still unbroken record that earned Olympic Stadium the enduring nickname of the Big Owe.

Toronto's new stadium, its planners promised, would learn from the mistakes of Montreal, with an improved roof design, and, most importantly, a financial plan that would pay for itself. "Before debt service, the project will throw off something like $30 million in the first full calendar year," promised Chuck Magwood, president of Stadco, the Crown corporation formed to run SkyDome, shortly before the building's grand opening. In 10 years, he figured, that level of revenue could pay off the building's debt.

The good news lasted less than a year. By the time Bob Rae's NDP took power in October 1990, it had become clear that Magwood, who left

SkyDome shortly after its opening, had been unbelievably rosy in his predictions: operating profits from the Dome's first full year in business were a mere $17 million, while debt service amounted to $40 million. To fully pay off its annual debts, it was estimated, the Dome would have to be in use 600 days a year.

The stadium's exorbitant price tag was largely to blame, though what precisely sent those costs Sky-rocketing is something of an official mystery. Late-'80s grandiosity played a role, no doubt—in the midst of construction, Stadco abruptly decided to add a hotel and health club to the building, a move that tacked on an additional $112 million to the price. And as with Olympic Stadium, rush charges to meet the planned opening day (it missed anyway, by nearly two months) added costs.

None of these added charges were passed on to SkyDome's consortium of private investors—the 28 companies that kicked in $5 million apiece to construction costs as part of the Dome's much-ballybooed "public/private partnership." For that $5 million, investors gained ownership of one of the Dome's 161 Skyboxes—and, where applicable, preferential vending rights to the building. The exclusive rights earned some public criticism—especially when consortium member McDonald's turned out to be paying a low yearly fee and charging exorbitant prices for stadium food—but another element of the original deal may have been even more damaging to the public's interest.

Someone, at least, had foreseen the possibility of cost overruns gobbling up Dome profits; unfortunately for the public, it was corporate takeover king (and current senator) Trevor Eyton, head of the private consortium. "The arrangement [we] had was that assuming the stadium was completed satisfactorily, and the related debt was less than $165 million," the private companies would take partial ownership of the Dome, explains Eyton today. "As you well know, by the time SkyDome was completed, the debt was significantly ahead of $165 million, so we had no responsibility to form the joint venture that we had contemplated. That meant that the province had the stadium entirely, and we were off to the sidelines."

Unable to cover even interest payments on its bonds, Stadco (the Crown corporation) saw its staggering debt continue to rise, to nearly $400 million by the end of 1993. If a debt-ridden stadium was a liability, one whose debt load *grew* each year was an unacceptable one. In March 1994, the Rae administration finally paid off the remaining debt from the provincial treasury, then sold off SkyDome to a new consortium of private corporations (including Jays' owner Labatt, later purchased by Interbrew) for a bargain-basement price of $151 million. "It was important to get the Ontario taxpayer off the hook for a deal made by people I'd love to play poker with" commented then-Finance Minister Floyd Laughren at the time.

Just who were those people? Magwood headed the Crown corporation and so presumably had the authority to sign the cheques—an option he apparently exercised with impunity. As for who else was involved and how, even the experts appointed by Bob Rae to address the Dome's growing debt—University of Toronto Athletics Director Bruce Kidd, and then-Canadian Auto Workers president Bob White—can't shed much light. "We didn't look as much into the reasons for the cost overruns as we tried to solve the problems," explains Kidd. There was talk of a public inquiry, he says, but ultimately, "we thought it was more productive to just get out of the damn thing."

By the time the government finally rid itself of the Dome, the Ontario public had taken a $262.7-million bath.

It would be one thing if the Dome's story were an anomaly, the result of poor deal-making by a few individuals—and good deal-making by others. But stories like this have become all too familiar in the sports-stadium craze that's swept North America since SkyDome's opening. Today, there are plenty of contenders giving the Big Owe a run for its money. Seattle's new Safeco Field, originally tabbed at $320 million (U.S.), has already passed the $500-million mark on its way toward its July opening, the bulk of it paid by the people of Washington state. Milwaukee's Miller Park, originally budgeted at $250 million, is likewise nearing the half-billion-dollar mark, even as its opening has been delayed from 1999 to 2000.

There are several reasons for the exorbitant costs. Economic down times can cut into projected revenue; boom times can drive up the cost of construction. The sheer size of modern stadiums, which are packed with high-tech gadgetry and can easily take up two to three times the land area of a traditional ballpark, inevitably leads to exploding price tags. Perhaps most significantly, stadium builders tend to lowball estimates to get a project approved, confident that once a hole is dug and a foundation poured, no one will be willing to pull the plug. One stadium consultant recalls researching costs for an architect on a publicly funded minor-league ballpark project. When he pointed out that the team owners' exorbitant demands for luxury suites were driving the price up he was waved aside: "They really want to get this team," the architect explained. "They'll find the money." He added that strict economics were not a priority, because "public projects are always better funded than private ones."

Stadium boosters argue that these mammoth public investments have a broader payoff. The fans who crowd into a sports stadium or arena, they claim, also stay at local hotels, eat at local restaurants, and otherwise generate economic activity far beyond the ticket revenue earned by the building itself. But "generating spending" is a dodgy concept. If fans are spending money in and around a ballpark, many economists ask, where aren't they spending it? Might increased tax revenues for restaurants near a new stadium, say, be offset by a drop in other neighborhoods, as people save their consumer dollars for a night at the ball game? This "substitution effect" is almost never addressed in estimates of spin-off stadium spending. After consultants Ernst & Young conducted one particularly rosy economic analysis for the Expos, Hautes Études Commerciales economist François Richer remarked that the study assumed that if the Expos left town, "people who spent in relation to the team's presence in Montreal [would] put that money into their mattresses."

The body of independent economic studies—studies not paid for by sports teams or their political allies—backs him up. In what is probably the most comprehensive of these, Lake Forest College professor Robert Baade looked at 30 cities that had built stadiums or arenas over a 30-year period, and found no sign of an increased economic activity as a result. As far as job creation goes, stadium projects routinely clock it at well over $100,000 spent per full-time job—one of the worst ratios of any industry, and a figure that has prompted University of Chicago economist Allen Sanderson to remark that if the money were "dropped out of a helicopter over [your city], you would probably create eight to 10 times as many jobs."

So, who profited from SkyDome? True, for its $300 million, the Toronto public got a more modern stadium than the Ex, one sheltered from frigid April and October nights on the lakefront. But, as with many modern stadiums, most of the innovations were in selling things: cavernous concession areas and in-house restaurants, all priced for an upscale clientele. The Dome's $7 hotdogs would become internationally infamous. And even most of the stadium's lowest-priced tickets were twice as expensive as those at the Ex.

For the stadium's primary tenant, though, SkyDome was a windfall beyond belief. Spared the trouble of risking their own money on a stadium venture, the Jays were the envy of the baseball world, with a state-of-the-art ballpark packed to the rafters with money-making machinery. "I'd seen the ultimate marriage between government, which builds these facilities, and the corporations and the people who tie into them," then-Seattle Mariners owner Jeff Smulyan raved upon visiting SkyDome soon after its opening. "You take the suites, the signage, throw the media on top, and you have an economic juggernaut."

Indeed, even as SkyDome and its provincial backers swam in red ink, the Blue Jays were on top of the baseball world, raking in World Series championships and record profits alike. In 1989, the year SkyDome opened, the Jays saw their gross revenues double, with yearly attendance topping a then-incredible 4 million. Team owner Labatt was launched into baseball's elite as the team's value soared to an estimated $180 million, ranked behind only the New York Yankees and Dallas Cowboys in all of pro sports. All this for consortium member Labatt's single $5-million

private investment share in the Dome, the same put up by McDonald's for the concessions rights.

But in the sports stadium biz, even sweetheart deals have a limited honeymoon period. Smith College economist Andrew Zimbalist, author of the book *Baseball and Billions*, estimates a new stadium's term at the top of the heap at somewhere between three and 10 years, depending on the team's performance. If all goes well, he says, the team can use the increased ticket revenues to buy better players; more success on the field translates into more fan interest, and keeps ticket sales high. It's that simple—but there is a limit. "[Eventually,] there will be a new tier of stadiums above yours that will be able to earn more money, and will enable those teams to draw the better players," he says.

For SkyDome, "eventually" came sooner rather than later. Within two years of SkyDome's opening, Baltimore introduced its Oriole Park at Camden Yards, an artful blend of exposed steel and luxury club seating bankrolled by a pair of state lotteries. It sent ballpark architects back to their drawing boards, and Oriole revenues soaring into the stratosphere. (Not coincidentally, the Jays' star second baseman Roberto Alomar left for the Orioles a few years later.) Two years after that, Cleveland's Jacobs Field opened, with still more exposed steel and luxury seating. From there, teams everywhere threatened that the new sports palaces would leave them uncompetitive or force them to move, and largely credulous local governments plunked down the money. In the 1980s, less than $2 billion in public money had been spent on stadiums in North America; in the following decade, that figure would top $11 billion.

In 1994, the year SkyDome turned five, new tourist-friendly ballparks opened in Cleveland and Texas; the Jays went from World Series champion to division cellar-dweller—and baseball went on strike, wiping out a third of the season and sending fan interest into a nosedive from which it's only now recovering. For the Jays, this meant dwindling revenues at a time when other teams' lucrative new playpens were flooding the sport with money, driving up the price of player contracts. The Jays now couldn't afford to bid for new stars to replace older and retired players. Last year, they claimed to have lost a whopping $40 million. And though there's some reason to be skeptical of the figure—Zimbalist recently calculated that the Florida Marlins' claims of $34-million yearly losses were actually hiding a $14-million profit, and Interbrew's ownership of the Jays' TV outlet, TSN, leaves plenty of room for similar bookkeeping—it's clear that the Blue Jays' days among baseball's economic elite are behind them.

So, with their 10-year lease at SkyDome expiring and their four division rivals either residing in or negotiating new ballparks, the Jays played the Ex card. If the threat made for plenty of public snickering, it also landed Interbrew (which has 90 percent ownership of the Jays) what it was looking for: a new 10-year lease that would redirect an estimated $72 million from SkyDome to the baseball team over the next decade. (At press time, there were conflicting reports on whether that lease will still stand when the new owners take over.) That Interbrew itself owns half of the stadium was no obstacle—when you are talking about tens of millions of dollars, better to get (almost) all the money than just half.

The same week as the new lease with the Jays was announced, SkyDome filed for bankruptcy protection.

To hear SkyDome's outgoing CEO Patrick McDougall tell it, the Dome's dire straits (even with its debt load reduced by half, to $151 million, the stadium is still losing money) are a result of low exchange rates and high taxes. The exchange rate, he says, affects ball players' salaries, as well as prices for musical acts and other imports from the U.S. "Also, the tax situation is quite strenuous here—we pay in excess of $12 million in [property] taxes a year."

But many sports economists openly wonder whether any large stadium can be made profitable, no matter how little you spend on it. According to Allan Sanderson, the United Center in Chicago, which is privately financed (not counting some hidden tax breaks) comes close. "You can make a closer go of it there because you've got a hockey team and a basketball team, and a circus and an ice show and an Elton John concert." But most stadium owners with one main

sports team tenant are left in an impossible negotiating position. "The cartel element is that any money you potentially could have made, [the sports teams] extract from you up front as a condition for coming there, or as a condition for not leaving. At that point, you're pretty much indifferent whether they break your left arm or your right arm." As for a domed stadium with 60,000 or 70,000 seats, "there's almost no price at which one of these things would pay."

That hasn't stopped municipalities from continuing to sing the praises of the stadium-enhanced economy—and governments from buying (literally) into them with sports subsidies. U.S. tax subsidies to pro sports teams are thought to amount to nearly as much as the $1 billion in annual direct cash payouts for stadium construction. Hidden tax breaks such as business entertainment tax deductions for luxury suites are estimated at another billion. (San Francisco's new "privately financed" Pacific Bell Park will receive $15 million in property tax breaks.)

Tax breaks are now on top of Canadian sports teams' policy agendas too: since two hockey teams, the Quebec Nordiques and the Winnipeg Jets, left for greener pastures in Denver and Phoenix, respectively, some quarters are increasingly clamoring for Canada to catch up to its southerly neighbour in this area. The owners of the Expos have demanded "creative solutions"—$150-million worth—toward their dream of a new open-air ballpark, and so far have been rebuffed by the government of Quebec. Several Canadian hockey teams, including the Edmonton Oilers and Ottawa Senators, have demanded government bailouts in the form of free rent, tax breaks and tax-exempt bonds, to prevent them from bolting across the border. MP Dennis Mills' Sub-Committee on the Study of Sport in Canada, in its final report last December, recommended extending a 10-percent tax credit on pro teams' first $50 million in revenues. (The government has until April to formulate a response.)

Ironically, Canadian teams are trying to match American subsidies just when many U.S. politicians and community activists are making headway in eliminating them. Last year saw a nine-month span in which five consecutive U.S.

stadium deals were rejected overwhelmingly at the polls–despite backers' multimillion-dollar ad campaigns. Citizen activist groups are continuing to challenge stadium plans in Boston, Hartford, and elsewhere. And tax-exempt bonds, a gimmick that effectively allows U.S. teams to artificially lower stadium construction costs at the federal government's expense, may soon be eliminated by Congress. (They're a stated priority of Canadian sports teams.)

A less-publicized–some would say more constructive–recommendation of the Mills committee was to explore challenging U.S. sports subsidies as a violation of NAFTA. It's a tactic that the U of T's Bruce Kidd, for one, endorses whole-heartedly. "What Canadians should be doing, instead of digging deep to level that playing field, is taking advantage of the provisions of the free trade agreement to say, this is unfair subsidization, and it should be eliminated–the same way the Americans in the case of lumber and wheat, and a number of other products, say Canadian subsidies are unfair," Kidd says.

Meanwhile, it was business as usual at Sky-Dome–with one notable exception. A surprise bidder had joined the fray. In an effort to take a public investment back to the public, Toronto city councillors Jack Layton and Dennis Fotinos had brought forward a motion calling for the city to expropriate the Dome. The motion promised the owners "fair compensation" (though it wasn't clear yet if that meant full market value.) As this issue went to press, it was still waiting to be heard. "It's time the taxpayers of Toronto and Ontario gained control over a facility that they have mostly paid for," Layton said in a public statement.

The rationale of an expropriation motion is simple enough. But whether a public owner can succeed in turning the Dome into a viable venture, where others before it have failed, is anybody's guess. For someone like Kidd, who spent four years trying to unload SkyDome, that's the last thing in the world he'd like to see. "I'm greatly relieved that this is not a public responsibility," he says. "That needs to be said over and over and over and over again. When homelessness is a huge issue, when we need to restore the public sector in so many ways–housing, health, education, and so on–the people of Ontario need not to be concerned about the fortunes of one sector of the entertainment industry."

For now, SkyDome's fate rests in the hands of its new owners, Sportsco, the private group headed by Pat Gillick, former general manager of the Blue Jays. Sportsco, which had offered $100 million for the Dome in December and been rejected by its owners, was recommended as the winning bidder by the bankruptcy court.

Sportsco beat out Interbrew, who was hoping to gain full ownership with its own bid. The implications of Sportsco's takeover aren't lost on either bidder. When Sportsco emerges the official winner in March, it could use its possession of the stadium as leverage to buy the Jays themselves, much as Robert Kraft did with the New England Patriots. Kraft bought the team's stadium in Foxboro, Massachusetts in 1988, then imposed such onerous lease conditions that the team's owners sold him the Patriots at a reduced price. (Kraft later abandoned his initial prize, parlaying it into promises of a $375-million publicly financed stadium in Hartford, Connecticut.) On the other hand, it wouldn't be an unprecedented move for the team owner, Labatt, to simply seek out a new (government-subsidized) stadium for its stars. Either way, the end of "SkyDome" (Sportsco has already announced plans to rename the ill-fated stadium), could mark a new era for both athletes and fans.

Source: Neil DeMause is co-author, with Joanna Cagan, of *Field of Schemes: How the Great Stadium Swindle Turns Public Money into Private Profit*. This article was originally published in *This Magazine*, March/April 1999, pp.17-23. Reproduced with the permission of the author.

39.

The Ski Cabin and the Private Box

Laura Robinson

Public funding of pro sport is a multimillion-dollar affirmative action program for men

I am writing this from inside the cabin built by the Georgian Bay Nordic Ski Club at the base of the Bruce Peninsula in Ontario. The cabin is situated on Grey-Sauble Valley Conservation Authority land, with ski trails that branch out from its front door. Each year the owners of adjacent parcels of land sign agreements with the ski club, giving the club a path of access through the land and responsibility for anything that may happen while we are skiing on it. Thousands of people–club members and day users–have skied this winter land, kicking and gliding through a relationship built on trust and 22 years of good intentions.

The day is clear and bright with temperatures hovering around the freezing mark–difficult for waxing, and dangerous for parts of the ski trail exposed to the glorious sunshine that makes Nordic skiing even more fun than it already is. Earlier my friend Sarah and I transferred snow from the woods onto a partially bare slope called "the Chute" so people wouldn't come flying down a ridge only to find themselves stopped dead by warmed-up dirt. Like the collective labour that built the cabin, our little contribution to the trail comes out of an overwhelming belief in this club that sport, physical activity and the great outdoors belong to all of us. The club provides me with beautiful trails, interesting people and a warm cabin. In return I pay my $25 annual fee, instruct when the club asks me to, and cover up bare spots if need be. The landowners receive a free membership and are content with the pleasure of knowing they contribute to the good health and happiness of other human beings.

When finally I must return to Toronto, I leave behind one of the best and simplest models of sport that works, only to trade it for a place where a colossal monument was built to house a few dozen men who play three sports, and can't even be counted on doing that well. This cement fortress, better known as the SkyDome, has had hundreds of millions of public dollars spent on it, and at the time of writing needs bankruptcy protection. Here in a nutshell is the saga of the SkyDome, also known as "the world's greatest entertainment centre":

- 1983: Ontario and Metropolitan Toronto contribute $60 million towards an original construction price tag estimated at $235 million. Paul Godfrey, then Metro Toronto's chair, persuades then-premier Bill Davis to shell out the money. It's the start of a long-term insider relationship with the SkyDome on the part of Godfrey and Senator Trevor Eyton. Private investors who purchase $5 million in shares receive contracts for monopolies on goods and services that are much more expensive than the SkyDome could have negotiated on its own.

- 1989: Costs skyrocket to $580 million when the stadium opens and Ontario taxpayers are stuck with a debt of $321 million, which they are legally bound to pay thanks to a sweetheart deal with the owners. Private investors receive control of revenue, while the province is responsible for the stadium's debt.

- 1994: The government sells the stadium for $151 million, and Eyton and Godfrey are first in line for the bargain-basement price.

- 1996: The SkyDome pays $15 million to the Bitove Corporation–owned by Steve Bitove, another insider–and takes over catering to the boxholders after years of complaints of overpricing.

- October 1998: The SkyDome owes the Ontario government approximately $25 million. After the stadium does not pay its property taxes, the province declares it may exercise its collection right. The stadium's $100 million debt, much of it accumulated over the last three years, includes approximately $70 million owed to insurance companies who purchased bonds when money was borrowed to finance the $151 million purchase in 1994.

- November 1998: Owners seek bankruptcy protection and receive an emergency $3.5 million loan from their major tenants, the Toronto Blue Jays, who are also in debt. The agreement puts the Jays ahead of all others in terms of repayment. Eyton and Godfrey quietly resign from the stadium's board of directors just after the news breaks. Meanwhile, immediate repairs and renovations to the SkyDome will cost more than $1.3 million.

- December 1998: More than $1.2 million is owed in back taxes to the City of Toronto. A new investment group offers $100 million for the SkyDome, but infighting among creditors and owners opens up the market and more bids are expected. By mid-December, an Ontario Court judge issues an order to sell the SkyDome at auction. Credit protection continues until January 29, 1999, to ensure an open bidding process. The winner will be announced in March.

- 1999: Leases on 124 of 161 private boxes come due. The last year's rent was paid ten years ago, so that there is next to no income during the last year of the lease. The boxes had brought in $1-2.5 million each to the SkyDome, but now the Blue Jays want an increased share of revenue from new leases.

- 2001: The JumboTron will need to be replaced. It cost S17 million in 1988.

The SkyDome's major tenant, the Toronto Blue Jays, aren't in much better shape. From the early 1990s when four million fans would watch the jays each year, support dwindled to 2.4 million in the 1998 season. The team estimates that since 1993 it has lost US$100 million. In 1998 alone, the *Toronto Star* reported, the Jays lost almost US$40 million. Even if the team added 10,000 fans per game, raising averages from 30,000 to 40,000, it would still lose money.

In the fanciful economics of pro sport, a team that loses money over the short term can still be sold at a profit later on. This increase in worth is based not on athletic performance, but on the mythology attached to masculinity and athletic triumph in our culture. This myth is regularly jarred by reality–from Ben Johnson testing positive for dope to O.J. Simpson being tried for murder to the Salt Lake City Olympic bid committee and International Olympic Committee members being caught up in fraud charges. In the case of the Blue Jays, the unpleasant reality checks have so far been of a lesser order.

José Canseco appeared in the lineup after being convicted of aggravated assault on his wife in California. Blue Jays management was silent about the issue, and offered him a $2-million contract. In October 1998, manager Tim Johnson finally admitted all the talk about killing women and children in Vietnam used to "motivate" his players were tall tales. He didn't go to Vietnam. The Blue Jays have forgiven Johnson and kept him on.

In December 1998, it was revealed that former Blue Jays president Paul Beeston "wrote in" illegal side agreements to Roger Clemens's contract. Just before this, Clemens transformed himself from a heels-dug-in stickler who insisted on being traded to a magnanimous guy who suddenly wanted to stay in Toronto. Beeston will be fined by baseball commissioner Bud Selig. Clemens, it appears, will stay.

Toronto is not alone in pouring huge amounts of money into the black hole of pro sport. It's a North America-wide phenomenon. If Canadians want to be competitive with the United States and have a team or two of men in each large city who collectively make hundreds of millions of dollars, then we'll have to cough up the cash to keep them. And as the sums involved snowball and the bills for yesterday's follies such as the SkyDome come due, keeping the cash flowing is an increasingly delicate political task. At the federal level, this task has been taken on energetically by MP Dennis Mills, chair of the House of Commons Sub-Committee on the Study of Sport in Canada.

In his recent report *Sport in Canada: Everybody's Business*, Mills recommended that a "sport pact be initiated to protect, enhance and promote the vitality and stability of professional sport in Canada." This pact would include 100 percent write-offs for small businesses that buy pro sport tickets and private boxes in stadiums; rebates of up to 10 percent for teams paying a net of $30 million in combined taxes to all three levels of government; a Canada-U.S. tax equalization plan for professional athletes; and a relaxation of immigration standards for individuals and their families involved in the professional sports industry.

Sports journalists tend to overlook the fact that Mills is the father of Craig Mills, who plays hockey for the Chicago Black Hawks, and also the governor of a major junior team in the Ontario Hockey League with an annual budget of $750,000. The team is the Toronto St. Michael's Majors, based at a prestigious all-boys Catholic school. Mills refused to give me the names of the nine investors who bought the CHL franchise for a fee of 1.5 million, but he did say that most of them consider the fee a contribution to St. Mike's. According to Mills, these men will not ask for their money back if the school sells the team, preferring to reinvest the profits in the school. If their motives are as altruistic as Mills suggests, it's a significant donation—with no tax rebate—to an institution that caters to boys only. Mills believes fervently that "junior hockey builds fine upstanding citizens," though he forgot to mention that girls are not allowed on these teams, and can only watch while young men play.

Bill Davis, who as premier inaugurated the province of Ontario's involvement in the SkyDome, takes a similar approach. When asked by the *Toronto Star* why any public funds should go to professional sports franchises, Davis replied, "The Science Centre was publicly funded. The Royal Ontario Museum was publicly funded. The Art Gallery of Ontario was too, as is the general arts community. Culture has many aspects. Sport is also part of our culture." Like Mills, Davis upholds a version of the sporting culture that includes only the wearers of jockstraps. When he listed the other organizations that receive government funds, he forgot to add that they are nonprofit, charge only a few bucks for admission, and ultimately must be publicly accountable for all their actions. They could do better, but they have made efforts in recent years to recognize the role women play in culture and to eradicate the previous "museumization" of people of colour and First Nations.

The world of male pro sport does not worry about such inconsequential details. While Mills's report endorses more equitable treatment of girls and women in sport, it does not recommend any enforcement mechanism to ensure that this happens. Only two pages of the 137-page report are devoted to this subject. We are given no guarantee that the owners of publicly funded stadiums and arenas will do anything but blow all the money that comes their way—still less that they will free up ice surfaces and ball diamonds for girls and women.

Ironically, the economic and political ethos among the men who run the world of pro sport is highly laissez-faire: let market forces determine all, and to hell with everything and everyone else. But when it comes to their baby—the very male world of professional sport—it's one big affirmative action program for men, paid for by you and me. Such are the paradoxes of this particular culture. These men also exercise what could be called soft love. They may take a law-and-order stance towards lawbreakers outside the sacrosanct doors of the sports arena, but boys will be boys. What's a beaten-up woman or two, a fantasy motivational speech about civilian murders and an illegal contract compared to what these swell guys do for a world-class city that houses the world's greatest entertainment centre? And as I said, it's not just Toronto.

The citizens of Edmonton may use other adjectives to describe Hogtown, but they too have used public funds to save their beloved NHL team, the Oilers, from being bought by Americans who have access to countless millions of taxpayers' dollars. The Coliseum that houses the Oilers is part of an area called Edmonton Northlands—an organization and geographical location that first started as a nonprofit agricultural society 123 years ago. Today the Northlands is a quasi-publicly owned, quasi-nonprofit entity that includes the Coliseum, the AgriCom (used mainly for trade shows), a race track, and buildings called the Sportex, the Silver Slipper and the Golden Garter. All of these installations are located on city-owned land.

Much of the activity in the area began with the addition of the Oilers in the 1970s, along with a deluge of demands on the public purse from Peter Pocklington, the owner of the team. In the early 1990s as players' salaries began to increase, Pocklington informed the country that he wasn't going to pay the $2.8 million annual rent to Northlands. He had already traded Edmonton's standard-bearer and greatest player ever, Wayne Gretzky, crying poverty as the impetus for his actions. Eventually the City of Edmonton and Northlands agreed that he could have all the revenues from the building's events, except for Klondike Days and the Canadian Finals Rodeo Championships, if he would pay the $2.8 million out of those revenues.

This, of course, was not good enough, and Pocklington eventually obtained a deal in which he paid no rent at all. Instead, fans paid a new ticket surcharge ($2 per ticket by 1994), which was passed on to Northlands in lieu of rent. Now the Oilers' home ice was 100 percent subsidized by the people of Edmonton, and yet Pocklington continued to bemoan the unfairness of it all. By this time all three levels of government had kicked in $5 million each in improvements to the Coliseum, but Pocklington started making noises about selling the team.

At the same time, Pocklington was being investigated after he repeatedly missed payments on a $120 million loan from the Alberta Treasury Branches. At the present time Pocklington is suing the Branches, saying that they plotted to put him into receivership and that they don't have a charter to exist in the first place. Pocklington's financial tentacles are long and tangled, and we may never know how much of this public money went to the Oilers and how much went to his other interests such as the unionbusting Gainers Meats and Fidelity Trust.

At the last minute the Oilers were bought by a group of more than 30 individuals, each of whom put in a contribution of $1 million or more for a total of $75 million. This amount has been written against what Pocklington owed the Treasury Branches, and the tale will continue to unfold in courtrooms and arenas, as the new owners also benefit from continuing concessions from the city and Northlands.

Economic considerations alone do not explain why men pay for the privilege of losing money, or why we support these men with public funds. Today's professional sport is the latest chapter in the history of the male athletic body, a history that reaches back beyond ancient Greece and the first Olympic Games. Piled on top of this body are the ghosts of all the earthly battles men have fought and the shadow of those yet to come. It's a very emotionally charged body for any man who believes masculinity and power are related to physical strength and athletic prowess.

For many men who have painful memories of their youth, the male athletic body takes the form of the guy back in the schoolyard who automatically got to choose who would be on his team. Other boys silently assumed and deferred to his leadership, praying he would cast a glance in their direction and give that wordless nod of approval that meant they could join him, if only for 15 minutes at recess. They could stand by him and be a teammate—a chosen one, basking in his radiant maleness.

Now a new group of men, a group whose status is defined by wealth, gets to choose the team. Those who never got to be captain, who waited with desperation to receive the silent nod, are now in charge. For all those boys who grew up feeling as if this magic mythology somehow excluded them, and who went on to join the other male clubs of the financially powerful and politically connected, a boyhood dream can come true. They can finally be part of the team. And when there isn't enough private wealth to sustain their dream, their friends in government will pitch in. As any plastic surgeon will tell you, in this world money can buy you a new ending.

Women and their bothersome demands for equal access to ice and fields, and salaries and divorces, don't inhabit this world. The only kind of man in this world is a man's man. The sports arena allows men to be physically close to one another in ways that our society disallows in any other venue. The hugs (in the stands or on the field), the bumpatting, the sharing of physical space—all these are celebrations of what York University sports history professor Greg Malszecki refers to as the "homosocial" culture of the sports arena.

In this world, a man can entertain in his own private box, go to practices and be waved through by staff, invite athletic men over for barbecues and play charity golf tournaments with them. Politicians and star athletes alike return his calls, and warm the seats next to him at games. He can wear a team jacket or an Italian silk suit, and take calls on his cellphone at rinkside. Such a man matters. The overlooked little boy on the sidelines, now grown up, has an unquenchable need for membership, and this is what we are paying for when the owners of our SkyDomes and Coliseums come calling with their empty change purses opened wide.

It's a new day on the ski trail, with a high of -16. The snow has been falling nonstop since the day after Sarah and I patched up the Chute, but the sun is shining now and everyone is skiing. Two guys who have finished skiing nail the last of an aluminum covering over the wiring that runs at the base of the cabin. Now they consider it a finished building at $20,000 in materials, and plenty of sweat.

I ask them to name the starting lineup of the Toronto Blue Jays. "Pardon?" they reply. Neither has a clue. One finally mentions he thinks Roger Clemens plays for them. I spend the next 25 kilometers of skiing doing a survey of each skier I meet. "Can you name the starting lineup of the Blue Jays?" Clemens, Canseco and one other guy I can't remember, because I don't know them either, are the only names anyone here can summon.

These people care deeply about sport. They dedicated the autumn to building this cabin —before it we skied with no shelter at all. There are as many women as men on these trails, and plenty of kids. People can ski as fast or as slow as they want. Some stop for a moment and watch the racers training—in lycra suits they look as graceful as ballerinas as they fly among the trees, breathing in time with the rhythm of quick heart. Perhaps the spectators become inspired and shuffle along at a slightly faster pace. Or perhaps they just appreciate the beautiful combination of the finely tuned human body moving with nature, unencumbered by entertainment centres, private boxes, private deals, and men who have an insatiable need to make the team.

Source: Laura Robinson is a former national-level cyclist and cross-country ski racer. She is the author of two books about sport, *She Shoots, She Scores: Canadian Perspectives on Women and Sport* and *Crossing the Line: Violence and Sexual Assault in Canada's National Sport*. This article was originally published in *The Canadian Forum*, March 1999, pp.14-18. Reproduced with the permission of the author.

40.

Citizens, Cities and Sports Teams

Philip White, Peter Donnelly and John Nauright

Sport spectators as citizens

Ice hockey has been called "the Canadian specific"—*the* metaphor for Canada. Hockey, and to a lesser extent football, are ritual activities that have brought Canadians together as an imagined community—as players, officials, spectators, television viewers or radio listeners. The professional and amateur versions of hockey and football form a seasonal calendar of belongingness that affects how many Canadians shape their sense of who they are as a people and who they have been in the past.

Following World War II and the construction across Canada of numerous, and oftennamed "Memorial" arenas, hockey became one of the main focal points of civic communities. Following another spate of "Centennial" arena building in 1967, in larger towns and cities, professional sport franchises became symbols of the community as a whole. Sport, it seems, is powerfully linked to civic, regional and national representativeness. A sense of belonging to a community is often an emotional issue that can be linked to nostalgic perceptions about what the world used to be like—a world thought, correctly or incorrectly, to have been closer, warmer, more personal and more stable.

In the case of hockey, the past is constantly invoked to impart a sense of continuity to the culture of the game. The drama of Paul Henderson's winning goal in the 1972 Canada-Soviet Union series, or of Bobby Orr's diving Stanley Cup winning goal, are deeply etched into Canada's social memory. Because of this legacy in contemporary Canada, playing or watching hockey at all levels still has a tendency to make people "feel" Canadian. Football is also connected with national identity, despite the history of its English origins and its American-influenced modifications. There is a nationalist sense of ownership for the "Canadian" version of football. Until the late 1960s, Canadians held many prominent positions on CFL teams and the Grey Cup was one of the major events on the annual sporting calendar.

Recently there has been growing concern about an erosion of interest in football, and about the Americanization of both football and hockey. The process through which this has occurred is primarily associated with the complex social and cultural changes resulting from "globalization," and with a related ambivalence among Canadians toward American cultural products. The current popularity of Major League Baseball and the National Basketball Association in Canada's major cities, and the large crowds attracted to the occasional National Football League exhibition game held in Canada, speaks volumes about the appeal of American cultural products for many Canadians. Conversely, many of those same Canadians, whose national identity is often defined as being that which is "not American," advocate protective policies, subsidization or other structures of ownership as viable ways to protect professional hockey and football in Canada.

Free trade, debt reduction, the instantaneous transfer of capital and ideas about the need to be "globally competitive" have resulted in crises of identity, and have placed countries, provinces and cities in competitive relationships. Identity crises have brought the local and the global into conflict, resulting in a type of wilfully nostalgic attempt to hold on to cultural products that are deemed to "define" a community or a country. In this time of rapid social, cultural and political-economic changes, Canadians are drawing on elements of their past cultural identity in order to cope with perceived or real instability. Recollections can help reconstruct the past as a time when the world was more stable and organized, and when people had more individual or collective power. Competition between cities has resulted in increasingly zealous bids to host "hallmark events" such as World Fairs and the Olympics, and to attract professional sport franchises so that a city may be identified as "world class."

Canadian identity has been affected by both the ambivalence about the appeal of American culture and uncertainties about the long-term relationship of the province of Quebec to Canada as a nation. In recent years, as part of this debate, there has been some discussion about the extent to which sport has had, and continues to have, cultural significance for national identity. In the 1990s this relationship has come under increasing scrutiny with: the Americanization of the NHL (through relocation of the league offices to New York, the appointment of an American commissioner and expansion into American "sunbelt" markets), and its clear globalizing ambitions; abortive attempts to locate CFL teams in U.S. cities; and frequent rumours about the financial woes of Canadian sport franchises. Recently, the Québec Nordiques and the Winnipeg Jets of the NHL relocated to the U.S. cities of Denver and Phoenix respectively, and the Edmonton Oilers and Ottawa Senators are reporting the type of financial problems that resulted in the relocation of Québec and Winnipeg. These developments have elicited some concern. Canadian social critic Rick Salutin, for example, argued that: "In a general sense hockey is one of the few things that make this place coherent.... Here there's a sense that the country is falling apart. With free trade, the threat of Quebec separation, issues of national sovereignty, hockey assumes a sense of national loss."

Despite the intense cultural significance of sport, and state involvement in other realms of culture, the use of public funds to subsidize professional sport franchises has been a contentious issue. On the one hand it is argued that subsidizing professional sport teams is consistent with other government subsidies of, for example, amateur spoil and high culture. On the other hand it is argued that professional hockey is not important enough to warrant public subsidy. As Jim Carr of the *Winnipeg Free Press* argued, when the future of the Jets was in the balance, "It is the Winnipeg Jets–a hockey team–that is leaving the city, not our hearts and souls." Arguments about the use of public funds are particularly problematic at a time of high unemployment and massive cuts to social programmes.

The future of the Jets was even debated on the editorial pages of *The Globe and Mail*: "One could argue that hockey is the national game, that it enriches our culture and reflects our experience, even that it promotes unity in a country with very few shared values." Beyond the media, the anxiety among Canadian political elites was reflected in the fact that NHL Commissioner Gary Bettman, and the respective owners of the Québec Nordiques and the Winnipeg Jets, Marcel Aubut and Barry Shenkarow, were summoned to Ottawa to confer with Federal Human Resources Minister Lloyd

Axworthy and Finance Minister Paul Martin to discuss the failing franchises. This was an unprecedented move in the relations between the NHL and the Canadian federal government.

The current financial crisis of several CFL and NHL franchises, and the loss of the Winnipeg Jets and Québec Nordiques has had a negative impact on local, regional and national confidence. Many Canadians, from a variety of backgrounds, reacted emotionally to the potential loss of "their" team, even if they were not paying customers. Local sport franchises, like many other symbols that promote feelings of collectivity, often seem to be taken for granted until their existence is threatened (e.g., the campaigns to "save" various CFL teams—Ottawa, Hamilton, Winnipeg, Calgary, etc.). Which raises the question of the implications for Canadians of the Americanization and potential globalization of the NHL, and the ongoing Americanization of the CFL. What options, if any, do Canadians have in order to reserve their cultural products?

The American style of sport has become the international benchmark for corporate sport— "show-biz," spectacular, high scoring or record-setting superstar athletes, the ability to attract sponsors by providing desired audiences, the ability to attract high-paying audiences by providing new stadia or arenas with luxury accommodations, and by having the characteristics necessary for "good" television coverage. We now have the spread of marketing practices and business structures in sport that are often U.S. in origin but are now being applied everywhere and, when they are effective, serve to obscure national origins and render them irrelevant.

The league-franchise system, corporate ownership and transnational investment capital have tended to obscure ideas of community and local ownership. Alternatives to corporate ownership are rarely proposed despite their obvious success for several Western Canadian teams in the CFL and for the current Superbowl Champions in the U.S., the Green Bay Packers. When Winnipeg media were boosting a "Save the Jets" fundraising campaign to raise $140 million to build a new arena, a local radio station informed Doug Smith that money raised would also be used to buy the team. When he asked if a donation would mean he owned part of the team, he was told no, the current owner (Shenkarow) would still maintain control. Several

recent studies have shown how the desire by cities to become "world class" by having a professional sport franchise has rendered them susceptible to "blackmail" by team owners. Tax-funded stadia built for private use, tax holidays and other deals are used to transfer public funds to private hands, all with questionable economic justifications regarding job creation, the way in which a "big league image" will attract other businesses to the city, and the "damage" to an economy that would result from the loss of a team.

Community ownership as an alternative may resolve some of the concerns regarding identity and cultural loss that are raised by the economic woes of CFL teams and the uncertainty of NHL teams in smaller communities such as Ottawa, Edmonton and Calgary. Nauright and Phillips have outlined several Australian alternatives to the private ownership model that pervades North America. These include:

- *Membership-based clubs*: Club members democratically elect a board, who employ professional managers and coaches to run the team. This model provides some control to club members on major decisions, and ensures accountability on the part of board members and employees. Nauright and Phillips have documented several examples where clubs have been able to fend off, through democratic and community action, attempts to move or merge a team.

- *Shareholders:* The best example of public ownership is the Green Bay Packers of the NFL. Some 1,800 shareholders own 4,700 shares, 90 percent of them live in the Green Bay area, and no individual may own more than 200 shares. This is the only publicly owned team in the NFL.

- *Combined membership and shareholding:* Several membership-based clubs have staved off financial crises by selling shares. In one case there was a stipulation that no individual or group of shareholders could own more than 10 percent of the shares.

Since there is little recent precedent for membership-based clubs in Canada, the shareholders model makes more sense, but it could be employed eventually to develop a membership-based model. It is likely that any alternative would be resisted by the leagues who obviously prefer a private owner-ship model. However, a community ownership/shareholder model would be ideal for the CFL, and the various campaigns to save fran-chises and generate season ticket sales suggest that supporters of the teams would delight in owning a share of their team. Appropriate restrictions could be imposed to ensure community ownership and prevent large blocks of shares accumulating in too few hands.

It is also likely that such a model would be popu-lar with hockey fans, although it might be best implemented in a Canadian professional league first before attempting to take on the NHL. How-ever, Peter Pocklington–owner of the Edmonton Oilers, and notorious for selling Wayne Gretzky to the Los Angeles Kings–has recently opened the door to the possibility of public ownership in the NHL. As a current alternative to selling or moving the team to a U.S. city, he has announced a sale of 40 percent of the team in a public share offering. Of course, control is maintained at this time–but it is interesting to speculate how a shareholders' meet-ing might have reacted to the sale of Wayne Gretzky!

Two fundamental principles of public broadcast-ing–guaranteed diversity and universal *accessibility* –would then appear to apply in the case of commu-nity and public ownership of sport teams. Alternative ownership structures would have the potential for generating diversity from the perva-sive Americanized/globalized pattern of modern sport–producing a wider range of sport(s) genres, products and practices.

Accessibility would counter the restrictive effects of privatized corporate ownership, and produce live sports events sympathetic to Canadian sport audiences. More importantly, in a reformulated relationship between citizens, cities and sports teams, the Canadian sport spectator would be rede-fined as a citizen rather than as a consumer.

Source: Philip White is a professor in the Department of Kinesiology at McMaster University, Hamilton. Peter Donnelly is a professor and Director of the Centre for Sport Policy Studies in the Faculty of Physical Education and Health at the University of Toronto. John Nauright is a senior lecturer in Sports Studies at the University of Queensland, Australia. This article was origi-nally published in *Policy Options*, 18(3) May 1997, pp.9-12. Reproduced by permission.

41.

Indy Dreams in the World Class City

Mark Douglas Lowes

Sports events like the Indy have become surrogates for, and mobilizers of, civic identity

In today's climate of relentless inter-urban competition for the major public and private investments that contribute to economic growth, spending on image-making and public relations is often perceived to be as important as spending on urban infrastructure and other upgrades. The rationale behind this is that the more a city such as Vancouver can appear "on the same stage," or "in the same league" as New York and Los Angeles, the stronger their chances of growing and prospering will be–or so the civic leaders believe.

In the broader context of an increasingly global sports entertainment industry and its seamless integration with mass media that reach global audiences, the annual Molson Indy Vancouver (MIV) motor race has become a fixture in a growth strategy whereby Vancouver seeks to pro-ject itself as a " world class" city. Sports events like the Indy and sports franchises like the Grizzlies have become surrogates for, and mobilizers of, civic identity, in Vancouver and other North American cities. Indeed, civic officials in both Canada and the United States have apparently bought into the idea that major-league sports teams, international sporting and cultural events, and the "world class" facilities associated with them, help a city to project images of cultural sophistication and economic dynamism.

In media coverage of the Molson Indy, a recur-rent theme is that the event puts Vancouver "on the world stage." This representational ambition is also manifest in suggestions that hosting this spectacular international event could make Van-couver "the Monaco of North America, Canada's Monte Carlo." This allusion, of course, trades on the glitz and glamour of Europe's Monaco: with its celebrity Royal Family, its elite hotels and casinos, and its breathtaking Mediterranean landscapes. Monaco and Monte Carlo are signified in popular discourse as a playground for the global rich and famous. Their annual Formula One race, the Monaco Grand Prix, is one of the most anticipated stops on the F-1 circuit, drawing the attention of the world.

Promoters argue that the Molson Indy —showcasing as it does the European and South American stars of elite motor sport racing, in the spectacular harbourfront venue of False Creek— confers upon Vancouver similar connotations of international chic. "The Molson Indy Vancouver has gotten to the point where it's more than just a race. It has become a world-class event," gushed one Tourism Vancouver official. Indeed, the MIV is seen by boosters as a signifier of Vancouver's arrival as a world-class city, providing the city with an occasion to show itself off: "It is Canada's Monte Carlo, pure and simple, a stunning setting where the Coast Range meets the Pacific Ocean." Vancouver's claims here to "Monte Carloness," it might be suggested, reflect both international pretensions, and the perceived importance of cities showcasing themselves as sites of affluent lifestyle pursuits. The latter are visible, in Vancouver, in the concentrations of galleries, designer clothing and accessory boutiques, and gourmet coffee shops and restaurants that saturate the city's downtown and False Creek districts (where the race takes place). Motor racing appeals to affluent audiences, and coverage of the Indy gives Vancouver widespread international exposure. Reporters and television crews from around the globe may spend several days in the city, filing stories on the race and its star personalities, but also conveying the cosmopolitan atmosphere of the city and its varied lifestyle attractions.

So, as a promotional vehicle, the MIV is highly valued by Vancouver's "new economy" oriented elites. They want the revenues the event itself brings into the civic economy; they also believe it contributes in important ways to Vancouver's image as a world-class tourist destination. The Indy generates a purported $19 million in economic spin-offs (according to Tourism Vancouver and Indy officials), pumping more than $500,000

into the city's tax base. Vancouverites are also reminded of the value of having Vancouver's scenery appear, even in the background, on television screens in an estimated 100 million homes around the affluent world. For this is a truly international event—no other show in town even dreams about an audience of this size, or this global distribution: not the Grizzlies, not the Canucks, and certainly not the B.C. Lions of the Canadian Football League.

Each year an estimated 160,000 people flood the stands during the Indy's Labour Day weekend run, including 70,000 for the final day. All this helps to create more than a thousand temporary jobs and approximately $2.4 million in contracts for local contractors. Moreover, though there is little hard evidence to support claims that the presence of "world-class" sports has an influence on residential (let alone business) relocation decisions, these events do contribute to the tourist industry, as well as to a cumulative image of a wealthy, globally oriented city. And it is in terms of these themes that Vancouver's political, business, and other civic boosters make the case that hosting the Molson Indy is a matter of economic and cultural "common sense." Entertainment spectacles are depicted as necessary to gain world recognition and "world class" status for the city.

Now, my objective here is not to dispute these claims, at least not on narrow economic grounds; the MIV does generate a lot of business over the Labour Day weekend, and perhaps has a more general "imaging" effect that benefits Vancouver's tourism industry. Rather, my criticism is of the "world class city" discourse that surrounds the event, and the fact that it is now very difficult in Vancouver to ask publicly what this means, and to create a public debate about the vision of Vancouver that is promoted here. Certainly there is no public forum where critics of the Molson Indy can make their voices heard and articulate an oppositional discourse. In this regard, I especially want to single out the Vancouver media for their relentless promotion of the event. For example, leading up to the race weekend, both the *Province* and the *Sun*, Vancouver's daily newspapers, produce extensive "Special Indy Supplements," each running 30-40 pages. In addition to this pre-event hype, both papers provide exhaustive race coverage, and a great deal of post-event "wrap-up." Local radio stations likewise contribute to the promotional atmosphere by airing 30-second "Eye on Indy" information spots, up to 25 times per day through the eight weeks leading up to the race.

The problem is that nowhere in this volume of media coverage is there a serious (or even half-hearted) engagement with concerns that have been raised repeatedly by Indy critics. Criticism has come from neighborhood residents' associations, from environmental groups, and from anti-poverty activists. Their concerns include things like the noxious air and noise pollution that are inevitable by-products of urban auto racing, the congestion of people and cars that the race weekend annually brings to False Creek, the celebration of car culture in a city endemically affected by smog and traffic jams, and most of all the allocation of public resources to an event aimed at affluent tourists, while public services remain under-funded and poor peoples' needs go unmet. Indeed, what is often obscured in the boosterism surrounding the Indy is the fact that there are voices in Vancouver who have tried to argue that their city would be better served if it invested in affordable and good quality public services, and in locally oriented public spaces such as parks and community recreation centers. But against the promotional clamour of the Vancouver media, such voices have a hard time making themselves heard.

Here I am struck by Andrew Wernick's proposal, in *Promotional Culture*, that we live amid a "vortex of promotional signs"—an endless circulation of messages and images in which virtually every aspect of social life has become part of a sales pitch. This is especially manifest in the promotional discourse that surrounds the idea of the "world class" city, and in the upmarket goods and events that supposedly confer this status on cities. In a world increasingly permeated by promotional culture, we find that consumer goods and entertainment have become the currency of urban public life. The sports entertainment industry, in particular, has become a site for the promotion of popular commodities and styles, and for the construction of both individual and civic identities. Yet these new sources of identity have, in the process, become ever more closely tied to market forces, and to the creation of meaning through consumption and display. In these discourses of consumption, the "consumer" has replaced the "citizen" as the focal point of urban life and economic strategy. Moreover, in cities like Vancouver, it is the buying public, and in particular that part of the buying public with globally oriented tastes and interests (and the incomes to support them), which is of paramount concern to those with "world-class" pretensions. Such are Vancouver's Indy dreams. Such is life in the "world class" city.

Source: Mark Douglas Lowes is a lecturer in the Communication Department of the University of Ottawa, Ontario. This article was originally published in *Canadian Issues/Themes Canadiens (CITC)*, Autumn 1999, pp.18-19. Reproduced with the permission of the author.

42.

The Globetrotting Sneaker

Cynthia Enloe

New world order

Four years after the fall of the Berlin Wall marked the end of the Cold War, Reebok, one of the fastest growing companies in United States history, decided that the time had come to make its mark in Russia. Thus it was with considerable fanfare that Reebok's executives opened their first store in downtown Moscow in July 1993. A week after the grand opening, store managers described sales as well above expectations.

Reebok's opening in Moscow was the perfect post-Cold War scenario: commercial rivalry replacing military posturing; consumerist tastes homogenizing heretofore hostile peoples; capital and managerial expertise flowing freely across newly porous state borders. Russians suddenly had the "freedom" to spend money on U.S. cultural icons like athletic footwear, items priced above and beyond daily subsistence; at the end of 1993, the average Russian earned the equivalent of $40 a month. Shoes on display were in the $100 range. Almost 60 percent of single parents, most of whom were women, were living in poverty. Yet in Moscow and Kiev, shoe promoters had begun targeting children, persuading them to pressure their mothers to spend money on stylish, Western sneakers. And as far as strategy goes, athletic shoe giants have, you might say, a good track record. In the U.S. many inner-city boys who see basketball as a "ticket out of the ghetto" have become convinced that certain brand-name shoes will give them an edge.

But no matter where sneakers are bought or sold, the potency of their advertising imagery has made it easy to ignore this mundane fact: Shaquille O'Neal's Reeboks are stitched by someone; Michael Jordan's Nikes are stitched by someone; so are your roommate's, so are your grandmother's. Those someones are women, mostly Asian women who are supposed to believe that their "opportunity" to make sneakers for U.S. companies is a sign of their country's progress—just as a Russian woman's chance to spend two month's salary on a pair of shoes for her child allegedly symbolizes the new Russia.

As the global economy expands, sneaker executives are looking to pay women workers less and less, even though the shoes that they produce are capturing an ever-growing share of the footwear market. By the end of 1993, sales in the U.S. alone had reached $11.6 billion. Nike, the largest supplier of athletic footwear in the world, posted a record $298 million profit for 1993—earnings that had nearly tripled in five years. And sneaker companies continue to refine their strategies for "global competitiveness"—hiring supposedly docile women to make their shoes, changing designs as quickly as we fickle customers change our tastes, and shifting factories from country to country as trade barriers rise and fall.

The logic of it all is really quite simple; yet trade agreements such as the North American Free Trade Agreement (NAFTA) and the General Agreement on Tariffs and Trade (GATT) are, or course, talked about in a jargon that alienates us, as if they were technical matters fit only for economists and diplomats. The bottom line is that all companies operating overseas depend on trade agreements made between their own governments and the regimes ruling the countries in which they want to make or sell their products. Korean, Indonesian, and other women workers around the world know this better than anyone. They are tackling trade politics because they have learned from hard experience that the trade deals their governments sign do little to improve the lives of workers. Guarantees of fair, healthy labour practices, of the rights to speak freely and to organize independently, will usually be left out of trade pacts—and women will suffer. The recent passage of both NAFTA and GATT ensures that a growing number of private companies will now be competing across borders without restriction. The result? Big business will step up efforts to pit working women in industrialized countries against much lower-paid working women in "developing" countries perpetuating the misleading notion that they are inevitable rivals in the global job market.

All the "New World Order" really means to corporate giants like athletic shoemakers is that they now have the green light to accelerate long-standing industry practices. In the early 1980s, the field marshals commanding Reebok and Nike, which are both U.S.-based, decided to manufacture most of their sneakers in South Korea and Taiwan, hiring local women. L.A. Gear, Adidas, Fila, and Asics quickly followed their lead. In short time, the coastal city of Pusan, South Korea, became the "sneaker capital of the world." Between 1982 and 1989 the U.S. lost 58,500 footwear jobs to cities like Pusan, which attracted sneaker executives because its location facilitated international transport. More to the point, South Korea's military government had an interest in suppressing labour organizing, and it had a comfortable military alliance with the U.S. Korean women also seemed accepting of Confucian philosophy, which measured a woman's morality by her willingness to work hard for her family's well-being and to acquiesce to her father's and husband's dictates. With their sense of patriotic duty, Korean women seemed the ideal labour force for export-oriented factories.

U.S. and European sneaker company executives were also attracted by the ready supply of eager Korean male entrepreneurs with whom they could make profitable arrangements. This fact was central to Nike's strategy in particular. When they moved their production sites to Asia to lower labour costs, the executives of the Oregon-based company decided to reduce their corporate responsibilities further. Instead of owning factories outright, a more efficient strategy would be to subcontract the manufacturing to wholly foreign-owned—in this case, South Korean—companies. Let them be responsible for workers' health and safety. Let them negotiate with newly emergent unions. Nike would retain control over those parts of sneaker production that gave its officials the greatest professional satisfaction and the ultimate word on the product: design and marketing. Although Nike was following in the footsteps of garment and textile manufacturers, it set the trend for the rest of the athletic footwear industry.

But at the same time, women workers were developing their own strategies. As the South Korean pro-democracy movement grew throughout the 1980s, increasing numbers of women rejected traditional notions of feminine duty. Women began organizing in response to the dangerous working conditions, daily humiliations, and low pay built into their work. Such resistance was profoundly threatening to the government, given the fact that South Korea's emergence as an industrialized "tiger" had depended on women accepting their "role" in growing industries like sneaker manufacture. If women reimagined their lives as daughters, as wives, as workers, as citizens, it wouldn't just rattle their employers; it would shake the very foundations of the whole political system.

At the first sign of trouble, factory managers called in government riot police to break up employees' meetings. Troops sexually assaulted women workers, stripping, fondling, and raping them "as a control mechanism for suppressing women's engagement in the labour movement," reported Jeong-Lim Nam of Hyosung Women's University in Taegu. It didn't work. It didn't work because the feminist activists in groups like the Korean Women Workers Association (KWWA) helped women understand and deal with the assaults. The KWWA held consciousness-raising sessions in which notions of feminine duty and respectability were tackled along with wages and benefits. They organized independently of the male-led labour unions to ensure that their issues would be taken seriously, in labour negotiations and in the pro-democracy movement as a whole.

The result was that women were at meetings with management, making sure that in addition to issues like long hours and low pay, sexual assault at the hands of managers and health care were on the table. Their activism paid off: in addition to winning the right to organize women's unions, their earnings grew. In 1980, South Korean women in manufacturing jobs earned 45 percent of the wages of their male counterparts; by 1990, they were earning more than 50 percent. Modest though it was, the pay increase was concrete progress, given that the gap between women's and men's manufacturing wages in Japan, Singapore, and Sri Lanka actually *widened* during the 1980s. Last but certainly not least, women's organizing was credited with playing a major role in toppling the country's military regime and forcing open elections in 1987.

Without that special kind of workplace control that only an authoritarian government could offer, sneaker executives knew that it was time to move. In Nike's case, its famous advertising slogan—"Just Do It"—proved truer to its corporate philosophy than its women's "empowerment" ad campaign, designed to rally women's athletic (and consumer) spirit. In response to South Korean women workers' newfound activist self-confidence, the sneaker company and its subcontractors began shutting down a number of their South Korean factories in the late 1980s and early 1990s. After bargaining with government officials in nearby China and Indonesia, many Nike subcontractors set up shop in those countries, while some went to Thailand. China's government remains nominally Communist: Indonesia's ruling generals are staunchly anti-Communist. But both are governed by authoritarian regimes who share the belief that if women can be kept hard at work, low paid, and unorganized, they can serve as a magnet for foreign investors.

Where does all this leave South Korean women—or any woman who is threatened with a factory closure if she demands decent working conditions and a fair wage? They face the dilemma confronted by thousands of women from dozens of countries. The risk of job loss is especially acute in relatively mobile industries; it's easier for a sneaker, garment, or electronics manufacturer to pick up and move than it is for an automaker or a steel producer. In the case of South Korea, poor women had moved from rural villages into the cities searching for jobs to support not only themselves, but parents and siblings. The exodus of manufacturing jobs has forced more women into the growing "entertainment" industry. The kinds of bars and massage parlors offering sexual services that had mushroomed around U.S.

military bases during the Cold War had been opening up across the country.

But the reality is that women throughout Asia are organizing, knowing full well the risks involved. Theirs is a long-term view; they are taking direct aim at companies' nomadic advantage, by building links among workers in countries targeted for "development" by multinational corporations. Through sustained grassroots efforts, women are developing the skills and confidence that will make it increasingly difficult to keep their labour cheap. Many are looking to the United Nations conference on women in Beijing, China, this September [1995], as a rare opportunity to expand their cross-border strategizing.

The Beijing conference will also provide an important opportunity to call world attention to the hypocrisy of the governments and corporations doing business in China. Numerous athletic shoe companies followed Nike in setting up manufacturing sites throughout the country. This included Reebok—a company claiming its share of responsibility for ridding the world of "injustice, poverty, and other ills that gnaw away at the social fabric," according to a statement of corporate principles.

Since 1988, Reebok has been giving out annual human rights awards to dissidents from around the world. But it wasn't until 1992 that the company adopted its own "human rights production standards"—after labour advocates made it known that the quality of life in factories run by its subcontractors was just as dismal as that at most other athletic shoe suppliers in Asia. Reebok's code of conduct, for example, includes a pledge to "seek" those subcontractors who respect workers' rights to organize. The only problem is that independent trade unions are banned in China. Reebok has chosen to ignore that fact, even though Chinese dissidents have been the recipients of the company's own human rights award. As for working conditions, Reebok now says it sends its own inspectors to production sites a couple of times a year. But they have easily "missed" what subcontractors are trying to hide—like 400 young women workers locked at night into an overcrowded dormitory near a Reebok-contracted factory in the

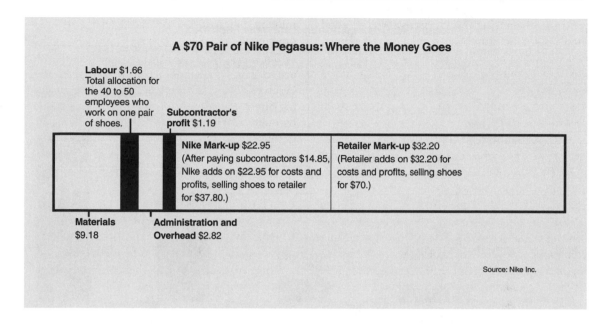

A $70 Pair of Nike Pegasus: Where the Money Goes

Labour $1.66
Total allocation for
the 40 to 50
employees who
work on one pair
of shoes.

Subcontractor's profit $1.19

Nike Mark-up $22.95
(After paying subcontractors $14.85,
Nike adds on $22.95 for costs and
profits, selling shoes to retailer
for $37.80.)

Retailer Mark-up $32.20
(Retailer adds on $32.20 for
costs and profits, selling shoes
for $70.)

Materials $9.18

Administration and Overhead $2.82

Source: Nike Inc.

town of Zhuhai, as reported last August in the *Asian Wall Street Journal Weekly.*

Nike's cofounder and CEO Philip Knight has said that he would like the world to think of Nike as "a company with a soul that recognizes the value of human beings." Nike, like Reebok, says it sends in inspectors from time to time to check up on work conditions at its factories; in Indonesia, those factories are run largely by South Korean subcontractors. But according to Donald Katz in a recent book on the company, Nike spokesman Dave Taylor told an in-house newsletter that the factories are "[the subcontractors'] business to run." For the most part, the company relies on regular reports from subcontractors regarding its "Memorandum of Understanding," which managers must sign, promising to impose "local government standards" for wages, working conditions, treatment of workers, and benefits.

In April, the minimum wage in the Indonesian capital of Jakarta will be $1.89 *a day*–among the highest in a country where the minimum wage varies by region. And managers are required to pay only 75 percent of the wage directly; the remainder can be withheld for "benefits." By now, Nike has a well-honed response to growing criticism of its low-cost labour strategy. Such wages

should not be seen as exploitative, says Nike, but rather as the first rung on the ladder of economic opportunity that Nike has extended to workers with few options. Otherwise, they'd be out "harvesting coconut meat in the tropical sun," wrote Nike spokesman Dusty Kidd, in a letter to the *Utne Reader.* The all-is-relative response craftily shifts attention away from reality: Nike didn't move to Indonesia to help Indonesians; it moved to ensure that its profit margin continues to grow. And that is pretty much guaranteed in a country where "local standards" for wages rarely take a worker over the poverty line. A 1991 survey by the International Labor Organization (ILO) found that 88 percent of women working at the Jakarta minimum wage at the time–slightly less than a dollar a day–were malnourished.

A woman named Riyanti might have been among the workers surveyed by the ILO. Interviewed by the *Boston Globe* in 1991, she told the reporter who had asked about her long hours and low pay: "I'm happy working here…. I can make money and I can make friends." But, in fact, the reporter discovered that Riyanti had already joined her co-workers in two strikes, the first to force one of Nike's Korean subcontractors to accept a new women's union and the second to

Hourly Wages in Athletic Footwear Factories

Figures are hourly estimates based on 1993 data from the International Textile, Garment, and Leather
Workers Federation; International Labor Organization; and the U.S. Bureau of Labor Statistics

United States
$7.38 -7.94

South Korea
$2.02 -2.27

China
$.10 -.14

Indonesia
$.16 -.20

Thailand
$.65 -.74

compel managers to pay at least the minimum wage. That Riyanti appeared less than forthcoming about her activities isn't surprising. Many Indonesian factories have military men posted in their front offices who find no fault with managers who tape women's mouths shut to keep them from talking among themselves. They and their superiors have a political reach that extends far beyond the barracks. Indonesia has all the makings for a political explosion, especially since the gap between rich and poor is widening into a chasm. It is in this setting that the government has tried to crack down on any independent labour organizing—a policy that Nike has helped to implement. Referring to a recent strike in a Nike-contracted factory, Tony Nava, Nike representative in Indonesia, told the *Chicago Tribune* in November 1994 that the "troublemakers" had been fired. When asked about Nike policy on the issue, spokesman Keith Peters struck a conciliatory note: "If the government were to allow and encourage independent labour organizing, we would be happy to support it."

Indonesian workers' efforts to create unions independent of governmental control were a surprise to shoe companies. Although their moves from South Korea have been immensely

profitable [see chart], they do not have the sort of immunity from activism that they had expected. In May 1993, the murder of a female labour activist outside Surabaya set off a storm of local and international protest. Even the U.S. State Department was forced to take note in its 1993 worldwide human rights report, describing a system similar to that which generated South Korea's boom 20 years earlier: severely restricted union organizing, security forces used to break up strikes, low wages for men, lower wages for women—complete with government rhetoric celebrating women's contribution to national development.

Yet when President Clinton visited Indonesia last November [1994], he made only a token effort to address the country's human rights problem. Instead, he touted the benefits of free trade, sounding indeed more enlightened, more in tune with the spirit of the post-Cold War era than do those defenders of protectionist trading policies who coat their rhetoric with "America first" chauvinism. But "Free trade" as actually being practiced today is hardly *free* for any workers—in the U.S. or abroad—who have to accept the Indonesian, Chinese, or Korean workplace model as the price of keeping their jobs.

The not-so-new plot of the international trade story has been "divide and rule." If women workers and their government in one country can see that a sneaker company will pick up and leave if their labour demands prove more costly than those in a neighbour country, then women workers will tend to see their neighbours not as regional sisters, but as competitors who can steal their precarious livelihoods. Playing women off against each other is, of course, old hat. Yet it is as essential to international trade politics as is the fine print in GATT.

But women workers allied through networks like the Hong Kong-based Committee for Asian Women are developing their own post-Cold War foreign policy, which means addressing women's needs: how to convince fathers and husbands that a woman going out to organizing meetings at night is not sexually promiscuous; how to develop workplace agendas that respond to family needs; how to work with male unionists who push women's demands to the bottom of their lists; how to build a global movement.

These women refuse to stand in awe of the corporate power of the Nike or Reebok or Adidas executive. Growing numbers of Asian women today have concluded that trade politics have to be understood by women on their own terms. They will be coming to Beijing this September ready to engage with women from other regions to link the politics of consumerism with the politics of manufacturing. If women in Russia and Eastern Europe can challenge Americanized consumerism, if Asian activists can solidify their alliances, and if U.S. women can join with them by taking on trade politics–the post-Cold War sneaker may be a less comfortable fit in the 1990s.

Source: Cynthia Enloe is Professor of Government at Clark University. She is the author of *The Morning After: Sexual Politics at the End of the Cold War*. Reprinted by permission of *Ms.* Magazine, (c) 1995. This article was originally published in the issue of March-April, pp.10-15. This article draws from the work of South Korean scholars Hyun Sook Kim, Seung-kyung Kim, Katharine Moon, Seungsook Moon and Jeong-Lim Nam.

43.

Bad Call

John Palmer

Why Canadians should blow the whistle on recommendations by a Commons committee advocating tax breaks for pro sports teams and parents of amateur athletes

On Dec. 3. a House of Commons committee headed by Dennis Mills released a report on the state of sports in Canada. Among the many recommendations in the report were several designed to enrich the owners of professional, major league sports teams in Canada. The most controversial of these recommendations was the one providing tax breaks for the owners of these teams, with the hope that these tax breaks would provide an incentive for the teams to stay in Canada.

It isn't as if the owners need the money. They may be crying about their reported losses, but don't believe them. It doesn't make sense that people are lining up to offer more than $100 million for a franchise, even though they expect to lose money in the business. And it doesn't make sense that current owners are unwilling to sell their franchises for such large prices if they think they are going to continue to lose buckets of money. If a current franchise could be sold for, say, $100 million, then the owner could easily put that money in a safe investment and earn at least $5 million a year in interest. It would be unusual for an owner to forego this $5 million a year just so he or she can invest in a perpetually losing operation.

Paul Beeston, former president of the Toronto Blue Jays, once said, "Show me a $4-million profit and I can (using widely accepted accounting tricks) turn it into a $2-million loss and have that loss approved by every major auditing firm in Canada." He came to regret that statement during the labour negotiations in 1994, but when I asked him about it, he agreed that he had said it and that it was true.

Owners of major sports franchises have a myriad of techniques for disguising their profits. As Andrew Zimbalist detailed so clearly in his analysis of the Florida Marlins' books in an Oct. 18 article in *The New York Times*, these techniques include paying themselves and family members very high salaries, undercharging their ancillary operations for services provided by the franchise and overcharging the team for services provided by the ancillary operations.

For example, Bud Selig is reputed to have numerous friends and relatives on the payroll of the Milwaukee Brewers; the Atlanta Braves notoriously undercharge WTBS for the television broadcast rights to their games; and the Marlins are grossly overcharged for playing in the stadium owned by Wayne Huizenga who, coincidentally, also owns the Marlins.

In each of these examples, the teams' profits are reduced but the owners' profits stay high as the owners siphon off profits from the team and put them somewhere else.

The major argument invoked by anyone who wants subsidies from taxpayers is that their business provides enormous spinoffs that benefit the entire community. Owners of sports franchises are no different. They point to all the jobs created by their business, to all the restaurant and hotel business that they claim comes as a result of their business and to all the peripheral businesses that would disappear if they left town.

At the risk of overstating my position: horse hockey.

What would people spend their money on if the team left town? The answer is lots of different things. But they'd still spend their money. And their spending would create just as many jobs and generate just as much tax revenue as happens when people attend a major sporting event. It's difficult to know how each fan would spend his or her money, but it would not likely be to travel with the team to its new town and watch games there. Instead, the spending would continue at about the same rate in the local community, but it would be diffused throughout the city, creating jobs and tax revenues that would roughly offset those lost if the team left town.

It probably is naive of me, but I am constantly amazed that arguments about the spinoff effects continue to be taken seriously by politicians. If people would just stop to ask, "What would people spend their money on if the team weren't here?" they would realize that the alleged spinoff effects are very small.

Having a major league team in a city does, I admit, attract fans from surrounding areas. And these fans do, indeed, spend money in the city. But is that good for the home towns of the fans who go to see the game? Why should the provincial and federal tax dollars of residents of London, Ont., be used to pump business into Toronto and suck business away from London? If big cities want to enact all kinds of hand-outs for the owners of sports teams, that's one thing; but it is grotesquely unfair to ask people not living in those cities to contribute to the folly.

Another complaint of the owners of major league sports franchises is that they are losing money because of the recent drop in the Canadian dollar. They signed big contracts with their stars a year or more ago, when the Canadian dollar was worth 75 cents US, but now, with the Canuck buck worth only 65 cents US, the Canadian owners have to pony up more Canadian dollars to pay the stars. Because nearly all player contracts are written in terms of US dollars, this drop added roughly 15 percent to the wage bill of the Canadian franchises—an extra 15 percent that their U.S. competitors don't have to pay.

But there is no reason that taxpayers should have to bail out or subsidize private entrepreneurs who take risks and then lose. After all, these owners are choosing to take these risks. They don't have to bear exchange-rate risk if they don't want to. They can fully hedge their player contracts by dealing in what are called the foreign exchange forward markets. If they chose not to use the forward markets to hedge these risks, that means they chose to speculate about foreign currency movements. They speculated and they lost. If the taxpayers are going to bail out all speculators who lose money, watch out. We will turn into a nation of speculators and gamblers who expect that we can keep our winnings, but that we can have our losses covered by other taxpayers. And one more thing: if the value of the Canuck buck had gone up instead of down, do you think the owners would gratefully have paid more than their tax bill? Nah, I don't think so.

What bothers me about the Mills report is that it attempts to form a coalition from causes that should be kept separate. It says, "We will offer these tax breaks, but only if you do something for amateur sports." That is a really inefficient way to help amateur sports. If the members of Parliament really want to help amateur sports, they should do so directly rather than filtering the money through the pockets and balance sheets of the owners of major league sports franchises. Taxpayer support for amateur sport should be judged on its own merits, not on whether it is coupled with some other government handout. This plan is just an indirect way to give money to team owners while trying to enlist the support of all the families involved in amateur sports in the scheme. Most people seem not to be falling for the trick.

Eventually, we are going to have to face the fact that it will be difficult to keep all our major league sports franchises in Canada when there are so many markets south of the border which are much bigger and hence potentially so much more profitable for the owners. Recent data indicate that Canadian cities are big enough to support two, or perhaps three, major league franchises in baseball and basketball, probably just one franchise in the NFL and, at most, maybe only four franchises in the NHL. Calgary, Edmonton and Ottawa are all very small markets compared with cities in the U.S. that don't have teams and would like to have one. Not all these teams are likely to remain where they are.

It is, of course, in the best interests of the remaining owners to keep those bigger markets in the U.S. in a state of limbo, so that everyone else can threaten to move there if their home cities don't cough up more money for stadiums, parking, etc. It is also in their interests to keep current owners from moving into the more lucrative markets so that the league can sell new franchises in the richest markets for the most money. So while the threat of losing a couple of teams is real, keep in mind it may not be as serious as owners argue.

In the end, the arguments in favour of tax breaks to owners of sports teams are misleading at best and often pernicious. Most of the alleged benefits are negligible. The only argument of merit is that we all get some civic and national pride from knowing these teams exist.

And while I'm pleased to know there are major league teams in all these cities, I would feel even more civic pride from knowing we have really top-flight lawn bowling teams in Yorkton, Sask., world-class ballet in Chester, N.S., and a top-ranked university in Clinton, Ont.

Source: John Palmer is a professor in the Department of Economics at the University of Western Ontario, London. This article was originally published in *The London Free Press,* Saturday, December 12, 1998. Reproduced with the permission of the author.

44.

Is This Any Way to Work Out?

James Christie

Amateur athletes can't afford to concentrate on their sport full-time. Maybe some of the $95-billion budget surplus can help

The news hit Arturo Huerta like a falling tree. One of his national track-and-field teammates was leaving Canada to compete for another country. Scottish-born distance runner Kathy Butler was shedding the maple leaf because Britain treats its elite athletes better.

Her decision this month was disquieting for Mr. Huerta, who is Canada's top race walker. After all, he had chosen to come here from his native Mexico. Canada was his land of opportunity. Why would other athletes choose to leave?

"I worry about those things," he said. "They have been brought up in Canada, started their athletic career in Canada, and when they're at their prime, they leave because there's not sufficient support...."

"If we keep losing these athletes, the sweat is going to dry up."

As Canada's reigning 5,000-metre champion, Ms. Butler collected about $7,200 a year in Athlete Assistance Program payments from Sport Canada. In Britain, she is eligible for 5 1/2 times that much –about $40,000 a year–in training and living expenses.

She is not the first athlete to flee for better treatment. Last winter, Canada's top luge slider, Clay Ives, a dual Canadian-U.S. citizen, went south, where national-team members receive $6,000 (U.S.) stipends from the U.S. Olympic Committee and the U.S. luge federation. As well, they are assigned a corporate "parent" from a pool of sponsors to pick up other expenses. Beyond that, an Olympic medal would be worth $20,000 to $40,000 from the USOC.

"If you want to be a full-time athlete in Canada," Mr. Ives noted, "you better have rich parents or rich friends."

Elite athletes in most developed countries can concentrate on being just that–full-time athletes. Pure amateurism is long dead and governments or Olympic organizations funded by corporate contributions see to it that Olympic-bound athletes have one job only–their sports.

That's not the case here. Canadian athletes–with the exception of corporate sponsor magnets such as sprinters Donovan Bailey and Bruny Surin and swimmers Joanne Malar and Curtis Myden–must take jobs to support themselves, their families and their sport dream.

Sport Canada, the federal government's funding agency, is paying out about $57.9 million a year–no more than it spent 10 years ago–and critics question whether the money is being spent wisely.

More than $9 million goes to athletes in direct payments (monthly living allowances range from $185 to $810). That's twice as much as a decade ago, but still a pittance compared with the money available to British, Italian, French or Australian athletes.

Meanwhile, the federally supported national training centres were told this week that they must make their services available in both official languages. And there will be no additional money to help make it happen. With the next Olympics looming, other programs may have to carry the load.

Watching Canadian athletes depart for greener pastures troubles Denis Coderre.

In August, he became Canada's first Sport Minister in seven years. Since taking the job, the Montreal MP has called himself "the promoter and watchdog of sport" and has tried to make himself the athlete's friend.

He has had a grim legacy to overcome. Two devastating budget cuts and a revision of Sport Canada funding during the previous seven years resulted in the number of national sport organizations that received government support being slashed to 38 from 57.

Some Olympic sports, such as weightlifting, were lopped entirely under the government's accountability framework. Many of the survivor sports stumbled ahead, but had to cut their programs–and most often the grassroots of sport suffered. The Canadian women's basketball

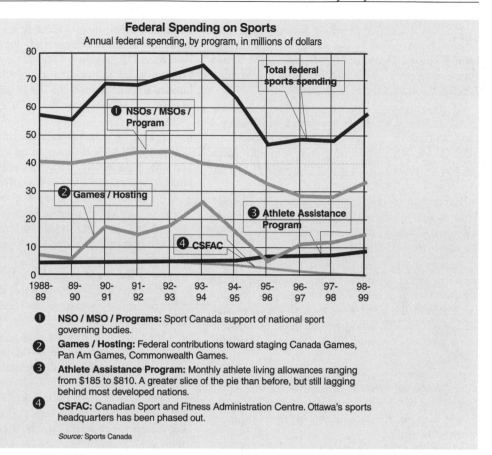

Federal Spending on Sports
Annual federal spending, by program, in millions of dollars

Total federal sports spending

❶ NSOs / MSOs / Program

❷ Games / Hosting

❸ Athlete Assistance Program

❹ CSFAC

(x-axis: 1988-89, 89-90, 90-91, 91-92, 92-93, 93-94, 94-95, 95-96, 96-97, 97-98, 98-99)

❶ **NSO / MSO / Programs:** Sport Canada support of national sport governing bodies.

❷ **Games / Hosting:** Federal contributions toward staging Canada Games, Pan Am Games, Commonwealth Games.

❸ **Athlete Assistance Program:** Monthly athlete living allowances ranging from $185 to $810. A greater slice of the pie than before, but still lagging behind most developed nations.

❹ **CSFAC:** Canadian Sport and Fitness Administration Centre. Ottawa's sports headquarters has been phased out.

Source: Sports Canada

program went for a few years without even having a junior team.

The federal contribution to the Canadian Centre for Ethics in Sport–Canada's vaunted antidoping organization–was cut by more than half.

The Canadian Sport and Fitness Administration Centre–which was to have been the national nerve centre for amateur sport and a place where disciplines could cross-pollinate with great training ideas and shared services–was phased out entirely.

Sport Canada's outlay plummeted to $47.2 million in 1995-96 from a peak of $75.8 million in 1993-94. In the past four years, since the Atlanta Olympics, it has climbed to just under $57.9 million.

Canada's rebound of $10.7 million since 1996 contrasts with Britain's World Class Performance Program, launched in the post-Atlanta misery when Britain won only one gold medal. The British

government amended its lottery laws to allow for payments to athletes and not simply bricks-and-mortar sport projects. The result was a $64 million handout, half of it in direct funding to athletes.

Canada's cuts were entirely justified. Every federal department and program suffered cutbacks in the days when the government was wrestling with the national deficit and trying to balance the budget.

But recent reports of a massive $95 billion surplus over five years has athletes–who have always been a low priority compared with social programs–thinking: "Now it's our turn."

Mr. Huerta could cry into his apron–the orange one he wears while working in the aisles of a Home Depot lumber department.

Like most would-be Olympians, he works an eight-hour day, then tries to squeeze in four to five hours of training.

He has a flexible working arrangement with Home Depot under the Canadian Olympic Association's Career Opportunities Program that allows him to support his wife Heather, sons Esteban and Michael, and an Olympic dream.

"I'm fortunate. The program has been very good in letting me have the time I need when I have to travel to compete or train elsewhere," he said. "It takes the stress off getting a bit of income for the mortgage, but it doesn't cover 100 percent of life and the training expenses."

According to one estimate, an athlete like Mr. Huerta will need nearly $20,000 over and above his Sport Canada handout to complete his training for the Sydney Olympics.

Riches have never been a goal for the 35-year-old athlete, who became a Canadian citizen shortly after the 1996 Atlanta Olympics. (Not an athlete in his homeland, he took up his sport once he got to Canada, found he was good at its shambling gait and earned a place on several national teams.)

He was happy to represent his new country. Last year, he trained in brutal heat and smog to toughen himself up for a silver-medal performance in the jungle-heat of Kuala Lumpur at the Commonwealth Games.

"I will go through it all, just to wear the colour of Canada, anywhere, under any circumstances," Mr. Huerta said.

Still, the disparity is always there in front of him, in the stride and strut of walkers from the countries who finished ahead of him at the Pan American Games and world championships this year.

"All the guys who beat me at the world championships, they're supported 100 percent by their country and don't need to work. That's what they do in Italy, Mexico, Ecuador, Russia, Spain, China."

Mr. Coderre refuses to see the departure of a top Canadian athlete for Britain as a symptom of failure. "It's unfortunate we lost Kathy Butler. I was not happy to see that happen. It happens often, however, in the way that other countries lose their athletes to Canada," he said.

"When we talk of funding being called 'inadequate,' I believe she was getting $7,200, but you also have to calculate the value of services, such as the seven multisport centres across Canada and the

Coaching Association of Canada. It's a matter of support for athletes. Remember, here they are not employees of the state."

But as for athletes believing the sport system needs a transfusion from the federal surplus, Mr. Coderre said he will be first in line with his sleeve rolled up.

He said the amateur-sport community had taken its hit to fight the deficit and he urged athletes to bombard politicians with the message that sport brings important values to Canadian society.

"It's clear, now that amateur sport has a specific minister, that sport is becoming a priority. We have to look at ways to get some of that surplus. I'll go to the Minister of Finance to say we need some more money.

"But I also want to go through the process and see if we can change the way we do things better with the money we have with management and accountability."

One thing that will not change, however illogical it may seem to some of the national training centre administrators, is the primacy of the federal bilingualism policy.

Even if there were only a single athlete request for French-language services at the Calgary training centre, the capacity must be there, Mr. Coderre said.

"I spoke to Dale Henwood (president of the Calgary centre] and met everyone from the centres and repeated the same message. It's a matter of providing tools [in an athlete's preferred language]. I never said I'll cut off your funds now.

"But bilingualism is an issue, I'm firm on that. I said that to the NSOs [National Sport Organizations] yesterday. I visited people from Hockey Canada and they hired a translator. The Canadian Soccer Association agreed to changes on their Web site.

"To carry a flag is also to carry the values attached to it."

And if you're Arturo Huerta, it means carrying a lot of lumber as well.

Source: James Christie is a staff reporter for *The Globe and Mail*. This article was originally published in *The Globe and Mail*, Thursday, November 11, 1999, A2O. Reproduced with the permission of *The Globe and Mail*.

45.

Should the Athletes Take the Money and Run?

Mark Tewksbury

We shouldn't be shocked when our Olympic hopefuls decide to compete for a country that makes them a better offer, says Canadian medallist Mark Tewksbury

There is a fundamental principle that underlies every athlete's life. It is so important it has been enshrined in the Olympic Charter, the Bible of amateur sport. This fundamental principle states: "Every athlete must have the possibility of practising sport in accordance with his or her needs."

An elite amateur athlete competing on the world stage has very specific needs indeed: suitable training facilities, world-class coaching, technical expertise and financial support are almost as essential as food and water if an amateur athlete really wants to be competitive with his or her peers around the globe.

But what happens when those needs are not being met? The amateur athlete's primary job is his or her sport. Across the globe most of these athletes rely heavily on government funding. When their country can no longer support their personal pursuit of excellence, what is an amateur athlete to do?

As we witnessed last week in the case of Kathy Butler, a top middle-distance runner, it is to move to another country, namely Britain, where Ms. Butler will receive up to $40,000 to support her training and living expenses, compared with the $7,200 she was receiving in Canada. If Ms. Butler wins gold or any other medal at the next Olympics, it will be for Britain, not Canada. Although the numbers speak for themselves, Ms. Butler's decision must have been a hard one.

The Olympic movement thrives because of the emotional equity we have invested in nationalism: the Parade of Nations, the victory ceremonies and the close-ups of athletes crying as they sing their national anthems are almost as important to the survival of the Olympics as the physical competition itself.

It is exactly this emotional response from the athlete that strikes a chord with those watching at home. In this moment there is a magic that enables viewers to share in the wonder of the Olympics. They feel as if they have swum, run or sailed with the athlete themselves. It is more than just personal pride when the national flag goes up—it is being raised for each one of us.

I was hooked as a kid, from the moment I saw the 1976 Montreal games. Throughout my career, the honour of competing for my country paralleled the importance of my own personal pursuit of excellence. I recall watching the 1984 Los Angeles Games on television as an up-and-coming 16-year-old and feeling outraged when U.S. commentators noted after a Canadian athlete's victory that the competitor had trained at a U.S. college, implying that the performance was the product of a superior American system.

When the recruiters from Stanford, Berkley and Texas came calling on me the following year, I flatly declined. I will be the product of a Canadian system, thank you very much.

Being so fiercely patriotic, I was disheartened that Ms. Butler chose to compete for another country, but my anger was directed toward the state of funding in her sport rather than toward Ms. Butler herself.

My decision to stay in Canada was made 15 years ago, and it was based on the knowledge that everything I would need to be competitive on the world stage was available to me here.

Forgoing the honour of representing Canada was probably a sacrifice for Ms. Butler, but in making a commitment to herself and to her sport, why shouldn't she go where the opportunity was best for her to fulfill her dream? As the Olympic Charter states, she was just trying to practise sport in accordance with her needs.

And then the bomb dropped.

On the heels of Ms. Butler's decision, it was reported by the CBC and in *The Globe and Mail* that in the lead up to the Sydney Olympic Games next year, Australian authorities have recruited more than 300 athletes and coaches from around the world, including Canadians, to compete for their country.

Some of Canada's top amateur athletes, including shot-putter Georgette Reed, swimmer Joanne Malar and world champion white-water kayaker David Ford, were approached with promises of ideal training conditions and complete financial, technical and moral support in their quests for Olympic glory, if only the athletes would take the fast track to Australian citizenship.

I reacted quickly and angrily. This was unacceptable. This was going way too far. A line had been crossed. This is not what the Olympic Games are all about.

Or is it?

I had to ask myself some hard questions. For how long have I let my emotional attachment to national pride blind me to the realities of the Olympic movement? And what is the difference between Ms. Butler seeking out a country that meets her needs to fulfill her Olympic dream and a country seeking out amateur athletes that meet its needs to fulfill its dream of having its best performance at an Olympic Games? One might argue that Ms. Butler is the victim of a system that is poorly funded, while Australia is systemically victimizing those who are vulnerable. In the end it all boils down to the same thing.

Perhaps it is because I am a romantic or an idealist but for most of my life I chose to believe that the Olympics were a public trust that embodied noble virtues such as peace, beauty and respect for universal fundamental ethical principles. To believe this today would be naive.

The Olympic movement is run like a private enterprise. It is a business where billions of dollars are at stake; so why shouldn't a country's amateur sports heroes be seen as free agents?

As an amateur athlete I took great pride in participating in sport for the honour of achieving my best and for competing for my country. But what should I have done if that emotional attachment to nationalism had hindered me from pursuing my dream? Should we let that sense of pride the Olympics instill in many of us keep athletes from making the best choices to see their own dreams fulfilled? Should we be outraged at Australia for attempting to steal our talent?

Why should an amateur athlete be any different from a computer programmer who is paid market value for his or her talent? Is Australia any worse than a professional team like the Toronto Blue Jays, who load their baseball team with the best players they can afford? I don't recall having a sense of outrage when the Blue Jays won the World Series and the vast majority of the players were foreign-born.

Are the Olympics different? Are they about more noble ideals?

Maybe it's time we looked at the Olympics for all that they really are. Yes, they are about nationalism. They may even be about the noblest of ideals. But let's not kid ourselves, the Olympic Games are a big business.

We can't expect our athletes to train in impoverished conditions and then expect them to compete with the finest elite athletes in the world. When presented with the opportunity to meet their needs elsewhere it is not necessarily wrong to leave.

But understand that we are losing more than just an athlete. If we ever want to see an Olympic medal draped over the neck of a Canadian, if we want to feel that magic and have that sense of pride, then we cannot ignore the reality that the games are a business. This is going to cost money. If we don't pay to meet the needs of the athletes, I am afraid there will always be countries like Australia who will.

Source: Mark Tewksbury is a three-time Olympic medallist and a member of the Canadian Sports Hall of Fame. This article was originally published in *The Globe and Mail*, Monday, November 15, 1999, A15. Reproduced with the permission of the author.

Part 11
Sport and the Media

The freedom of the press belongs to those who own one. This old adage is a cautious reminder about the power of the institution we know today as "the media." Although the media has claimed, for much of this century, to be objective—to report just "the facts"—a growing body of research, known as media studies, is continually showing how events are "mediated." That is, they are selected, edited, ordered, and framed, perhaps for the purposes of "entertainment," but perhaps also at the behest of the owners and/or sponsors in order to provide a particular "take" on the event.

Many sport sociologists now use the term "sport-media complex" to refer to the symbiosis between the sport and the media. Research has shown how sport has been shaped by the media (e.g., tie breakers in tennis), but also how sponsors are a powerful part of the complex. For example, the CBC experienced pressure from sponsors to broadcast the Nagano Olympics in the same format as NBC/Atlanta—a tape delayed/"plausibly live" presentation of major events interspersed with numerous sentimental up-close-and-personal interviews with athletes (Christie, 1997). The CBC resisted the pressure in favour of 18 hours a day of live broadcasting from Japan, but it is experiencing similar demands for its Sydney broadcasts.

The vast majority of media research in sport has been concerned with gender issues, and this section mirrors that trend. The first article involves the Canadian Association for the Advancement of Women and Sport and Physical Activity (CAAWS), an Ottawa-based advocacy group, and Canadian newspaper sports departments. In November 1994, CAAWS released its fourth annual one-week survey of Canadian newspaper sports sections, indicating the respective proportions of the sports pages devoted to men's and women's sports. The results revealed that 13 of the 20 newspapers surveyed had even less coverage of women's sports than the previous year. These surveys are naturally not popular with sports editors, but they had the good grace to invite CAAWS to address their annual meeting in Ottawa in January 1995. Marg McGregor's speech provides some powerful reasons, and constructive means, for increasing the coverage of women's sports. That newspapers (and other media) have a long way to go in addressing women's sports is highlighted in the Metro (Toronto) Interschool Athletic Association survey of coverage of high school sports in the *Toronto Star* and the *Toronto Sun* during the 1994-95 school year.

Bruce Kidd then addresses a forum that is not usually considered as "media"—Halls of Fame and museums (and even athletic department display cases). It seems that even in these places, the displays are selected, edited, ordered and framed (i.e., mediated) for us by others, and Kidd makes it quite clear that the gender bias in other media is also evident here. Finally, Melisse Lafrance analyzes ("deconstructs" or "unpacks" to use media studies terminology) the famous Nike advertisement known as, "If you let me play..."

Each article in this section is easily adapted to serve as a student project.

Reference

- Christie, J. (1997). CBC to resist sap in Olympic coverage. *The Globe and Mail,* 11 April, p.C16.

Additional Sources

Videos:

- *Lindros,* TV Ontario's "Medium Close Up" analysis of the coverage of Lindros's refusal to play for the Québec Nordiques by the Francophone and Anglophone media.
- *Producing the Olympics,* Scanning TV series production analyses the way in which television produces and presents the Olympics to a worldwide audience.

Print Resources:

- Don Cherry is perhaps the most significant media creation in Canadian sport. The folowing two articles indicate the complexity of what he represents. Salutin, R. (1993). Quotations of Chairman Cherry. *The Globe and Mail,* 7 May, p.C1; and an article by Gillett, J., White, P., & Young, K. (1996). The Prime Minister of Saturday night: Don Cherry, the CBC, and the cultural production of intolerance. In H. Holmes & D. Taras (eds.), *Seeing Ourselves: Media Power and Policy in Canada.* Toronto: Harcourt Brace, pp.59-72.

46.

Canadian Sports Editor's Speech

Marg McGregor

"Girls hit the wall at about age 11"

Thank you very much for providing me with the opportunity to speak with you today. It's a real pleasure to be able to have your ear. This is a great opportunity to have a relaxed discussion–to learn from one another, to share issues, concerns, ideas, and to have some fun in the process.

I will make several suggestions today–some of what I say may strike a chord with you and some may not coincide with your experiences; nevertheless I encourage you to extract the messages that are meaningful for you, put them in your back pocket and maybe even try them out in your newspaper.

Some of the assumptions I'm basing my talk on are that everyone here:

- loves sport and cares about how it affects our family and friends;

- wants to make newspapers as interesting as possible;

- wants to sell more newspapers. Your markets are dwindling and you have open minds about exploring other mechanisms to tap markets which haven't traditionally been considered.

The four keys areas of my presentation this morning will be:

1. Why women in sport coverage is important. I hope to be able to convince you that increasing your women in sport coverage is (a) the right thing to do from a social perspective and (b) the right thing to do from a business perspective.

2. How newspapers are doing in terms of the quantity and the quality of women in sport coverage.

3. A discussion of some of the issues/obstacles that impede print journalists from running more women in sports stories, and some suggestions as to how we can work around these obstacles.

4. I'll offer some suggestions on how to enhance the quality and quantity of women in sport coverage. And I'm eager to hear your suggestions for ways we can work together to increase coverage for women in sport.

We'll then break for a coffee and stretch break followed by a panel discussion. We have two panelists this morning–Sue Scherer and Phyllis Berck. Also in the audience is Sheila Robertson–CAAWS' communications consultant. Following the panel we'll have the opportunity for some interaction in the form of a question and answer session. I expect we'll be able to engage in some lively discussion and debate.

Before I get to the core of my presentation, I would like to provide a 30-second sound bite about CAAWS:

- we are in business to encourage girls and women to get out of the bleachers and cheerleading uniforms and onto the fields, rinks, gymnasiums, locker rooms, and sport board rooms of this country;

- we work with other organizations in the sport community to build a better sport system, a sport system which is: free of racism and sexism, which shows respect for indigenous peoples, which welcomes athletes with a disability, and which is committed to the empowerment of women and men.

Why is media coverage of women and sport important?

I'd like to share a story with you that relates to a friend and colleague of mine–a person most of you will be familiar with–Sue Holloway. Sue was speaking to a group of Grade 3 kids in an inner-city school in Toronto. She asked the kids to name all the female athletes they could think of. Their response gave new meaning to the term "invisible women." There was total silence in that school library ... utter silence for the longest time. The Grade 3's were trying ... One of them suggested

"Alwyn Morris?" Alwyn of course is a fine Olympian, and a fine MAN.

So the kids were trying ... they simply had no names to offer. As Sue Holloway explained later they just don't see any athletes who are women ... they just don't hear about them.

Why are women so invisible? Media coverage plays a big part in this. Insidiously our society's reverence for men's pro sports and its silence about women's accomplishments shapes, defines, and limits how we feel about ourselves as women and men.

As sports journalists you have an incredible platform to shape and define public attitudes and beliefs. Let me give you an example. My four-year-old daughter and I spent hours glued to the TV watching the Commonwealth Games this past summer. The images we saw went way beyond communicating statistics of winners and losers. My daughter saw able-bodied athletes competing alongside athletes with a disability, she saw men and women athletes competing shoulder to shoulder. This exposure had a tremendous impact in terms of shaping my daughter's viewpoints. The subtle message was that sport is for the able-bodied and athletes with a disability, and for men and women. I like to think that what my daughter saw will stay with her as she matures.

Girls hit the wall at about age 11 in this country. The once boisterous playful kids reach the cusp of adolescence and begin to drop out of physical activity in record numbers, take up smoking in droves, and their self-esteem takes a tremendous kicking. They are really vulnerable at this point in their lives.

I believe that you have it within your power to curb these depressing trends. I believe we owe it to the fresh-faced, ponytailed, knobby-kneed girls in this country to give voice and exposure to the many excellent female athlete role models they might emulate. Tell the fascinating and compelling stories of strong, athletic, powerful women in this country, so that at Sue Holloway's next speaking engagement, the Grade 3's can readily identify several women athletes within their community and their country.

I am not advocating token coverage based solely upon the gender of the athlete. Far from it. I believe there are more than enough story angles to go around. Canada has outstanding women athletes. There are no shortage of fascinating stories to be told. Beyond the obvious examples of Silken Laumann, who left a powerful and indelible image in the minds of all Canadians, and Sylvie Frechette, who overcame adversity—we have:

- Myriam Bedard–2 gold medals at Lillehammer
- Susan Auch–silver medal in speed skating at Lillehammer
- Nathalie Lambert–2 Olympic silvers and 3 world championships in short track speed skating
- Women's hockey team–three time world champions
- Sandra Peterson–2-time world champion in curling; a model of perfection on the ice
- Ljiljana Ljubiisik–world champion and world record holder in blind athletics
- Joanne Muncz–6 gold medals in swimming at the 1992 Paralympics
- Tanya Dubnicoff
- The Canadian women's cycling team's extraordinary performance in the Women's Tour de France
- Marnie McBean's silver medal performance in rowing last year
- Kennedy Ryan's extraordinary accomplishments in freestyle skiing
- Annie Pelletier–diving

Women receiving coverage in the media is not an end in itself. For most women athletes this is not even a goal; personal excellence is. But through the media an individual's accomplishments become validated. Individuals become "newsworthy." Their presence on the sports pages puts them on an equal footing with their male peers. In whatever area women choose to excel, they wish to be deemed significant. Their stories are captivating.

Increasing your women's sports coverage makes good business sense: it will help you sell more papers, and it will help your bottom line.

This is not news to you. Bob Sparks from the University of British Columbia surveyed the national population of Canadian dailies (117 newspapers) in 1993. He looked at trends affecting sports reporting. Responses from 74 dailies indicated that they are under increased pressure to be more competitive and cost effective in a constricting marketplace. Many sports departments are looking at changing their section contents to capture more young people, more women, and in some cases broader ethnic representation.

Other business sectors have cottoned on to the marketing reality that women, who make up 52 percent of the population, represent a significant marketing opportunity. The clever business sectors such as the auto industry have looked at mechanisms for tapping a huge market that they haven't traditionally served.

TSN has recognized the marketing opportunities and is running a "Women in Sports" series. In the United States there's talk of a 24-hour women-in-sports channel.

Beer companies have realized that women are becoming more powerful as consumers, and their buying power is becoming stronger. Freda Colbourne, manager of communications for Molson Breweries captured this point nicely when she said, "Over the last 5 years if you look at a reel of commercials there has been a dramatic shift in the use of women and men in beer commercials. Women were becoming consumers of beer and by no means did we want to offend the consumer" (*Ottawa Citizen*, October 14, 1992). Labatts pulled an ad a few years ago in less than a week after numerous complaints. It featured a man who goes to LaBar, meets LaBabe, gets LaRing ... LaRing through LaNose.

I am convinced that more people would read your sports sections, and your existing readers would be happier, if you placed more emphasis on amateur sport and women in sport. All the indicators suggest the truth of this conviction.

Some of you may tell me that women don't care about sport. Omitting the NBA scores gets you countless calls from irate readers, but when you ignore the world rowing championships, no one calls or writes or complains—hence the assumption that no one cares.

If women want more coverage, why don't they write to complain, you ask? Well, my theory is that women may very well be expressing their opinions by simply not buying your paper or reading your sports section, turning to other sources such as community newspapers for their sport news.

It may be that women are too busy. Or perhaps they think their comments will go unnoticed. A number of things have incensed me over the past year—things about which I have never taken the time to phone or write the organization involved.

The clever marketer will tell you the importance of anticipating consumer and potential customer wants and needs, and not simply responding to existing customers' demands and complaints.

You may also suggest that women are not interested in sports. Well, take a look at a crowd shot of a football or hockey game next time you're watching TV or are at a game. Women are every bit as visible as men in the bleachers. In fact a survey by the NHL found that more than 40 percent of its fans are women (source: Canadian Press). Almost half of the tickets sold at NBA and baseball games are purchased by women. The interest is there.

You may want to tell me that you don't cover a story because of the gender of the athlete. We're not asking you to do that, but we do wish you would explore the possibilities. The economic returns might surprise you.

By not making a conscious business decision to pay attention to including both genders, by default you continue to cover men's pro sport at the expense of amateur women's and men's sport stories. I believe that you could sell more papers if you wrote more stories about women.

I also think you would be able to attract advertisers by diversifying the demographics of your readership. The Bob Sparks survey revealed that many papers are under siege. Advertising revenue is declining, your travel budgets are being whacked, the space devoted to sports is shrinking, staff size is declining.

At this point in the decade the information super-highway is just around the corner. The way people access information will be dramatically different in 10 years time. Not to get left behind, the clever newspapers will be looking at how to deliver a better product to the new markets they have courted.

How are newspapers doing?–quality and quantity

Let's look at how Canada's newspapers are doing now in terms of the quantity and quality of their coverage of women in sport.

Quantity

Think back to the list of athletes I mentioned earlier. Reflect upon the type of coverage these women athletes received in your papers: Did the stories get covered? To what depth? Did they get mentioned in the agate, in the BRIEFS segment only, or was there a feature story? Did you run any photos with the stories? What was the nature of the photos? Was it a podium shot with women smiling and hugging each other, or did you run a shot of the women doing what they do best–competing–a photo which emphasized the athlete's strength, power, skill and determination? Let's see more action shots–you know … muscle, expressions of strain, and gruelling training sessions.

I have an anecdote I'd like to share with you. Kay Worthington–double gold medallist from the 1992 Olympic rowing team–was speaking to a gym full of school children in rural Ontario and one little girl raised her hand and asked "Will you show us your muscles?" Isn't this great? Little girls wanting to see more muscles! Think of that little girl the next time you're selecting photos!

CAAWS did a survey of 20 daily newspapers from Victoria to Halifax in 1994. That survey showed that sports sections in newspapers devote an average of 5 percent of their space to stories about women athletes.

Five percent. Of course, the NHL, NBA, CFL, NCAA, PGA, have to be covered, but 5 percent! Stories about women and their accomplishments simply are not being told.

This year's survey was our fourth, and it is interesting that it always generates a reaction. Some of you welcome it and are sincerely interested in how your paper did, how you can do better, and what stories we think you missed.

Some of you scoff at it, say it's silly, even inaccurate. You question our right to even do the survey. And some of you wonder what on earth we want.

Some sports journalists say they write what their readers want to read about, and people just aren't interested in women in sports.

It's interesting to note that 20 years ago the organizers of the Professional Women's Tennis Association were told that people would not watch women's tennis on TV because women couldn't hit the ball as hard or run as fast as the men. Today the women's matches enjoy tremendous popularity and occasionally draw higher audience ratings than the men's games!

My experience suggests that the public is tired of hearing stories of striking players, striking referees, on-court brawls, seasons that go on forever, exorbitant salaries, rioting fans, O.J. Simpson, O.J.'s lawyers, etc., etc., ad nauseam…. As the *Ottawa Citizen* so aptly put it: "The entire NHL went off the air for 3 months–and so what? Kids got on with their games, grown-ups explored other diversions" (January 12, 1995, *Ottawa Citizen*).

I am convinced that the public would respond to stories of local heroes, of real people in real time–the women and men in our communities who organize the leagues, drive the car pools, run the bingos and bakesales, and provide encouragement and consolation–all for the love of our kids and the simple joys of sport. And stories, too, about the athletes who flourish because of these efforts, athletes who may become the stars of the future.

I suggest you look to the *Ottawa Citizen* which runs a first-rate weekly Sports Roots feature which focuses on everyday people in our community and gives voice to their accomplishments.

Tied into the issue of quantity of coverage is the issue of the pervasiveness of professional sports. After you've covered professional sport there's really not much space left over for amateur sport.

Let's ask ourselves who loses when the public domain is so dominated by stories of professional sports that they eclipse all mention of swimmers and divers, field hockey and basketball and volleyball players.

Why not expand your horizons, expand the types of sports you cover, cultivate new audiences?

Quality

Some papers have done a first rate job in terms of the quality of their women in sport coverage.

By and large the Canadian media did the Canadian women and their performances justice at the last winter and summer Olympics. Most journalists refrained from adjectives such as sexy, leggy, cute and refrained from references to girls and ladies. Instead the Canadian women had a powerful presence built on performance.

For example, the *Calgary Sun*'s article on Kerrin Lee-Gartner:

> No, Kerrin Lee-Gartner did not need steroids to become an Olympic Champion. She did it with an inner strength that knows no measure. She did it by refusing to quit, despite physical and mental anguish. She did it while growing up, far from home and family. And she did it in the best Canuck fashion of all: Purely crazy.

The Globe and Mail made reference to Silken Laumann's stalwartness by headlines such as "Laumann offers lesson in courage" and "Laumann has already proved her medal." Even Sylvie Frechette was spared reference to feminine stereotypes of grace and beauty by the *Globe*. The *Globe* asserted that Frechette set strong precedents in sport. "If a single athlete has the power and magnetism to define sport, then Sylvie Frechette defines synchro swimming."

During the Games women athletes get to demonstrate their mettle and enjoy the media spotlight. But the heady days of Olympic media coverage only occur every two years. If readers enjoy that coverage, why not see if fair and interesting media coverage can occur continuously?

Canadian women athletes seemed to fare as well as their male peers in the press during these major Games. Both genders had to deal with the media's impatience for medals and a big story to break.

And by and large the Canadian media outperform their American counterparts in terms of how women are portrayed. Allow me to repeat some American gems garnered by Mary Hynes, former host of *The Inside Track* on CBC Radio Sports.

You're about to hear descriptions of some very remarkable women, athletes who rank among the best in the world. Each is strong, powerful, dedicated, driven. Here's how some media portray them:

"She's so fresh faced, so blue eyed, so ruby lipped, so 12-car-pile-up gorgeous. 5 feet 5 inches and 114 pounds worth of peacekeeping missile."

"She" is also a world and Olympic champion. "She" is Katarina Witt, as seen through the eyes of *Sports Illustrated.*

And more recently ... this week's issue of *Sports Illustrated* featured a letter from a reader asking how he could possibly get excited about the Cowboys when the magazine hasn't even run a photograph of their cheerleaders yet? Incidentally the *Sports Illustrated* editors obliged the reader by running the requested photo.

Sports Illustrated also has a roll of honour. It's a list of the 173 men and 8 women who have appeared on three or more covers of *Sports Illustrated.* Of those 8 women, 3 were on the cover of a swimsuit issue.

What I love about this roll of honour is that in one statistic you have in a nutshell what's wrong with this picture, what's wrong with the way some media portray athletes who are women. The amount of coverage is pitiful, but then all too often, the kind of coverage is even worse.

"She cooks and sews and washes clothes, just like most wives do." Yes, we're talking about that renowned cook and seamstress Greta Waitz as seen through the eyes of ABC television. When she's not darning socks or making soup, she's one of the best distance runners in the world.

These examples have a common thread running through them—the achievements of female athletes being undervalued and undermined by some media's emphasis on their appearance, their attractiveness to men, or, amazingly, their skill as homemakers.

This emphasis on attractiveness is ironic to me because sport is one of the few places where our bodies are ours to do with as we please. Lunging for a soccer ball we don't worry if we are having a bad hair day; exploding out of the starting gate we don't care how nubile we appear; in the final desperate kick to the finish line we don't smile and wave. While playing most sports, our bodies are ours to do with as we please; and if in the process we sweat, and grunt, or get bloody or look "unattractive" it doesn't matter to us.

Unfortunately Americans don't hold the sole franchise on portraying women athletes as baby dolls. Let me share some examples that are closer to home, in which strong, powerful, courageous athletes are sold short. Let me illustrate my point:

"She is a comely nubile with hazel eyes, a glowing complexion, and a decidedly feminine grace. There's no hint of testosterone in her nature." This is goalie Manon Rheaume as described on the pages of *The Toronto Star*.

I am reminded of that notorious Kerrin Lee-Gartner episode. When Kerrin powered her way to a gold medal in the women's Olympic downhill in Albertville, it wasn't her skiing prowess that dominated some sports pages. Some media were more impressed with what she had done before the race. Some reporters ignored her strength and power and courage and insinuated she won because she had sex with her husband before the event. The titillating story originated in Europe but it was quickly picked up and carried by some Canadian media.

Another story which comes to mind is an article I read in the *Toronto Sun* (Feb. 17, 1994) referring to the moguls freestyle ski venue in Lillehammer: "It looks like a field of breasts, doesn't it? A good crop too."

Examples come to mind from the broadcast media as well. When little girls tuned in to watch Elizabeth Manley on TV at the Olympics in Calgary in 1988, what messages did they hear? Well, Elizabeth was dubbed a kewpie doll more than once—one of the cutest Olympians in recent memory—one who had charmed her way onto the medal podium.

But just imagine if the commentary had focused on the excellence, the power, the strength, the sense of sheer triumph. Then a little girl watching the Olympics and dreaming her own Olympic dream wouldn't just see a cutie pie in Elizabeth Manley. She'd see a powerful, determined skater who overcame ridiculous odds to win the silver medal.

Issues/challenges we face

Access to information

During the baseball strike and hockey lockout we certainly had an opportunity to give more play to high-school, college, and community sport. I would acknowledge that national sport organizations failed by not inundating you with facts, information, and story ideas about their athletes during the labour unrest.

But let's face it—not-for-profit sport organizations will never have the resources to match the type and quality of information you receive from professional sports. It will always be quicker and easier for you to run the pro sport story. But because of the labour unrest I think the public's preoccupation with pro sports has waned. Many people have remarked to me that they have started to read the sport sections again because the coverage related to community and amateur sport, areas of interest that they are rediscovering.

Perhaps the way to get the information about who is competing where and when is to simply call the national sport organization. They'll give you the information you need and probably the phone number of the athlete you're interested in. Establish relationships with these organizations. Unearth the stories. Take the initiative.

And what about creating a multi-sport national team, made up of athletes from your community who are on National Teams? Why not identify 6 to 10 athletes at the beginning of a year? Introduce them to your readers. Follow their highs and lows throughout the year. Track their progress.

There are lots of exciting amateur events that take place in North America. The World Rowing Championships in Indianapolis, the World Hockey Championships in Lake Placid. The World Cup Skiing events in Whistler. The World Cup Speed Skating events in Quebec City. These are events within low-cost traveling distance for most of your papers, and each had few Canadian media in attendance. What about using some of the money that you saved during the labour strikes to send reporters to amateur events in the upcoming year? This type of coverage would also help better acquaint your reporters with amateur sport—so they would be in a position to do a better job when covering high profile events such as the Olympic and Paralympic Games.

Athlete education

Margaret MacNeill, a professor at the University of Toronto conducted a survey of the members of the Canadian Athlete's Association. Her results, which haven't been published yet, show some interesting findings. She found that most athletes do not understand the media. Many athletes withhold information from the media. They are often scared of the media. Many athletes truly think the media are supposed to be a part of a booster club, and are supposed to be writing positive things about athletes. So misunderstandings occur when the coverage is not always positive.

These observations suggest that athlete education is key. How can we work together to overcome these issues?

Questions women athletes like to be asked

Marg MacNeill's survey found that women athletes don't want to be asked about motherhood. They may be a mother but, at that moment in time, they are athletes first, and that's the world they want to talk about.

Real world pressures

TV broadcasters have more access to competition sites at major Games. Newspaper reporters are barricaded out and shoved aside. When you're under pressure to make deadlines, you often will go for the quickest story. CAAWS Media Kits may help by providing hero notes on Canada's top women athletes.

Suggestions—a few quick tips (source CP)

- Why not lead with the women's competitions in events such as marathons, where both sexes compete? If separate stories aren't warranted, the most competitive and exciting race deserves the lead—and that's certainly not always the men's event. This approach has worked in ski coverage in recent years when the women's team out-produced the men. No doubt the pendulum will swing back as the men improve, but surely the best results deserve the greatest coverage.

- Any sports reporter who refers to a female gymnast as a pixie, or a basketball player as an amazon, is being sexist and patronizing. *Time* magazine said it best in an article by Jill Smolowe headlined, "Don't call them pixies": "Avoid reaching for adjectives like huggable, perky, cute—sort of like puppies. Let's get real. Female gymnasts who vie for medals are among the toughest athlete's in the world. They are not only strong, powerful and agile, they also have a discipline, dedication and determination that would put many athletes to shame. Two times daily, six days weekly, often year after year they labour in airless gymnasiums to master and reinvent the most difficult flips, twists and spins. Often they work in spite of strains, sprains and stress fractures" (*Time*, Summer 1992).

- Physical descriptions of athletes—male and female—are sometimes appropriate, and their personalities will enliven quotes. But avoid gratuitous descriptions that have sexist undertones. The simple technique of reversal will help you judge. Ask yourself: Would this type of thing be written about a male?

The print media enjoy an amazing opportunity to dig in at a deeper level than broadcast media. I suspect that most people aren't buying papers to read who won last night's game. They already know that from the TV or radio. The added value of the newspaper is the feature story. So features are key.

Features on events and athletes are great. But you could also write features on women in sport issues. *The Winnipeg Free Press, Calgary Herald, The Vancouver Sun,* Mary Ormsby, the *Ottawa Citizen,* and *The Montreal Gazette* in particular have done well in this area.

Some feature story ideas

Why not take a look at sex discrimination in sport? Does it exist? If so, how far have we come? If a woman was discovered at the ancient Olympic Games she was thrown off a cliff. The founder of the modern Olympic Games said in 1896 that women did have a role to play and that role was to applaud the performances of men. Thirty years ago prospective women participants were presented with rules and traditions that effectively said women can't do this or that. Women can't play soccer, or ice-hockey or rugby. The reasons given included the danger to child-bearing capabilities—organizers were worried women's uteruses would fall out! Women weren't allowed to wrestle or run more than 800 metres. It's the 1990s. Just how far have we come?

What about a story on the extent, variety and accessibility of facilities to women, or harassment in sport, or eating disorders, or what about equipment? Does equipment designed for boys and men work equally well for girls and women? Should women play with men's equipment or should it be retooled to meet the needs of women?

What about taking a look at sports halls of fame? The Canadian Sport Hall of Fame—the self-proclaimed "shrine of sports." Only 12.5 percent of individuals in the Hall of Fame are women. We could boost this figure to a little over 13 percent if we include fillies and some of the speed boats named after women. Despite the fact that women have excelled in ice hockey for more than a century there are no women at all among the honoured members of the Hockey Hall of Fame.

Conclusion

Thanks very much for your attention today! I hope you enjoyed my presentation. It is my hope that many of you possess the fresh thinking it will take to increase your coverage of women in sport, and in turn attract more readers, and enable more girls and women to enjoy the magic of physical activity and sport.

Source: Marg McGregor was Executive Director of the Canadian Association for the Advancement of Women and Sport and Physical Activity and is now Executive Director of the Canadian Interuniversity Athletic Union (CIAU). This article was originally published in *Action*, Spring 1995, p.7. Reprinted with permission of the Canadian Association for the Advancement of Women and Sport and Physical Activity.

47.

Metro Schools' Female Athletes Angered by Lack of Media Attention

Metro Interschool Athletic Association

Missing in action

TABLE 1: High School Sports Articles in the *Toronto Star*, **September 13, 1994–April 8, 1995**

Total Articles (including Mini)	**158**
Boys Football	48
Boys Basketball	39
Boys Hockey	24
Other Male Sports	8
Total Male Sports	**119**
Girls Basketball	16
Other Female Sports	11
Total Female Sports	**27**
Non-Gender Specific	**12**

TABLE 2: High School Sports Pictures in the *Toronto Star*, **Sept. 13, 1994–April 9, 1995**

Total Pictures	**109**
Boys Football	45
Boys Basketball	24
Boys Hockey	14
Other Male Sports	7
Total Male Sports	**90**
Girls Basketball	8
Other Female Sports	8
Total Female Sports	**16**
Non-Gender Specific	**3**

TABLE 3: High School Sports Articles in the Toronto Sun, Sept. 12, 1994–April 5, 1995

Total Articles (Including Mini)	98
Boys Football	31
Boys Basketball	36
Boys Hockey	12
Other Male Sports	4
Total Male Sports Articles	83
Girls Basketball	5
Other Female Sports	4
Total Female Sports Articles	9
Non-Gender Specific	6

Table 4: High School Sports Pictures in the Toronto Sun, September 12, 1994–April 9, 1995

Total Pictures	44
Boys Football	17
Boys Basketball	17
Boys Hockey	5
Other Male Sports	4
Total Male Sports	43
Girls Basketball	1
Total Female Sports	1

Source: Reprinted with permission of the Metro Interschool Athletic Association.

48.

Missing: Women from Sports Halls of Fame

Bruce Kidd

A women's sports hall of fame?

There are only 48 women (13 percent) among the 377 athletes and builders celebrated in Canada's Sports Hall of Fame, and only 56 women (21 percent) among the 247 recognized in the Canadian Olympic Hall of Fame!

Despite the fact that women have excelled in ice hockey for more than a century, there are no women at all among the honoured members in the Hockey Hall of Fame. As Allison Griffiths of the CBC's *Inside Track* has pointed out, the profligate James and Bruce Norris, who virtually destroyed strong franchises in Chicago and Detroit, are included in the Hockey Hall, white their innovative sister Marguerite, who presided over the Red Wings during five profitable seasons and three Stanley Cups, has been ignored.

Halls of fame play a strategic role in the public remembering and interpretation of sports. Through their annual, often well-publicized selections and inductions, they confer status (and lifetime bragging rights) upon those selected, singling out in the process particular sports, skills, practices, and values for praise or blame, legitimation or derision.

Thousands visit the new high-tech Hockey Hall in Toronto's commercial core. Other halls have become important sources of reference for school children, journalists, and amateur and professional historians. To the extent that their selection decisions shape the records they maintain—the excellent archives of Canada's Sports Hall of Fame in Toronto only actively collects materials on inducted members, for example—their judgments shape the primary data available for research.

Can you imagine what Canadian sport would be like today without the contributions of Abby Hoffman, Marion Lay, Betty Baxter, and Diane Jones Konihowski, all inspirational Olympians who have significantly improved the opportunities for many others? It would be impossible to write about the "Golden Age of Women's Sport" in the 1920s without an entire chapter on Alexandrine Gibb, who single-handedly initiated Canadian women's participation in international competition, created the women's Amateur Athletic Federation, and wrote about women's activities in her daily column in the *Toronto Star*. Yet none of these women, and many others I could mention, are included in Canada's Sports Hall of Fame, which aspires to be the most inclusive and comprehensive of the Canadian halls, or the Olympic Hall of Fame, administered by the Canadian Olympic Association.

The myopia is not limited to the 30 or so formal halls of fame across Canada. Virtually every school, college and university has trophy and display cases extolling the highlights of its sports history. Women are just as invisible in most of them, too.

The dearth of women in so many halls and exhibits is hardly innocent. It contributes to the "symbolic annihilation" of women through the public discourse. In the case of the displays in athletic facilities, it may well send out the message that the efforts of girls and women are unworthy. That was certainly the conclusion arrived at by the Gender Equity Task Force at the University of Toronto last year.

Some halls base selection on high performance, but that should hardly be a problem. As University of British Columbia sports historian Barbara Schrodt has often pointed out, when the number of events and size of teams are considered, Canadian women have usually outperformed Canadian men in international competition. An even more pressing case can be made in response to the ambition of many institutions to provide "popular ethnographies" of the history of sport. The Alberta and Manitoba halls even include the word "museum" in their titles. Given the rich history of girls and women competing in sports, it is simply inaccurate not to include them.

One explanation might be the predominance of male broadcasters and sportswriters on selection committees. What counts as "sports" on most broadcasts and newspapers is male professional sports. There are only two women—Jones-Konihowski and Susan Nattrass—among 13 selectors at Canada's Sports Hall of Fame. But individual selections are also structured by a pervasive undervaluing of women's contribution throughout Canadian society.

In the past, it's primarily been feminists who have initiated the recognition of Canadian female athletes. In the 1930s, when the now familiar traditions of "athletes of the year," all-star games, and halls of fame were invented, the Women's Amateur Athletic Union of Canada created the Velma Springstead Trophy to honour the best female athlete of the year. In our own time, CAAWS inaugurated the moving, annual Breakthrough Awards. Much more needs to be done, so it will have to be feminists (and their allies) who seize the reins again.

It would be nice to have a Women's Sports Hall of Fame in a well-travelled location in every Canadian city, but given the scarcity of resources, that is not likely to happen. We should step up the pressure on existing institutions.

Every hall of fame has its own selection criteria, process, and culture, so some legwork is necessary, but it shouldn't be too hard for members of the CAAWS Network to increase the number of well-researched applications each year, and to raise the eyebrows of funding agencies and sponsors if they get turned down. It's also time to start pushing for gender parity on selection committees.

Another target should be the historical displays in those halls with facilities. Most curators are professionally trained and accept the obligation of "getting it right."

Perhaps the most accessible to the CAAWS Network are the historical displays in schools, college and university athletic departments where women make up a significant percentage (sometimes the majority) of the population. Do the displays adequately reflect the experiences and accomplishments of sportswomen, and serve to affirm their interest and abilities? If not, how might such displays be made more accurate and inclusive?

Although the recommendation of the University of Toronto Gender Equity Task Force—to make a dent upon the long history of "symbolic annihilation" with a year of women-only displays—was not accepted, just raising the above questions had an educational effect.

The full story needs to be told!

Source: Bruce Kidd is Dean of the Faculty of Physical Education and Health at the University of Toronto. This article was originally published in *Action*, Winter 1994, pp.4-5. Reprinted with the permission of the Canadian Association for the Advancement of Women and Sport and Physical Activity.

49.

What's the Problem?

Mélisse Lafrance

Nike's "If you let me play" campaign

Nike's advertisement: A sweet, powerless, almost destitute little girl sits pensively on an outdoor swing. Her hair is blondish-brown, her eyes appear close to black against her otherwise depressed complexion. She has a freckle on her left cheek, adding to the generally infantilized texture of the mise-en-page. She is wearing a white corduroy top, decorated with pink and blue floral patterns. Her small, weak hands feebly clutch the only part of the swing visible on the page: a large, protruding black chain. Superimposed is the Nike swoosh and the text "If you let me play." At the bottom of the page, in much smaller print, one can read the alleged benefits of "playing sports": "I will like myself more. I will have more self-confidence. I will suffer less depression. I will be 60% less likely to get breast cancer. I will be more likely to leave a man who beats me. I will be less likely to get pregnant before I want to. I will learn what it means to be strong."

For the critically inclined, the "If you let me play" advertising campaign represents an insidious reformulating of conservative body politics. The explicit request for permission by a young girl to a presumed white male reader/consumer is complicated and problematic when viewed in progressive theoretical terms. Indeed, the request for permission seems sufficient in itself to render impossible a feminist reading of the advertisement. The dubious implications of this advertising strategy, however, range far beyond the problematic plea for permission. In this brief article, I will endeavor to discern the often elusive mechanisms through which the "If you let me play" campaign reproduces dominant forms of masculine, racial, and sexual privilege. To do so, I will examine the subtle insinuations contained within each section of the advertisement's textual content.

"I will suffer less depression"

To better tackle the implications of this narrative, one must first examine some of the causes of women's depression: violence, poverty, and the kinds of work typically performed by women (Walters et al, 1995). When these are taken into consideration, one realizes that Nike trivializes the sociostructural roots of women's depression with the suggestion that if you let women play sports, "[they] will suffer less depression."

In Canada, recent studies (Comité canadien, 1993; Statistics Canada, 1995) show that violence against women is endemic, despite the fact that 62 percent of sexual assault victims do not report assaults to police. A recent Canadian study (Comité canadien, 1993) notes that: "taking all three kinds of sexual assault as defined in the Criminal Code into account ... two out of three women, well over half the female population, have experienced what is legally recognized as sexual assault" (p.28). Moreover, "The short- and long-term effects of sexual assault include depression, anxiety, trouble with interpersonal relationships, reduced job effectiveness, diminished sexual satisfaction, sexual dysfunction and sleep disorders, and increased use of sedatives and sleeping pills ... with that comes a profound loss of self-esteem and self-worth" (Comité canadien, 1993, p.29).

In terms of poverty as a cause of depression, it is noteworthy that recent studies (e.g., Health Canada, 1996; National Council of Welfare, 1996; Walters et al., 1995) have confirmed socioeconomic status as the major determinant of physical and mental health. Even in a country with an almost universally accessible health care system, inequalities in health status persist. The latest Report on the Health of Canadians could not be clearer: "The rich are healthier than the middle class, who are in turn healthier than the poor" (Health Canada, 1996, p.iii). It is also germane that women are over-represented among the poor, and this trend is worsening. This is because when one examines the current research on the Canadian work force, one finds that women dominate the lower ranks of all types of employment. Women are paid substantially less than their male counterparts, and women's work in both private and public sectors is more often than not defined by monotony, low pay, job insecurity, and poor working conditions (Armstrong & Armstrong, 1994; Clement & Myles, 1994; Ng, 1993). In these circumstances, it is entirely understandable that "on measures of self-rated health, psychological well-being, stress, and depression, women do not score as well as men" (Health Canada, 1996, p.27). When some of the structural causes of mental illness among women are seen and understood, Nike's suggestion that playing sports will resolve the problem of female depression appears simplistic and even insulting. I would argue that Nike's advertisement tends to trivialize and obscure the structural oppressions that many women experience, and how these contribute to depression.

"I will be 60% less likely to get breast cancer"

Recent medical studies show that heightened breast cancer rates are largely attributable to environmental pollutants and to drugs commonly prescribed to women (e.g., hormone replacement therapy), and not to individual predisposition (Castleman, 1994; Worcester & Whatley, 1992). There is little evidence that exercise is a significant factor in breast cancer, land Nike's contention that "playing sports" will significantly reduce breast cancer occurrence again misrepresents women's illness as an outcome of individual choices, an individual problem with individual solutions.

"I will be more likely to leave a man who beats me"

"I will be less likely to get pregnant before I want to"

The aforementioned statements intimate that women can freely and without difficulty leave the men who beat them, rape them, harass them in the workplace, and/or coerce them into sex. Indeed, the advertisement's text in this instance omits any suggestion of the economic realities associated with male domination, or the psychological manipulation experienced by abused women. Most importantly, these Nike narratives once again locate the source of crucial social-structural problems within individual, allegedly free-willed women. In this sense, the advertisement represents a textbook mobilization of the neo-conservative "blame-the victim" discourse.

"I will like myself more"

"I will have more self-confidence"

There is a well-known correlation between physical activity and a positive self-concept. However, both sociologists and those responsible for equipping themselves and their family members with sporting gear can attest to the increasingly exclusive and inaccessible nature of organized sports. Not only are the costs of sporting equipment and apparel increasingly intolerable, but Nike has contributed in a significant way to this escalation. It does not any longer suffice, in the imagery popularized by Nike and other major "leisure wear" brands, to throw on a pair of old running shoes, pick up a baseball bat and head to the park. Contemporary advertising has created norms whereby even recreational athletes feel they must suit themselves up in expensive attire, pay the bus fare to the closest sport complex, pay an entry fee, and then pay a fee for participating in the chosen sporting activity. For those women who have children, or who are balancing multiple jobs, these costs may also be compounded by the babysitter's fee. For many, then, the costs associated with regular sport or fitness-related activities become prohibitive.

Nike claims that improved self-esteem will result from girls and women being "permitted" to play sports. Even a cursory examination of the research conducted on female populations, however, reveals that girls and women do not need anybody's permission. What they need is concrete access to sporting spaces. According to Harvey and Donnelly (1996, p.4), what girls and women require is the eradication of the "systemic barriers" to physical activity. These include "infrastructural barriers" (e.g., high costs, lack of transportation, lack of time, etc.), "superstructural barriers" (e.g., sexist policies, lack of role models and/or pro-women facilitators, etc.) and "procedural barriers" (e.g., lack of social support, lack of rights to services or opportunities, etc.).

Given the existence of these systemic barriers, it is possible to suggest that adult women who do participate in physical activity and sports are a "breed apart." In Canada, women who participate in sports are most likely financially comfortable, and probably enjoy decent living and working conditions and access to regular leisure time, and it is most likely these positive socioeconomic conditions that explain the higher level of self-esteem, self-confidence, and mental and physical health that are found among physically active girls and women.

General problematization of Nike narrative(s)

First, one must interrogate Nike's obscuring of class-related issues. Those most acutely affected by the issues highlighted in the "If you let me play" campaign inhabit the economic periphery of Western societies. Yet, Nike proposes a solution (i.e., the consumption of expensive sporting goods) that is realistically open only to those who make up the dominant economic class. This attests to the paradoxical if not bogus character of Nike's "concern."

Second, the Nike advertisement is a blatant appropriation of "women's" issues. That is, Nike has managed to effectively re-articulate the solution of "women's problems" with individual, consumer choices (Cole & Hribar, 1995). In each section of the advertisement's text, the gendered problem delineated is individualized, de-politicized and naturalized. Where grass-roots movement feminism saw unwanted pregnancies, violence against women, and low self-esteem as assuming an inherently systemic and historical character, Nike remakes these phenomena into issues of personal choice remedied by individual agency. Where movement feminism asked women to interrogate their sexual identities and beliefs, and to fight against the complex systems that oppress them, Nike proposes a far easier and more comfortable solution: no trouble in the classroom, no clothing or food boycotts, no late-night strategic meetings, no stress when reading the newspaper, no perplexing critical thought.

All Nike asks for is your money. When one sits down with the facts in front of her, Nike's "pro-woman, pro-self-esteem" image emerges as fraudulently immoral.

Source: Mélisse Lafrance is a graduate student at the University of Oxford in England. This article was originally published in *Canadian Issues/Themes Canadiens*, Autumn 1999, pp.20-22.

Part 12
The Crisis in Hockey

The poor performance of Canada's men's national hockey teams in recent years–at the World Championships, the Junior World Championships, and the "Dream Team" of NHL players at the Nagano Olympics in 1998–is only one symptom of a broader crisis in the game in Canada.

Concerns have been expressed about the player development system, which seems to emphasize player size and aggression over skill, defensive rather than offensive play, and playing games rather than practising. Concern has also been expressed about violence and injury, with a growing number of well-publicized concussions, and other eye and head injuries, some resulting from deliberate violence in what is thought of as the "Canadian style" of play. And concern has been expressed about the globalization and the Americanization of the game, which is draining off Canadian talent, opening the game to many nationalities, and taking NHL teams away from this country.

There has been much discussion about these issues, and a major conference called "Open Ice" was held in Toronto in 1999 in order to produce ideas to resolve the "crisis." Because of all this attention, and because this is a major topic of interest in Canadian sport sociology, this concluding section examines the various issues in the "crisis."

The Globe and Mail newspaper, until recently Canada's only national newspaper, has been a major forum for this discussion, and this section opens with a 1998 (post-Nagano) editorial outlining some of the issues of concern. This is followed by three articles addressing the issue of violence and injury. James Deacon examines Don Cherry's promotion of violence in hockey, and then examines the role of dirty play and violence in producing injuries. Then Cam Cole exposes the hypocrisy of fans who cheer fights, but were "shocked" by the recent Marty McSorley/Donald Brashear incident.

Another editorial from *The Globe and Mail* summarizes a series on the crisis in Canadian hockey.

The series itself (William Houston's "A Game in Crisis"), a twelve-part series of articles focusing on player development problems in Canada, is also presented in full here. (See also **Youth**.)

Finally, there are four articles dealing with various aspects of globalization and Americanization. Howie Meeker is outraged that the federal government would consider using taxpayers' money to support NHL franchises in Canada (and keep them from moving to the United States), rather than supporting the grassroots game. Jim Silver notes how little changed in Winnipeg as a result of the loss of the Jets to the United States–despite the dire consequences that were predicted if the provincial and federal governments did not use taxpayers' money to maintain the team in Winnipeg.

David Shoalts's three-part series of articles on the economics of the NHL ("Hockeynomics") is also presented here in full. The selection presents interesting data on the league and the potential use of the Internet. The overview of the crisis in Canadian hockey concludes with a brief examination of the turnaround by Federal Industry Minister John Manley, who announced federal support for the Ottawa Senators and then withdrew that support in the face of public outrage about the plan.

What will become of this crisis in Canadian hockey remains to be seen. Perhaps by the time of the next edition of this book, the direction of change will be clearer and we will be past the worst aspects of the current crisis.

Additional Sources

Videos:
- *The New ice Age*, a six-part CBC television series that takes a look at a year in the life of the NHL.
- *The Game of Her Life*, a NFB video on the lead-up to Nagano for the Canadian women's hockey team.

Print Resources:
- Hockey Twilight in Canada: An International Exchange: Part I: Klein, J.Z. and Reit, K.E., "Our tarnished past." Part II: Teitel, J. "Their glorious future." *Saturday Night*, December 1998, pp.30-44.

50.

Who Killed Canadian Hockey?

Editorial, *The Globe and Mail*

If we want it back, we're going to have to fight for it

Watch the guys who block the shots, who go into the corners, who go stand in front of the net and take the poundings, who grind it out for 82 games of the year, and nobody really knows who they are except their team mates—and they're appreciated by their team mates and their coaches and the people who appreciate that kind of hockey. And that's a Canadian hockey player.—Team Canada manager Bob Clarke, speaking on national TV after he announced his selections for the 1998 men's Olympic hockey team.

Want to know why we lost in Nagano? Read Bobby Clarke's credo one more time. There it is, in black and white: We are the grinders, the clutchers, the hangers, the no-name role-players, the men with heart enough to make up for shoddy skills. Yes, this is what Canadian hockey is all about. Here in the Church of Don Cherry, blessed are the toothless muckers, for they shall inherit a National Hockey League contract.

How did this happen? Cast your mind back a mere 20 years, to an NHL whose rosters were all close to 100 percent Canadian. The top players were of course Canadian to a man as well, and all the individual awards–highest scorer, most valuable player, best defenceman–had always been exclusively our turf. With the exception of the Soviet Union, no one could even touch us. At the first Canada Cup, in 1976, Canada defeated Finland in the opening game by a score of 11-2. At the 1998 Olympics, Finland beat Canada 3-2.

It hasn't been a great couple of years for Canadian hockey.–Wayne Gretzky, after the loss to Finland.

No, it hasn't. We were beaten by the American all-stars at the World Cup in the fall of 1996. At the Olympics, the Canadian women took on the United States twice and lost both times and the men wound up in fourth place. At the recent world junior championships, our guys finished eighth.

The quality of Canadian hockey is not merely declining, it is in free fall. With the exception of the junior team's stumble against Kazakhstan, the abysmal international results are no fluke. Remember the 100 percent Canadian NHL of a generation ago? Cherish the thought: the league's makeup is now only 60 percent Canadian-born and dropping.

And worse yet, Canadians are a minority where it really counts, in the ranks of star players. Remember when every one of the top scorers was one of us? History. Just before the Olympic break, the list of the NHL's top 25 scorers included only nine Canadians. The leading point-getter was a Czech, second was a Swede, third was a Finn, fourth was an American. The captain of the Toronto Maple Leafs is a Swede. The best player in Edmonton is American. The top scorer in Vancouver is Russian. Our game? Not anymore.

I think you have to be somewhat cautious after the disappointment we all shared after the Olympic experience in Nagano that we don't have the knee-jerk reaction that something is wrong… The Olympics have emphasized that the rest of the world has caught up to Canada, but that doesn't mean we're behind.–Dev Dley, vice-president of the Canadian Hockey League and commissioner of the Western Hockey League.

See, nothing is wrong. Nobody panic, nobody worry, nobody change what you're doing. Next time, we will simply try harder, and our vaunted Canadian heart will carry the day. We will play "our" game, only this time it will work. They say the definition of stupidity is doing the same thing over and over again and expecting different results. Welcome to Canadian hockey.

The first step in treating the illness must be acknowledging that we have one. So here goes: Canadian hockey is sick. Now on to figuring out what the problem is, and how to cure it.

To yours from failing hands we throw the torch; be yours to hold it high.–passage from "In Flanders Field," inscribed on the Montreal Canadiens' dressing room wall.

Clever stickhandling, pretty passing plays, lightning on skates: this is what made Beliveau and Lafleur and Hull and Orr great. And yet, in a few short years, those who weave such magic have come to be described as "European style" players. European style? No, such skills were always part of our game, yet we seem to have suddenly misplaced them.

As Gretzky, Mario Lemieux, Mark Messier and others retire, there are far fewer talented players to whom the torch can be passed. Compared to past national squads, Team Canada '98 was notable for its lack of creative offensive stars. With Paul Kariya and Joe Sakic injured, we were left with almost no other possessors of those delicate puckhandling and playmaking skills that not only sell tickets in the NHL, but also win games in the Olympics. Hence the final result.

All the interference, the holding, the hooking; it doesn't allow the good players to flourish… It's the main reason I didn't return.—Mario Lemieux, on why one of the greatest players of all time chose to retire early.

The NHL's insistence on not enforcing its own rules diminishes the quality of the game at the hightest level—and what's more, the style of play is emulated in junior, midget and bantam leagues throughout Canada. As a result, the players produced by Canadian youth hockey are very different from the best European players. The Canadian player is robust, used to seasons of 100 games, used to pounding the boards and enduring nightly physical abuse. He may lack finesse, but his hardiness makes him a great trench warrior, ideal for the bottom 50 percent of the jobs in the NHL.

Indeed., a division of labour is slowly setting in: if current trends continue, each team's four or five marquee players will be mostly non-Canadians, while Canadians continue to hold down most of the less skilled posts, the on-ice hewers of wood and bearers of water.

And even this part of the game the Europeans are learning, as the Czechs so ably demonstrated. That is no surprise. It's not that tough to teach a bunch of experienced players to play a system, using the defensive neutral-zone trap or boxing opponents out from the front of the net. Far harder is learning how to make the puck dance while skating at full speed and turning on a dime. Such skills take thousands of hours of practice.

And Canadian youngsters no longer practice, no longer play for fun, no longer simply get out there and *play.* Instead, you have elementary school-age kids slogging through seasons of 80 games and few practices. Coaches in these leagues actually think the objective is not to develop basic skills, but to win. Nothing could be more harmful to this country's progress in hockey, or more destructive of the individual youngster's enjoyment of the game. And success and enjoyment are inseparable: ever wonder why kids begin abandoning hockey in droves at 12 and 13 years of age? Because it's not fun anymore.

Canadians were so distraught over the loss in Nagano because we are, secretly, a nation of deep passions. Hockey is our passion, a place where a quiet people reveals its fire. This is our game. If we want it back, we are going to have to fight for it—with our hearts; but above all with our heads.

Source: This editorial was originally published in *The Globe and Mail,* Feburary 28,1998, D6. Reproduced by permission of *The Globe and Mail.*

51.

Over the Top: Has Don Cherry Gone Too Far?

James Deacon

Is Don Cherry what's wrong with Canadian hockey?

Ian Cobby and James Harris are excited as heck. Down from suburban Georgetown, they're spending Saturday night at the main CBC building in Toronto, and they've talked their way into meeting Don Cherry. *Grapes*! The two boys, both 10, and Ian's dad, John, follow a CBC staffer into a private lounge adjacent to the *Hockey Night in Canada* set where Cherry, preparing for "Coach's Corner," is resting before going on camera. The kids step into the dimly lit room and, wham, it hits them. "Hi guys, how ya doin'?" comes the familiar bellow. It's Don, all right, loud and proud. He's wearing gray flannels, red blazer, red shirt and red tie–can't miss him.

Cherry usually keeps to himself before his between-periods sessions with host Ron MacLean, but for the boys he makes an exception. He likes kids, and they like him. "You hockey players?" he asks, rising to greet them. "*I* am," says Ian, explaining he plays on an atom team. "That's great," says Cherry. He's too distracted for small talk, but he signs a pair of postcards of himself with his beloved English bull terrier, Blue. "Thanks for stoppin' by," he says, "and enjoy the game, eh?" The door closes and the boys pause behind the set to examine their freshly minted autographs. James says it was cool meeting the big TV star. "Yeah," agrees Ian. "My mom doesn't like what he says, but I think he's great."

Out of the mouths of babes, eh? The 64-year-old intermission icon is one of the most-watched men in Canada thanks to a remarkable talent for simultaneously entertaining and appalling millions of viewers who tune into *Hockey Night in Canada* on Saturday nights in season. With hockey on nearly every night during the playoffs, his exposure is tripled–since mid-April, he has been on every second night, and that will continue until the Stanley Cup is awarded in June. The appeal? Watching Cherry is like watching a bonfire burning next to a barn full of hay. Will he keep the blaze contained, or will all hell break loose?

Cherry, of course, thinks fighting is a good thing; European players are stealing jobs away from hardworking Canadian boys; Americans are ruining the NHL; and anyone who thinks differently is un-Canadian or an intellectual, or both. He has a strong rapport with players from atom to the NHL. "There's not a better guy to have on your side," says Toronto Maple Leafs' tough guy Tie Domi. "When he talks on TV, a lot of people listen." And when Cherry drops the bombast, he is a keen analyst who can pick apart a videotape replay to show how a goal was set up by an event at the other end of the ice. "Don's strength is dealing with the game," says *Hockey Night's* executive producer, John Shannon, "and when he sticks to that, everyone is happy."

But he doesn't stick to the game. He is notorious for his right-of-Reform rants on pet peeves ranging from taxes to immigration. And as for Quebec, well, don't get him started. He claims he is simply taking aim at the separatists, but more often than not national unity feels the pain. His tirades often sound anti-French rather than anti-Bloc–at the Winter Olympics last February, he took a cheap shot at Canada's opening ceremonies flag-bearer, 1994 Olympic gold medallist Jean-Luc Brassard, calling him "a French guy, some skier nobody knows about." The truth is, *Cherry* had never heard of Brassard, and knows nothing about freestyle skiing. Later, he compounded the insult, calling separatists "whiners." Rejean Tremblay, the prominent *La Presse* columnist, says Cherry appears to be crossing the line between nationalism and racism. "Don Cherry is a mystery to me," Tremblay says. "The man I've known personally for 20 years seems infinitely more warm, more open than the guy that we see on television."

Perhaps Cherry is self-destructing. He isn't sure himself. The death of his wife, Rose, of liver cancer last June nearly killed him, too. "And he's still not in great shape," worries Shannon. Cherry concedes his attitude about what he will or will not say on camera has changed since Rose died. "I don't give a shit now, I really don't," he says, his voice falling to a whisper. "Why should I care? People say, 'Don, you've gone too far now,' but I don't care."

He is used to people challenging his politics, but lately, they've been questioning something more sacred–his impact on the game. Cherry has come to symbolize Canadian-style hockey–which is to say, Rock 'Em Sock 'Em hockey, the name of Cherry's hugely successful video series–at a time when Canada's finest have suffered soul-searching losses at the World Cup in 1996 and the Olympics last February. Cherry says the problems are overblown. "To me, there's nothing wrong," he says. "I wish we handled the puck a little more, but that's it." He cannot stomach the oft-repeated suggestion that Canada take a lesson from the slick-stickhandling Europeans. "We're teaching kids to block shots, hit, God forbid *fight*–we're teaching them all the fundamentals," he says. "The Europeans hockey coaches and players just go out and score. As long as you get 50 goals, you're a superstar."

But in the post-Nagano world, Canadian officials and parents have acknowledged that minor hockey only teaches *some* fundamentals. Coaches bent on winning put more emphasis on size and so-called system hockey than imparting puck-handling and skating skills. At the NHL level, the shortfall in skills translates into a scoring race dominated by Europeans, who did not come up in a similarly stifling hockey environment.

Nor are the Europeans' successes limited to scoring. Despite Cherry's insistence that they cannot match Canadians for playoff competitiveness, it was a pair of imports, Russian Alexei Yashin and Swede Daniel Alfredsson, who led the small but swift Ottawa Senators to a stunning first-round playoff upset of the big, intimidating New Jersey Devils. (The Senators were among three Canadian teams to score first-round upsets–the Montreal Canadiens and Edmonton Oilers advanced as well.) Alfredsson did duck a direct question about Cherry, but it was clear he and the other targets of Cherry's derision were thrilled the Senators beat the Devils. "It feels great to come through like this against New Jersey," he said, "because they're the toughest team out there. Ask any of the other teams–no one wanted to play them."

Howie Meeker, the man Cherry replaced between periods, says Canadians should have

NHL Leaders in Penalty Minutes		
1.	Donald Brashear, U.S.	372
2.	Tie Domi, Canada	365
3.	Krzysztof Oliwa, Poland	295
4.	Paul Laus, Canada	293
5.	Richard Pilon, Canada	291
6.	Matthew Barnaby, Canada	289
7.	Denny Lambert, Canada	250
8.	Matt Johnson, Canada	249
9.	Sandy McCarthy, Canada	241
10.	Rob Ray, Canada	234

begun rethinking the way hockey is taught years ago. "I'd say 1972 was the time to start taking it more seriously, after the Russians showed us how to play the game," Meeker says. The need for that reassessment may have been lost in the euphoria surrounding Paul Henderson's momentous last-minute goal that saved the series for Canada. But now the reformers are having their day, and there is no escaping the shadow of Cherry. His bigger-is-life, take-no-prisoners ethic has become gospel to minor-hockey coaches and players. In that way, he has helped build a generation of competitors who are long on work ethic and size, but short on the stick skills and creativity that define truly great players. "That influence can be detrimental, particularly for people who hang on his every word," says Murray Costello, president of the Canadian Hockey Association. "And there are many who do."

Roy MacGregor, the respected *Ottawa Citizen* columnist, author and one-time minor-hockey coach, says he could see the Cherry effect on kids. "His thinking, and his extraordinary influence, has been the single most destructive influence on the development of Canadian hockey," MacGregor says. He adds that Cherry has that power not just because of TV, but "because hockey means so much in Canada, and because people believe in him."

All the outrage and controversy have built quite a little empire. While some may dismiss Cherry as an annoying but harmless redneck, like the loud-mouth at the end of the bar who might shut up if people just ignore him, it is a mistake to underestimate him. And even for committed hockey haters, it is almost impossible to escape him. He has an enormous audience–CBC's Saturday night games attracted an average of 1.5 million viewers this season–and he has been allowed to hurl his Cherry bombs unopposed, except when the affable MacLean, the host since 1986, can get a word in edgewise. His Rock 'Em Sock 'Em videos–the series now numbers nine–have sold over a million copies and counting. He does a nationally syndicated radio show and lends his name to a 12-restaurant chain, Don Cherry's Grapevine. Then there are his commercials–for several companies, including Nabisco's Mr. Christie products and Campbell's soup. Don Cherry–the self-styled voice of the regular guy–is a very rich man.

The fact is, Cherry's schtick is not buffoonery. He has an agenda. His high-decibel, over-the-top delivery may be TV-driven theatricality, much like his wardrobe, but the opinions, the issues he tackles, the edge, are genuine Cherry. He does not take calls on game days, using the time to put together a "game plan" for that night's show–"just like when I was coaching." He arrives late to the set so that Shannon and MacLean do not have time to rehearse. He does his own version of the old TV detective Columbo, playing dumb but speaking straight to his core audience–"my people," as he calls them. "He's just giving viewers what they want," says Shannon. "Don would not say the things he says if he didn't think they would be well received. And he knows his constituency better than most politicians know theirs."

Cherry did all the wrong things on his way to the top. A native of Kingston, Ont., he was a career minor-leaguer who laced up his skates for exactly one NHL game–no goals, no assists. He retired from the American Hockey League Rochester Americans at 33 to work on a construction crew at the Kodak plant there. Laid off, he became, by his own admission, the world's worst Cadillac salesman. He fell back on the only thing he knew–hockey–mounting a comeback with the Americans at 35. In mid-season, the general

Leading NHL Scorers, 1997-1998			
	Goals	Assists	Points
1. Jarmoir Jagr *Czech Republic*	35	67	102
2. Peter Forsberg *Sweden*	25	66	91
3. Pavel Bure *Russia*	51	39	90
4. Wayne Gretzky *Canada*	23	67	90
5. John LeClair *U.S.*	51	36	87
6. Zigmund Palffy *Slovakia*	45	42	87
7. Ron Francis *Canada*	25	62	87
8. Teemu Selanne *Finland*	52	34	86
9. Jason Allison *Canada*	33	50	83
10. Jozef Stumpel Slovakia	21	58	79

manager fired the coach and gave the reins to Cherry. Within 3 1/2 years, he was running the Boston Bruins. "I was coaching Bobby Orr," he says, still incredulous. "*Me.*"

He nevertheless squandered that windfall. Never one to button his lip, he feuded–foolishly, he now admits–with Boston general manager Harry Sinden and got fired after five seasons. He later coached the Colorado Rockies (now the New Jersey Devils) and was fired there, too. Ralph Mellanby, then the producer of *Hockey Night in Canada*, got him a job as a color commentator and, Cherry says, "I was in trouble all the time." He was saved from the unemployment line by Mellanby, who paired him with then-host Dave Hodge between periods. "Coach's Corner," and a star, were born.

A controversial star, of course: his scornful comments about Brassard, and remarks he made during the January ice storm about Quebec's language laws, prompted Bell Canada to pull its sponsorship of "Coach's Corner" in Quebec in April. But it goes against the TV grain to muzzle Cherry—the more outrageous he gets, the higher the ratings go. "The interesting thing about 'Coach's Corner' is that we set out to create intermissions that were entertaining," says Shannon. "What we've done is create programming that is actually more viewable than the games." Ross Brewitt, a Cherry booster from Mississauga, Ont., says "it's his penchant for blurting out what he thinks that has made him a national figure. And 95 percent of the time, he's right." That may be a stretch, but Ken Dryden, the former goalie who now is president and general manager of the Toronto Maple Leafs, agrees that Cherry has much to offer on the subject of hockey. "There is a lot of wisdom, a lot of knowledge, in what Don says," Dryden concludes.

The way critics see it, however, *Hockey Night in Canada* has allowed its star to get away with what might otherwise be seen as on-air conflicts of interest. He has worn a hat on camera with the logo of his soon-to-be-launched Mississauga Ice Dogs, a major-junior A team that is busy selling season tickets (and that will not include a single foreign player, Cherry vows). He recently supported NHL owners who were making pleas to Ottawa for tax relief that could ultimately help the profitability of his own team. He defends fighting in the game, yet he includes replays of two major fights in each Rock 'Em Sock 'Em video to boost sales. "Is that correct?" asks MacGregor. "The CBC would not stand for that in any other aspect of their business, presumably."

Worse for the game, says Bruce Dowbiggin, national sports correspondent for CBC Radio, is that Cherry has been allowed to deliver his one-sided message on how hockey ought to be played without rebuttal. "Kids take their messages straight," Dowbiggin says. "That's why I hold Hockey Night in Canada accountable. They do not offer a counterpoint. I'm not saying 'Take him off the air.' I'm just saying they should put someone on with a different point of view, someone who will say, 'Don, you're a clown.'"

Sitting back on an old sofa in the studio lounge, his on-air duties done, Cherry is watching two different playoff games on a bank of TV monitors. He's mad at MacLean, who inadvertently wore the same color tie. "It's the first time that's happened in 12 years," Cherry says grumpily. This has not been a happy time for him. It has been a year since Rose died, and he has not yet fully absorbed the hit. He struggled when he and MacLean took their show on the road, to Vancouver for the all-star game in January and to Nagano, Japan, for the Olympics. "I've been lost now for awhile, but I seemed to be more lost over there," Cherry says of his time in Japan. "I used to call Rose every morning, wherever I was, at 8:30 on the nose, and...." He doesn't finish the thought.

The real-life Don Cherry—the soft-spoken, painfully private guy rattling around in his now-too-big house in suburban Mississauga—does not want to talk about Rose. Or at least, that's the word before the interview begins. "I think it's a tender subject," explains CBC publicist Susan Procter. "And it may be that way for a long time." But Cherry brings it up himself. She was his best friend, the centre of his daily existence far more than work or hockey. All his adult life, he left the rink or the construction site or the car lot and went home to her, and now she's gone. He hardly knows what to do with himself, says fellow broadcaster Brian Williams, who delivered one of two eulogies at her funeral. "Rose," Williams says, "was his life."

Cherry's children, Cindy, 41, and Tim, 35, both live nearby, which is a help. Cindy has taken on Rose's old job, sorting the pile of mail that arrives daily via the restaurants and the CBC. She is also working with a group in Milton, Ont., on what they're calling Rose's Place, a hospice Cherry is helping to fund for families with terminally ill children. Keeping busy helps, but Cherry's loneliness is palpable. "I'm a lone guy. I don't go out. I, ah, I always...." His voice trails off. "When I got out of hockey, I never hung around with anybody. I still don't. I don't have a guy to say, 'Let's go fishin' or somethin'.' Maybe Tim, my son, but I don't have a friend like that. If I ever had advice for anybody, it's to have other friends, and don't isolate yourself or just stick with your wife all the time."

Then he remembers a story that cheers him up. Rose, among other things, was Don's censor. "One time on 'Coach's Corner,' I told Ron to shut up," he says. "Rose just hated it." She wouldn't talk about it when he got home that night, but he heard about it at breakfast. "She said, 'You are, without a doubt, the most ignorant human being. I'm embarrassed.'" Cherry laughs a little at the memory. But the smile soon fades.

Without Rose's moderating influence, he has been more provocative on "Coach's Corner," more out on the edge politically. He says he's just saying aloud what other people—his people—are thinking. "As far as Quebec's concerned, it's not fair," he says. "Everybody knows it's not fair, but they're afraid to say it. We have French signs, and they don't have any English—is that fair? Is it fair that you can't speak English down there anywhere in government, and we have to speak French for our government in Ontario? Everybody says the same thing. They whisper to me, 'If they want to leave, let them leave.'"

Cherry has turned his attention to the third period of the Montreal Canadiens-Pittsburgh Penguins game. His jacket is off, his tie is loosened, his three-storey collar is undone, and he's ripping into Jaromir Jagr, the gifted Czech centre who led the league in scoring this season, not to mention helping his country win Olympic gold. Jagr is the kind of guy people pay to see—six-foot-two, a powerful skater and larcenous stickhandler—but Cherry claims he's everything that's wrong with the NHL. "The guy can't hit, and never back-checks," Cherry sneers. "The joke is that he has to go down and introduce himself to his goaltender. But he'll get all the trophies and stuff like that."

While his private style is toned down from his TV persona, his opinions remain the same. He really does think European players are cowardly, that they take dives to draw penalties—conveniently ignoring the fact that "good, hardworking Canadian boys" do the same. The Philadelphia Flyers' Bill Barber was arguably the most prolific diver in NHL history, and he came from Callander, Ont. Czech defenceman Frank Musil, now with Edmonton, once called Cherry "a total idiot" for painting all imports with the same brush. Cherry has softened a little—he professes to like a pair of Russians, the Senators' Yashin and the Vancouver Canucks' Pavel Bure. But he is adamantly against imports on his junior team. "They call me a racist because I don't want any Europeans coming to play for my Ice Dogs," he says. He doesn't mind depriving his team of a young Yashin and Bure? "If a kid comes over here and becomes a Canadian, I'll put him on in a minute," he says. "But I will not parachute him in so that he can grab the money and run."

That, says Dryden, is where Cherry goes wrong, not just in political correctness, but in hockey, too. By declaring that the old-style Canadian game is best, and that all others are unworthy, he denies his players a chance to learn from the Europeans. "Don gets himself into a box," Dryden says. "The National Hockey League is a far, far better league now that the best players in the world all play here." Harry Neale, a former coach who has become CBC's top game analyst, agrees. "Anyone who thought that Canada was going to be the only supplier of NHL players had blinders on," Neale says. "It's a global game now."

Friends who have watched Cherry take ever-greater risks on camera wonder if he's trying to get himself fired. At times, he seems tired of the effort it takes to be Don Cherry, tired of the constant criticism. "I'd be lying if I said it didn't wear me down," he says. "You wake up in the morning, you're half-asleep, and you look at the paper and they're ripping you. I like to say I laugh it off, but it gets to me, it bothers me."

His approach to hockey and life, however, were forged years ago in the minor-league ice wars. Asked if the Cherry-bashers made him want to quit, he scoffs: "You don't understand—nobody understands. I don't *care* what they think. It's like a fight—I thrive on it. He leans forward, and suddenly his weariness and sadness are gone. He is again the guy on TV, pugnacious defender of all things Canadian, and of all things Grapes. "When somebody criticizes 'Coach's Corner,'" he goes on, "I'll come back twice as strong. That's what I did as a player. If I knew going into a game that the best fighter was on the other team, it got me pumped. I knew, sooner or later, him and me would be at it. It's the second-best rush in the world, fighting. You know what I mean? It keeps life going."

Source: James Deacon is a sports and lifestyle editor at *Maclean's*. This article was originally published in *Maclean's*, May 18, 1998, pp.46-50. Reproduced by permission of *Maclean's*.

52.

Thugs on Ice

James Deacon

Leagues are cracking down on illegal hits that injure players but they won't stop the fights

Todd Fedoruk looks terrible. The Regina Pats' winger is a strapping 19-year-old from Redwater, Alta., with sandy-brown hair and the usual sports-guy goatee, and he would be handsome if it weren't for an angry red-purple welt under his left eye, or the ripening bruise high on his right cheek. As for his nose, well, it's a story all by itself. There is a still-bleeding cut on what used to be the bridge, and the mashed cartilage hooks alarmingly to one side—presumably away from where the telling punch was thrown. Being a recognized tough guy in major-junior hockey makes Fedoruk the target of every other team's fighters and wanna-bes. So it was no surprise that the Lethbridge Hurricanes' six-foot, seven-inch enforcer, Mike Varhaug, would provoke a fight in the early minutes of a recent game at the Regina Agridome and exploit his reach advantage to rearrange Fedoruk's features.

Showered and heading home in a dark blazer, white shirt and tie, Fedoruk admits he got suckered into a fight he should have avoided. He took up Varhaug's challenge when another fight was already in progress, and in junior, combatants in the second fight are automatically thrown out of the game. It was a lousy trade for the Pats—Fedoruk is the more accomplished player. So his seventh broken nose in the past three seasons was for naught, and the only consolation was that Regina won anyway. "I shouldn't have..." he begins, the words trailing away as his shoulders droop in contrition. "I've got to pick my spots better—I can't help the team if I'm not on the ice."

In rinks around North America, hockey is slowly changing. The proof is that a junior tough guy like Fedoruk thinks he should have ducked a fight. The Western Hockey League is still a rugged circuit—Fedoruk's was one of three bouts in the game. But that is child's play compared with the late 1970s, when there were brawls during the pregame warm-ups, particularly when the Ernie (Punch) McLean-coached New Westminster Bruins were involved. The decline in fisticuffs is particularly evident in the NHL: there were 826 fights last season, an average of 0.77 per game, compared with two per game in the 1977-1978 season.

Fewer fights have not made hockey a safer game, however. For one thing, fighting has become more menacing in the NHL; enforcers are bigger, stronger and better trained in boxing. And for another, bodychecking and stickwork have become more vicious—hits from behind into the boards, slew-footing (kicking an opponent's feet out from under him), and high sticks and flying elbows. In 1997-1998, Anaheim star Paul Kariya's season ended with a crushing cross-check to the head; Toronto winger Nick Kypreos's career ended with a single punch. It was, players say, the NHL's meanest season.

That's saying something. Hockey in Canada has long followed the old Conn Smythe dictum—"If you can't beat them in an alley, you can't beat them on the ice." But now players show less regard for the safety of their opponents. It took the stomach-turning sight of Kypreos, unconscious and face-down in a pool of blood, to restart the age-old debate over whether fighting—severely punished in all other major team sports, not to mention society as a whole—should be allowed in hockey. This is more than just a moral and legal issue. The argument goes to the heart of how Canada is developing players at a time when, as the 1998 Nagano Olympics suggested, the country's preeminence in pucks appears to be waning. And it took the frightening hit on Kariya by Chicago defenceman Gary Suter, and Suter's laughable four-game suspension—a punishment that, in hindsight, hardly fit the crime—to spur leagues at all levels to reconsider the rules and how they are enforced.

To begin this season, the NHL announced it was introducing a system that, once it has enough trained officials, will put a second referee on the ice to help spot infractions behind the play. And last summer, NHL commissioner Gary Bettman hired former player and New York Rangers coach Colin Campbell as the league's senior vice-president and chief disciplinarian. In the first three weeks of the new season, Campbell slapped nine offenders with fines and suspensions for hits from behind and sticks or elbows to the head. It may take a while to get the message through: just last week, Montreal's Dave Manson earned a three-game suspension for a crushing elbow to the head of Boston's P. J. Axelsson, and Mike Ricci and Bernie Nicholls, both of San Jose, were badly cut by high sticks. "The players were allowed to do some things in the last few years," says Campbell, a native of London, Ont., "and when they were given enough rope, they began to hang themselves."

No one, however, is planning to ban fighting. Fans in junior-and minor-league arenas are used to a steady diet of fistic mayhem, and besides, those operators say they take their cues on rule changes from the NHL. The NHL, meanwhile, says it is already policing the pugilists. Rules introduced over the past 20 years have eliminated bench-clearing brawls and heaped extra punishment on instigators and players who jump off the bench to trade punches. Still, combatants in routine bouts get mere five-minute penalties, and Campbell echoes the attitude towards fighting expressed by the majority in the hockey world. "It's not something we can go and mess with right now," he told *Maclean's*. "It's part of the game that I think the NHL has controlled pretty good, and I don't think it is a huge problem."

No? In addition to the Kypreos incident, there was another heart-stopping scene at the end of the 1997-1998 season. Chicago defenceman Cam Russell, whose helmet had been knocked off while duking it out with Toronto tough guy Tie Domi, fell backwards and cracked his head on the ice. In stunned silence at Maple Leaf Gardens, Russell was carried off, and doctors say he was lucky to get away with nothing worse than a concussion.

Inside the game, there is growing concern for the welfare of the fighters themselves. "One of these days, a guy's going to get the upper hand in a fight and he's going to land a bomb in the wrong place, on a guy's temple or something, and boom, someone could die," says Michael Barnett, the influential agent whose roster of clients ranges from top draft picks to ageless superstar Wayne

Gretzky. "And then all hell will break loose because everyone will stand back and say, 'How did we ever let this happen?'"

Defeat weighs lightly on the 12- and 13-year-olds of the Tier II Flyers. Just off the ice after losing to the Rangers at Al Ritchie Arena in Regina, the boys are happily exchanging volleys of balled-up tape and yelling to buddies across the room, drowning out a long-suffering volunteer coach who is trying to get a consensus on which NHL jersey design they want this season. After much hollering, Nashville gets the nod. The expansion Predators are new, and new is cool.

Looking at the kids' cheerful faces, it is difficult to imagine that much of the violent behavior plaguing the sport is learned at that early stage of organized hockey. Sheathed in armor from helmet to skate blade, young players feel a false sense of invulnerability, hurling themselves around like projectiles and, too often, checking opponents headfirst into the boards. With masks protecting their faces, they crash into one another with elbows flying and sticks high. None of that seems to faze the Flyers who, in peewee, are allowed to bodycheck for the first time. "Hitting makes the game more interesting," says 13-year-old Mike Laberge. "We should be able to hit as soon as we start hockey."

But bodychecking can also be intimidating—boys that age can vary in height by a foot and in weight by some 60 lb., and the difference can be perilous to kids who are just learning how to take a hit. "You get lots of injuries that you didn't see before," says Flyers' coach Jim Lauten. Scott McGillivray, who coaches a Tier I peewee team in Regina, says he benches players for dangerous hits, even if the referee misses the play and fails to call a penalty. "There's definitely a lack of respect for their opponents," McGillivray says. "That's our biggest job as coaches at this level. We want them to hit, but hit cleanly."

Even checks that don't draw penalties can draw blood: in the NHL last week, Ottawa defenceman Andreas Dackell suffered a concussion and needed 30 stitches to the face after being crunched into the boards by Philadelphia's hulking Eric Lindros. "The players have lost respect for one another a little," a rueful Gretzky told *Maclean's*.

The Body Count

Fighting may be the most overt violence in hockey, but it is not the most injurious.
Hitting from behind and stick fouls such as cross-checking, slashing and high-sticking have made the
rink an increasingly dangerous place. Following is a sample of players who were seriously hurt—from
fighting, illegal checks and stickwork—during the past decade.

1988	Ron Sutter, Philadelphia Flyers: broken jaw and concussion from a cross-check.	1993	Pierre Turgeon, New York Islanders: separated right shoulder from a check from behind.
1988	Mario Lemieux, Pittsburgh Penguins: bruised sternum from a two-handed high stick.	1993	Mike Peluso, New Jersey Devils: concussion from a fight.
1988	Jeff Norton, New York Islanders: bruised ribs and internal trauma from a slash.	1995	Rob Ray, Buffalo Sabres: fractured orbital bone from a fight.
1990	Tomas Sandstrom, Los Angeles Kings: fractured facial bone, scratched right cornea and bleeding inside right eye from a fight.	1998	Nick Kypreos, Toronto Maple Leafs: severe concussion from a punch to the face.
		1998	Paul Kariya, Anaheim Mighty Ducks: concussion from a cross-check.

Now in his 20th season, the Great One recalls that when he was still an Edmonton Oiler, then-coach Glen Sather made the players practise without helmets to teach them to keep sticks down. "We used to protect one another more than we do in this day and age," he says. "You can call it what you want, but things have changed—you never saw anyone go for Jean Béliveau's head or Guy Lafleur's head."

In the stands at the Halifax Metro Centre, the 5,000 or so fans react to every stiff check and post-whistle confrontation between the home town Mooseheads and the Drummondville Voltigeurs. Ernest Dingle, a 21-year-old commerce student, is hoping for a fight—"It makes the game an adrenaline rush," he says—but is disappointed. "I think the refs were quick to stop the fights, too quick," Dingle says. "They should let them go." Another avid observer, Mike DiPenta, 49, says fights are inevitable when young men step on the ice. "You put skates on and a helmet and you turn into a different human being," DiPenta says. "It's true."

That, in essence, is one of the well-worn explanations for why fighting is allowed in hockey: that players need to blow off steam because of the unique intensity of the game. Then there is what Claude Ruel, the venerable ex-coach who now scouts for the Montreal Canadiens, said while watching the Pats-Hurricanes junior game. "Nobody ever gets hurt in a hockey fight," he argues, citing the difficulty of maintaining balance on skates. Another rationale comes from players, who insist the threat of having to fight an opponent helps discourage vicious stickwork.

Really? Consider:

- Is hockey so much more intense than, say, football that participants are compelled to smash their fists into opponents' faces? Anti-fighting advocates say no and, off the record, many players say no, too. The difference is that in football, anyone who fights is immediately ejected and is subject to fines, so it doesn't happen very often.

- To the old saw about no one getting hurt, well, Kypreos and Russell are recent rebuttals. "Don't believe it," says Kypreos. "Guys get hurt, absolutely." Enforcers routinely sustain concussions, broken fingers and jaws, smashed noses, and cuts to the eyes and face that require stitches. In 1996, Wendel Clark, then a key member of the Leafs, fractured his thumb in a fight and was lost for 16 games. And Detroit's Joey Kocur now has so much scar tissue on his right hand that the skin no longer has any elasticity.

- Anyone who believes fighting is helping keep sticks down should consult Paul Kariya, not to mention the dozens of players who get clipped for stitches in the face every season. And Suter's cross-check cost Kariya more than just months of headaches and short-term memory loss. It cost the sniper a place on Canada's Olympic team in Nagano, which in turn deprived Canada, which fell one goal short of the gold-medal game, of perhaps its best player.

There is no question that fighting is part of North American hockey, but it is emphatically not part of the world game, which hockey is increasingly becoming. And the Russians, Swedes and Czechs–who never had to drop their gloves at home–now dominate the scoring race in the NHL. Yet the beating goes on: every team from junior on up has at least two so-called tough guys on its roster. And Don Cherry, who routinely decries the foreign influence in hockey on *Coach's Corner*, proudly banned any Europeans from his expansion Mississauga Ice Dogs of the Ontario Hockey League. At the weekend, the Ice Dogs had won only once in 12 tries–and led the league in penalty minutes.

So what's the point of all that punching? Entertainment, pragmatists say. Brian Kilrea, the renowned coach of the major-junior Ottawa 67's, has guided such crowd-pleasing skill players as Bobby Smith, Doug Wilson, Mike Peca and Alyn McCauley towards the professional ranks, yet he believes strongly that fighting sells tickets. Fights quicken the pulse in any hockey crowd, getting otherwise demure customers onto their feet and screaming for their man. In that respect, hockey may be a bit like stockcar racing–NASCAR fans, the saying goes, pay to see the crashes, not to see the cars go round and round. "If we didn't have fights," Kilrea suggests simply, "the attendance wouldn't be as good."

Fighting is also important to some sponsors and TV networks. Advertising executives say the NHL's most important drawing card is its appeal to the prized beer- and truck-buying demographic, men between the ages of 18 and 35. They also happen to be the biggest fans of the more physical aspects of hockey, including fights. Then there are the sportscasts on TV: competing for viewers, The Sports Network and CTV Sportsnet, among others, now show clips from virtually every available fight.

The NHL has conducted polls to gauge public reaction to fighting, but its findings are not conclusive. The league does know that gloves-on hockey still sells on TV because it gets its best ratings during international tournaments and the NHL playoffs, when there is almost no fighting at all. Ken Dryden, the Leaf president who is on record against fighting, says no one knows if fighting is scaring away more fans than it attracts, perhaps because no one is asking the right questions. And the league will consider banning fighting only if it gets the right answers. "The determining factor," Dryden says, "is whether more people will watch if the fighting is taken away."

Even if they wanted to, however, the league's New York City-based leaders will not move quickly on the fighting issue. Traditionalists have been wary of Bettman, a former NBA executive, since he took control in 1993, fearing he would try to remake the NHL in the image of the hip-hop hoops league. He did, after all, approve Fox Broadcasting's hated blue- and red-streaked puck for U.S. consumption. But Bettman wants to build the league's fan base, not alienate longtime supporters, so insiders say that if he plans to take action on fighting, he will do so with a scalpel, not a sledgehammer. "He can't lead with his chin on this," said a senior NHL executive.

The NHL may not have to act. There are other forces at play in hockey that are gradually pushing pugilism aside. Nowadays, it is not just that there are fewer fights; there are fewer fighters, too. Gretzky says highly touted rookies such as the Rangers' top draftee, Manny Molhotra, are now exempt from the rough stuff. "Twenty years ago when I broke in, a kid like that would have had three fights in the first week of training camp," Gretzky says. "That's what happened to Mark Messier. Manny's a big, tough kid, and other guys would have challenged him, to see what he could do. Now, he comes in, people know he's a hard-nosed two-way player, but he's not a fighter, so they leave him alone."

The reason for the change? Dollars, mostly. "The rules have helped, but more than that, it's the money we're paying players now," says Campbell. "Owners don't want to be paying a guy millions of dollars and see him sit out with a broken hand or a broken jaw. You want your best players on the ice."

That leaves fighting to the specialists, typically players with borderline skills who have made themselves useful with their fists. Today's enforcers dwarf most of the old fighters. "They are as big as NFL linebackers, they're tough and they are out there bareknuckle boxing," Barnett says. "Real boxing stopped that years ago. If you asked Evander Holyfield to step into the ring with another heavyweight and fight without gloves, he'd say you were crazy. Yet for some reason, we let this continue in hockey."

That does not seem to deter juniors, for whom fighting is a means to a lucrative end: in the NHL, long-serving enforcers can take home $1 million or more in a season. It's how Fedoruk got into the Western Hockey League, first with the Kelowna Rockets and then with the Pats, and it helped get him noticed by scouts who, in addition to skill, look for size and "character"—a willingness to drop the gloves for the cause. In 1997, Fedoruk was drafted in the seventh round by Philadelphia.

Veteran fighters, though, acknowledge the risks. They do what they do knowing that what happened last season to Kypreos and Russell could happen to them. They have to accept that, in many cases, their families won't watch them play because they hate to see them get hurt. They know that, like Old West gunslingers, they are the

target of every tough new kid hoping to make a name. All of that goes with the territory. Then there's the fact that enforcers rarely get to use their playing skills because they have to concentrate on the grim job of trading punches. "That's why I always played my best hockey during the play-offs," the Leafs Domi says. "I didn't have to worry about fighting."

That in itself is a good reason to crack down on fighting. Another, says 11-year-old Whitney Eberle, is that it disrupts the flow of the game. And besides, she adds, most fights are boring—more clutching than punching. Eberle, who plays girls atom hockey in Regina and watched the Pats-Hurricanes game with her parents and her brother's novice team, thinks the Western Hockey League sets a bad example. "My little brother, he tries to fight and stuff because he sees these guys fighting," the sixth-grader says, gesturing towards the ice surface. "I find the NHL games are more interesting because there are not as many fights and it's faster."

The players themselves may yet decide the issue. Kypreos says the sports fan in him likes to see a good fight in a game, but when he steps back, he gets a different perspective. "Sometimes I just shake my head," he says. "I mean, it's 1998 and we allow fighting. It's part of the game, but don't you think it's kind of weird? I do that outside the arena and I know I'm spending the night in jail." But what to do? "There's such a fine line between what's right and what's wrong with fighting," says Gretzky. "Why isn't there any fighting in the play-offs? Because everyone is scared they'll hurt their teams. Somehow we have to figure out how to make that work the rest of the year, too." Hockey would be a better sport for it.

Source: James Deacon is a sports and lifestyle editor at *Macleans*. This article was originally published in *Maclean's*, November 9, 1998, pp.68-72. Reproduced by permission of *Macleans*.

53.

The Hypocrisy of Hockey Fans

Cam Cole

We cheer the fights—then we're shocked when they go too far

Violence sells. The National Hockey League has known it forever.

The media that covers hockey has known it forever. Don Cherry has made a tidy living selling it to kids, and enough of us love him for it that the CBC doesn't dare pull the plug on him. His videos aren't called *Hockey's Nicest Plays*, they're called *Rock'em, Sock'em*. You want to see concussions, kids? Watch this: Boom! That's old-time hockey!

Newspapers and talk radio and TV highlight shows aren't innocent, either.

There's nothing like a good, violent incident to stir up heavy opinions and passionate arguments, our stock-in-trade.

What are the two most replayed pieces of video tape from the past few days? Geoff Bodine's horrifying, blazing, cartwheeling crash at the Daytona race track, and one man clubbing another over the head with a hockey stick. Blood is good for ratings, just as war, some say, is good for the economy.

The NHL's vice-president of hockey operations, Colin Campbell, yesterday suspended the clubber, Marty McSorley, for the last 23 games of the regular season, plus all those payoff games the Boston Bruins aren't going to play–and I don't imagine you had to turn to the fine print on the results page to find out about it.

Just listen to us, this last couple of days, calling for Marty McSorley's head, because he almost handed us Donald Brashear's. As if we just discovered that thugs are employed by National Hockey League teams and we are shocked that they seem bent on behaving like thugs.

Look, this is not to defend McSorley, the Boston Bruins defenceman who crossed the ice to bludgeon the unsuspecting Vancouver Canucks enforcer across the temple with the business end of his hockey stick on Monday, surely one of the most heinous assaults of the post-expansion era.

I don't care if Marty is a decent guy off the ice, I don't care that I know him and like him, I don't care that he made himself into a hockey player through hard work, though the only tools he owned when he fought his way in the NHL's door were his fists and his willingness to use them.

I don't care if Donald Brashear beat him up earlier in the game, and his 36-year-old ego was bruised. I don't care if Brashear skated in front of the Boston bench and flexed his muscles. I don't even care all that much (and Campbell doesn't care at all) that the severity of Brashear's injury was exacerbated by his refusal to fasten his chinstrap properly, and so his helmet came off as his head struck the ice.

I don't know whether I even totally believe the words of contrition that came out of McSorley's mouth Monday night as he must have realized the enormity of the trouble he was in. There has always been just a little bit of con in Marty McSorley, a hint of calculation behind every emotion.

I feel for McSorley in the loss of his father last summer, and I wish some of his teammates, or a coach, had just grabbed him by the back of his shirt and said: "Cool it, Marty," the way his old Edmonton teammates used to do. But I don't see what any of that has to do with the act.

The act had no acceptable context. McSorley didn't just "snap" and suddenly have the devil possess his body. In the dying seconds of a game already irretrievably lost, he slammed his stick on the boards, begging to be sent out for a last chance at retribution, and his coaches let him go get it, and by God, he got it.

Well, he should be gone for a good, long time, and if 23 games and $72,000 (US) in forfeited salary doesn't seem enough, I suppose you could always vent your displeasure with the NHL by not buying tickets or watching the product on TV. It will be, by at least two games, the longest suspension handed down in league history, though the hunch is that if the Bruins had 30 or 40 games left in the season, the suspension would have been for 30 or 40 games.

But I wouldn't hold my breath, if I were you, waiting for the NHL to change of its own accord.

It is a league built on contradictions—the proximity of speed to danger, of skill to violence—but ultimately, it is played by men carrying weapons. And because it is good for business, the NHL has always winked at the occasional consequences.

Every now and then, a Really Big Mess happens, the NHL makes horrified noises and calls it an isolated incident, and life goes on.

What Marty McSorley did to Donald Brashear was premeditated, but on a violence scale, was no worse than defenceman Gary Suter's slash to the jaw of Anaheim's Paul Kariya before the Nagano Olympics. Kariya would miss the rest of the season, yet Suter, to the everlasting shame of the NHL, was suspended only four games by Brian Burke, who was the league's disciplinary chief at the time. The same Brian Burke, now Vancouver's general manager, who thinks the law should not get involved in an on-ice incident because the league knows how to police itself.

Oh, really?

"Does the punishment ever fit the act? I don't know," said Campbell.

Inevitably, some will believe the NHL missed a big chance here to send the ultimate message to the players and to the paying public, and to kids. Nearing the end of a career marked by penalty minutes, fights and prior suspensions, McSorley would have been the easiest fall guy ever. The NHL could have suspended him for life, and it might have turned out to be the same thing, but it would have sounded better.

"What do you think would happen if you ran down the hall in the NHL executive offices and smashed a hockey stick into the face of one of your co-workers?" a Vancouver hockey fan named Jeff Smith wrote to Campbell. "What if a baseball player took a bat, ran down the foul line and clubbed the third baseman in the face, rendering him bloodied and unconscious? What if a golfer took a club, ran across the 18th green and hammered a competitor in the head leaving him to lie unconscious and bleed in the grass? As ridiculous as these examples sound, I question whether Mr. McSorley's workplace should be any different."

But it is different. If it weren't, a Marty McSorley wouldn't have a job in it.

Campbell, asked what he would tell all the readers and viewers around North America who were sickened by this terrible image of hockey that played all over the continent the past two days, said: "We don't like it. We hope Donald Brashear recovers from it. But it does not represent our game."

Bruins' veteran defenceman Ray Bourque condemned McSorley's act, calling hockey "a game of respect."

They must be thinking of a different game.

Source: Cam Cole is a staff writer for *The National Post*. This article was originally published in *The National Post*, February 24, 2000, pp. A1-A2. Reproduced by permission.

54.

Putting the Canadian Back in Hockey

Editorial, *The Globe and Mail*

The solutions are radical, but simple

"I've never seen a country with so many arenas produce so few good players."—former National Hockey League player and member of Team Canada '72 Pat Stapleton.

The landscape is dominated by 3,000 of them. Every village, every hamlet, each borough and quartier of whatever social class has one, great old barrel-vaulted barns rising from the snowy Prairie, ancient arsenals straddling the Canadian Shield, places that beckon to a neighbourhood like a place of worship. There are more hockey rinks in Canada than in all of Europe. And yet these arenas, factories of hockey operating 18 hours a day, 12 months a year, produce fewer of the great stars than they once did, and less joy among children of all ages than they could.

Our game is sick. As William Houston detailed in his series on the trouble with Canadian hockey (which you can read on the Web Extra section of our website at www.globeandmail.ca), Canada is no longer the world hockey power it once was. Most of the National Hockey League's teams are located in cities south of the border, and this is no surprise. Demography and economics make it so. But for the first time, the NHL fraternity of players, long an exclusively Canadian club, is dominated by non-Canadian stars. Canadian brawn and heart can still impress and intimidate, and slightly more than half the league's players are Canadian (two decades ago, it was closer to 100 percent), but Canadian skills are ever less in evidence. The list of scoring leaders and the roster of all-star teams is top-heavy with Americans and Europeans.

The malaise has deep roots. Kids 8, 9 and 10 years old, kids with no plans of making the NHL, are forced to treat hockey from a very early age like a job. Seventy-five percent of those kids who start playing hockey at age 5 or 6 have dropped out by the time they hit 15. As a result, Canadian organized hockey is falling down on both counts: it doesn't win, and it isn't fun.

The solutions are radical, but simple. The answers start from the bottom up.

Hockey is for kids: It's not for parents, it's not for coaches, it's not for the aggrandizement of our national image. It is a game, created for fun, to be enjoyed by kids and the young at heart. The coach of a group of eight-year-olds should not care about how many games they win. He should care about how much they learn—and how much fun they have.

Such an attitude, in the world of hockey, is seen as subversive. As a result, more young Canadians now play organized soccer than play hockey. That sounds odd when you consider how much time most of this country spends covered in snow. Hockey in is our blood—but so unfortunately are hockey's ancient, Dickensian training techniques, which mistake humiliation for teaching.

The idea of, say, a tennis instructor, or a ski pro or an elementary school teacher belittling his young charges like a drill sergeant, forcing them to drop to the ground and perform push ups or otherwise degrading them any time they fail to learn quickly enough, is absurd. It would be described as child abuse and the teacher would be fired. In hockey, this is how eight-year-olds have always been trained. Negative reinforcement—catch the pass or you'll get a hiding—is the Canadian way. It's moronic.

Winning does not matter: It seems paradoxical at first: Canadians lose because they focus too much and too early on winning. But consider: would it make sense for elementary schools to devote three days a week, year round, solely to test-taking, and only two days to teaching and reading? Welcome to the school of hockey. It is quite normal for young kids to play seasons of 80 or 100 or more games, with few practices squeezed in amongst all this competition. Europeans reverse the ratio, with three or four practices to every game. It shows.

The average player in the average game will touch the puck for a grand total of 10 seconds. Games are about expressing skills, not learning them. What kids need is the chance to develop, to skate, to feel their stick on a puck. That can only come through practice and through playing hours of pick up and shinny, games where the concept of winning and losing does not exist.

The game is not about violence. Most leagues do not introduce body-checking until age 12, but some have talked about lowering the age to 8. That would be a serious mistake. Eight-year-olds have enough worries about school-yard bullies; they hardly need adult coaches encouraging the use of intimidation on the ice. That's what the return of checking will bring.

In the late pre-teen and early teen years, size starts to matter. Coaches egg on violence, which wins games, but also tends to end the careers of smaller, skilled players. The older kids get, the worse it gets. Canadian junior hockey, the province of 15- to 20-year-olds, is considerably more brutal than the NHL, and skilled players, generally left alone in the pros, are often targets.

And those targets, most too young to vote or buy a drink, are effectively slaves to a junior hockey monopoly that is run by a gang of buccaneers who would do Blackbeard proud. Kids are drafted at 14 in Western Canada and at 15 in the East, which means that they have to move to whichever city selects them if they want to keep playing hockey. They can be, and frequently are, traded, which means being repeatedly moved hundreds of miles. Kids in Grades 10 or 11 are forced to uproot their entire lives—and not to go to a team or a school of their choosing, but to labour in a league-assigned hockey factory. There, they are paid far below minimum wage, and are subject to dismissal or trade at the captain of the pirate ship's whim.

The Americans are more civilized. They think teenagers and their parents should have a choice about where they play hockey. Imagine. Americans play for a high school of their choosing, then a university of their choosing. In Canada, for those playing Tier I junior, there are no choices.

Our recommendations:

1. *For children under the age of nine, there should be no organized league play:* They should spend time practicing and scrimmaging with their teammates. Throw a bag of pucks on the ice and let them go.

Winning and losing don't mean anything when you haven't learned how to skate properly.

2. *Return hockey to the schools:* Children should be taught by teachers, not ambitious volunteers. As in the United States, elementary and high schools should be encouraged to set up proper hockey programs, as they do with other sports. Schools will be able to enforce high practice-to-game ratios, and encourage an ethos of learning.

3. *Pass legislation to end the junior draft:* The top young teens and their families should decide where they will play. If that hurts the business of junior team owners, tough. Universities should be encouraged to establish better hockey programs, as in the United States—where teams play half or fewer the number of games played by Canadian junior teams. The junior draft should be illegal.

Organized hockey in Canada is no longer successful. Organized hockey in Canada is no longer fun. Shame.

Source: This editorial was originally published in *The Globe and Mail*, Saturday, April 25, 1998, D6. Reproduced by permission of *The Globe and Mail*.

55.

A Game in Crisis

William Houston

A 12-part series on the state of hockey in Canada today

1. A need for change

The images linger: Paul Henderson, at the goalmouth, slapping in his rebound; Mike Bossy deflecting a shot by Paul Coffey; Mario Lemieux bearing in, shooting, scoring. At the highest level of international competition, Canada affirmed what we already knew: our country produced the best hockey players in the world.

But circumstances have changed and so has Canada's place in the game. The country that invented hockey no longer dominates the sport. The swagger disappeared after Canada lost three of four games to the United States in the 1996 World Cup of Hockey. Now, more questions are being asked after the Canadian men's fourth-place finish in the Nagano Olympics.

Though some cling to the memories of Canada's former glories, leading hockey figures say the game is in a crisis. Canada is a diminished force in international and professional hockey not as a result of advances made in Europe and the United States, but because the country no longer produces its own highly skilled players. Canadian youth hockey, which has a rich history of developing the game's stars, has become a wasteland for children who have been denied proper training.

Canada still sends more players to the National Hockey League than any country, but most of them are second- or third-line performers—checkers and role players, the "unskilled labour of the NHL," as former Hockey Canada head Derek Holmes calls them. The top talent, with the occasional exception, now comes from countries other than Canada.

"All the good kids, in terms of skill, are in Europe," said Paul Henry, the director of player development for the NHL's Florida Panthers. "It's just so clear cut."

Howie Meeker, a former player, coach and commentator, said: "We Canadians say, 'Hey, it's our game and we're better than everybody else.' But, in fact, every year we're slipping further and further behind."

Bruce Hood, a former NHL referee, says the notion that Canada is still No. 1 is based on nostalgia rather than reality.

"We've always had this pompous, arrogant attitude that it's our game and we're the best," he said. "But how many times are we going to get beaten [before] people understand we're not?"

Although some attribute Canada's international losses to the bad luck of facing two hot goaltenders, Mike Richter in 1996 and Dominik Hasek at Nagano, the performance of opposing goalies doesn't explain Canada's weak showing in both tournaments. In 1996, the team struggled to defeat Germany and was fortunate to get past Sweden. At Nagano, Canada was outplayed in the two big games that counted by smaller hockey countries, the Czech Republic and Finland.

"There are people who say that if Eric Lindros [didn't] hit the post [in the shootout against Hasek] or if somebody else [scored], we would have won," said former player Billy Harris, who has coached professionally in North America and Europe. "They're just rationalizing."

Moreover, the argument that Canada's decline is attributable to the growth of the game in Europe is less compelling than statistics that show 3.5 times as many children playing hockey in Canada's development system as children in the development systems of Sweden, Finland, Russia, the Czech Republic and Slovakia combined.

As recently as 10 years ago, Canadian players dominated all aspects of NHL scoring. Canadians still make up 61 percent of the league, compared with the Europeans' 20 percent. Yet it is European players who, for the most part, lead in offensive statistics.

This season, Europeans hold down the first three spots and four of the top five in NHL scoring. In goal scoring, Canadians are shut out of the top six spots and place only three in the first 10. The leading scorer among defencemen is a European.

A look at NHL all-star teams over the past 10 years shows a steady decline in Canadian content. In 1987-88, Canadians made up 83 percent (five of

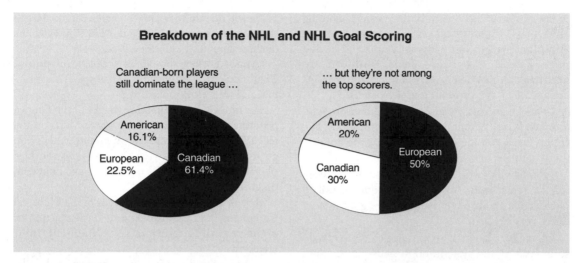

Breakdown of the NHL and NHL Goal Scoring

Canadian-born players still dominate the league …

American 16.1%
European 22.5%
Canadian 61.4%

… but they're not among the top scorers.

American 20%
Canadian 30%
European 50%

six spots) of the first all-star team. Europeans composed 17 percent (one spot).

But five years ago, Canada's percentage dropped to 66 percent (four players), while a European and a U.S. player filled the two remaining positions. Three years ago, Canadians were down to 33 percent. Europeans and Americans were also at 33 percent. And then last year, Europeans made up 66 percent, while Canadian content had shrunk to 33 percent. The projected composition of this year's all-star team has Europeans at 66 percent and 17 percent each for Canada and the United States.

"When 20 percent of the players in the NHL are European and the best 10 percent of the scorers are also European, that should be a wake-up call," said Ron Dussiaume, a former professional player and a master course conductor with Canada's national coaching certification program.

Hall of Famer Bobby Hull says Canadian hockey has ignored signs of decline for years.

"Do they have to be hit right between the eyes before they realize what's doing on?" Hull asked. "It's unforgivable what's happened to our game. We've gone so far backward we think down is up."

Hull and another Hall of Famer, Mike Bossy, both veterans of international hockey, watched the Nagano tournament and thought the Canadian team lacked talent. Hull said he was disheartened by the Canadian team's inability to carry the play to the opposition, a style that had been a Canadian trademark.

"I love the game," Hull said, "and I just feel bad that it has gotten to the point where you watch a Canadian team play in one of the greatest tournaments, and they were afraid to carry the puck. I'd never seen a Canadian team that was afraid to take the play to the opposition."

Said Bossy: "Obviously, nothing against the players who were there. I mean, they played their heart out and weren't able to win. But I think as far as individual talent, it left a little to be desired."

Edmonton Oilers president and general manager Glen Sather says he noticed a talent dropoff when he selected the 1996 World Cup team.

"When we were picking defencemen, Rob Blake and Al MacInnis were hurt," Sather said. "So we had to use other guys and they just didn't have the skill to play at that level."

Critics place the blame for Canada's decline at all three levels—professional, junior and youth. Junior hockey is a business in which revenue and winning games take precedence over developing players. Professional hockey emphasizes size and aggressiveness. Minor hockey, taking its lead from the pros, does the same, placing size and strength ahead of skill and creativity, even for eight-year-olds.

While children in Europe learn fundamentals from hours of practice and are taught by trained coaches, Canadian kids are thrown into games, as many as 140 in a season, and rarely practice. They are coached by volunteers, many of whom are inexperienced or incompetent.

For parents who dream of their sons becoming NHL stars, winning and playing games are more important than children learning skills and having fun. Instead of scoring goals, children are instructed to play defensively and to intimidate. At the age of 13, the dropout rate skyrockets.

"They're robots," said Marty Williamson, who coaches a Tier 2 junior team in Milton, Ont. "The creativity isn't in the game and maybe the fun isn't there, either."

John Neville, who has coached in minor hockey for 24 years, said: "We're not producing skilled players. It's an absolute reality. We've got a system that's very broken."

Canadian players who advance to the NHL do so in spite of the system, not because of it, critics say. And even those who are good enough to play in the NHL still can't match the Europeans in skill because they weren't adequately taught as children.

"We're sending players to the NHL, but we're not developing players," said Peter Martin, the head of the Hamilton minor hockey association. "The elite players are the ones advancing, but they would advance anyway."

Rick Polutnik, an executive with Alberta's amateur body, describes youth hockey in Canada as disorganized and leaderless.

"I would suggest most minor-hockey associations don't know what they're doing," he said. "Then I would suggest that if you interviewed every board member of every minor-hockey association in Canada and every provincial body, and you interviewed every board member of the national body, you would not get a clear consensus as to what we're doing with the game of hockey."

General managers of Canadian-based NHL teams say what's clear to them is a Canadian talent shortage.

"I think there is a problem," said Ken Dryden, president and general manager of the Toronto Maple Leafs. "Why is it that the European players are tending toward the top of the scoring list and on the all-star teams? The evidence would suggest that we're not doing as well in some ways as we need to do."

Sather says there's too much emphasis on winning and not enough time spent on teaching fundamentals.

"A lot of minor-hockey coaches think they're running NHL teams," he said. "They go with two or three lines and kids are left out.

"Minor hockey should be about development. That's exactly what they do in Europe. They practice and they work on skills."

Pierre Gauthier, general manager of the Ottawa Senators, said: "We need to get more kids on the ice. We need to change that mentality where you go to an atom game [11-year-olds] and the best players are always on the ice, and it's all about winning. It's totally ridiculous."

Réjean Houle, general manager of the Montreal Canadiens, says that stressing defensive tactics for eight-year-old children robs them of their creativity.

"You inhibit the imagination and artistry of the person," he said. "Let them experience emotion and spontaneity."

Although there is agreement that changes are needed in minor and junior hockey for Canada to get back on top, there is also skepticism about anything substantial being done.

"Nothing will happen," Meeker predicted. "This will pass over. You'll write an article, someone else will write an article, but it will not make one bit of difference to how minor hockey is run in this country, and it just breaks my heart."

Harris says Canadians will again experience the pride and thrill of their team winning a major international tournament, but it won't happen often.

"I don't think we will ever dominate hockey again," he said. "We will win a world championship once in a while, but we'll need a hot goalie and some lucky goals to do it."

Canadians will forever remember the achievements of Henderson, Bossy and Lemieux, but the memories might also divert attention from the reality of our failing game. The players who brought glory to Canada were products of another system, one in which children played more freely and practiced more frequently. The greatest obstacle to reform in Canadian hockey is the claim that nothing needs to be changed.

2. Win at all costs hurts children

The request appalled John Neville, but it did not surprise him. After his team was eliminated from the playoffs a few weeks ago, he was approached by the president of the winning Toronto Marlboro peewee club. The Marlboro president asked Neville to release the star goaltender of his team in Markham to the Marlies for the duration of the playoffs.

"He told me it was a great opportunity for my player," said Neville, who has been coaching in minor hockey for 24 years. "I looked at him and said, 'What about the opportunity for the goaltender you've got–the one who gets to sit on the bench while my guy takes you to the promised land?'"

The next day, Markham goalie Matt George turned down the offer, saying he did not want to be responsible for the Marlie goalie being removed from the lineup.

Marlboro officials had no such concern about the humiliation and betrayal of a youngster who came out to games and practices during the season and had been loyal to the team.

Neville and other coaches say minor hockey's obsession with winning is the most destructive element of the Canadian youth system. Moreover, it is one of the fundamental reasons the country is no longer producing top-level talent.

Canadian children play in an environment that stresses winning over developing skills. Coaches, desperate for victory, use only their best players in key games. They teach defence and intimidation rather than offence and creativity. Instead of learning the game, the focus is on playing.

In Canada, children as young as six participate in twice as many games as practices. Coached by volunteers, many of whom are inexperienced, they fall well short of the 3-to-1 practice-to-game ratio recommended by Canada's amateur body, Canadian Hockey.

In the old days, Canadian children learned fundamentals on rinks and ponds away from organized hockey. But in today's game-oriented system, there is no place for unstructured activity, and the practice time children receive is inadequate.

"If you're going to be skilled in anything, you must practice," said Ron Dussiaume, a former professional player who conducts master courses in Canada's national coaching certification program. "If your son or daughter wants to take music lessons, what you do as parents is make sure they are agreeable to practicing an hour a day to make it happen.

"We don't apply that to hockey. So the lack of practice hurts us tremendously."

The European system takes the other route. It places an emphasis on learning skills. While Canadians five and six years old play a 20-game schedule, children in Europe won't start playing games until they are seven. At earlier ages, they are taught to skate, pass and handle the puck.

In Canada, children 10 years old are already playing as many as 140 games in a season. In a game, even the best players handle the puck on average for about 45 seconds. In a well-structured 50-minute practice, a child will be working with the puck almost constantly.

In Europe, children play no more than 30 games and participate in more than 100 practices. They are taught by professional coaches. Skills are learned in high-tempo practices that incorporate game conditions.

"When you spend 9 or 10 years as a child under those conditions, you can play like Jaromir Jagr," said Dussiaume, who has developed a minor hockey practice curriculum that incorporates European techniques.

Few, if any, Canadians play at the level of Jagr, who helped lead the Czech Republic to a gold medal at the Nagano Olympics. Statistics show that Europeans lead the National Hockey League in most offensive categories.

The effectiveness of European training became clear to Paul Henry, the director of player development for the NHL's Florida Panthers, while he was watching a team practice earlier this season in Djurgarden, Sweden.

"They practice twice a day," Henry said. "In the morning, they work on nothing but skills for an hour and a half. It's all skill development. When I left the arena, I realized why European kids are better than Canadian kids."

Inadequate practice time is only one of the problems caused by Canadians' consuming need to play games and win. Instead of being taught offensive skills, eight-year-old children are instructed on defensive systems. They are discouraged from handling the puck or attempting offensive plays. A team is more likely to win if it plays safe, conservative hockey.

Lee Fogolin, a former NHL defenceman and now a minor hockey coach in Edmonton, said: "We wonder why our defencemen aren't mobile and can't handle the puck. Well, go to the rink and watch. The coaches are yelling, 'Get it out! Dump it in! Don't handle the puck!' The kids get the puck and as soon as it's on their stick, it's gone."

Toronto lawyer William McMurtry, whose 1974 report on violence in amateur hockey predicted that Canada would fall behind Europe in developing skilled players, remembers his son Tom playing minor hockey as a 12-year-old.

Although a good player at an elite level, Tom asked to move the next year to less competitive house-league hockey. The fact that he was clearly superior to his teammates in house league prompted McMurtry to ask him whether he missed playing at the higher level.

"He thought for the longest time," McMurtry recalled. "And then he said, 'No Dad. Sometimes I feel like skating in front of my own net with the puck.'"

At the elite level, even 12-year-olds weren't allowed to skate in front of their own net.

Canadians' obsession with hockey, once a stimulant that drove Canada to be a world leader, has given way to the pursuit of winning at all costs. It isn't children who insist on playing games and winning. It is, instead, the parent who dreams of seeing his son in the NHL. It is the coach who thinks he has a future in pro hockey. And it is the volunteer-association official who covets the bragging rights that go with being the head of a winning organization.

"It's all ego," McMurtry said. "Parents, coaches, organizers can call it anything they want, but it's ego.

"If they really cared about the standard of hockey in this country and they really cared about the kids, they wouldn't be doing it this way."

Ray Lalonde, who played university hockey in the United States and coaches in the Metropolitan Toronto Hockey League, said: "I sometimes think we should put pucks on the ice, leave a couple of parents to supervise and the rest of us go in and drink coffee.

"The kids would love it. They don't really care about winning and losing. You can ask the little ones and half can't remember whether they won or lost. But the parents remember.

"It's the parents who need the games. They say, 'Oh, I just find hockey so exciting.' Well, it's not really entertainment for the parents. It's supposed to be fun for the kids."

It's hard to imagine that there's much fun left in a system that summarily cuts or benches a 13-year-old.

3. NHL sad model for youth hockey

The problems that afflict youth hockey in Canada are learned and copied from the most influential organization in the game.

The National Hockey League sets the agenda, not just for professional leagues in North America, but for all levels of hockey in Canada.

Children imitate their favourite players, volunteer coaches use NHL strategies and association heads and parents look to the top pro league as the standard to which youth hockey should aspire. Today, that standard is based on size, aggression, obstructionism and, to a lesser extent, fighting.

"When we were winning, we brought a certain style to minor hockey and to junior hockey," said Mike Bossy, who starred for the New York Islanders in the 1970s and 1980s. "And when the Edmonton Oilers were winning, they brought their style of play. Since then, the style seems to be big players and hitting."

If hockey, as entertainment, has regressed because of defensive tactics and obstruction, Canadian hockey development has been devastated. By copying the NHL game, minor hockey has focused on winning rather than teaching skills. Learning defensive tactics is more important than working on offensive plays.

Canadian youth hockey, as a result, tends to produce poorly trained players who function best in an obstructionist system. Today, Europe, which stresses practice time and skills in its development

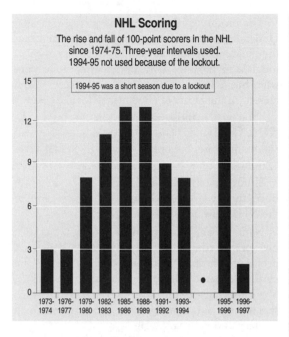

NHL Scoring

The rise and fall of 100-point scorers in the NHL since 1974-75. Three-year intervals used. 1994-95 not used because of the lockout.

1994-95 was a short season due to a lockout

system, supplies the NHL with most of its top talent.

Frank Mahovlich, who played from the 1950s to the 1970s, compares the NHL's evolution to a war of escalation. In the 1950s, the arms buildup started with the slapshot, which intimidated not only goalies but also defenders. The curved stick increased the element of the danger and was a major reason for goalies wearing masks and players putting on helmets.

In the 1960s, forechecking emerged as a key offensive strategy and, along with it, an increased emphasis on intimidation.

"If you look at game footage from the 1950s and early 1960s, there was no forechecking at all," said Toronto Maple Leafs president Ken Dryden, who played in the NHL in the 1970s. "Teams were allowed to get to centre ice almost unimpeded. I still have that phrase in my head from listening to games on the radio. It was Foster Hewitt saying, 'It's the Leafs at centre, three abreast.' What the heck does three abreast look like? There hasn't been three abreast in the NHL for the last 20 years."

The Boston Bruins were the first team of the modern era to use size and fighting, in addition to forechecking, as a tactic. But in the 1970s, the big bad Bruins were outmuscled by the Philadelphia Flyers, whose gang attacks on opponents took intimidation to a new level.

In Canada, fighting and brawling increased in the junior leagues and in minor hockey, prompting the Ontario government to commission a report on violence in amateur hockey in 1974.

The report's author, Toronto lawyer William McMurtry, a former amateur hockey player and boxer, wrote: "When coaches and parents hysterically demand victory at any price they seldom realize just how great the cost is…. Rather than a divisive force, fuelled by calculated animosities, [hockey] should be … a shared commitment to excellence."

In the NHL, excellence meant winning, and for the Flyers the key was intimidation. Ulf Nilsson, who played against the Flyers in the 1970s, says the Broad Street Bullies set back skill development in hockey 15 years. Bobby Hull, Nilsson's teammate in Winnipeg, describes the Flyer strategy as, "Bobby Clarke [the Flyers' captain] would send out the goons and the other kukaloos to beat people up, and then he and Bill Barber and Reggie Leach would go out and score the goals."

By the 1990s, obstructionism had surpassed intimidation as the most effective way for mediocre teams and players to compete in a league diluted by expansion. Minor hockey followed the NHL's lead in stressing defensive strategies. Children eight years old were taught the neutral-zone trap and left-side lock. Tactics became more important than creativity and learning skills.

In the NHL, teams became so proficient at neutralizing skilled players that the league's top star, Mario Lemieux, finally quit.

"All the interference, the holding, the hooking—it doesn't allow the good players to flourish," he told reporters in Toronto a few months ago. "It's the main reason I didn't return."

What astonished many was that a professional league would allow illegal tactics to drive its marquee player out of the game. Derek Holmes, the former head of Hockey Canada, said: "The NHL, in effect, forced him out. It's amazing, hard to fathom. Here's a guy who put people in the rinks, a superstar, and he quit."

Dryden admits the NHL is guilty of dummying down its product. With an average of 5.3 goals per game this season, league scoring is at its lowest point in 28 years. Last year, only two players scored more than 100 points, marking the first time since 1969-70 that fewer than three players reached 100 points.

"We're playing a style that makes players less skilled," Dryden said, "and that's outrageous."

The league cracked down on restraining fouls after the Olympic break in February, but skeptics believe obstruction will slip back into the game as four new teams are added to the league over the next three years.

Still, the NHL's task of ridding pro hockey of obstructionism pales in comparison to the challenge facing Canadian minor hockey. After decades of copying the NHL, it needs to throw out a win-at-all-costs philosophy and concentrate on skill development if it hopes to produce the best hockey players in the world.

4. Size beating out skill, even early on

The boy at tryout camp showed promise. He was a better skater and puck handler than many of the prospects. And when he was cut, the coach conceded he was one of the team's more talented players.

"But this year," the coach said, "we're really looking for more size."

The boy was eight years old.

The story, told by Toronto lawyer William McMurtry about a friend's child, helps explain why kids quit hockey and why Canada is falling behind other countries in producing the best players in the world.

Hockey at the minor and junior levels in Canada reflects play in the National Hockey League. Because the NHL values size, so too does youth hockey. In the NHL, players need to be large and strong enough to break through the obstructionism. Minor hockey also places a priority on big players.

The result, according to Hall of Famer Bobby Hull and other critics of the system, is a diminished skill level in the youth game. Small players with talent don't get picked for teams, and even if they do, they ride the bench. Those who do get ice time are larger and more aggressive.

The product of this exclusionary system is what Hull calls, with a mixture of disdain and humour, the kukaloo—a lumbering NHL player who is tough and hard-working but doesn't skate very well, has a low skill level and is hopelessly outclassed in the arena of elite international hockey.

"You watch those kukaloos on the ice in the NHL," Hull said. "They can't pass. Sure, they can shoot and skate, but only if they're given half a day to do it."

Unfortunately, Hull said, Canadian hockey produces mostly kukaloos these days. The top talent in the NHL now comes from Europe.

Nada Stajan, a parent in Mississauga, has seen her son, Matthew, cope in a system that places a premium on size. Matthew Stajan is skilled but small compared with other players in his league. Moreover, his birthday is in December, which means he is almost a year younger than peers with January and February birthdays.

"When he was cut from a team in peewee, he wanted to quit hockey, he was so upset," Stajan said. "We had to scramble to find him a team."

John Neville, a minor-hockey coach who also scouts for the Sault Ste. Marie Greyhounds of the Ontario Hockey League, said the late bloomers are written off in the Canadian system. "We're eliminating them because of the perception they can't survive or they don't bring to the table the things we need," he said. "And we're missing the boat."

Hull observed that, almost to a man, the finest hockey players Canada has produced have been 6 feet or less and under 200 pounds. They include Hull, Wayne Gretzky, Bobby Orr, Maurice Richard and Guy Lafleur. Gordie Howe was six feet and 200 pounds.

"We're bullying players of that size and skill out of the game," Hull said. "Why should they bother staying in? They'll have more fun taking up skiing and playing tennis. We've lost a generation of potentially great players."

At all levels of hockey, size is inexorably tied to intimidation. Hockey is a contact sport, so there is nothing wrong about playing physically. But in Ontario, parents are objecting to the provincial hockey federation's plans to introduce bodychecking for 8-year-olds, lowering the age level from 12.

"Bodychecking spells one word, intimidation, and everything that goes with that word," said Ron Tereshyn, who played minor hockey in Toronto and whose 10-year-old son is in the Scarborough association. "The whole idea is for kids to have fun."

The Ontario Hockey Federation defends its move by saying kids at the ages of 12 and 13 are suffering injuries from bodychecking. Better to teach them at an early age how to handle contact.

But Michael Clarfield, a sports-medicine physician and team doctor for the Toronto Maple Leafs, said the bodychecking issue obscures the real problem in minor hockey—children are not being taught how to skate, stickhandle and pass.

"You put bodychecking into a game and injuries go up," he said. "That's a fact at any age. Nobody can refute that. The issue of bodychecking isn't the real problem. From what I'm seeing, we're not developing skills."

Some parents do favour contact for children starting at eight years old. When the head of a hockey association in Ontario heard that the OHF was lowering the age for bodychecking, he was delighted. It would mean, he told a friend, that his 10-year-old son, who lacks talent but not size, would play at a higher level, because he would be able to "instill fear" in his opponents.

The element of fear may work for an unskilled player trying to impress a coach, but it inhibits smaller children with ability from developing.

Generally, an eight-year-old in contact hockey won't handle the puck as much as he should in a game or take chances that will put him jeopardy, but would otherwise improve his skills.

"I remember the year our son's team went from non-contact to contact," Leaf president and general manager Ken Dryden said. "There was just this absolute fixation on bodychecking.

"Once it becomes a fixation, then everything you do becomes a compromise. Your skating becomes a compromise, your stickhandling, your passing, your shooting.

"Bodychecking might improve psychological skills, make you mentally stronger, more competitive, the rest of it. But if you're not playing a style that encourages skills to get better, all you're going to do is improve in skills that aren't necessarily the ones you want to be better at."

Tereshyn said he will keep his child out of contact hockey next season. Bodychecking will come later, but the unanswered question for him is: Will his son meet the required size to get a fair chance in Canadian hockey?

5. Hockey establishment not keen to learn from setbacks

Howie Meeker watched Canada's fourth-place finish in the Nagano Olympic hockey tournament with his two sons, Howie Jr. and Mike.

After the Canadians lost the bronze-medal game to Finland, a country that has one-sixth the population of Canada and one-twelfth the number of children playing development hockey, Howie Jr. turned to his father and asked, "Do you think we'll learn anything from this?"

"Before I could answer," recalled Meeker, a former player, coach and commentator, "Howie Jr. said, 'Nah, not a snowball's chance.'"

Critics are skeptical about Canadian hockey's willingness to change an outdated development system that no longer produces the best hockey players in the world.

Hockey in this country has a tradition of resisting change and viewing new ideas suspiciously, especially when they come from outside the establishment.

Bruce Hood, a former NHL referee, called it "an arrogant attitude that says it's our game, we're the best, and how dare you tell us what to do."

Canadian hockey's hostility to new ideas can be traced back to at least the 1940s, when a young fitness guru in Toronto, Lloyd Percival, developed conditioning and training regimens, and published them in a book titled *How To Train For Hockey* and later in a second book, *The Hockey Handbook*.

The NHL disdainfully rejected Percival's theories, except for one team, the Detroit Red Wings. The Wings didn't win four Stanley Cups between 1950 and 1955 solely because of his training techniques, but Gordie Howe said it did help the players, particularly him.

"I was into a lot of his stuff, running and aerobics," he said. "He was so far ahead of his time they all thought he was a little wacko."

The Toronto Maple Leafs were particularly scornful. The two sides feuded, and Percival was moved to say at one point, "NHL players are the most primitively trained of all major athletes."

But sports organizations outside hockey listened to Percival. Bud Wilkinson, the legendary coach of U.S. college football's Oklahoma Sooners, implemented his systems. So did several National Football League teams, as well as track and field coaches.

In hockey, the Percival method was embraced by Sweden, Czechoslovakia and, most important to the future of the international game, the Soviet Union. His book became the foundation of Anatoly Tarasov's Soviet system. Percival stressed conditioning and proper diet. He taught balance, agility and lateral movement, the very qualities for which Russian players would become renowned.

By 1964, the Soviet Union was clearly the dominant power in international hockey. At the time, Percival said: "Today, Russian hockey players are skating an average of four miles an hour faster than NHL players and keeping up the faster pace twice as long or more. The Russian players are not only in far better shape than NHL players, but they are better coached in theory and technique of the game."

For most people, the idea that Russian players were superior to Canada's best professionals was ludicrous. Before the 1972 Summit Series, it was predicted by almost everyone that Canada would easily win every game.

Members of Canada's national team, amateurs who had consistently lost to the Soviet powerhouse during the 1960s, weren't so sure. All along, they had argued the Russians were better hockey players than Canadians believed.

Some national team members attended the first game of the 1972 series at the Montreal Forum. As the Soviet Union took control of the game, Derek Holmes, who played for Canada in the 1960s, said he and his teammates "quietly gloated."

"We were sitting near the bench," Holmes recalled. "I remember the Russian Valery Vasiliev, as he was leaving the ice, winked at me and nodded, as if it were an affirmation. The Canadian players' mouths were open and they were gasping for air."

The 1972 experience, according to popular Canadian mythology, opened the eyes of the hockey establishment to the innovations of European hockey.

In the years that followed, the NHL did pay more attention to physical conditioning. And as Europeans joined North American teams, lane changing and free-flowing offence increased. Some teams, such as the Edmonton Oilers, used European practice drills. But in the development of players, nothing changed.

"They didn't learn anything from 1972," Hall of Famer Bobby Hull said. "If they had learned anything, they would have gone back to teaching the basic fundamentals of our game."

But there was no motivation to change. After 1972, Canada held its own in the big international tournaments. It defeated Czechoslovakia in the 1976 Canada Cup. Although it lost the 1979 Challenge Cup two games to one to the Soviet Union, humiliated 6-0 in the last game, and was trounced 8-1 in the 1981 Canada Cup, Canada rebounded to win the tournament in 1984, 1987 and 1991.

As Canadian hockey entered the final decade of a century in which it had, for the most part, led the world, all was well with the Canadian game. Or so it seemed, until the breakup of the Soviet Union in 1991 freed Eastern Europe's best players to join the NHL.

Russian, Czech and Slovak players quickly established themselves among the league's best. The calibre of Swedish and Finnish players, no longer intimidated by Canadians, continued to rise. Today, Europeans lead the league in virtually all offensive categories.

But cracks were showing in Canada's development system long before 1991. Although Canada was able to defeat the Soviet Union in the 1984 and 1987 Canada Cups, the victories were excruciatingly narrow and Canada always had home-ice advantage. Canadian teams won not because they had more talent, but because they were tougher and more determined to win.

Today, Canada has no edge in toughness, and Europeans, with plenty of NHL experience, have learned how to win.

In 1974, Toronto lawyer William McMurtry, in his report on violence in amateur hockey, warned that if Canadian leaders in the game "continue to encourage the present trends in hockey where skill is secondary to physical intimidation, then it is likely every other hockey nation will surpass North America in actual hockey skills."

Canadian hockey, of course, paid no attention.

6. Competitive parents, coaches driving kids out of hockey

The question is a simple one, but it seems to baffle leaders of Canadian youth hockey.

What is the purpose of the kids' game?

To critics of the system, minor hockey may have more to do with providing entertainment for parents and coaches than engaging children in an enjoyable activity.

"I would suggest most minor hockey associations don't know what they're doing," said Rick Polutnik, a minor hockey coach and an executive with Hockey Alberta. "Many will say, 'Well, we're developing hockey players.'

"Well, if we're in the business of producing NHL players, we're a dismal failure. There aren't many of them making it to the NHL. And if the idea is to keep kids in the game, we're failing there, too."

Although Canada has more children playing hockey than any country in the world, about 475,000, the dropout rate skyrockets at age 12. Seventy-five percent of the kids who start by age five or six have quit by age 15. Soccer, with a youth enrolment of about 530,000, has surpassed hockey as the most popular participation sport in Canada.

The decline in hockey at the teenage level is one of the reasons Canada has fallen behind as a producer of top-level talent. For the most part, skilled players in the National Hockey League are European.

Adolescents leave hockey for reasons that include lifestyle, maturity, money and relationships. But they also drop out because they are old enough to make a decision independent of their parents. And by age 13, most of them don't want any part of what they consider a hostile environment.

In the early years, a child faces the problem of the overinvolved parent. At the arena they are called Screamer Dads and Screamer Moms.

Ray Lalonde, a minor hockey coach in Toronto, remembers one boy who insisted on carrying the puck down only one side of the rink. It turned out he was avoiding the other side because his parents were sitting there.

After a particularly loud father kept screaming orders to his child during a game, Lalonde approached him.

"I told him he was pretty loud," Lalonde recalled. "He said, 'Yeah, I get pretty excited.'

"I said, 'When your kid's on a swing in the school yard, do you stand behind him and yell, 'Swing! Swing! Swing!'?

"And when he goes in the sandbox, do you yell at him, 'Dig! Dig deeper!'?

"The kid's playing out there. Just let him play."

If a parent isn't yelling at a child, a coach probably is. A player, blamed for a loss, is berated in the dressing room. He may be cursed, grabbed, shaken or slapped.

Almost from the start, a child deals with rejection. In important games, a player, if he is not among the best on the team, will be benched and probably won't be told why. A tiering system that places children in different competitive levels, beginning at age eight, conveys to most kids that they're not good enough.

Dave Henderson, a 26-year-old investment banker in Toronto, went through the Metropolitan Toronto Hockey League and played some Junior B, but quit for a year at age 13.

"I got sick of the parents yelling, or a coach coming back after a game and blaming you for losing a game," he said. "A lot of good hockey players are destroyed at the age of 10 years old, not because they don't have the talent, but because they're turned off. You've got coaches who think they're running an NHL franchise and parents who put a lot of pressure on kids.

"It's brutal. It's almost mental abuse.

"They forget that hockey is played because it's supposed to be fun. And then they wonder why kids drop out and hockey is slipping a bit in this country."

By the time a child is 12 or 13, intimidation becomes an important coaching tactic. Players are instructed to be aggressive and in some cases start fights. If they don't follow orders, they are benched or perhaps humiliated.

"I see it at the junior level where kids are sent out to fight their friends," said Marty Williamson, who coaches a Tier 2 junior team in Milton, Ont. "Then they phone up and apologize to the friend, saying the coach made them do it and if they didn't he was going to kick them off the team. It's bizarre."

A story that circulated in the MTHL this season was about a top-level 13-year-old who was his team's biggest player but wasn't aggressive enough to satisfy his coach. As punishment, he was required to wear a pink sweater and carry a purse in practice.

"It's win at all costs in minor hockey," said John Neville, a youth coach in Markham, Ont. "It's insanity."

Given the environment, the massive exodus of kids beginning at age 12 is not a surprise, but it is a concern to people in the system.

"Wake up, man," is Polutnik's message to minor hockey volunteer coaches and organizers.

"Hockey isn't as enjoyable as it should be. When there is that amount of pain and frustration, and a high dropout rate, something is wrong."

He says minor hockey associations need to understand that they exist not to entertain parents or sustain the ego of coaches. They are there to provide an activity for children, to teach them a game, give them some enjoyment and perhaps help build character.

"I believe that if our goal is to raise good citizens, and if we have good values and the children have good experiences in the game, more will stay in and more will make it, if that's what's important. So why not emphasize those values instead of winning?"

7. Junior stars either must suffer goons or quit

Richard Peacock scored his second goal of the season and also got into a fight during a rancorous engagement between his junior team, the Prince George Cougars, and the Tri-City Americans.

After the February game, Peacock told an interviewer that one-punching Regan Darby of the Americans, cutting him near the eye and sending him to the dressing room, was more rewarding than scoring a goal.

As those who watched Peacock play will attest, Canadian junior hockey, the major feeder system for the National Hockey League, produces plenty of hard-nosed competitors who can fight and check. But for pure skill, Canadian players today cannot match Europeans who lead the league in most scoring statistics.

Critics say an ineffective development system for players aged 6 to 16 is the main cause of the poorly trained Canadians. But junior hockey, which emphasizes size and aggression and condones fighting, is also blamed.

Some of the finest players Canada has produced, including Hall of Famer Mike Bossy, considered quitting hockey because of attacks in the junior leagues.

"When you know the intention of the opposing team is to get you out of the game, when you know that when you start a game you're going to get speared and you're going to have to fight, and you're going to have a goon lined up next to you, that's intimidating and it takes a lot of the fun out of it," Bossy said.

After Wayne Gretzky completed his first and only year of major-junior hockey with the Sault Ste. Marie Greyhounds, his agent, Gus Badali, advised him to jump to the professional World Hockey Association, and not just for the money. Badali, concerned Gretzky might get hurt in an attack, felt his 17-year-old client would be safer in the pros where skilled players are generally left alone and heavyweights battle it out against each other.

Lee Fogolin, a former NHL player and a product of the Ontario major-junior league, says a young player at the wrong end of a punchup may never recover emotionally.

"Sixteen is a tender age for a kid," he said. "And now all of a sudden he has some guy hanging a beating on him. It's a pretty fragile situation. Is he strong enough at that age to say, 'Okay, well, that was a learning experience and I'm going to continue,' or does he go into a shell and never come out of it?"

Cory Cross, a 6-foot-5 defenceman, played junior hockey at Lethbridge, Alta., but refused to fight. He finally quit, opting, instead, for the University of Alberta and a spot on the varsity team. He's now one of the better defencemen for the NHL's Tampa Bay Lightning.

There are reasons, other than fighting, for good athletes to quit junior hockey or seek an alternative system. Sixteen year olds are almost always required to move away from home to play for the team that owns their rights. Unlike scholastically based development systems, the junior leagues reserve the right to trade players or demote them to a second-tier farm team in another city.

Fogolin says adapting to living away from home, competing to keep a spot on a team and finding time for a high school education are difficult enough for a teenager playing in a high-pressure elite league, never mind dealing with a trade midway through the school year.

"I can remember some real down times at that age," he said. "When you're with one team and all of a sudden they move you to another, it's that much worse."

Howie Meeker, a former NHL player, coach and commentator, calls junior operators "pirate slave traders." He says the old pre-1967 junior setup in which NHL teams owned the junior affiliates and, for the most part, recruited players from the region in which the teams were situated, was a more humane system. Generally, players stayed closer to home and weren't traded.

Although junior hockey is deemed to be a development league, it is, foremost, a business. Local ownership is dependent on gate revenue and revenue production is dependent on playing games. Winning is the key to selling tickets, and for a coach, a winning season could be his ticket to the NHL.

But games and winning, alone, do not advance a player's skill level. Even the stars handle the puck for only about 45 seconds in a game. Practice is needed to improve the fundamentals, but junior hockey's 2-to-1 practice-to-game ratio falls below the European 3-to-1 and sometimes 4-to-1 ratio.

In junior hockey, the margin of profit for the clubs is small, so owners cut costs by piling extra duties on the coach, such as managing, marketing and promoting the team, as well as scouting. As a result, the training of players suffers.

For several years, an additional source of income for owners has been expansion, in which existing clubs share in the entry fees charged to new teams. Junior leagues at all levels have expanded rapidly. Canada's three major-junior leagues have added 15 teams in 17 years.

But expansion dilutes talent, and the stars today are denied the opportunity of working together on the same team. The days are long gone when a couple of top junior prospects, such as Bobby Clarke and Reggie Leach of the Flin Flon Bombers, played on the same line and helped each other develop.

Moreover, the thinning of talent forces teams to recruit younger players. The Ontario Hockey League now drafts youngsters at 15. The Western Hockey League takes them at 14 years of age. Drafting that early not only discourages late bloomers, but it also removes good players from levels below junior and weakens the development structure.

Still, junior hockey's rough environment and long 66-game schedule prepares players for a gruelling professional career. A growing number of top European juniors come to Canada's leagues to toughen up for a year or two. But for them, skills have already been learned in Europe's prejunior youth systems.

For the Canadian prospect who hasn't been taught as effectively in youth hockey, the junior leagues reinforce his primary skills of checking and playing aggressively.

Billy Harris, a former pro player and coach, says: "Junior hockey, to me, stands for survival of the fittest. The problem is, if you're a top athlete and you're getting the crap kicked out of you because you're a good player, most are going to say, 'I'm going to play tennis and learn how to ski.'"

8. Getting to the root of hockey's problems

It is a hockey factory. It has more children enrolled in its amateur leagues than most countries, including Sweden, Finland, the Czech Republic, Slovakia and Russia, have participating in youth hockey. It is well financed and influential, and in the high-pressure environment of elite amateur hockey, it is a continuing source of controversy.

The Metropolitan Toronto Hockey League, with a membership of 50,000, reflects much of what is good about Canadian hockey. And it mirrors, in fact magnifies, the problems that plague the country's youth game.

The MTHL, at its elite level, is often hostile territory for children. It excludes many, traumatizes some and turns away potentially great players from the game.

The story of two elite atom teams (11-year-olds) helps illustrate why some good athletes quit hockey at an early age and why Canada has declined as a developer of the best players in the world.

"I could write you a story that would be headlined At What Price Victory?" said a parent, who requested not to be identified. "The players here have been devastated."

The team is the North York Canadians, who won the MTHL major atom championship last week and on the weekend were competing in the Ontario playoffs.

The Canadians were built for the sole purpose of winning a title. The idea of developing players outside the team's core of stars was never a consideration. Five skaters, among the best in the country, were recruited from the Toronto area and promised as much ice time as they could handle.

"It was set up as a National Hockey League team," another parent said.

The central figure was Devereaux Heshmatpour, a defenceman who towers over his teammates and scored 74 goals in 40 regular-season games, according to his father. Devereaux, who is enrolled at Upper Canada College, also plays elementary-school hockey. On the weekends, he is trained for hours in skills and skating by Yasha Smushkin of Toronto, who is from Russia and is among the top hockey teachers in the world.

The budding career of Devereaux is guided by his father, Allen, a powerful parental influence on the North York Canadians who has been known to rent ice time for the sole purpose of putting his son through a regimen of drills. A former athlete who wrestled and played football for Penn State in the 1970s, Allen Heshmatpour is a developer from Los Angeles who moved his family to Toronto so that Devereaux could play in the MTHL.

Devereaux quickly emerged as the Canadians' star this season, but when it became obvious that only five or six players were getting ice time, the supporting cast started to drop out. Eventually, the number of players on the team shrank from the required roster of 14 to as few as 9. Over the course of the season, the club was fined hundreds of dollars by the MTHL for not icing a full lineup. Heshmatpour says the fines were picked up by the Canadians' association.

Ice time wasn't the only problem for the Canadians. Of far more concern to some parents was the hostile environment for the players. There were accusations of profanity.

"There were kids who left because of the language," one parent said.

A parent of one player who quit several months ago said his child could not continue after a dressing-down on the bench.

"My son was devastated," he said. "He's quit the game altogether. You've got a kid who, for the first time since he was five, can't watch *Hockey Night in Canada*, doesn't want to skate."

Robert Law, general manager of the North York executive overseeing the Canadians, said allegations were brought up during the season, once during a hearing in which a player tried to get released from the team.

There were no return telephone calls received last week from the Canadians' coach, John Caranci, and Law declined to discuss the allegations, although he did say the coaching staff would not be returning next season.

One parent said the damage has already been done. "I have a kid who's going to be 12, and he's hung up his skates and he'll never play again. So what did hockey and the MTHL do for him? And at what price victory? In the end, the team ended up with a ringer trophy and a lot of casualties."

When Sandra and Steven Radcliffe heard complaints about the coach of their 11-year-old son, they weren't sure how to react.

Steven Radcliffe, manager of the North York Rangers major atom team, felt that Lorne Rappaport, the 24-year-old coach, was doing a good job.

But then he received calls from parents who complained about profanity. Said one parent, who requested not to be identified, "It was all swearing. He was calling the children [obscene names]. To my son, in particular, he would say you're too small, too weak, too slow, you're never going to make it in minor peewee. You shouldn't be in hockey in the first place. Maybe his whole strategy was to motivate through humiliation."

During the Christmas break, the Radcliffes noticed a change in their son, Andrew, the team's goalie.

"He turned from a normal, sunny, happy kid to being belligerent at home and miserable," Sandra Radcliffe said. "He didn't want to go to hockey or do school work."

When pressed by his mother to reveal what was wrong, Andrew broke down and cried. He said Rappaport had warned the players not to discuss anything said in the dressing room. Finally, the child said the coach had used profanity toward him and other players.

Sandra Radcliffe said she confronted Rappaport twice, the second time after she says he cursed Andrew for letting in two goals early in a game.

Rappaport said he was never approached by Sandra Radcliffe, although he confirmed telling the kids not to discuss remarks uttered in the room, a practice that demands silence from children and creates an unhealthy environment, according to sports psychologists.

"It's the boys' time," Rappaport said, explaining the code of silence. "This is Triple-A hockey. They're 11-year-olds, and when they come to the arena, it was their time in the dressing room."

Rappaport declined to comment on whether he cursed his players, but Steve Davis, the top executive with the amateur body overseeing the North York team, said, "Up until Christmas, he had used some language in the dressing room."

In January, at the behest of the players, two parents joined Rappaport behind the bench for games. The coach's conduct improved, parents say, morale shot up and the team climbed from 11th to 9th place.

Still, an upbeat conclusion could not prevent the breakup of the team at the end of the season. Several parents pulled out their kids, not wanting them to be coached by Rappaport for another season. Other children were told they weren't wanted back. Sandra Radcliffe quoted Rappaport as telling her that he was looking to have the best team possible.

Concerns about Rappaport's conduct prompted the Radcliffes and the parents of four other players to send letters at the end of the season to the club executive outlining the problems and asking that he be removed.

Davis said the letters were interpreted as sour grapes from parents whose children were not invited back for next season, but Sandra Radcliffe said her motivation was to simply rid the organization of a problematic coach.

"We were already leaving," she said. "We wanted to try to avoid 15 other kids going through this same thing next year."

In its investigation, the association executive did not talk to any of the letter writers because, Davis said, their positions were already made clear. Parents of other players were called. No one had a complaint, Davis said. One thought everything had been "normal" by the standards of minor hockey.

The executive group ruled that Rappaport could stay. If conditions had been as bad as some parents alleged, Davis said, they should have issued a formal complaint at Christmastime.

Davis said a letter was sent to Rappaport warning him that verbal abuse would not be tolerated.

Rappaport said, "I'm absolutely disgusted about what these parents are trying to do."

In explaining the decision not to release Rappaport, Davis said, "In hockey, you get two sides to everything, right?"

Looking back, Steven Radcliffe said he agrees that action should have been taken earlier, although both he and his wife did express concerns to team officials during the season.

"I guess everybody at the elite level is afraid to make too much noise for fear of repercussion," Steven Radcliffe said. "If you're a complaining parent, they take it out on your son."

What concerns Sandra Radcliffe is the message sent to the players by the association's support of Rappaport.

"We tried hard to get him removed to show to our kids that when you come to us and there's a problem, we listen," she said. "We wanted to say to them, 'We believe you, and we'll go forward with it and people will fix it.'

"What our kids have seen is that when they did all they're supposed to do, they weren't believed."

9. Europeans make serious practice of development

Pat Stapleton, who played for Canada in the 1972 Summit Series and now teaches hockey to children, surveyed the landscape of Canadian hockey and said, "I've never seen a country with so many arenas produce so few good players."

Stapleton was counting the 3,000-plus arenas that are used for hockey in Canada compared with 1,000 in all of Europe. He was also observing that there are 3.5 times as many children playing in this country's development system as in Sweden, Finland, the Czech Republic, Slovakia and Russia combined.

Despite these resources, Canada has declined in the development of top players. Today, Europeans lead in most National Hockey League scoring statistics.

At the Nagano Olympics, the Czech Republic, which has 1/19th of Canada's numbers in youth hockey participation, won the gold medal. Finland, with 1/12th Canada's numbers, knocked off this country in the bronze-medal game.

Anders Hedberg, a Swede and assistant general manager of the Toronto Maple Leafs, suggested in a radio interview last year that if Canada, which has 475,000 children playing youth hockey, used the European system of developing players, it would win international games 10-0.

Hedberg was perhaps overstating his case, but the question remains: What is Europe doing that Canada is not?

For starters, European countries take their time teaching players. In Canada, it's a rush. Canadian children as young as five are thrown into a schedule of 20 games a season. In Europe, children don't play until they are at least seven. From the age of five to seven, they are taught skating and hockey skills in training schools twice a week.

The practice-to-game ratio is consistently higher in Europe than in Canada's game-oriented system. A Canadian eight-year-old may practice once for every two games played. In Europe, the ratio is turned around, so a child gets three practices to every game.

For the most part, European countries use professional coaches to teach children. Canada has a volunteer system that yields good, but too often bad results behind the bench.

At the age of eight, Canadian children are funnelled into a tiering system that grades them and places some in elite divisions. This sends out the message to most children, particularly the late bloomers, that they are not good enough. They may quit. Tiering doesn't begin in most European countries until children are at least 10.

An 11-year-old child will play 30 games in a season in Europe and participate in at least three times as many practices. In the high-octane environment of elite minor hockey in Canada, an 11-year-old might play 140 games in leagues and tournaments. Canada's system does produce, for the most part, the best goaltenders in the world because they face shots that count in so many games.

A top-level player in Canada participates in hockey 12 months of the year. During the summer months, he will play in weekend tournaments and during the week he will be taking power-skating classes.

Critics say this approach burns out players or makes them into one-dimensional athletes. The way to develop a great athlete is to have him participate in more than one sport as a youth.

In Europe, children are in a hockey program 11 months of the year, but the four-month off-season is used for dryland training. Soccer complements hockey and develops a child's agility, balance and footwork. Both Mats Sundin and Peter Forsberg, the two best Swedish forwards in the NHL, were excellent soccer players and, in fact, met for the first time as children at a soccer tournament.

Russia, and to a lesser extent the Czech Republic and Slovakia, uses the old Eastern European hot-housing system of developing players. Top athletes are identified at age seven and placed in sports schools, where they receive professional training in a high practice-to-game ratio. This intense streaming process has produced some of the most skilled athletes to have played the game.

Still, the Russian system and other European training programs aren't without problems. There is no mass participation in Russian hockey. Potentially great hockey players, specifically slow developers, are never given a chance to play in this exclusionary setup.

In Sweden, hockey officials are concerned about the phlegmatic nature of their junior players. They lack competitiveness and determination, two qualities that have made Canadian players winners.

Still, the European, by the time he reaches the NHL, is enormously talented, and after a period of adjustment, the competitive instincts flow.

The United States has based its player development on Canada's system, with a few significant differences. U.S. hockey is game-oriented, and, as in Canada, children play too many games and do not practice enough. But U.S. hockey differs from the Canadian game in that it is often part of a school's athletic program. Players in a high school and a college system get more practice time than counterparts in junior hockey.

In addition, U.S. hockey is played, in some regions, on Olympic-sized ice, at the youth, junior and college levels. The larger surface requires a skater to be faster and more mobile, and it provides the time and space needed for a player to use stick skills in games.

Despite it's humiliating sixth-place finish at Nagano, the United States has the resources to emerge as the dominant hockey country in the world. USA Hockey is well financed, partly by the NHL, and has the fastest-growing youth system in the world. When USA Hockey's annual budget of $20 million (U.S.) is converted into Canadian funds, it is almost three times that of Canadian Hockey's $10-million budget. At its current rate of growth, U.S. youth participation in hockey will surpass Canada's in four years.

Still, Canada's advantage over all countries is its passion for the game. If the required changes were made in Canada's development system, Hedberg's estimation of its potential may not be far off.

10. Big ice surface cited as key to europeans' success

In the 1960s, Anatoli Tarasov, the head of hockey in the Soviet Union, was asked who would win a one-on-one competition between Bobby Hull, Canada's greatest offensive player, and Anatoli Firsov, the legendary star of the Soviet national team.

"Probably Hull would win," Tarasov said. "But if they played two on two, it would be more interesting. Three on three, Firsov would win. Four on four, Firsov would win easily. Five on five, it wouldn't even be a game."

Whether five Anatoli Firsovs would rout five Bobby Hulls in a make-believe Canada-Russia game played in 1963 is esoteric stuff of hot-stove debate.

Tarasov's point was that Hull's terrific individual skills and sensational slapshot would be countered and bettered by the passing, playmaking and teamwork of the European player.

Today, Europe produces most of the top offensive players in the world, partly because of superior passing and playmaking. Canada has slipped as a developer of talent because of weak training, but also as a result of a factor over which Canadian coaches and players have no control: Europeans learn the game on big ice; Canadians do not.

"The Olympic-size rink helps in skill development, there's no question about it," said Lou Vairo, an executive with USA Hockey and a former U.S. Olympic coach.

In the 1980s, Vairo advised U.S. communities to build European-sized rinks (200 by 100 feet) instead of the smaller National Hockey League surfaces (200 by 85 feet).

"I had three reasons for that," he said. "It wouldn't cost that much more, the large ice might attract international competitions and the players coming up would develop into top-level international players."

Ron Dussiaume, a master coach conductor with Canada's national coaching certification program, says big ice helps development in all key areas.

"The larger ice surface gives you more room," he said. "But large ice also corresponds with more speed. If there is more room, you have to be faster to cover the distance, like the defenceman moving from the middle lane to the boards. His speed and acceleration must increase. The larger ice forces you to be extremely fast, because if you are not, you'll never get there on time."

The time and space that becomes available to players on the large ice surface also allows them to hone puckhandling, passing and creative skills.

"It gives you room to stickhandle and you can take a little longer to make plays," Vairo said.

"Players get better at passing and stickhandling, and they get more comfortable with the puck. They [Europeans] handle the puck a lot more than our players do. Our players on the small rink don't have the time to handle the puck, even in a peewee game [13-year-olds], because they're being banged by someone."

NHL players today are at least 15 percent larger than they were when the league started up in 1917-18. They are also faster, but they are still playing on the same-sized sheet of ice used 80 years ago. The result is a constricted, over-heated game that critics call pinball hockey. The forecheck makes everything happen quickly. The puck bounces off a player's stick onto another, or caroms off the boards. There is little time to carry the puck and limited space in which to make a play.

The Nagano Olympics, played on the large ice, opened the eyes of hockey fans unaccustomed to international hockey. Several in the U.S. media wrote approvingly of the Olympic game, observing that it was more artistic and creative than NHL hockey. For similar reasons, aficionados such as Dussiaume, a former pro who once played for Don Cherry, and Billy Harris, the former player and coach and an author, prefer the style of hockey played on European ice.

Still, NHL executives say the league would never consider switching to the European surface, not only because it is virtually impossible to add ice to an arena without subtracting seats, but also because the league considers the European game dull.

"The NHL is built around forechecking and action in front of the net," said Glen Sather, the president of the Edmonton Oilers. "In the European game, everything is from the outside. A lot of European games become boring–technical, but boring. And there's not enough hitting."

Even Vairo said, "Hockey's not as exciting on the big rink as the small rink."

Given the advantages of developing players on large ice, one solution could be for youth hockey in Canada to use big ice for training kids 11 years old and up. The smaller children could play on a half a surface. Pro hockey, because it's committed to the frenzied, constrained game, could continue with its 200 by 85 sheet.

Another solution, albeit radical, is for the NHL to use four skaters a side instead of five. Not only would this open up the game, said Vairo, but clubs would save money on salaries because they would not need as many players. Not that the NHL Players Association is likely to agree to roster deductions.

The solution, most say, is for the International Ice Hockey Federation, the European-based governing body, and the NHL to get together and establish dimensions acceptable to both sides.

Peter Martin, the head of the Hamilton amateur hockey association, observes that hockey is the only international sport that does not have a standard surface. The size of baseball parks vary, but the fundamental dimensions, from plate to mound, base to base, are consistent.

A compromise makes sense to Toronto lawyer William McMurtry, who played university hockey and wrote the 1974 Ontario report on violence in amateur hockey.

"There's no question ours is too small and theirs is too big," McMurtry said. "I remember saying this to John Ziegler [the former NHL president] in the 1980s. I said, 'You don't have to go to 100 feet across. But go to 92 feet.' It would be recognition that the players have gotten bigger. And it would make the perfect game."

11. Cherry admits all is not rosy with hockey

Not long after the Canadian men's hockey team finished out of the medals at the Nagano Olympics, former National Hockey League referee Bruce Hood spoke to a group in Oakville, Ont.

During his speech, Hood addressed Canada's decline as a hockey power. Confronting a touchy subject, he said Canadian hockey was in bad shape and the country's development system needed an overhaul.

The crowd gave him a standing ovation.

Michael Clarfield, a sports medicine physician and Toronto Maple Leaf team doctor, says virtually everyone he talks to believes Canadian hockey needs to be reformed as a training ground for kids.

"I talk to hockey people every day, people at the high and low levels of the game, parents, etcetera, and everyone agrees the system is wrong,"

Clarfield said. "They don't want their kids playing that much. The kids are overcoached. That's the big majority."

In interviews, minor hockey coaches, parents, former players, some commentators and even NHL general managers agreed the youth training in Canadian hockey isn't doing the job.

"Everybody I talk to says the same thing," said Hood, who works part time as a hockey commentator. "Nagano was a wakeup call, because our game of hockey in Canada sucks."

Still, the sports media, particularly in hockey, have steered clear of the issue. Commentators are more likely to say Canada's poor showing at Nagano was caused by poor coaching or faulty player selection than a lack of talent.

"It is a very sensitive area," says Billy Harris, a former player and coach, and an author. "I agree that there is something wrong with our system, but you hate to be critical of volunteers who keep our minor system going."

One of the strongest supporters of the status quo is the CBC's *Hockey Night in Canada*, despite the network's concern over the declining quality of play in the NHL. Commentator Don Cherry has built his reputation on promoting tough, aggressive hockey, admiring a good fight and denouncing European players. In addition to being the host of *HNIC*, Ron MacLean is also an amateur referee and a participant in the hockey development system. He defends the Canadian game whenever he feels it is under attack.

After the Nagano Games, MacLean and Cherry rejected the notion the Canadian team was outplayed and, instead, offered a variety of explanations for its weak performance. They included: We didn't play our game. We didn't hit. Too many centres. Wayne Gretzky should have been selected for the shootout. A hot goalie. Eric Lindros hit the post.

Prodded by MacLean, Cherry chided those who thought Canada's loss reflected poorly on the country's development system. He compared Canadian hockey to baseball in the United States.

"How about the States?" he asked. "The States and the world. How about the MVP? For the National League, it was Larry Walker—foreigner. Now we have the most valuable player in the World Series. A Cuban. We have the guy pitching

that gave up the hit—a Cuban. The guy that made the hit that scored the winning run—Colombian or something. Another foreigner. And the guy that scored the run was a foreigner.... And you don't see the States saying they're bad like we are here. We lost. But we'll be ready next year."

"I agree," MacLean said.

Cherry's argument was echoed by at least one other commentator. When a sports journalist was asked on TSN if Canadians should be concerned about its hockey system, he said, dismissively, they should not. Countries such as the United States and Russia have not commissioned inquiries, so why should Canada?

But hockey is not the U.S. national game and Russia fared relatively well at Nagano. For Canada, hockey is the country's invention and passion. If a Dream Team of U.S. baseball players lost a World Cup tournament and then bombed out in the Olympics two years later, U.S. sports fans would want answers. Furthermore, the decline of baseball in the United States, particularly among African Americans, is already an issue.

Cherry's contention that Canada still produces the best players in the world frustrates those who see him as a potential spokesman for reform. As hockey's most influential media figure, he could, from his pulpit in his bullying style, tell parents and coaches that more practice time is needed for children, teaching skills is more important than winning, and fighting should be left to the pros.

"He just keeps up that circus act and keeps insisting that everything's just great," said Howie Meeker, a former player, coach and commentator. "He is a great entertainer and he's got an act going, but he's hurting the development of hockey."

Cherry reacts predictably to the fact that Europeans lead the NHL in most scoring statistics. Points are not the sole measure of a great player, he said.

"Hockey is not just getting points and skating like Sonja Henie. Hitting is skill, body checking is a great skill, back checking is a great skill. And—I know people hate fighting—but fighting is a skill."

But then a surprise: He agrees that changes are needed in the development of Canadian players.

"We do have faults; there's no doubt about it," he said. "The one thing I would like to see is more practices. I would like to see less games and I would like to see them handling the puck more—but I've always felt that way."

Then why hasn't he said this on the air?

"I'm going to have a statement on that," he said. "My son and I have talked it over."

He says the momentous occasion will occur during the NHL playoffs.

Has the mountain moved?

"I always have to end it this way," he said. "We're still the best."

12. Correcting hockey woes is child's play

It was invented in Canada, nurtured in this country and showcased to the world by Canadian players. Hockey is Canada's game and for years the nation's stars dominated the sport.

But today the game is in trouble. Canada has declined as a producer of top-level players and it has also alienated its greatest resource—the children who participate in the sport. Too many drop out, and those who stay cannot match their European counterparts in talent.

Most of the leading offensive stars in the National Hockey League these days are from European countries, although Europeans make up only 22 percent of the league while Canadians account for 61 percent. Canadians are increasingly relegated to second-line and third-line positions on NHL teams.

Murray Costello, president of the Canadian Hockey Association, the amateur governing body, sees problems in the country's youth development system and says reform is long overdue.

"I don't think anybody can take issue with most everything you're saying [in *The Globe and Mail* series]," he said. "It's not as good as it used to be and it's not as good as it should be overall."

While observing that Canadian hockey still provides a healthy and wholesome experience for many children, Costello acknowledges that a pervasive win-at-all-cost attitude is choking the youth game and denying children an opportunity to learn skills.

No trend better illustrates the extent to which parents and coaches will go to win games than the parental approval of steroid use among 14-year-old hockey players.

Phil Zullo, a fitness instructor and personal trainer in Toronto, says he has been approached on several occasions by parents seeking steroids for their sons in minor hockey.

"It's happened three or four times now, fathers asking me about it," said Zullo, who warned them against steroid use. "And at least one father, I know for a fact, put his son on it."

The consuming need to win not only cultivates drug use, but also physical and emotional abuse of children. Participants in minor hockey have cited incident after incident of children as young as 10 being hit or profanely humiliated by parents and coaches.

One coach in the Metropolitan Toronto Hockey League forced his 11-year-old players this season to take off their helmets, get down on their hands and knees and push pucks along the ice with their noses. This was punishment for the team's weak passing in a game. After a parent pulled his son off the ice, the boy was handed a one-game suspension by the coach for not participating in the so-called practice.

"It's compete, compete, compete, win, win, win at all costs," Costello said. "Parents and coaches and minor-hockey associations have to accept that the game is for the kids. And as long as they're having fun—with or without competition—they'll still develop."

There are no quick fixes for a broken volunteer system that has grown increasingly elitist, obsessed with winning, hostile to the people it is supposed to be serving and ineffective in developing skills. Still, there is a way to turn it around, coaches, former players, administrators and parents say.

For starters, the CHA needs to speak out strongly against the pervasive win-at-all-cost attitude that is driving children away from the game. The association, perhaps enlisting the help of Canada's best players, should launch a campaign to get its message out to Canadians.

Coaches and parents should be told to de-emphasize winning and intimidation, play fewer games, practice more and make it enjoyable. This will be the challenge facing CHA executive Bob Nicholson, who will succeed Costello as president in June.

Toronto Maple Leafs president Ken Dryden and others believe a national forum would be a useful way to discuss problems in minor hockey, seek answers and, perhaps most important, publicize the issue.

Local minor-hockey associations are often controlled by a small group of people whose values and motives may or may not be appropriate to child development and skill training. Rick Polutnik of the Alberta amateur hockey association says pressure needs to be placed on these organizations to widen participation and get new voices into the decision-making process.

Other recommendations include:

• Enforce zero tolerance for coaches who abuse children. Too many club executive bodies give coaches accused of emotional or physical assaults the benefit of the doubt.

• Reduce elitism. Children are tiered into levels of ability at the age of eight. The message conveyed to a player cut from a team is that he is not good enough. Many will drop out. Junior hockey drafts players at 14. Tiering should not begin until the age of 12 and adolescents should not be drafted into junior hockey until age 16.

• Take fighting and stickwork out of minor and junior hockey. Pro hockey condones fighting because it appeals to a core demographic, but there's no place in the amateur game for violence outside the rules. Fighting in junior hockey should bring a game misconduct, with graduated suspensions to repeat offenders. Suspensions for fighters in children's hockey should be increased. Coaches who assemble goon teams should be fired.

• Cut back on the number of games children play. During a season, a 10-year-old may compete in as many as 140 games, counting weekend tournaments. He won't come close to meeting the 3-to-1 practice-to-game ratio recommended by the CHA. Canada should take its lead from the European model. Have kids participating in three or four practices for every game. Teach them offensive skills. Top-level Canadian children play 12 months of the year. In the summer, it's weekend tournaments and power-skating classes during the week. Instead of playing year round, borrow from the Europeans. Use the off-season for dryland training and participation in sports other than hockey to improve a player's athleticism.

• Keep bodychecking out of the game until children are 12. That will give players a chance to practice skills in game conditions without fear of injury.

• Move toward a larger ice surface. The European sheet, which is 15 feet wider than North American ice, forces children from the age of 11 to become better skaters. And big ice gives them the time and space needed to apply skills in games. Costello supports the idea of new community arenas being built to European size, if it is affordable. "It would be great," he said. "I think that as an organization, the CHA board could be convinced fairly quickly to make that recommendation–that every renovation, every new building should have international ice."

• Return hockey to the schools. In the old days, the game was played at the elementary and high-school level. But for a variety of reasons, the practice ended, for the most part, 25 years ago. Costello approves of schools getting back into youth hockey. Arenas for the most part are empty on weekdays and classroom schedules built around ice time would not only keep the arenas in use, but provide valuable practice time. High-school hockey, because of peer recognition, would also provide an incentive for adolescents to stay in the game and an alternative to junior hockey. "Hockey should be in the schools," said Howie Meeker, a former player, coach and commentator who has operated hockey schools for years. "That's where you have control, that's where you have half-sensible people who can develop a child physically and intellectually." The financing of public- and secondary-school hockey would be accomplished as it is in minor hockey, through fund-raising efforts and participation fees.

• Provide more government funding. The U.S. amateur body has an annual budget of $20 million (U.S.). When converted to Canadian funds, it is nearly three times larger than the $10 million that the CHA receives from Ottawa. Meeker says money should be spent to improve the calibre of the volunteer coach. He proposes a degree program for hockey teachers. Graduates would work at the grassroots level. They would instruct volunteers on how to teach and coach and would supervise the training of children.

- Reduce the cost of hockey. Once a blue-collar sport, the game is now affordable only to the affluent. It can cost parents $5,000 a year and more to keep a child in elite minor hockey. "Some of the best players in our history have come from the low end of the economic scale," Costello said. "They're being lost to the game because of the elitism."

Costello, Meeker, Polutnik and others are optimistic that hockey can find its way back, but the focus needs to be on the child rather than the ego of a parent or coach, one of whom dreams of a son playing in the NHL and the other a pro career behind the bench.

Minor hockey is for children. It is about playing a game and learning appropriate life skills. If a child in Canada dreams of an NHL career, it's not as a fighter or checker, which too often is the final product these days. He aspires to be Wayne Gretzky or Jaromir Jagr. Minor hockey owes the child a chance to achieve the goal and also enjoy playing a game.

Source: William Houston is a staff sports writer for *The Globe and Mail*. This series was originally published in *The Globe and Mail*, April 4, 6, 7, 8, 9 10, 11, 13, 14, 15, 16, 17, 1998. Reproduced with permission from *The Globe and Mail*.

56.
Why I'm Outraged
Howie Meeker

If we're going to put money into hockey, it's most needed at the grassroots level

A portion of my tax dollar going to help NHL teams! I don't know whether to laugh or cry. At every opportunity for over 40 years I've said that hockey, the way it has been run, has to be the greatest game in the world to survive. Our decisions at every level over the last half century have *never* been what's best for the game or the players.

At least 80 percent of those involved in the game in this great country are under 14 years of age or in beer leagues or on old timers' teams. The ones who should be playing hockey at their skill level at least twice a week are the teenagers. We've purposely driven them out by introducing violence and checking at the ages of 12 and 13. Kids of average size and toughness then have nowhere to play. Kids need to learn to play the puck, not the man.

Those who do continue through the system get very little, if any, individual physical or mental instruction. So most of the players we develop are somewhat behind the players of other nations. The country's minor hockey systems are run by parents who have absolutely no love or feel for the game, rather than professionally trained coaches who have the time and resources to devote to a comprehensive hockey program and teach skills. Once their own children move on, the coaches go, and teams have to start over.

God help us. In fact, in the amateur participation and development field, I don't even think the big guy upstairs could help.

As I stood helplessly by and watched the educator and bureaucrat destroy our wonderful game at the community level, I thought, "Well, what's at the top isn't half bad." Then came the Soviets in '72. Swedes, Finns, Czechs and Americans followed, and hockey expanded to a total of 22 NHL teams in the United States. Our 90-cent dollar fell below 66 cents.

Most of the above could have, or should have, led to better things, but as great a game as it is, hockey didn't satisfy many of the new U.S. owners. Despite being the leaders of business with huge assets and community status, they had wanted national recognition. With football, basketball and baseball teams hard to come by, they said, "Let's try hockey."

During my short career as an NHL general manager, I was privileged to attend only three or four owners' meetings, but I went one-on-one with GMs and owners at every opportunity over those three years. One thing that came through loud and clear was that, as an owner, if you ran your hockey operation with the same philosophy and made the same business decisions that worked in every other venture, *you would go broke.* During the last owners' meeting I attended, at about 2 a.m., big Jim Norris, then owner of the Detroit Red Wings, raised his glass and said, "Gentlemen, it's a wonderful game but a very different kind of business."

Ninety percent of the yearly cost per player is the fault of U.S. owners, not the player. They continue to give in during collective-bargaining agreements and salaries have skyrocketed. The Ottawa Senators have not been part of the solution though, they played a large role in escalating salaries when they signed teenaged rookie Alexander Daigle to a 2.5-million-a-year contract in 1993. Now they have their hats in their hands.

All the existing financial problems were in place when the current owners of most Canadian teams took command. I suggest they should have sent their bank managers and head accountants to vote on the deal. With their eyes wide open they walk into a no-win situation and when asked to ante up again, they cry for help. And they are going to get it, can you believe it? My and your federal tax dollars. And some provincial ones too.

I wouldn't mind if our governments spent 100 times what this folly is going to cost them on a national skill-training program with a master coach for every community and the adoption of a philosophy designed to keep every teenager, boy and girl, in the game as long as they wanted to play recreational hockey. In five years we would raise the skill level of those in our top junior leagues by at least 25 percent and have 250,000 more teenagers playing for *fun.* Win-win, both ways.

Absolutely no way would we miss those NHL teams who couldn't pay their bills. Rod Bryden, John Manley, Jean Chrétien and Wayne Gretzky, are you listening? It's not the owners of NHL teams that need help, it's the Canadian grassroots game of hockey that's at risk.

Source: Howie Meeker played for the Toronto Maple Leafs from 1946 to 1953, winning four Stanley Cups. He was the voice of the Montreal Canadiens on CBC's Hockey Night in Canada for 20 years and is the author of *Stop It There, Back It Up!* about the state of Canadian hockey. This article was originally published in *The Globe and Mail,* Thursday, January 20, 2000, A17. Reproduced with the permission of the author.

57.

The Jets Are Gone But Not Much Has Changed

Jim Silver

"We just couldn't afford to keep them"

The jets left Winnipeg in 1996. Their many supporters claimed that, as a result of their departure, Winnipeg would become a "second class" city: young people would leave, business would dry up, life would never be the same. None of this has happened. Winnipeg is no more nor less a second-class city than when the Jets were here. Out-of-province migration, long a problem in Manitoba, has continued at roughly the same pace, and the provincial government–the same government that predicted economic disaster if the Jets were to leave–claims that business is booming. The dire predictions have simply not been borne out by the experience.

What is more, there is a broadly based agreement in Winnipeg, even among avid Jets supporters, that the Jets' departure was, in the end, inevitable. "We're sorry they're gone," most people say, "but I guess we just couldn't afford to keep them here." There is an acceptance, albeit reluctant, of what is now seen to have been inevitable. But what is interesting about the Jets saga is how little was learned from it.

Opposition to spending vast sums of public money to save the Jets was led by a small citizens' group calling itself Thin Ice, of which I was a member. Thin Ice argued consistently that if there were many tens of millions of extra public dollars kicking around, they should be invested in the community, where they were sorely needed, not in NHL hockey. It was an argument about social justice and equity.

It was also an argument about urban economic development. Supporters of the "Save the Jets" campaign, and especially the city's business establishment, claimed that public expenditure to save the Jets was justifiable, indeed necessary, for the city's economic future. That claim has now been shown to be without foundation, but the faith of the corporate elite in this type of economic strategy remains unshaken.

The strategy is the megaproject approach to urban economic development. Build or do something big, something that has a high profile and can boost the city's image. Build a tall office building, or a large downtown mall. Even better, build a new arena to save the Jets and "put Winnipeg on the map." Putting Winnipeg on the map is important because urban economic development is all about creating a "good business climate" and boosting the city's image in order to attract capital from afar.

Their failure to save the Jets has not given the city's decision-makers a moment's pause as far as the merits of this approach to urban economic development is concerned. As I write this, we are six weeks away from the 1999 Pan Am Games, which Winnipeg will host. If one big, high-profile, image-oriented sports project fails, the city's business establishment has said, then let's try another. In excess of $150 million in public funds will be spent to enable Winnipeg to host the Pan Am Games for two weeks. It will, we are told, put Winnipeg on the map. The Jets may be gone, but the megaproject mentality remains firmly intact. One megaproject failed, so we're trying another. And if it fails, there will undoubtedly be yet another.

Spending vast sums of public money on glitzy megaprojects to boost the city's image and breathe life into the local economy is a flawed way to promote urban economic development. It's not that it doesn't "work." It achieves what it is intended to achieve. It creates benefits of various kinds for some, and drags many of the rest along with its boosterism and its appeals to civic pride. Winnipeg's business establishment has successfully used variants of this strategy throughout the entirety of the twentieth century. It's a safe bet that they will continue to do so in the twenty-first century. It's all they know, and from where they view the world, it works.

The problem is that this approach to urban economic development does not get at the roots of the city's most serious problems. In fact, it adds to those problems. It deflects public concern and scarce public dollars away from, to give just one example, the issue of high poverty rates. In 1996, the year the jets left Winnipeg, over 50 percent of all households and over 80 percent of Aboriginal households in Winnipeg's inner city had incomes below the Statistics Canada low-income cut-off. This represents a very significant increase since the 1991 Census, and is a huge and appalling problem (Black, Luzubski, Shaw and Silver, forthcoming). The United Way, an organization not wont to make public statements that might be seen as political, issued a report in early 1997 saying that United Way organizations were unable to meet the massive and growing needs in the community created by ever-increasing levels of poverty (United Way of Winnipeg, 1997). A 1996 survey at Child and Family Services Winnipeg and CFS Central found that 92 percent of social workers who responded believed that demand for their services had exploded to such an extent–largely attributable to growing levels of poverty–that it was no longer possible for them to comply with all aspects of the Child and Family Services Act (CUPE, 1996, Appendix 4, p.6). Many more such sources could be cited (see Silver, 1999).

There is, in Winnipeg, a desperate need for creative initiatives to turn around the rapidly escalating levels of poverty. That is why Thin Ice was opposed to using tens of millions of scarce public dollars to save the Jets. There were more pressing needs for that money.

Those needs still exist. In fact, they are growing. But the message continues to go unheard. In that regard, as in others, the Jets' departure has brought no change. It is not just that the predictions of mass exodus and business collapse have proved hollow, and that in fact many of those who made such predictions are now boasting about Manitoba's purportedly strong economy. It is also that poverty and the many problems it creates continue to grow, and even to approach crisis proportions, and yet these issues continue to be ignored by those who boast about the economy's strength. Far from having learned anything useful from the Jets fiasco, the city is about to bring to fruition yet another megaproject by hosting the Pan Am Games.

Those of us who opposed the spending of vast sums to save the Jets, on the grounds that there were better uses for the money, may have won that battle, but it seems we have lost the war. That there are more pressing needs for the city's and the province's money and attention are among the lessons not yet learned from the battle over the Jets' departure. The worrisome thing is that, so long as decisions about urban economic development continue to be made by the local business establishment, that lesson will never be learned. Glitzy megaprojects funded with other peoples' money work just fine for them.

References

- Black, Errol, Darren Luzubski, Lisa Shaw, and Jim Silver. *The Growth of Poverty in Winnipeg's Inner City, 1981-1996* (Winnipeg: Canadian Centre for Policy Alternatives-Manitoba, Forthcoming).
- Canadian Union of Public Employees. *What We Owe To Our Families: A Brief On Child Welfare in Manitoba* (Winnipeg: Canadian Union of Public Employees, 1996).
- Silver, Jim. *Thin Ice: Money, Politics and the Demise of an NHL Franchise* (Halifax: Fernwood Publishing, 1996).
- –––. *Solutions That Work: Fighting Poverty in Winnipeg's Inner City* (Winnipeg: Canadian Centre for Policy Alternatives-Manitoba, 1999).
- United Way of Winnipeg. *Trends, Issues and Innovations in Winnipeg's Human Care Services: A Report on Discussions Amongst United Way of Winnipeg* Member Agencies (Winnipeg, February, 1997).

Source: Jim Silver is a professor in the Department of Political Science at the University of Winnipeg, Manitoba. This article was originally published in *Canadian Issues/Themes Canadiens (CITC)*, Autumn 1999, pp.12-13.

58.

Hockeynomics

David Shoalts

A three-part series looking at the national Hockey League's bottom line

1. Is NHL as sound as made out to be in Bettman's books?

Gary Bettman bragged when Wal-Mart heir Nancy Laurie and her husband, Bill, recently became the latest billionaires to buy a National Hockey League team. "The ownership of franchises has never been stronger and the value has never been higher," the commissioner said in welcoming the new owners of the St. Louis Blues.

The NHL has become a league of financial contradictions. Owners whine on one hand that escalating players salaries are driving them to the edge of bankruptcy.

But Bettman and others point to rapid expansion and rising franchise values as a sign of robust health.

A clue to the real state of the game's finances came recently when Bettman let it be known his league is willing to receive a cut of sports-betting revenue. It was a stark contrast to his previous stand on sports betting. "I am totally against sports betting," he said in 1994. "That has always been my position."

The financial problems of Canada's small-market NHL clubs have been well documented. But what really plagues the NHL now goes beyond the Ottawa Senators, Calgary Flames and Edmonton Oilers. The entire league has become a contrast of big markets versus small markets.

And that is worse news in the NHL than in other major leagues. Small-market clubs in the National Football League and National Basketball Association have their coffers enriched by a share of billion-dollar television deals. NHL teams rely on ticket revenue, and in many U.S. markets the news on attendance is not good.

Yes, official figures are up. The NHL claims its average crowd rose from 15,987 in 1995-96 to 16,262 last season. But a league insider says attendance is significantly inflated throughout the league to make the NHL look more healthy than it is.

For example, Pittsburgh Penguins financial documents obtained from the U.S. Bankruptcy Court show a significant difference between the club's paid attendance and what it announced publicly. For the 1997-98 season, according to NHL records, the average attendance at a Penguins game at the Civic Arena was 15,071. The records from the bankruptcy court list the club's average attendance as 13,988. That's more than 1,000 seats a game, a difference of 7 percent.

The difference is greater for the 1998-99 season, when the NHL's records list the Penguins' average attendance as 14,825. The actual attendance was 13,255 a game, a difference of 1,570 (11 percent).

Washington is another city in which there has been a significant difference between announced and actual attendance.

In the 1998-99 season, after the Capitals' appearance in the Stanley Cup final, the club said its average attendance at the MCI Center was 17,281. It also claimed 20 sellouts in 41 games at the 19,740-seat arena.

By the end of last season, Capitals management admitted the attendance numbers included tickets that had been given away. Reporters were told the number of season-ticket holders was down to 6,000.

Shortly after Ted Leonsis, president of America Online's Interactive Properties Group, bought control of the Capitals in June, he told a Washington reporter that attendance for 1998-99 was among the bottom four in the league, along with the Carolina Hurricanes, Tampa Bay Lightning and New York Islanders. Leonsis also indicated that season tickets could be in the neighbourhood of 3,000.

Other small-market U.S. clubs have large pockets of empty seats, too, and much of the problem can be tied to the cost of attending an NHL game for a family of four, which is now more than $230 (U.S.).

"It's a $200 bill for an evening of entertainment just about any way you cut it," said Dean Bonham, a sports marketing consultant in Minneapolis who deals with the four major professional sports on behalf of corporate clients such as IBM and Federal Express.

"I don't know how many hockey fans from a macro perspective can continue to pay those kinds of dollars."

At least some of the new owners Bettman boasts about make it clear they're not buying teams because fans are dying to spend money on hockey. William Davidson, who owns the Detroit Pistons of the NBA among other things, bought the Lightning because the club came with a good arena lease and six acres of land around the Ice Palace in downtown Tampa.

"We think the main attraction was the arena," Tom Wilson, the president of Davidson's sports conglomerate, told the *Tampa Tribune.*

Wilson called the purchase of an NHL franchise alone a dangerous investment.

John Rigas has pumped money into the Buffalo Sabres for years through his company, Adelphia Communications, the fifth largest cable television firm in the United States. He is now the majority owner of the club, but hasn't officially taken command because of the dispute with some of the holdover owners over the arena debt.

The Rigas family says the club's debt is now $80 million, mostly because revenue at the Marine Midland Arena, which is jointly owned with the city, has not been high enough to pay the loans used to pay the club's share. Rigas has let it be known to politicians in Buffalo that if they are willing to write off most of the arena debt and renegotiate the lease, his cable company will go ahead with a technology park on the waterfront that would bring 1,500 jobs to the city.

The city is still mulling over that proposal with at least one other development plan for Buffalo's waterfront.

At the same time, television ratings in the United States have decreased during the past five years, although the league is in the first year of a new five-year, $600-million deal with ABC-ESPN.

Bettman, who did not respond to requests for an interview for this story, maintains attendance is strong. "Attendance is not a problem," he said when asked directly earlier this year.

In baseball, clubs can only announce the number of tickets sold. The NFL announces the number of tickets sold, the no-shows and the number of people actually in attendance. The NHL does not have a rule concerning how clubs must post their attendance. An NHL spokesman said the figure is left to each club.

It is difficult to verify the announced attendance in the NHL, just as it's difficult to verify any financial information put out by the clubs because the true numbers are found only in the Unified Report. That report contains the revenues and expenses for every club and is distributed quarterly.

The league's passion for secrecy is such that it won't even identify the clubs in the report to its own members. Each club is identified by a number.

A second NHL executive who has regular access to the reports says the numbers in them are scary.

The league office frowns on owners veering from the company line, and now, after several months as an owner, Leonsis doesn't like discussing specific figures. "I don't know where you got those numbers from," he said. "No, [season-ticket totals] were five to six thousand when we got here, and we got 2,500 more without even marketing aggressively."

Leonsis believes the Capitals are a growing business and the asset will appreciate, although, "except for a small handful of teams, the NHL as it's structured now can't make money."

Season tickets, which owners count on for a solid base of revenue, are a problem in more places than Washington. Indeed, if they had to, many clubs could not meet the NHL's requirement of 12,000 season tickets for expansion franchises.

Among them are the Ottawa Senators, who recently announced their latest drive had upped the number to 10,808. Others thought to have fewer than 10,000 are the Calgary Flames, Los Angeles Kings, the Lightning, Islanders, Penguins and Carolina Hurricanes.

Even though they are about to move into a new arena—every owner's panacea for all financial ills—the Hurricanes decline to disclose their season-ticket totals. *The Raleigh News and Observer* said the number could be as low as 5,000. However, the NHL executive who pointed out the discrepancies in average attendance also says some clubs play

Comparing the Cost of Attending an NHL Game

Arena	Team	Average Ticket	Fan Cost Index
Air Canada Centre	Toronto Maple Leafs	$72	$355*
Fleet Center	Boston Bruins	$54	$295
Continental Airlines Arena	New Jersey Devils	$51	$274
First Union Center	Philadelphia Flyers	$53	$273
Miami Arena	Florida Panthers	$50	$273**
MCI Center	Washington Capitals	$50	$273
Civic Arena	Pittsburgh Penguins	$54	$267
McNichols Arena	Colorado Avalanche	$49	$267**
Nassau Coliseum	New York Islanders	$47	$266
United Center	Chicago Blackhawks	$44	$262
Madison Square Garden	New York Rangers	$39	$257
Kiel Center	St. Louis Blues	$45	$239
Joe Louis Arena	Detroit Red Wings	$44	$237
Arrowhead Pond	Mighty Ducks of Anaheim	$41	$232
Great Western Forum	Los Angeles Kings	$35	$223**
San Jose Arena	San Jose Sharks	$34	$210
Greensboro Coliseum	Carolina Hurricanes	$38	$207**
America West Arena	Phoenix Coyotes	$33	$206
Ice Palace	Tampa Bay Lightning	$36	$203
GM Place	Vancouver Canucks	$36	$201
Molson Centre	Montreal Canadiens	$35	$195
Nashville Arena	Nashville Predators	$48	$194*
Corel Centre	Ottawa Senators	$34	$185
Marine Midland Arena	Buffalo Sabres	$31	$184
Reunion Arena	Dallas Stars	$27	$179
Canadian Airlines Saddledome	Calgary Flames	$29	$164
Skyreach Centre	Edmonton Oilers	$26	$150
	Average	**$42**	**$232**

Fan Cost Index: *Four average-price tickets, two beers, four small soft drinks, four hot dogs, two caps, two programs and parking.*

All funds in U.S. dollars, numbers are rounded off. All numbers except Toronto Maple Leafs and Nashville Predators are from the start of the 1997-98 season. Ticket prices are game-day prices, which do not include discounts.
*Represents current prices obtained by the *The Globe and Mail*.
**These teams have moved into new arenas during the last two years.
Source: Team Marketing Report, Inc.

with their season-ticket numbers as well. The total doesn't always include only those who buy all 41 games, but even packages for as few as five games.

The trend is for season-ticket holders to attend fewer games, Toronto Maple Leafs president Ken Dryden said not long after the club moved to the Air Canada Centre. Many sell some of their tickets, even in hockey-mad Toronto.

"I think our average season-ticket holder attended about 11 games [in 1997-98]," he said. "What has happened, I think, is because of other [entertainment] choices and the cost of tickets, people have come to approach going to games the way they do going to *Les Miz [Les Miserables]* or *Phantom of the Opera*. It's something you do once or twice a year."

Based on prices taken at a recent pre-season game, the Maple Leafs have jumped to the top of the NHL since moving into the Air Canada Centre. With an average ticket price of $72, the family cost index for a Leafs game is an eye-popping $355.

"Now, even the bigger-market teams have figured out you can't grow much more [ticket] revenue," Hurricanes owner Pete Karmanos said. "We can't get ticket prices any higher."

That, NHL Players' Association executive director Bob Goodenow says, is what the NHL owners have to figure out. He also says at least one club has admitted that "prices have nothing to do with [player] salaries. It's how much fans are willing to pay."

The NHL also has to contend with declining television ratings in the United States. The Fox Network shared the rights with ESPN for the past five years. But it declined to match a $600-million offer from ABC-ESPN for an exclusive deal and bowed out of the NHL in June. Fox saw its regular-season ratings drop from 1.9 million households in 1995 to about 1.4 million in 1999, a decrease of 5.3 percent.

"They paid about four times as much as we thought [the NHL rights] were worth," said Lou D'Ermilio, vice-president of media relations for Fox. "Economically, the numbers as presented did not make sense. Hockey's popularity never really grew outside of areas of historic interest."

Diane Lamb, a spokeswoman for ESPN, said the cable network's playoff ratings were up significantly last spring. She feels that sharing the NHL rights with ESPN's corporate sibling, ABC, will boost ratings because of "cross-promotion and increased exclusivity."

But the $4.3 million that the U.S. television contract pays each club every year is minuscule compared with the five-year, $2.8-billion NBA television contract or the six-year, $18-billion deal enjoyed by the NFL. Each NFL team received $73 million this year–before a single ticket was sold.

"When you look at the extraordinary levels of revenue that broadcast-driven leagues enjoy and then compare that to what the NHL is trying to survive on, it's clear you have a much smaller pot of money to pay salaries," Bonham said.

But as long as people such as Leonsis see the NHL as a good investment, Goodenow says, it's hard to believe owners' tales of woe. The NHL's accounting is a very complex matter, he said.

The union leader points to Bettman's remark about strong ownership and franchise values for an answer. "That's a pretty important statement," he said.

Maybe so, a high-ranked executive with an NHL club said, but the situation is still bad enough that he thinks a price will be paid by someone, even if it's for no better reason than to send a message about labour costs.

"I get the feeling the league would not mind if a franchise went down because of salaries," he said. "Then you could say to the players, 'You see?'"

2. Cyberspace represents gold mine for NHL, new owner believes

Rather than crying about rising player salaries, the National Hockey League should begin exploiting new revenue possibilities.

That's the view of one of the league's newest owners, Ted Leonsis, who parlayed an early stake in Internet giant America Online into enough money to buy the Washington Capitals and a piece of the MCI Center and the Washington Wizards of the National Basketball Association.

Most NHL clubs are already developing new ways to make money, usually through new arenas and the increased ticket, advertising and luxury-box income they offer. There are also innovative schemes, such as silent auctions, which have become significant moneymakers for teams such as the Toronto Maple Leafs.

Leonsis agrees with his fellow owners that salaries are getting out of hand. But at the same time, the NHL is in position to reap many economic rewards, he said.

"I'm very optimistic about hockey for five reasons," Leonsis said. "One, it's the most global of the four major [North American] sports. I don't think the global heart of it has been tapped, and as distribution channels like the Internet get more global, that can be tapped.

"Second, the demographics for hockey are very strong. We're finding in our market that our [audience] is very upscale.

"Third, I think the Internet represents huge new revenue streams for teams in the coming years. The good news is that the NHL and its teams own their own Internet rights.

"Fourth, I think the NHL brands are undermarketed, and I'm accustomed to a world like AOL where you build the brand with every fibre.

"And last, I think the tension between the league and the NHL Players' Association is short-lived, and we can work together."

Leonsis isn't the only one who thinks the NHL does a relatively poor job of marketing itself. A recent survey by *The Sports Business Journal* of 300 executives at companies that sponsor various sports asked which organizations were best at marketing their sport.

The NHL wound up 10th, with only 21.7 percent of the respondents saying it does a good job. NASCAR, the stock-car racing association regarded as a group on the rise, was first with 100 percent, followed by the NBA at 86.7 percent.

One of the areas the NHL should begin working on, according to Bob Goodenow, executive director of the NHL Players' Association, is its U.S. television package. The Fox Network gave up its contract after five years of declining ratings and now ABC-ESPN has an exclusive $600-million, five-year contract.

"The situation with Fox and the league was that they tried to experiment by moving games from Sunday to Saturday and back to Sunday," Goodenow said. "There was no regular pattern. It's difficult getting a national audience like that."

What the league should do, Goodenow says, is work on developing one or two teams that fans across the United States can identify with.

"Hockey doesn't have a Dallas Cowboys or Chicago Bulls with significant fans from coast to coast that can be reflected in national ratings," he said. "I think now with ABC and ESPN there's an ability to cross-promote and develop a more focused broadcast pattern."

Television revenue discussions always get around to pay TV. The NHL has a pay-TV package in the United States and recently launched one in Canada. But the culture of hockey on free television is entrenched in Canada, where the market for pay TV is small. And south of the border, the appetite for hockey on pay TV is equally small.

"I think we've turned over every stone in our market," Vancouver Canucks general manager Brian Burke said of panning revenue streams. "Pay TV is a possibility in the future, but will it solve our million-dollar losses? No. There's only four million people in British Columbia."

The global reach of the Internet, then, is the most intriguing possibility. Leonsis sees exploring the World Wide Web as more important than the traditional method of spending money on free-agent players to improve the team and its ticket sales.

"We feel we can be competitive [on the ice]," Leonsis said. "So if it's a choice between a right winger and a world-class database and a Web site, we'll build the database and Web site."

Along with the Capitals, Leonsis bought the Washington franchise of Ticketmaster from former owner Abe Pollin. He feels that can be combined with a Capitals Web site to build "a global hockey portal which we can use to get into other things like ticketing and other sports."

The Capitals recently relaunched their Web site (www.washingtoncaps.com), and in addition to the usual statistics and stories about the team, fans can buy game tickets and team merchandise on-line. Eventually, Leonsis hopes to have a site that draws millions of visitors a day and attract big advertisers.

"I'm going to spend a lot of money establishing a one-to-one relationship with the fans and building a Web portal," he said. "I'm going to give all the players laptop computers with access to the Internet. The players will be the stars.

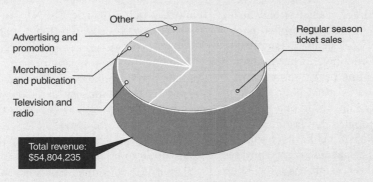

Where the Money Comes From

As part of a public company, the Vancouver Canucks are one of the few hockey teams forced to disclose their revenue. But they are typical of NHL teams in that the lion's share of that revenue comes from ticket sales.

Other

Advertising and promotion

Merchandise and publication

Television and radio

Regular season ticket sales

Total revenue: $54,804,235

Source: Nortwest Sports Enterprises Ltd. 1998 annual report

Richard Palmer / *The Globe and Mail*

"I've been at America Online for six years and seen it grow from 6,000 members to 18 million, so we have nowhere to go but up."

For the Maple Leafs and their corporate sibling, the Toronto Raptors of the NBA, silent auctions are speaking loudly when it comes to the bottom line.

Since the start of their 1997-98 seasons, the weekend games for both teams have allowed fans to submit written bids on merchandise from hats and sweaters to framed prints of historic occasions such as the closing of Maple Leaf Gardens. Almost all of the items have been autographed by the sports stars who have worn the item or are on the print.

In the beginning, there was some internal disagreement in Maple Leaf Sports & Entertainment, which owns both teams, over the purpose of the silent auctions. Questions had been raised about people bidding on items in the belief a good portion or all of the proceeds were going to charity.

However, Maple Leaf Sports executives say raising money for the company, not charity, was always the motivating factor.

"Auctions are an age-old way of doing business," said Jeff Newman, Maple Leaf's director of consumer products. "Auctions go on every day in every city, both silent and not so silent. To assume with every silent auction the money goes to charity is wrong.

"We are in the business of making money for this wonderful facility and for the athletes who play in it. A silent auction is another means of transacting ourselves."

While Maple Leaf executives played down the notion, the auctions have turned into a significant moneymaker. One estimate has placed the take from sales at Leafs games as high as $40,000 a week.

"It's okay, but in the grand scheme of things it's not what we would call a huge part of our merchandising," said Maple Leaf vice-president and project director Tom Anselmi, who also said the company's prime motivation for the auctions was not to help charities. "We do it to make money."

Discussions with several fans at the silent-auction booth at a Maple Leafs game at the Air Canada Centre showed the enormous revenue potential of the auctions. None of the people interviewed were under the impression this was a charitable venture.

"We don't care whose pockets the money goes in," said Jeff Schimp of White Lake, Mich., whose friend Tim White bid $300 on a framed picture of Detroit Red Wings captain Steve Yzerman holding the Stanley Cup. "We like the exchange rate."

Some people were concerned that some items were not clearly marked with the information they were not one of a kind but one in a series.

"I had the impression these are one-ofs, but they're not," Morris McDowell of Brampton, Ont., said. "That could mislead a few people."

The auction has several booths—one on each level of the Air Canada Centre. The booth visited by *The Globe and Mail* had 22 items up for bids, from a signed Tie Domi T-shirt and baseball cap for a minimum bid of $50 to an autographed photograph of Muhammad Ali standing over prone Sonny Liston in a world boxing championship bout for a minimum bid of $600.

The revenue potential is astonishing. One item could gross as much as $500,000 in one season.

For example, one popular item is a framed picture of the opening faceoff at the final game at Maple Leaf Gardens. The picture is signed by three of the participants. Three commemorative coins are mounted in the frame.

The Maple Leafs commissioned 500 of the pictures and paid the principals to sign them. One went on sale each week at each booth at the Air Canada Centre, and the sale prices were as high as $1,100.

Terry Busch of Cardiff, Ont., was looking at the print and said the booth attendant told him it went for $1,100 the previous week. "You say there's 500 of them and this one is No. 10," he said. "Well, the guy told me they got $1,100 for one last week. So they sell it and put up another one."

Maple Leaf Sports makes no apologies for the auctions, which are becoming common among professional sports teams. Company executives also say customers can count on their products to be authentic in an industry rife with counterfeiting.

"Because of our access [to athletes], people can be sure what we sell is genuine," Anselmi said.

3. Revenue sharing unpopular idea in NHL: players' fingers in financial pie remain bugbear for club owners in any discussion of economic woes

Whenever the National Hockey League's economic problems are discussed, talk invariably turns to player salaries.

And many of the league's problems would certainly be solved if the players would simply take less money. The Calgary Flames would be more likely to compete with the New York Rangers, whose payroll will hit $59 million (U.S.) this season.

It's not often suggested that the burden should be put on the owners, that the Rangers might share some of their revenue with the Flames.

When the current collective labour agreement was negotiated in the fall and winter of 1994-95, the union made several revenue-sharing proposals. They were rejected by the owners, and revenue sharing—both among themselves and with the players—remains unpopular with the owners.

Shortly after the agreement was reached in January of 1995, the NHL put together two revenue-sharing plans for the small-market Canadian teams. One sees a pool of $10 million divided each year by clubs that meet a number of criteria, including ticket sales and corporate sponsorships. The other pays the difference in the values of the Canadian and U.S. dollars for Canadian clubs that want to match an offer from a U.S. club for one of their restricted free agents.

However, since NHL clubs now rarely bid on each other's restricted free agents, the compensation plan has not been used in recent years. As for the other plan, the payouts were relatively small because they were shared by the Edmonton Oilers, Calgary Flames and Ottawa Senators. They got even smaller "because Vancouver got into it last year," Oilers president Glen Sather said.

"No chance," New Jersey Devils owner John McMullen said yesterday when asked about expanding revenue-sharing plans.

McMullen was vilified during the 1994-95 player lockout that preceded the current collective agreement when he was accused by the NHL Players' Association of saying "to hell with the small-market teams. This isn't about small-market teams."

The years have softened mcMullen's stand only slightly. He said the existing revenue-sharing plans, which help the Canadian teams, are enough. He is also opposed to sharing revenue with small-market teams in the United States.

"It's a necessary evil," he said of the money shared by the Canadian teams. "I feel it's unfair to have the rest of the teams supporting Canada."

At this point, McMullen went into the standard NHL owner's speech of how the problems of small-market Canadian teams are tied to the higher U.S. dollar and player salaries. If there is to be revenue sharing, he said, it should come from Canadian lottery funds or the Canadian taxpayer, or both.

Each side of the labour-management argument accuses the other of not caring about the small-market teams.

"Until recently, Bob Goodenow would say, 'If a small market can't make it, move,'" Carolina Hurricanes owner Peter Karmanos said. "Sooner or later, we're going to run out of those places."

In reply, the NHLPA's executive director brings up the revenue-sharing proposals he and his negotiating team presented to the NHL during the 1994-95 labour talks.

"We made proposals in the last round of negotiations that would have generated revenue, and there was a revenue-sharing plan that was significant, beyond anything that was mentioned publicly," Goodenow said. "Frankly, Pete's wrong.

"The lack of concern with small markets begins with his fellow owners who don't want to share revenues."

In the National Basketball Association, 55 percent of the gross revenue goes to the players under their latest collective agreement, which includes salary caps. Actually, McMullen said, he'd be all for revenue-sharing if that was the percentage the NHL players would get.

"But as it is, they get 70 percent of the revenues now," McMullen said, echoing Boston Bruins president and GM Harry Sinden, who said earlier this year that player salaries were eating up 72 percent of league revenue.

However, the matter of how revenues and expenses are accounted for leaves so much leeway that not even NHL commissioner Gary Bettman would back up Sinden's claim. All he would allow is that in the past two years, salary growth has outstripped revenue growth to the extent that payrolls are now well above 50 percent of revenue.

Revenue sharing between the owners and players involves trust. But trust is in short supply between the owners and the NHLPA.

The owners accuse Goodenow of directing every player's contract negotiations in order to extract the maximum amount of money from the clubs. Players and agents look at the growing number of unrestricted free agents sitting at home and the fact no club, aside from the Rangers, went after restricted free agents this summer and mutter darkly about collusion by the owners.

"Clearly, there's evidence of a league-wide effort to rein things in [on player salaries]," said Gordon Kirke of Toronto, a lawyer and player agent. "The only thing we don't know is whether that's a concerted effort with subtle pressure brought to bear or whether coincidentally owners in different cities independently decided they are going to show restraint.

"I'm not suggesting there's collusive conduct here, because I don't know. But there are certain indications that make you wonder. When a general manager says to you a player should go down the street and see what offers he gets, and he says so with great confidence, it makes you wonder what he knows."

Even if there is collusion among the NHL owners, they are getting more and more sympathy from hockey's beleaguered fans, who have to deal with rising ticket prices and long contract hassles with some of their favourite players.

Until this summer, the NHLPA had enjoyed a long winning streak over the owners in contract negotiations.

In his eight years as head of the union, Goodenow has built the NHLPA from a paper tiger under disgraced Alan Eagleson to a forceful advocate for the players, with 55 employees and programs ranging from agent certification to group licensing to career assistance.

Player agents say Goodenow has never issued marching orders when it comes to contract negotiations, but he has ensured that all representatives are well armed with information because of the realization that one player's contract has an effect on all.

When owners complain the current collective agreement, which they agreed to in 1995 and won't expire until 2004, is the reason for the explosion in player salaries, most complaints concern salary arbitration. After five years as a professional, most NHL players are eligible for arbitration, in which an independent arbitrator decides to accept the player's or the team's salary proposal.

The owners admit that thanks to the NHLPA's efforts to inform agents and their clients, they lost far more arbitration hearings than they won during the 1990s. Each victory helped drive up salaries.

Since the lack of a big television contract means the NHL is a gate-driven league, the owners have faced pressures unique to their sport. Much of their profit comes from making the playoffs, when the salaries have been paid out and expenses are relatively low.

"Every year, only 16 teams make the playoffs, a bunch of them miss and then eight teams go out in the first round," one player agent said. "Then the media in those cities kick the crap out of those teams. So in those cities, there's all kinds of pressure on teams to improve right away.

"That's one of the big things putting pressure on teams to spend money."

The agent said the NHLPA's attitude when it comes to contracts is "there's a bottomless pit of money, so go get it. That's been their attitude for a decade. They have a lot of players believing that. A certain mindset develops and the players in turn put pressure on their agents. I think even if you only have a cursory knowledge of economics, you know [payroll inflation] can't go on forever."

While the agent believes Goodenow has done an excellent job as a union leader, he says a growing number of his colleagues believe it may be time to relax the militant attitude.

At the same time, many NHL players judge Goodenow's performance on how much their salaries go up each year. "Yeah, I think that's probably weighted pretty heavily," Vancouver Canucks player representative Trent Klatt said, although he added that players should also take into account "all the things [the NHLPA] does, like disability insurance, and other ways they look out for our interest."

Goodenow doesn't see a problem with his or the union's approach, and "ultimately the players are the boss and I do what the players tell me to do. So if the agent's displeased with his role, he can negotiate less for the client or decline to represent the client."

As for his performance being judged on salary inflation, Goodenow said, "I don't have that same take. I think the players judge by looking at the job the association does for them based on their understanding of the industry and the compensation they get as a group."

While the owners have made attempts to reopen the collective agreement, the most recent during negotiations for NHL participation in the 2002 Winter Olympics, most realize there is as much chance of the NHLPA agreeing to that as there is of them adopting full revenue sharing.

So, with both sides amassing multimillion-dollar war chests in preparation for the next round of collective bargaining in 2004, should NHL fans resign themselves to a labour war that would wipe out at least one season?

One NHL owner who came to the league from a different business doesn't think so. In fact, he says, he rather likes the current agreement, which gives teams control of their players from the age of 18 to 31 because of the right to match other contract offers.

When he was negotiating to buy the Washington Capitals last spring, Ted Leonsis said, "the CBA [collective bargaining agreement] for me was a plus, not a minus. You can spend what you want. If you want to spend a lot of money, you can. And if you don't want to spend a lot, you don't have to."

Leonsis made his fortune as a senior executive with the Internet giant America Online. He feels that if new revenue possibilities such as the Internet and marketing the NHL brand are exploited, everyone in the league–players and clubs in large and small markets–would profit, as long as costs were under control.

"There's enough here for all of us to thrive," he said.

Source: David Shoalts is a staff writer for *The Globe and Mail*. This series was originally published in *The Globe and Mail*, October 6, 1999, S1; October 7, 1999, S3; October 8, 1999, S4. Reproduced with permission from *The Globe and Mail*.

59.

People: 1, NHL: 0

Peter Donnelly

It's nice to win one against the poor sports

In December 1998, Liberal MP Dennis Mills released the report of his Parliamentary Sub-Committee on Sport in Canada. The report, *Sport in Canada, Everybody's Business*, contained 69 recommendations. Sixty-eight concerned assistance to the amateur Sport Community in Canada: one concerned government funding for professional sport, specifically NHL hockey.

A number of us felt that this recommendation was the primary purpose of the report. The other recommendations, while mostly admirable, were merely a vehicle for carrying the idea of public funding for Canadian NHL teams, particularly the Ottawa Senators.

The Faculty of Physical Education and Health held a forum to respond to the Mills Report. We sent a strong message endorsing many of the recommendations, modifying others, and indicating clearly why it would be a travesty to direct public funding to an American-dominated private sport league which already receives substantial public subsidies. In an era when governments have viciously slashed all types of social programs, including welfare, such generous corporate welfare hardly seems "sporting."

It seems even less fair when the other subsidies from federal, provincial, and municipal governments are taken into account, such as the 50 percent tax write-off claimed on the purchase of the best seats and corporate boxes. (If you feel that welfare fraud is a concern, consider the tax fraud that occurs at every Maple Leafs/Raptors/Blue Jays/etc. game when friends and family members attend on tickets for which a tax write-off is being claimed.)

Surprise! John Manley announced federal support for Canadian NHL teams last Tuesday—the only recommendation from the Mills Report on which the government has acted! Surprise!! He withdrew that support last Friday, in the face of overwhelming public opinion against the deal.

Some of the media have done a great job establishing the background of the proposed subsidy: the land development deal in Kanata that ended up, almost accidentally, in the construction of a new arena and an NHL team; the hubris of the NHL in locating a team in Ottawa rather than the better-prepared Hamilton; the American-style blackmail ("give us 'X' or we'll move our team to a city that will"); the powerful financial and political connections between Senators' owner Rod Bryden and the Liberal government; the way in which the New York-based NHL is bankrupting the league by greedy expansion (the owners get to share $50 million each time a new team is added), etc.

The people spoke, loudly, and its nice to win one. Wouldn't it be nice now to have a little concerted action on health care and education funding? The farm and housing crises? The environment and GM food? The globalization of trade and unemployment?

Source: Peter Donnelly is a professor and Director of the Centre for Sport Policy Studies in the Faculty of Physical Education and Health at the University of Toronto. This article was originally published in *The Independent Weekly*, January 27-February 2, 2000. Reproduced with permission of the author.

Notes on Articles

Swimming with the Big Boys?
Douglas Booth and Colin Tatz

Notes

1. *The Olympics: A History of the Modern Games* (Urbana: University of Illinois Press, 1992), p.4.

2. While many commentators considered Sydney second favorite, Beijing was the clear front runner.

IOC Voting for the 2000 Olympic Games

	Votes	City				
		1st	Ber	Man	Bei	Syd
1	89a	7(0b)	9	11	32	30
2	89		9(7)	13	37	30
3	88c			11(8)	40	37
4	88				43	45

(a) There are currently ninety-one members of the IOC. The President votes only in the event of a tie and Bulgerian Ivan Slavkov was under house arrest, charged with misappropriating sports funds during the Zhivkov regime. (b) Numbers in brackets redirected to Sydney in the following round. (c) David Sibandze (Swaziland) left midway during the vote to return in time for his country's general election two days later.
Sources: "Voting" and "Good at games," *Australian*, 25 Sept. 1993; "Green scarf clue in the two-city voting race," *Sydney Morning Herald (SMH)*, 25 Sept. 1993.

3. Robert Paddick, "Sport and Politics: The (Gross) Anatomy of Their Relationships," *Sporting Traditions*, (1)2, 1994, pp.51-67.

4. AM, ABC Radio, 24 Sept. 1993; "Keating pledges substantial aid," *Australian*, 25 Sept. 1993.

5. Christopher Finn, letter, *SMH*, 28 Sept., 1993.

6. Comprising Serbia and Montenegro, contemporary Yugoslavia succeeds the pre-1941 royalist and the post-1945 Titoist nation. The United Nations now recognises the other former provinces as independent states.

7. Vyv Simson and Andrew Jennings, "The China Syndrome," *The Lords of the Rings* (London: Simon and Schuster, 1992).

8. Andrew Jennings, "The China Syndrome," *Inside Sport*, Sept. 1993, pp.20-1.

9. Simson and Jennings, *Lords of the Rings*, pp.103-106, 260, 271.

10. The Inquiry Commission reports on: national and international characteristics, support in the country for the city's bid, immigration and customs facilities, meteorological conditions, environmental protection, security, health, Olympic and media villages, accommodation, transport, competition sites, media facilities, telecommunications, data processing, finances, marketing, and legal issues. The Commission does not offer formal rankings although it identifies its preferred city. "The power of 12," *SMH*, 6 Mar. 1993.

11. John Rodda, "How Sydney bought the winning votes," *Guardian Weekly*, 3 Oct. 1993.

12. United States House of Representatives, Text of the resolutions opposing Olympics in China, 27 July 1993; Interview, Tom Lantos (U.S. Congressman), AM, ABC Radio, 24 Sept. 1993.

13. "IOC boss warns U.S. against meddling," *Australian*, 26 June 1993.

14. Interview, Perry Crosswhite (Secretary General, Australian Olympic Committee), 3 Dec. 1993.

15. "Elder urges black support for games," *Australian*, 21 July 1993.

16. Interview. AM, ABC Radio, 25 Sept. 1993.

17. Letter, Aboriginal Legal Service, Redfern, to IOC members, 26 Oct. 1992.

18. "Govt told: Olympics need $100 poll tax," *SMH*, 15 Oct. 1993.

19. Greenpeace offered an exemplary lesson. It participated in the design of the Olympic village as a strategy to advance its environmental cause and gain wide influence. Interview, John Walter (Research officer, Greenpeace), 8 Oct. 1993.

20. "Wrestling over China's Olympic bid," *National Journal* (Washington), 11 Sept. 1993.

21. The term "potential" is stressed here. The actual economic performance of recent hosts is discussed below. Moreover, financial rewards are unevenly spread across different sectors. Tourism has generally not benefited as much, for example, as construction.

22. The burial place of Shih Huang-ti, China's first sovereign emperor.

23. "$100m bribe to Olympics," *Sun Herald*, 14 Mar. 1993.

24. Simson and Jennings, *Lords of the Rings*, pp.241-2.

25. "No pain in Spain for the five-star Samaranch gang," *Financial Review*, 5 Aug. 1992.

26. "No pain in Spain for the five-star Samaranch gang," *Financial Review*, 5 Aug. 1992.

27. "Games rort slashing to save $1m for Sydney," *Australian*, 28 Aug. 1991.

28. Simson and Jennings, *Lords of the Rings*, pp.240-1.

29. "Sydney's bid for 2000 is all money down drain," *Age*, 28 July 1992.

30. John Rickard, *Australia: A Cultural History* (London: Longman, London, 1988), pp.264-6.

31. Interview, Perry Crosswhite, 1993; John Coates, The process of bidding for an Olympic Games, paper presented at SOBC meeting, 6 Mar. 1991, pp.6-8; The Games People Play, *Four Corners*, ABC Television, 19 July 1993: Barry Cohen, "Africa in no position to point finger on rights," *Australian*, 9 May 1994.

32. Interview, Perry Crosswhite, 1993; Rodda, "How Sydney bought the winning votes."

33. "How Games chief wooed the man who didn't vote," *SMH*, 30 Sept. 1993.

34. "Sydney's golden touch," *Sunday Age*, 14 Mar. 1993.

35. "How Games chief wooed the man who didn't vote," *SMH*, 30 Sept. 1993.

36. "Games rort slashing to save $1m for Sydney," *Australian*, 28 Aug. 1991.

37. "No glass empty in 'big Australian crawl'," *Age*, 24 Sept. 1993.

38. "No glass empty in 'big Australian crawl'," *Age*, 24 Sept. 1993.

39. "Sydney poised to win Olympics," *Australian*, 23 Sept. 1993.

40. Interview, John Coates, AM, ABC Radio, 25 Sept. 1993; John Rodda, "How Sydney bought the winning votes," *Guardian Weekly*, 3 Oct. 1993.

41. "A lean, mean, green machine," *Sunday Age*, 26 Sept. 1993.

42. "World soccer boss backs Beijing's bid," *Australian*, 23 Sept. 1993.

43. "A lean, mean, green machine," *Sunday Age*, 26 Sept. 1993.

44. "Good at games," *Australian*, 25 Sept. 1993; The World Today, ABC Radio, 27 Sept. 1993; "A lean, mean, green machine," *Sunday Age*, 26 Sept. 1993.

45. Sydney and Manchester had a "mutual understanding" to persuade their supporters to direct second preferences to the other. "Sydney in deal with Olympic city rival," *Sunday Age*, 19 Sept. 1993.

46. "For some, the postman never ever rings," *SMH*, 25 Sept. 1993.

47. The freeing of prominent dissidents before the vote may have assisted China's image. "Games-hungry China frees third dissident," *SMH*, 18 Sept. 1993.

48. "Beijing bid chief threatens boycott of U.S. Olympics," *SMH*, 19 Sept. 1993.

49. Bruce Kidd, "From 'excellence' to 'bread and roses': The transformation of the Toronto Olympic bid," paper presented to the Australian Society for Sports History conference, Canberra, July 1991.

50. "Sydney—the logical choice," This Week (supplement to the *Sun-Herald*), 21 Mar. 1993.

51. Interview, Susan Tuckerman (Olympic Promotions Officer, Department of Education), 5 Oct. 1993; "Gold medal effort by schools," *Sun-Herald*, 26 Sept. 1993.

52. NSW Department of School Education, Sydney 2000 Information Kit, Feb. 1993.

53. "Back to the game of politics as Jumpin' John looks to 1995 election," *SMH*, 27 Sept. 1993.

54. PM, ABC Radio, 16 July 1993.

55. Wendy Bacon, "Watchdog's Bark Muffled," *Reportage*, Sept. 1993.

56. PM, ABC Radio, 1 Oct. 1993. In August 1994 the NSW Government embargoed all official documents pertaining to the bid. These documents can no longer be obtained under Freedom of Information.

57. Max Walsh, "Olympic figures just do not add up," *SMH*, 25 July 1993; "Sydney 2000 report attacked," *SMH*, 26 July 1993.

58. Saulwick poll, *SMH*, 6 Nov. 1993.

59. "$1.3bn budget blowout proves it's a big games," *SMH*, 14 Oct. 1993.

60. Editorial, "A republic in time," *Age*, 28 Sept. 1993.

61. "Olympics to tune world to Mabo, human rights, say black leaders," *SMH*, 27 Sept. 1993; "Mabo: blacks to call for Olympics boycott," *SMH*, 29 Sept. 1993; "Blacks seek Queen's help, urge games boycott," *Australian*, 29 Sept. 1993.

62. Editorial, "The Mabo Olympics?" *SMH*, 30 Sept. 1993.

63. "Catalans to raise banner of independence at Olympics," *SMH*, 25 July 1992.

64. SOBC, Security Fact Sheet, 19 Mar. 1992.

65. "Sydney's Olympics—the class issues," *Workers News*, 1 Oct. 1993. Surprisingly few commentators remarked on the uncertainty associated with predicting the Australian economy seven years hence.

66. Michael Kjaerbye, "More than Simply Sharing the Spirit," *Reportage*, Sept. 1993, p.11.

67. "Viable bid unlikely, Treasury warned," *SMH*, 15 Oct. 1993.

68. Clifford Geertz, "Deep Play: Notes on the Balinese Cockfight," *Daedalus*, (101)1, 1972, p.24.

Index